OXFORD STUDIES IN LANGUAGE CONTACT

Series Editors: Suzanne Romaine, Merton College, Oxford,
and Peter Mühlhäusler, University of Adelaide

Language Contact and Change

D1601610

OXFORD STUDIES IN LANGUAGE CONTACT

Most of the world's speech communities are multilingual, making contact between languages an important force in the everyday lives of most people. Studies of language contact should therefore form an integral part of work in theoretical, social, and historical linguistics. As yet, however, there are insufficient studies to permit typological generalizations.

Oxford Studies in Language Contact aims to fill this gap by making available a collection of research monographs presenting case studies of language contact around the world. The series addresses language contact and its consequences in a broad interdisciplinary context, which includes not only linguistics, but also social, historical, cultural, and psychological perspectives. Topics falling within the scope of the series include: bilingualism, multilingualism, language mixing, code-switching, diglossia, pidgins and creoles, problems of cross-cultural communication, and language shift and death.

Language Contact and Change

Spanish in Los Angeles

CARMEN SILVA-CORVALÁN

CLARENDON PRESS · OXFORD

This book has been printed digitally and produced in a standard specification in order to ensure its continuing availability

OXFORD
UNIVERSITY PRESS

Great Clarendon Street, Oxford OX2 6DP

Oxford University Press is a department of the University of Oxford.
It furthers the University's objective of excellence in research, scholarship,
and education by publishing worldwide in

Oxford New York

Auckland Bangkok Buenos Aires Cape Town Chennai
Dar es Salaam Delhi Hong Kong Istanbul Karachi Kolkata
Kuala Lumpur Madrid Melbourne Mexico City Mumbai Nairobi
São Paulo Shanghai Singapore Taipei Tokyo Toronto

with an associated company in Berlin

Oxford is a registered trade mark of Oxford University Press
in the UK and in certain other countries

Published in the United States
by Oxford University Press Inc., New York

ISBN 0-19-823644-1

To my brother

Hernán Silva-Corvalán

(1935–1987)

Nuestras vidas crecieron junto al Maule
y el Maule va a dar a la mar . . .

Acknowledgements

The research on which this book is based was financed primarily by two grants from the National Science Foundation (BNS-8214733 and BNS-8721453) and by grants from the University of Southern California Humanities Faculty Research Support Grant (1982–3) and Faculty Research Innovation Fund (1985–6). Part of the research and writing was carried out while I was a guest researcher at the Max-Planck-Institut für Psycholinguistik, Nijmegen (1986). The support of these three institutions is gratefully acknowledged.

The research for this study would not have been possible without the co-operation of the Mexican-Americans who gave generously of their time, their intuitions, and their attitudes about language and bilingualism, and who more than once allowed me to invade the privacy of their homes with the ominous tape-recorder. I wish to express my appreciation for their hospitality and their help.

The following previously published articles have been incorporated into various sections of this book in an adapted and substantially revised or expanded form: 'Bilingualism and Language Change: The Extension of *Estar* in Los Angeles Spanish', *Language*, 62 (1986), 587–608; 'Tense–Mood–Aspect Across the Spanish–English Bilingual Continuum', *Variation in language: NWAV-XV at Stanford*, in K. Denning, S. Inkelas, F. Mc-Nair-Knox, and J. R. Rickford (eds.), (Stanford, Calif., Stanford University Department of Linguistics, 1987), 395–410; 'Oral Narrative Along the Spanish–English Bilingual Continuum', in John Staczek (ed.), *On Spanish, Portuguese and Catalan Linguistics* (Washington, DC, Georgetown University Press, 1988), 172–84; 'Past and Present Perspectives on Language Change in US Spanish', *International Journal for the Sociology of Language*, 79 (1989), 53–66; 'Current Issues in Studies of Language Contact', *Hispania*, 73 (1990) 162–76; 'Cross-Generational Bilingualism: Theoretical Implications of Language Attrition', in T. Huebner and C. A. Ferguson (eds.), *Cross-Currents in Second Language Acquisition and Linguistic Theories* (Amsterdam, John Benjamins, 1990), 325–45; 'Spanish Language Attrition in a Contact Situation with English', in H. W. Seliger and R. Vago (eds.), *First Language Attrition: Structural and Theoretical Perspectives* (Cambridge, Cambridge University Press, 1991), 151–71; 'On the Permeability of Grammars: Evidence from Spanish and English Contact', in W. Ashby, M. Mithun, G. Perissinotto, and E. Raposo (eds.), *Linguistic Perspectives on the Romance Languages* (Amsterdam, John Benjamins, 1993), 19–43.

I wish to thank the editors and publishers for granting permission to use this material.

I am especially grateful to my colleagues Nancy Dorian, Suzanne Romaine, and

Roger Wright for their friendship, for reading the manuscript, and for offering valuable critical observations and meticulous editorial suggestions which I have done my best to take into account. Nancy and Suzanne deserve special recognition for nurturing my initial interest in the topic of language contact, and for their intellectual support during every phase of this project. It will be obvious to the reader that Nancy Dorian's work has had a profound influence on my own work. I also very gratefully acknowledge Nancy's careful scrutiny of each of the seven chapters of this book, as well as her enlightening comments on practical and theoretical issues.

My indebtedness to many other colleagues and friends over the years is great. William Labov and Benji Wald have inspired and encouraged my efforts to carry out sociolinguistic work. For comments and discussion about earlier versions of individual chapters, I give thanks to Roger Andersen, Edouard Beniak, Lucía Elías-Olivares, Charles Ferguson, Susan Gal, Mary Ellen García, Jane Hill, Thom Huebner, Flora Klein-Andreu, Yakov Malkiel, Raymond Mougeon, Ricardo Otheguy, Ellen Prince, and John Staczek. For thought-provoking questions about some of the premises and conclusions presented in Chapters 1 and 7, I convey my thanks to Sarah Thomason. I also owe an extended thanks to Erica García, who offered incisive observations and invaluable advice on various papers which were later incorporated into different sections of the book.

The research and writing of this study have taken several years. During this time a number of students, too numerous to mention individually, have assisted me with some of the research projects discussed here, have made helpful comments during seminars, and have at all times encouraged me with their enthusiasm for the issues related to language contact. I give them special thanks.

I wish to recognize my indebtedness to my parents, Fernando and Felisa, and to my sons Diego, Fernando, and Rodrigo, for giving me the love, encouragement, and emotional support which I needed to pursue my professional life. My brother Fernando and my extended family (including Nicolas, the latest addition) have also contributed to making my progress smoother. Finally, more than thanks are due to my husband, Scott Dahlberg, who in the last few years has had to put up with innumerable questions about English, and with linguistic issues as a frequent topic of conversation. By dedicating this book to Hernán, I know they feel I am dedicating it to all of them.

C.S.-C.

Pacific Palisades, California
July 1992

Contents

Contents

Abbreviations

Cl	verbal clitic pronoun	PerCond	periphrastic conditional
Cond	conditional	Perf	perfect
exp.	expected	PerFut	periphrastic future
Fut	future	PI	present indicative
FutRef	future reference	Pluperf	pluperfect indicative
HP	historical present	PluS	pluperfect subjunctive
Imp	imperfect indicative	PPS	present perfect subjunctive
Imper	imperative	Pres	present
Ind	indicative	PresP	present participle
Inf	infinitive	PresPerf	present perfect indicative
IS	imperfect subjunctive	PresRef	present reference
lit.	literal(ly)	Pret	preterite indicative
P	participle	PS	present subjunctive
PastP	past participle	Sub	subjunctive
PastRef	past reference		

List of Tables

I

Language Contact and Change

1.1. Theoretical Preliminaries

IN THE past thirty years, sociolinguistic research has been concerned, among other questions, with the examination of language change (Romaine 1982). Labov (1972a; 1981a; 1981b), in particular, has successfully challenged the traditional structuralist position, which argued that change in progress could not be observed, by developing the necessary methodological techniques to identify and study possible changes in progress in apparent or real time. During this period, one of the most debated questions within the field of historical and socio-historical linguistics has been the interaction between internal linguistic factors and external social forces (including as such a different language) in what Weinreich *et al.* (1968: 186–7) call the *actuation or motivation of linguistic change*, i.e. the role that both society and the structure of language may play in stimulating or constraining linguistic change. With respect to this dilemma, these authors observe that if the theory that linguistic change is change in social behaviour is taken seriously, then it may not be possible to postulate predictive explanatory hypotheses. Rather, it is conceivable that all explanations may have to be offered a posteriori.

Most neogrammarians and post-Saussurean structuralists, including generativists, view change as motivated and governed by internal factors.[1] Structuralism conceives language as a system whose elements are defined by the place they occupy in opposition to other elements, or as a system controlled by language specific rules and universal principles. This concept of language underlies the explanation of change, on the one hand, in relation to the existence of structural spaces and of incomplete or unbalanced correlations within the system and, on the other hand, on the basis of processes of reanalysis essentially motivated by rule opacity. Also considered to be internal are a number of cognitive factors which constrain possible changes; for instance, it is suggested that changes which may lead to the neutralization of important oppositions or which may cause comprehension difficulties will tend to be resisted (cf. Martinet 1962). In contrast, sociolinguistics focuses on the social forces which shape language structure and use, as well as on internally motivated variation. Sociolinguists have shown that language is inherently and systematically heterogeneous and variable, and that the seeds of change lie precisely in the existence of this variation. In regard to change, therefore, most

---

[1] In the diffusion of change, dialect geography, areal linguistics, and wave theory all consider the role of social communication, but a strong structuralist point of view disallows structural dialectology (Anttila 1972: chs. 14–15).

analysts agree with one of the general principles postulated by Weinreich *et al.* (1968: 188):

Linguistic and social factors are closely interrelated in the development of language change. Explanations which are confined to one or the other aspect, no matter how well constructed, will fail to account for the rich body of regularities that can be observed in empirical studies of language behavior.

Despite changes of perspective and methodological advances, however, Labov (1982) notes that we are still far from reaching a solution to the problem of causality. The question of what forces, whether internal or external, have motivated a specific change at a given time and place continues to haunt sociolinguists as well as structuralist historians. In this respect, Malkiel (1983: 251) justifiably observes that the answers proposed depend to a large extent on the linguist's theoretical inclination. Accordingly, the linguist will 'favor either external or internal factors . . . either an explanation allowing for the intervention of speakers, at varying levels of consciousness, in the events affecting their speech or the rival explanation operating with unguided clashes of blind forces'.

In the context of this continuous controversy, increasing attention has been focused on pidgin and creole languages, on the acquisition of first and second languages, and on the linguistic phenomena which develop in situations of societal bilingualism and multilingualism. In language-contact situations, developing languages, receding languages, and maintenance of languages lend themselves to the examination of hypotheses about linguistic change, because they are characterized by constant and rapid changes which may be observed as they arise and spread in the linguistic and social systems. Among the important theoretical issues dealt with by those concerned with these studies have been the possible universality of the linguistic processes characteristic of these situations, and the role that a model, primary, or superordinate language may play in the shaping of the developing, secondary, or subordinate language—as against the possibility of autonomous developments constrained by the linguistic system of each of the languages in question and/or by human cognitive processes.

In regard to the issue of universality, it has been observed that some of the phenomena characteristic of bilingualism and multilingualism, namely *simplification, overgeneralization, transfer, analysis,* and *convergence,* are indeed attested across different situations of linguistic stress. This observation has motivated the proposal of a number of corresponding theories (theory of transfer, theory of simplification, etc.) valid for all these language situations (e.g. creolization, language acquisition, language loss). Different scholars conceptualize and define these universal phenomena in somewhat different ways. It becomes necessary, therefore, to state explicitly how I understand them in the context of my work.

Researchers have not yet come to an agreement about the meaning of simplification. Indeed, Ferguson (1982: 58) has pointed out that 'the notions "simplicity" and "simplification" are among the most elusive concepts used in the characterization of language'. However, he adds that, despite this difficulty, there is general consensus regarding what in fact constitutes linguistic simplification. Included as such are, for instance, reduction of the inventory of linguistic forms, semantic range, or language functions, and the elimination of alternative structures at certain levels (p. 59).

Note that the phenomena referred to by Ferguson, reduction and elimination of alternatives, are end-states that imply the existence of more complete varieties with which the 'simplified' ones are being compared. In a situation of languages in contact, simplified varieties of a given language may develop as a result of incomplete learning and/or language attrition. In the latter case, reduction and elimination of alternatives must necessarily involve a classical stage of variation in the use of all available forms, followed by the gradual disappearance of some forms, functions, and/or alternatives. Variability and gradual simplification should in principle be observable in the speech behaviour of individuals as well as across individuals.[2]

Accordingly, I consider reduction and elimination the *result* of a complex process of linguistic simplification which also implies rule generalization, in the sense that the use of a form is being expanded to a larger number of contexts. Note that my definition of simplification as a process differs from Ferguson's (1982) view of this concept as referring to an end-state. It also differs in some respects from definitions of simplification offered by other authors (e.g. Meisel 1977; 1983*a*; Mougeon *et al.* 1985; Mühlhäusler 1981; Trudgill 1983: ch. 6).

Viewed as a process, then, simplification involves the higher frequency of use of a form X in context Y (i.e. generalization) at the expense of a form Z, usually in competition with and semantically closely related to X, where both X and Z existed in the language prior to the initiation of simplification. Thus X is an expanding form, while Z is a *shrinking* or *contracting* form. If simplification reaches completion, its final outcome is reduction or loss of forms and elimination of alternatives, i.e. a *simplified* system with fewer forms and possibly, though not necessarily, loss of meanings.

This definition of simplification appears to correspond to the notion of *overgeneralization* (cf. Preston 1982; Silva-Corvalán 1990*a*) as the more extensive use of a form than expected in ordinary practice. The only difference is that simplification explicitly refers to contraction, that is, the less frequent use of a competing form. Overgeneralization, on the other hand, may affect contexts where no corresponding competing form exists, i.e. where we may have XY extending to $X\emptyset$ or vice versa (e.g. $\emptyset + V_i \rightarrow se + V_i$ in Spanish examples such as $\emptyset$ *murió en un accidente* '(he) $\emptyset$ died in an accident' $\rightarrow$ *Se murió en un accidente* '(he) *se* died in an accident'). A related term is *regularization*, which I use to refer to those cases where the forms extended or overgeneralized are those with a wider structural distribution in the language in question.

---

[2] Incomplete acquisition of the mother tongue (L1) or of a second language (L2) in a contact situation may also involve simplification, i.e. a period of variation leading to reduction and elimination. Cf. Meisel (1983*a*) for an in-depth discussion of simplification as a strategy of L2 acquirers. I do not concern myself with the issue of incomplete acquisition here.

Transfer is undoubtedly a controversial notion as well. It may be simply defined as the incorporation of language features from one language into another, with consequent restructuring of the subsystems involved (cf. Weinreich 1974). This definition accounts for the obvious cases of transfer, usually at the lexical, morphological, and phonological levels of analysis. By contrast, at the syntactic level it may be more difficult to identify direct transfer and to prove permeability of a grammatical system to influence from a different system. For instance, even an obvious candidate for an explanation based on direct transfer from English into Spanish such as the non-expression of *que* 'that' in complement clauses in Los Angeles (LA) Spanish, as in *Creo ∅ te hubiera gustado* 'I think (that) you would've liked it', does not constitute an unquestionable case of incorporation of a foreign feature. (The non-expression of *que* is discussed in Chapter 5.)

Despite these difficulties, I consider that transfer may have occurred whenever one or more of the following phenomena is present in the data:

(1) The replacement of a form in language S with a form from language F, or the incorporation from language F into language S of a form previously absent in S. In both cases, the form from language F may be incorporated with or without its full associated meaning, and it may undergo various degrees of morphophonological adaptation to language S. Examples: In LA Spanish *bye* replaces *adiós*, *chao*, and other forms of leave-taking; *lonche* is incorporated to refer to a noon meal. This type of transfer is usually referred to in the literature as 'borrowing'; I consider it an instance of *direct transfer*.

(2) The incorporation of the meaning of a form R from language F, which may be part of the meaning of a form P in S, into an already existing form, structurally similar to R, in system S (cf. Weinreich's 1974: 30 'extension or reduction of function'). This is also a case of *direct transfer*. Example: *registrarse* incorporates the meaning of *to register* (in school), thus making obsolete the Spanish words *matricularse/inscribirse* 'to register in a school/for a course'.

(3) The higher frequency of use of a form in language S, determined on the basis of a comparison with more conservative internal community norms, in contexts where a partially corresponding form in language F is used either categorically or preferentially. This constitutes an instance of *indirect transfer* from language F into language S. Example: the more frequent use of progressives by Puerto Rican bilinguals as compared to monolinguals (Klein-Andreu 1986a; cf. also Morales 1986: ch. 4; Mougeon *et al.* 1985; Schachter and Rutherford 1979; Silva-Corvalán 1986).

(4) The loss of a category or a form in language S which does not have a parallel category or form in the system of F (cf. Weinreich's 'neglect' or 'elimination' of obligatory categories). An example is the loss of adjective gender marking in some varieties of Los Angeles Spanish. This is a form of indirect transfer.

Transfer leads to, but is not the single cause of, *convergence*, defined as the achievement of greater structural similarity in a given aspect of the grammar of two or more languages, assumed to be different at the onset of contact (cf. Gumperz and Wilson 1977). Indeed, convergence may result as well from pre-existing internally motivated changes in one of the languages, most likely *accelerated* by contact, rather than as a consequence of direct interlingual influence (Silva-Corvalán 1986).

A change in a language L is considered to have *accelerated* in the speech of a group X when both the number of context types (as opposed to tokens of the same context), and the frequency of use of the innovation in a token count in the various contexts are higher as compared to an older age group Y in the same speech community as X, and when this increase is in turn higher than any possible increase of the same instance of change identified in the speech of a group P who speak the same language as X, as compared to an older age group Q in the same speech community as P.

This definition follows from the assumption that change-related variation observed in apparent time (Labov 1972*a*), i.e. across generations, may reflect stages of diffusion in real time. Crucially, in the case of language contact, I consider the language proficiency continuum (see section ii below) to stand for apparent time in the manner in which different age groups are considered to represent apparent time in sociolinguistic studies of variation. The claim that synchronic variation across age groups may constitute evidence of change is debatable, since any variation identified as a change on the basis of differential distribution of the variants across age groups could also be interpreted as corresponding to age grading or to stable variation in the different age groups. This problem does not affect our study, however, because acceleration is established with respect to groups differentiated by length of contact with English and proficiency in Spanish (the proficiency continuum) rather than by age.

Analysis is the process which underlies either the preferential use or the creation of analytical or periphrastic constructions as opposed to synthetic ones. This accounts, for instance, for the much more frequent use of the periphrastic future and conditional forms (*ir a* 'go to' + Inf.) rather than the corresponding synthetic ones (*-rá*, *-ría*) in all varieties of Spanish.

At least three of these processes, simplification, overgeneralization, and analysis, which characterize change in the languages of monolingual communities as well, may frequently be accounted for on the basis of cognitive and intralinguistic factors (see Chapters 2–5), rather than as the result of direct transfer. There is a general consensus, however, that intensive language contact is a powerful external promoter of language change. Nevertheless, perhaps owing to the fact that the acknowledgement of contact-induced changes poses a threat to some of the methods of historical linguistics (as discussed by Thomason and Kaufman 1988), it is only rather recently that linguists have challenged the view that a grammatical system is impermeable to direct transfer of elements which do not correspond to its internal structure or tendencies of development (cf. Jakobson 1938). In this regard, Thomason and Kaufman (1988) argue that there is evidence from a large number of contact situations in support of their hypothesis that 'it is the sociolinguistic history of the speakers, and not the structure of their language, that is the primary determinant of the linguistic outcome of language contact' (p. 35).

While I am basically in agreement with this hypothesis, the results of my investigation of bilingualism in a situation of family and individual language shift indicate that, even under conditions of intense contact and strong cultural pressure, speakers of the receding language simplify or overgeneralize grammatical rules but do not introduce elements which would cause radical changes in the structure of the language. Rather, these changes occur step by step in real time, and across the proficiency continuum in the receding language. Since ultimately they may lead to the development of a language which is essentially different from its non-contact ancestor, I favour a slightly different hypothesis: that the structure of the languages involved, to a large extent constrained by cognitive and interactional processes, governs the introduction and diffusion of innovative elements in the linguistic systems; the sociolinguistic history of the speakers is the primary determinant of the language direction and the *degree* of diffusion of the innovations as well as of the more distant (in terms of time-span) linguistic outcome of language contact (i.e. after several generations of normal language transmission; cf. Thomason and Kaufman 1988). This hypothesis accounts for the changes attested in numerous situations of language maintenance and/or shift involving normal transmission across generations.

This book follows this tradition of language contact studies, dealing with some of the changes undergone by a particular variety of Spanish in a situation of intensive contact with English in Los Angeles. Approximately 150 hours of recorded Spanish language data from an intergenerational sample of 50 adult bilinguals are examined. Whenever relevant, monolingual spoken Spanish is also studied for comparison purposes.

The general hypothesis investigated is that, in language contact situations, bilinguals develop strategies aimed at lightening the cognitive load of having to remember and use two different linguistic systems. In the use of the subordinate language, beyond phonology,[3] the strategies suggested by the data include:

(1) Simplification of grammatical categories and lexical oppositions.
(2) Overgeneralization of forms, frequently following a regularizing pattern.
(3) Development of periphrastic constructions either to achieve paradigmatic regularity or to replace less semantically transparent bound morphemes.
(4) Direct and indirect transfer of forms from the superordinate language.
(5) Code-switching, which involves the use of two or more languages by one speaker in the same turn of speech or at turn-taking points.[4]

---

[3] No phonological phenomena are examined here.

[4] Code-switching has been shown to be a characteristic communicative mode of skilled bilinguals (Poplack 1979). However, some forms of code-switching also appear to function as a strategy to compensate for diminished proficiency in a language, for memory lapses, etc. (Silva-Corvalán 1983*b*). I do not deal with code-switching in this book.

The result is more or less massive changes in the secondary language. The extent of these changes correlates with the speakers' level of bilingual proficiency and with extralinguistic factors. The occurrence of the changes is further favoured and accelerated by (*a*) absence of normative pressures on the subordinate language; (*b*) restriction in the range of communicative uses of the subordinate language; and (*c*) speakers' positive attitudes towards the superordinate language combined with either neutral or negative attitudes toward the subordinate one.

This book examines in depth the linguistic strategies listed in (1)–(4). I determine the patterns of diffusion of a number of changes in the linguistic system, and examine their correlation with the extralinguistic favouring factors postulated. I give special attention to the issue of permeability at different stages of attrition or distance from the Spanish dominant norm. By analysing and comparing the speech behaviour of an intergenerational sample of speakers in apparent time and along the Spanish proficiency continuum, I attempt to characterize and explain processes and stages of language attrition. Thus, I expect to provide here one of the baselines for the universal generalizations that may be possible when enough comparable studies are available concerned with constraints on deviations from target or source languages, about the relationship between the sequences of development/learning and the sequences of loss, and about the strategies employed to compensate for the lack of certain linguistic devices available to the users of the non-restricted systems.

1.2. The Socio-Cultural Setting of Spanish in Los Angeles

This study is based on data obtained from Mexican-American bilinguals living in a mostly Hispanic area of Los Angeles County (inner rectangle in Fig. 1.1) between 1983 and 1988. According to the US Census of 1980,[5] Los Angeles County was a multi-ethnic area of 7,477,503 persons, slightly over 30 per cent of the total population of California (23,667,902). There were 4,544,331 persons of Spanish origin in this state; 3,597,065 persons five years old and over declared speaking Spanish at home. Almost 50 per cent (2,066,103) of the Hispanic population resided in the Los Angeles County, and of these, 80 per cent (1,650,934) were of Mexican origin. The US Census of 1990 indicates an overall increase in the population of California, to 29,760,021. Of these, 25.4 per cent are of Hispanic origin. In 1990, a total of 5,478,712 persons five years old and over speak Spanish at home in this state, i.e. almost a 2 million increase in ten years. With respect to the density of Hispanic population in the areas studied (inner rectangle in Fig. 1.1), the *Los Angeles Times* of 25 July 1983[6] reports that it ranged from 30 per cent in Monterey Park to over

---

[5] The figures from official Censuses are necessarily conservative, in that they do not include many persons of Spanish origin who are undocumented immigrants in California.

[6] In all cases the statistics provided are the most recent available. Since I conducted most of the fieldwork in this community between 1983 and 1985, the figures from 1980 and 1983 are quite relevant for the present research.

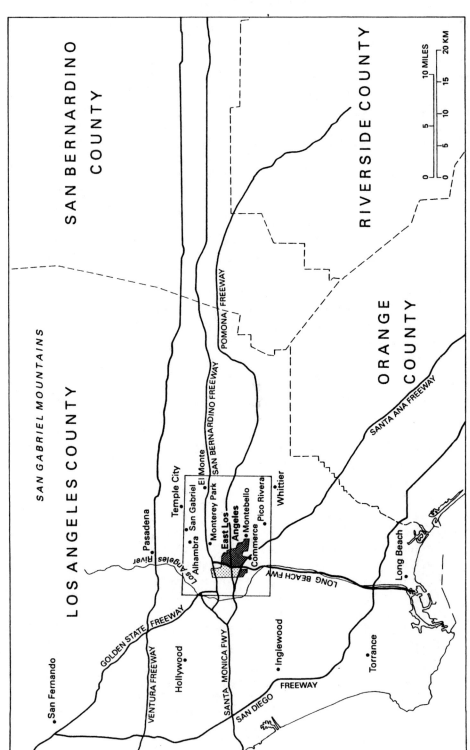

FIG. I.I. Area of Residence of Speakers Studied

70 per cent in East Los Angeles, Commerce, Pico Rivera, and other suburbs adjacent to East Los Angeles.

Contact between Spanish and English in the bilingual communities of Los Angeles has been intensive and has involved large numbers of individuals (currently it is estimated to include about 3 million persons in Los Angeles County). Spanish was the language of prestige, associated with the Spanish conquerors, until California was annexed to the United States in the late 1840s, i.e. for about 200 years. Since then, Spanish has become subordinate to English, not because of linguistic reasons but because of the socio-political and historical factors which have made English officially, socially, practically, and economically superordinate, a status which this language to a large extent enjoys at the international level as well. This unequal status accounts for the almost complete diffusion of English in urban Hispanic communities, as well as (though to a lesser extent) in non-urban areas.

Los Angeles is not easy to classify neatly into one category of bilingual community with reference to its genesis, boundedness, and stability (see Lewis 1978 for a discussion of typologies of bilingualism). Nevertheless, certain features related to the history and permeable boundaries of this community bear upon the linguistic picture.

The city of Los Angeles was founded in 1777 by the first Spanish governor of Alta California. The first public school, however, was opened only in 1855, seven years after the end of the Mexican/American War. The rapid change from a Spanish-Mexican to an Anglo-controlled cultural, economic, and political environment is reflected in the fact, among others, that in this public school 'only English was permitted for instruction' (Romo 1983: 25). During the second half of the nineteenth century Los Angeles attracted a variety of immigrant groups, including Anglos, Blacks, Jews, Chinese, and Germans. The Spanish-Mexican population stayed at first in the original core area of the city, but increasing industrial construction and new waves of immigrants from Mexico created the need for moving to the east. From a town of 100,000 people in 1900, Los Angeles grew to a metropolis of over a million by 1930, of whom approximately 100,000 were Mexican (Romo 1983: 5, 61), and to a megalopolis (Los Angeles County) of over 7 million in the years following the Second World War. By the end of the 1960s, 'Los Angeles had become the major destination for Mexican immigrants and Mexican in-migrants from other areas of the southwest' (Romo 1983: 170).

Although the Hispanic community of Los Angeles is basically a geographically stable urban community, bound together by historical, social, linguistic, and cultural factors which differentiate it from other bilingual and English-only speaking communities (e.g. of European or Oriental background), both its boundaries and its internal structure are impermanent and undergoing constant change. Interstate movements and changes from rural to urban centres by Spanish speakers in the US quite often lead to a rapid shift to English, easily observable by comparing the linguistic behaviour of these migrants with that of their offspring in the new environment. A similar situation of language shift is created by movement from inner city to suburban areas, where ethnic and linguistic identity are more diffuse. Other immigrant groups (e.g. Chinese, Vietnamese, Korean, Philippine) settle in formerly exclusively Hispanic areas, for instance, causing some disintegration and movement to other areas. By contrast, permanent and continuous migration of groups of individuals from Hispano-America, as well as yearly seasonal migrations, have been an important positive factor in the maintenance of Spanish. These migrations reinforce links with non-restricted varieties of the language, and they facilitate frequent intermarriage between bilinguals with reduced degrees of proficiency in Spanish and nearly monolingual Spanish speakers. This social phenomenon undoubtedly motivates increased conscious and unconscious efforts to maintain Spanish as a community language.

Indeed, Spanish in the United States illustrates both maintenance and shift to English. The maintenance of Spanish at the societal level is unquestionable. Despite efforts to reassert the status of English as the dominant language through the passing of state laws which establish English as the official language (e.g. in California in 1986 and Arizona, Colorado, and Florida in 1988), my direct experience of the situation in the south-west indicates that Spanish is being spoken by ever larger groups of individuals; new publications in Spanish appear on the market; television programmes in Spanish increase their audience; important business companies advertise in Spanish and provide customer services in this language (e.g. telephone companies, law offices, hospitals, health centres, department stores).

Sixty per cent of the Hispanic population of the United States (close to 9 million according to the 1980 US Census) resides in the five states referred to as 'the Hispanic south-west', namely Arizona, California, Colorado, New Mexico, and Texas. Of the 6.5 million people who speak Spanish at home in these five states, over 3 million live in California, nearly 2.5 million in Texas, and under 500,000 in each of the remaining three states. An analysis based on these and other 1980 Census figures leads Bills (1989), however, to conclude that, although Spanish speakers are the overwhelmingly dominant linguistic minority in each state, there is no evidence 'that the Spanish language is being strongly maintained in the United States Southwest' (p. 26). Indeed, at the individual or family level, shift to English is common in such urban centres as Los Angeles. The children of first-generation Hispanic immigrants acquire Spanish at home, but most of them gradually become dominant in English as they go through either a transitional bilingual education programme or an English immersion programme.

The typical family situation is one in which the older child acquires only Spanish at home, and maintains a good level of communicative competence in this language throughout his life, with more or less attrition depending on a number of extralinguistic factors, while the younger children acquire both Spanish and English at home. These younger children are more likely to develop and maintain a contact variety characterized by greater distance from the norms of first-generation immigrants. When first-generation immigrants become grandparents and are close to their grandchildren, these may acquire Spanish at home; but this case is rare in large urban centres. At best, these third-generation children may be exposed to Spanish from birth if they live in a Spanish-speaking community and are in contact with Spanish-speaking family members and friends. They may develop proficiency in understanding Spanish, but do not often speak this language with any degree of fluency. However, there are exceptions to this average scenario. One may occasionally come across a second-generation speaker who either never acquired Spanish, or acquired it and lost it altogether, or stopped using it for years, and is in the process of 'reactivating' it, a phenomenon that I refer to as *cyclic bilingualism* (cf. Torres 1989). Likewise, a third-generation speaker may exceptionally have acquired Spanish from birth, and maintained it.

This dynamic situation of cyclic bilingualism, added to the fact that the socio-historical information regarding such contact is recoverable, make Spanish–English contact in Los Angeles a singular situation for the study of the processes underlying both possible stable changes in language maintenance and changes generally characteristic of language shift or loss. I will examine some of these changes in the following chapters.

It has been shown (e.g. Dorian 1981; Elías-Olivares 1979; Silva-Corvalán 1991a) that in these situations of societal bilingualism an oral proficiency continuum may develop between the two languages in contact. This continuum resembles in some respects a creole continuum, inasmuch as one can identify a series of lects which range from standard or unrestricted Spanish to an *emblematic* use of Spanish and, vice versa, from unrestricted to emblematic English. At the individual level, these lects represent a wide range of *dynamic* levels of proficiency in the subordinate language. Speakers can be located at various points along this continuum depending on their level of dominance in one or other of the languages or in both, but it is in principle possible for an individual to move or be moving towards (hence 'dynamic' level) one or the other end of the continuum at any given stage of his life. The following examples illustrate three different points in the Spanish continuum, from full proficiency in Spanish to emblematic Spanish:

[1] Researcher = C; Silvia (2) = S[7]
C: ¿Y tenían una casa grande para la familia o era chiquita? ¿Cómo - ?
S: Bueno, cuando - murió mi papá - vivíamos en una casa bastante, muy grande, donde había, este, muchas huertas - frutales, alrededor. Estaba en el centro la casa y estaba rodeada de puros árboles, puros, puros árboles frutales. O sea que

---

[7] See s. 1.3.1 for an explanation of speakers' groups and numbering. In the examples, a series of dots stands for language material omitted because it is not relevant to the discussion; one or more dashes represent short to longer pauses; a slanting line stands for interruption; a series of xxx is inserted when something said is incomprehensible to the transcriber. Square brackets in the English translation stand for material (one sentence or longer) not included in the translation because it was originally said in English. The information given in parentheses at the end of the examples corresponds to speaker's name initial and number, sex, age, Group (1, 2, or 3), and tape (ELA no.) where the example occurs. In [2], italicized words lack gender agreement.

saliamos de allí y - con una canasta o algo así. La llenábamos de duraznos, manzanas, toda clase de, de fruta. Y verdura también que - se sembraba allí. Rábanos, lechuga, todas clases de verduras . . .   (S2,f24,1,ELA37)

C: 'And did you have a large house for the family, or was it small? How - ?

S: Well, when - my father died - we lived in quite a, in a very big house, where there were, uh, many orchards around. The house was in the center and it was surrounded by just trees, just, just fruit trees. So we went out and - with a basket or something. We filled it up with peaches, apples, all kinds of fruit. And vegetables also - that they grew there. Radishes, lettuce, all kinds of vegetables . . .'

[2] Researcher = H; Robert (24) = R

H: ¿Y tu tortuga cómo la conseguiste?

R: Un día yo y mi papá estábamos regresando de, de, de un parque con, con un troque de mi tío. Y estábamos cruzando la calle. Y nos paramos porque estaba un STOP SIGN. Y mi papá dijo, 'Ey, Roberto. Quita esa tortuga que está en la calle.' Y no le creí, YOU KNOW. Y miré. Y creí que era *un piedra*, pero grande. Y no le hice caso. Entonces me dijo, 'Apúrele. Quita esa tortuga', YOU KNOW. Y me asomé otra vez. Y sí era tortuga. ¡Estaba caminando *ese piedra* grande! [risa] Pues me salí del carro, del troque. Y fui y conseguí *el tortuga*. Y me *lo* llevé pa' mi casa.   (R24,m20,2,ELA50)

H: 'And your turtle, how did you get it?

R: One day my dad and I were coming back from, from, from a park in my uncle's truck. And we were crossing the street. And we stopped because there was a STOP SIGN. And my dad said, 'Hey, Roberto. Remove that turtle from the street.' And I didn't believe him, YOU KNOW. And I looked. And I thought it was *a stone*, but big. And I didn't pay attention to it. So he said, 'Hurry up. Remove that turtle' YOU KNOW. And I looked again. And yes, it was a turtle. *That big stone* was walking! [laughter] So I got out of the car, the truck. And I went and got *the turtle*. And I took *it* home.'

[3] Researcher = C; Nora (40) = N

C: ¿Y cómo lo haces para poder entender todo en español y hablar en inglés? ¿Cómo lo haces?

N: *Ay, ya no sé,* I don't know. I'm surprised to be able to do that.   (N40,f21, 3,ELA48)

C: 'And how do you manage to understand everything in Spanish, and to speak in English? How do you manage?

N: *Ay, I no longer know,* [   ]'

Note that in [2] a speaker from Group 2 uses the expressions *you know* and *stop sign* in English, fails to establish feminine gender agreement in a few noun phrases and in one clitic pronoun (all italicized in [2]), and uses only *estar* 'to be' as an auxiliary in all the progressive constructions where Mexico-born speakers would most likely use other semi-auxiliaries (e.g. *venir* 'to come', *ir* 'to go'). Despite these deviations from the norms, his Spanish appears only slightly non-native, and it is perfectly understandable. By contrast, in [3] the use of Spanish is mainly emblematic of the speaker's ethnicity, and of her cultural ties with the Hispanic community to which she belongs. This speaker is at the very bottom of the proficiency continuum.

Studies which claim to be describing a given aspect of bilinguals' competence will necessarily be invalid if they do not take into account the place that bilinguals occupy in the continuum illustrated in the examples given. Indeed, the absence of this information constitutes a serious methodological problem which weakens the validity of numerous group studies of the languages spoken by bilinguals.

The case of language attrition has been referred to as 'creolization in reverse' by Trudgill (1983) in his study of Arvanitika (a variety of Albanian spoken in Greece), a term which captures the observation that while certain pidgins and creoles move toward a higher number of grammaticalized distinctions, in language loss the reverse is true; for instance, speakers at the lower levels of proficiency rely on contextual and/or lexical strategies to communicate certain grammatical meanings (e.g. temporal or aspectual distinctions).

The type and degree of reduction found in pidgins, however, is different from that found in language attrition in situations of language shift (Romaine 1989*a*). As observed by Dorian (1978, 1981) in East Sutherland Gaelic, in these situations a language dies 'with its morphological boots on', i.e. with a certain degree of complexity which pidgins do not seem to develop. I have observed the same in the Los Angeles community. Indeed, speakers with the lowest levels of Spanish proficiency are most fluent in English and do not need to use Spanish for any practical purposes. However, the little Spanish they use, most frequently contained in long passages of discourse in English, does retain some verbal inflections, gender, number, case, and prepositions, as illustrated in [4]. This example, produced by José R., a young man of seventeen, further illustrates the characteristic pattern observed for US-born youngsters: they would like to talk to their elders only in Spanish but in fact use mostly English.

[4] Researcher (R), José R. (J, 44, Group 3)[8]
R: ¿Pero tu, tu abuelita está en un hospital ahora?
J: No. Mi abuelito 'stá - 'tá en (a) hospital de/
R: ¿Tu abuelito? ¿Y tu abuelita dónde está?
J: 'stá (b) a la casa 'orita. No, 'stá, mmhm, ella, ella no la, la, o, yo (c) vive con mi, mmhm. *Well, see. I, I want to speak Spanish, but like I don't know everything to, you know, speak it, but I understand it.*
R: . . . ¿Pero con quién hablas en español tú, a veces, digamos?
J: (d) Hable yo - yo, a ver - yo (d) hable con mi a, abue, abuela - (e) más de (f) mi a, abuelo, porque cuando yo (d) hable con mi abuelo él no (g) entende, él

---

[8] Letters (a), (b), (c), etc. indicate a point of deviation from standard norms; the standard form is given in the corresponding notes immediately following the example.

tiene (h) uno problema - eso - *ears. So whenever I have a chance to speak, I speak
to my grandparents. So, I don't speak, I just - listen to what they're saying, and
then I, I - - hear it in my brain and, and - and try to understand instead of speaking
back at them because I - they understand English as much.*

R: 'But your, your grandma's in a hospital right now?

J: No. My grandpa is - is in (a) hospital.

R: Your grandpa? And your grandma, where is she?

J: She's (b) at home now. No, she is, mmhm, she, she doesn't the, the, oh, I (c)
live with my, mmhm. [   ].

R: . . . But who do you speak Spanish with, sometimes?

J: I (d) speak - I, let's see - I (d) speak with my g, grandmother - more (e) than
with my g, grandfather, because when I (d) speak with my grandfather he
doesn't (f) understand, he has (g) a problem - that - [   ].'

Notes: (a) Article *el* 'the' is missing; (b) Preposition *a* 'to' used instead of *en* 'in, at'; (c) *vive*
'live-3sg' used instead of *vivo* 'live-1sg'; (d) *hable* 'speak' used instead of *hablo* 'speak-1sg';
(e) *más de* 'more of/than' used instead of *más que* 'more than'; (f) preposition *con* 'with' is
missing; (g) Verb stem is not diphthongized; (h) numeral *uno* 'one' is used instead of
article/quantifier *un* 'a'.

There are certainly many deviations from the standard norms in [4]. Yet the
passages in Spanish also contain the expected verb agreement with third-person
singular subjects, gender marking (*la*-fem *casa* 'the house'), subordinate clauses,
and correctly used prepositions (*porque cuando yo hable con mi abuelo* 'because when
I speak with my grandfather').

The most critical extralinguistic factors which seem to account for the amount
of attrition attested at the lowest levels of the proficiency continuum include the
highly infrequent or steadily decreasing use of Spanish; its restriction to the
domain of the family and close friends; and neutral or negative subjective attitudes
towards the maintenance of Spanish. These factors evolve quite naturally in urban
areas without a strong Hispanic presence where the population of Spanish origin
is more educated than in rural areas and has a higher income level (cf. Bills 1989).
In this respect, the situation in Los Angeles is rather complex. While the levels
of education and income remain on the whole below Anglo and Asian averages
(1980 Census), the strength of the Hispanic presence is indisputable. It is evidently almost impossible to forecast how strongly the Spanish language will be
maintained.

The long and sustained contact between English and Spanish in the USA has
given rise to numerous changes in the system of Spanish (and no doubt also in the
English spoken in Spanish communities), some of which have been investigated
and reported in the literature. At first, research focused mainly on phonological
and lexical aspects. In contrast, since the mid-1970s morphological and syntactic
aspects have been explored, as well as the very interesting phenomenon of code-
switching (e.g. various articles in Amastae and Elías-Olivares 1982; Bergen 1990;

Bills 1974; Bowen and Ornstein 1976; Elías-Olivares 1983; Fishman and Keller 1982; Hernandez-Chavez *et al.* 1975; Peñalosa 1980; Sánchez 1983; Wherritt and García 1989). This book aims at contributing to this tradition of studies of Spanish in the USA. In the following chapters, I will examine a number of lexical, semantic, and syntactic changes at different stages of the Spanish proficiency continuum of bilinguals within the broader frame of general language-contact and language-change studies.

1.3. Research Methodology

1.3.1. Speakers and Language Data

The studies to be presented here are based on samples of data obtained through recordings of conversations made mainly between 1983 and 1985. A few additional recordings were made in 1987–8. Approximately 150 hours of audio-recorded conversations with 50 Mexican-American bilinguals living in the eastern area of Los Angeles were collected and transcribed (see Fig. 1.1). Of these, about 20 hours were recorded by student assistants who are themselves members of the Mexican-American community; the rest correspond to conversations between the author and the subjects included in the study. In addition, two further techniques were employed: (*a*) fill-in-the-gap questionnaires designed to obtain supplementary information about the speakers' use of various tenses, as well as of *ser* and *estar*; and (*b*) a set of questionnaires which explore speakers' attitudes towards English and Spanish. These questionnaires were applied between 1987 and 1988.

The speakers for the study were chosen to fill in an intergenerational sample including men and women of different ages, categorized in three groups (1, 2, and 3) according to the length of time that the speakers' families have lived in the USA. Appendix 1 displays the distribution of the speakers in these three groups, the sociolinguistic coding for each speaker, and the meaning of the codes used. It should be obvious (see my discussion of the proficiency continuum above) that the separation into three discrete groups does not correlate directly with three discrete groups in terms of Spanish oral language proficiency. Indeed, because of their social histories, different speakers in Groups 2 and 3 have acquired different levels of fluency in Spanish.

Group 1 includes speakers born in Mexico, who immigrated to the USA after the age of eleven. This age cut-off point was established for two reasons. It is usually considered that the 'critical age' by which the structures of one's native language are firmly acquired is around 11–12 (Lenneberg 1967). Secondly, since the sample was to include adolescents, the cut-off point was made as low as possible to allow for at least five years of residence in the USA for those in Group 1. This length of residence seemed necessary for the development of some degree of bilingualism and for adequate exposure to 'Los Angeles Spanish'.

Group 2 encompasses speakers born in the USA or those who have immigrated from Mexico before the age of six. Group 3 also comprises speakers born in the USA; in addition, at least one parent responds to the definition of those in Group 2.

The places of origin in Mexico of the speakers in Group 1, and of the parents of those in Group 2, include Mexico City (3 persons) and eight states north of it (see Fig. 1.2), namely Guanajuato (2 persons), Jalisco (15), Zacatecas (1), Nuevo León (1), Durango (1), Chihuahua (3), Sonora (3), and Baja California (6).

Only those speakers in Group 1 have received more than three years of formal instruction in Spanish, in Mexico, although only one person in this group completed secondary education in Spanish (see Appendix 1). Most speakers in the younger age group (15–29) have taken 2–4 semesters of Spanish in the USA to fulfil their high-school foreign-language requirement. It is unlikely, however, that this period of study had any significant effect on their proficiency in Spanish, except in the case of Rod (no. 42, Group 3), who did not acquire productive proficiency in Spanish before adolescence.

The level of education in English varies in every group: six speakers in Group 1 have received no formal education in this language, five have received their high-school certificate in Los Angeles, two are attending high school, and three are attending college. Only two of the sixteen speakers in Group 2 did not complete secondary education. In Group 3, one speaker has achieved a doctoral degree, one did not complete secondary education, three will soon complete this level of schooling, seven have completed it, and the remaining six have continued studies beyond high school.

The choice of speakers was restricted to include first-generation immigrants from Mexico who had lived in Los Angeles for at least five years in the case of the younger group, and fifteen years for the older age group. The same restriction applied to speakers in Groups 2 and 3. In addition, US-born Mexican-Americans should have acquired Spanish or at least been exposed to this language from birth. On the whole, speakers in Group 2 were able to converse in Spanish with ease. In contrast, seven of the eighteen speakers in Group 3 spoke Spanish with difficulty; indeed, nos. 40, 44, and 46 (see App. 1) spoke with me mainly in English and sporadically produced a few passages of spontaneous Spanish.

The eastern Los Angeles area was chosen because of its high concentration of Hispanics, mostly of Mexican ancestry, and because approximately 40 per cent of the population aged five years and over living in this area claimed Spanish as their home language in the 1980 US Census. My initial contact with these communities was facilitated by some of my students. I communicated with all the speakers beforehand; they were aware of my interest in bilinguals and 'the life of Spanish in the community'. I established a friendly relationship with most of them (for instance, by maintaining at least some telephone contact between the recording sessions), especially so with a number of families, which included two and sometimes three different generations of immigrants (see family groupings in Appendix 1). The speakers were recorded twice, with an interval of about six months between

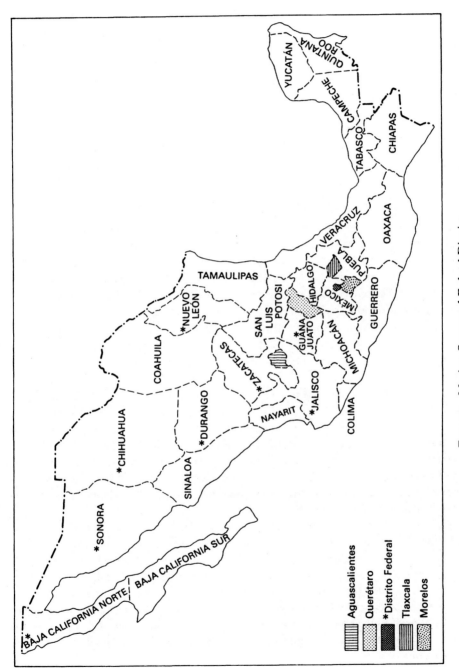

Fig. 1.2. Mexico: States and Federal District

Aguascalientes
Querétaro
*Distrito Federal
Tlaxcala
Morelos

the two recordings, for periods ranging from 75 to 100 minutes each time. The questionnaires were filled in after all the recordings were completed.

The goals of my studies required the use of careful sociolinguistic fieldwork methodology in order to succeed in obtaining comparable data across speakers, while at the same time maintaining an atmosphere of 'social conversation' during the recordings. Crucial to a study of the impact of language contact on both form and function of such aspects as verb morphology and the *ser/estar* opposition, for instance, are spoken data ranging along a wide variety of topics and discourse genres, which ensure the creation of contexts for the use of every form of the verb system hypothesized to be available in the language of first-generation immigrants. Despite a few drawbacks, the data obtained from every speaker represent the variety of topics/discourse genres expected. These include, but are not limited to: exposition of past events, narratives of personal experience, route directions, descriptions of people and places, argumentative discourse, and discourse about hypothetical situations.

This variety of data was obtained quite naturally and with ease from first and most second-generation immigrants, but it became a somewhat more difficult enterprise with some of the speakers in Group 3. For instance, when talking about counterfactual events, one of these speakers (no. 50) tended to switch to English for long stretches of conversation, and had to be asked to switch back to Spanish. Other speakers in the larger sample explicitly stated: *No me gusta hablar hypothetically* 'I don't like to speak hypothetically'. The reasons for this dislike may not have been exclusively linguistic, however. Indeed, when asked why, one of these speakers explained to me that he only liked to talk about or say what he could be certain of.

The analysis of hypothetical reference further requires topics which elicit both past and non-past time reference, as well as the expression of various degrees of possibility. These necessary data were obtained by introducing such topics as (*a*) for past reference: life in Mexico if X had not come to the US, life in the USA if X had chosen a different career/job/school; and (*b*) for non-past reference: speaker's response to the possibility of X dating/marrying someone from a different race/religion/cultural background; situations which would justify abortion; or the possibility of having a lot of money.

The recorded conversations were all transcribed by bilingual students at USC, and edited by me and by some of my graduate students. The analyses of these data, presented in the subsequent chapters, are based on these transcribed materials. I have studied the speakers' productive proficiency in Spanish. In a bilingual community like the one illustrated by Los Angeles, however, the ability to understand the minority language by far exceeds the ability to use it productively. My impression is that all the speakers included in this study understood me, although it is likely that at times I may have unconsciously modified my Spanish to adjust to my interlocutors.

1.3.2. Analytic Framework

In the following chapters I will approach some specific questions motivated by the data and by the hypotheses put forth in the preceding sections, through qualitative and quantitative analyses of the oral corpora collected. In some instances, the qualitative analysis will be supplemented by descriptive statistics (including tabulations, cross-tabulations, and analysis of variance), as well as by information stemming from ethnographic observations.

For the quantitative treatment of the data I have used the Statistical Package for the Social Sciences (SPSS-X) and VARBRUL (explained by Rousseau and Sankoff 1978), computational programs which allow me to examine the statistical significance of the correlations proposed as existing between a given linguistic variable and a number of internal and external variables. While quantification is relatively simple when one is dealing with phonological variables, it is more delicate when the phenomena involved are syntactic-semantic, as pointed out, among others, by García (1983), Lavandera (1978), Romaine (1981), and Silva-Corvalán (1989: ch. 4); it requires a much more careful contextual analysis, and the total linguistic context from which the observation is drawn is more difficult to identify. Quantification is crucial, however, since, as I have shown elsewhere (Silva-Corvalán 1986), the influence of one language on another, and the discontinuities along the bilingual proficiency continuum, may be more evident through differences in the frequency of use of a certain structure rather than in its categorical occurrence or non-occurrence.

I will explain the procedures followed in the qualitative linguistic analysis of each study conducted as it becomes necessary. Suffice it to say here that this analysis has been far from simple. On the one hand, it involved pioneering work on the linguistic issues under examination as they occur in spoken Spanish. On the other hand, the claim that a bilingual speaker no longer has available for productive use a given lexical item or syntactic construction had to be based on careful comparison of the linguistic behaviour of speakers across the continuum in clearly similar discourse contexts. I have been performing this painstakingly slow scrutiny of the data for seven years. This book is the result.

2

Tense–Mood–Aspect Across the
Spanish Continuum

2.1. The Tense–Mood–Aspect Continuum

THIS CHAPTER focuses on simplification and loss of tense–mood–aspect morphology in the Spanish spoken by adult Spanish-English bilinguals representing
different degrees of Spanish language attrition. Specifically, it addresses three
research questions. What type of simplification and loss affects the Spanish verbal
system? What factors, linguistic or extralinguistic, account for the type and stages
of simplification and loss attested in the data? What is the universality of the
systems and processes identified in this study across other language-contact situations, as well as in creolization and language acquisition?

2.1.1. Tense in Spoken Los Angeles Spanish

Let us briefly examine the verb system of Spanish,[1] presented in Table 2.1. Following Comrie (1985: esp. ch. 1), I consider *tense* to be 'the grammaticalisation of
location in time', and include as such those forms discussed under the labels
of '*preterite*', '*pluperfect*', '*future*', '*non-finite forms*', etc., regardless of the fact that
these forms are usually used to convey mood and aspect distinctions as well as
tense. Though it is not current practice, I have included the so-called 'periphrastic
future' and the 'periphrastic conditional' (formed with the PI and the Imp of *ir* 'to
go' + Inf, respectively) as tenses, on the basis (*a*) that 'morphological boundness is
not in itself a necessary criterion' (Comrie 1985: 11) to decide whether a given
category is grammaticalized and (*b*) that they are by far the most frequent forms
used to locate situations in the future (the PerFut, as in *Va a llamar mañana* 'he's
going to call tomorrow'), or in the future of the past (the PerCond, as in *Dijo que
iba a llamar mañana* 'he said he was going to call tomorrow'). I examine two uses
or functions of the morphological Fut, namely its use as tense: *Estará aquí mañana*
'he'll be here tomorrow', and its modal use in reference to a hypothetical situation
in the present: *Estará enfermo* 'he must be ill [at the moment of speaking]'. Likewise, two functions of the morphological Cond are differentiated; tense: *Dijo que
llamaría más tarde* 'he said he'd call later', and modal: *Estaría enfermo* 'he must have
been ill' (possibility in the past), *Si tuviera tiempo llamaría mañana* 'if I had time
I'd call tomorrow' (unlikely possibility in the future).

[1] Statements about uses of this verbal system do not necessarily apply to varieties of Iberian Spanish.

TABLE 2.1. Verb Forms Examined Across the Continuum

Simple	Compound
Non-finite forms	Perf Inf: *haber mirado*
Inf: *mirar* 'look at'	(Perf PresP: *habiendo mirado*)
PresP: *mirando*	
PastP: *mirado*	
Finite forms	
Indicative mood:	
Pres: (*él*) *mira* '(he) looks at'	PresPerf: *ha mirado*
Pret: *miró*	(Past Perf: *hubo mirado*)
Imp: *miraba*	Pluperf: *había mirado*
Fut: *mirará*	(Fut Perf: *habrá mirado*)
PerFut: *va a mirar*	
Cond: *miraría*	Cond Perf: *habría mirado*
PerCond: *iba a mirar*	
Subjunctive mood:	
Pres: *mire*	PresPerf: *haya mirado*
Imperf: *mirara/mirase*	PluS: *hubiera mirado*
Imperative mood:	
Pres: (*tú*) *mira* '(you-sg) look'	
(*usted*) *mire* '(you-sg-polite) look'	

I also follow Comrie in the classification of tense forms into absolute, absolute-relative, and relative. Comrie incorporates the notions of relative, absolute, and absolute-relative tenses in his cross-linguistic study. Absolute tenses locate a situation in time relative to the present moment; absolute-relative tenses locate a situation in time relative to a reference point which is in turn established (absolutely) to be before or after the present moment; with pure relative tense, the reference point is some point in time given by the context, not necessarily the present moment. In Spanish, I consider absolute tenses the PI, Pret, Imp, Fut, and PresPerf (semantically 'past with present relevance', Comrie 1985: 77–82). Absolute-relative tenses include the Cond (as future in the past), the PS and IS, and Ind and Sub compound forms. Relative tenses comprise the non-finite forms. [1–4] illustrate Sub absolute-relative tenses.

[1] Dice/dijo que vengas. (PS, fut. in the present/past)
    'He says/said for you to come.'[2]

---

[2] Subject pronouns are not obligatorily expressed in Spanish. When it is important for the discussion to signal that there is a non-expressed subject in the Spanish example, I will indicate this by placing the English subject in parentheses. Otherwise, the English translation will appear with the corresponding pronoun.

[2] Dijo que vinieras. (IS, fut. in the past)
   'He said for you to come.'

[3] Si me hubiera dicho, hubiera venido. (PluS, fut. perf. in the past)
   'If he had asked, I would've come.'

[4] Quiere que hayas cenado (PPS, past of fut. in the present) a las 7.
   'He wants for you to have eaten by 7.'

The Perf PresP, the Past Perf, and the Fut Perf Ind are in parentheses in Table 2.1 to indicate that they are never used by any of the speakers in the sample. In fact, the Past Perf is not used in any variety of spoken Spanish and is quite rare in written Spanish, and the Perf PresP appears to be restricted to the written mode. Their absence in spoken Mexican-American Spanish is, therefore, not surprising. The Fut Perf is still used in spoken and written Spanish to refer to past hypothetical *situations* (as shown in [5];[3] following Comrie (1976), I use situation as a technical term to refer inclusively and indistinctly to actions, processes, events, states, etc.), as well as to future situations viewed as completed after a reference point also located in the future ([6]).

[5] A: Los Castro se han ido ya.
   B: *Habrán vendido* su casa entonces.
   A: 'The Castros have already left.'
   B: 'They must have sold their house then.'

[6] Ya se *habrá ido* cuando lleguemos ahí.
   'He will have already left when we get there.'

Furthermore, the morphological Fut (*-rá*) is used to refer to future time only in a restricted number of registers in Hispano-American Spanish (e.g. threatening/strong commands: *Te quedarás aquí hasta que yo diga* '(You)'ll stay here until I decide to the contrary'; religious register). Likewise, the Cond is extremely rare in its tense function, i.e. when it is used to refer to future in the past, as in reported speech. The tense function is performed almost exclusively by the periphrastic constructions. In the Mexican-American data, the Cond and the Fut occur with a very low frequency in the speech of first generation immigrants,[4] especially so in their tense function. Given acceleration of change in languages in contact, the early loss of these forms in the other two groups is predictable.

To identify patterns of simplification and loss in the verb system I have compared the linguistic behaviour of speakers in Groups 2 and 3 with that of those in Group 1, i.e. with the speech of members of the same family, or at least of the same bilingual community (see Appendix 1). In the qualitative analysis I have used discourse analysis techniques for the identification of form functions and of the expected changes along the continuum.

---

[3] Examples without a reference to a speaker are made up by me. I am a native speaker of Chilean Spanish.
[4] I refer to speakers in Group 1 as 'first-generation immigrants'.

This linguistic analysis is often complex. Indeed, it is well known that among the important functions of verb morphology are those of indicating aspectual and mood oppositions. Thus it would be possible to argue that, in syntactic contexts which allow more than one form (as [7–8] illustrate), a speaker who uses Ind instead of Sub, for instance, has done so to communicate a higher degree of assertiveness rather than because of lack of the Sub; or that a speaker who uses Pret instead of Imp views the situation as a dynamic, unanalysed whole, and not as temporally suspended in its existence (cf. Silva-Corvalán 1991*b*).

[7] No te creo que *viene* (Ind)/*venga* (Sub) mañana.
'I don't believe you that he's coming/he may come tomorrow.'

[8] Mi país *fue* (Pret)/*era* (Imp) hermoso antes.
'My country was/used to be beautiful before.'

Since these are indeed possible arguments, I have tackled the questions they raise by considering the possibility of simplification or loss in three different linguistic contexts: obligatory contexts (i–iii; cf. Brown 1973: 255); discourse-pragmatic contexts which favour a form (iv); and 'optional' contexts (v), as follows:

(i) First, obligatory syntactic contexts, i.e. those requiring one or another verb form, were considered, e.g. contexts which impose *consecutio temporum* constraints in a number of subordinate clauses. Thus, the PluS provided by the researcher in the protasis of [9A] limits the choice of verb form in the apodosis to PluS or Pluperf or to Cond Perf. The choice of other verb forms (as in [9B]) is considered to indicate simplification or loss of these perfect forms. Likewise, failure to use Sub in certain subordinate clauses ([10]) which require it in Group 1 is ascribed to simplification or loss.

[9] A: ¿Y qué me dices de tu educación si tus padres se *hubieran quedado* en México?
    B: No *estudiaba* (Imp) mucho, yo creo.
    A: 'So what can you tell me about your education if your parents *had stayed* in Mexico?'
    B: lit.: 'I *didn't study* much, I think.'

[10] Lo voy a guardar antes que *llega*. (Pres)
'I'm going to put it away before he *comes* home.'

(ii) Obligatory contexts created either by intrasentential linguistic material (e.g. an adverbial expression) or by the verb form used in the preceding sentence were taken into account to determine whether the form under examination was correct. Accordingly, the use of Imp in [11–12] and of Pret in [14*b*] are regarded as signs of simplification of the Pret/Imp opposition. This is because the adverbial expression *el año 69* 'the year 69' and the complement *un accidente* 'an accident' in [11–12] force an interpretation of the situation as singular and perfective so that the Pret is required. Examples [13*a*] and [14*a*], on the other hand, have created an

imperfective frame of repeated situations in the past which [13*b*] and [14*b*], being
part of the same temporal-aspectual sequence, should—but fail to—maintain.

[11] El año sesenta y nueve *tenían* (Imp) el World Cup en Toluca, en fútbol.
(D36,m45,3,ELA43)[5]
'The year sixty-nine they had the World Cup in Toluca, in soccer.'

[12] Iba a ser profesional, pero creo que *tenía* (Imp) un accidente.   (R24,m20,
2,ELA50)
'He was going to become professional, but I think he *had* an accident.'

[13] a. Después mi hermano *era* (Imp) el que *iba* (Imp) a misa
b. y *entregó* (Pret) el sobre.   (S38,f19,3,ELA66)
a. 'Afterwards my brother *was* the one who *went* to church
b. and *handed* in the envelope.'

[14] a. Porque este mejicano no *sabía* (Imp) el inglés,
b. no más *habló* (Pret) español,
c. pero *era* (Imp) muy bravo y muy macho.   (D36,m45,3,ELA43)
a. 'Because this Mexican *didn't know* English,
b. he *would* only *speak* Spanish,
c. but he *was* very tough and very macho.'

(iii) Discourse constraints on the occurrence of a form in a given context can
provide information needed to evaluate the correctness of the form used. For
instance, narrative abstracts and statements which orient or evaluate the narrative
events as a whole must be coded in the Pret in Spanish (Silva-Corvalán 1983*a*). This
rule, never broken by first-generation immigrants ([15]), is frequently violated by
speakers in Groups 2 and 3 ([16–17]), who use Imp instead.

[15] Dicen que *fue* (Pret) muy trágico. Yo no *alcancé* (Pret) a ver lo demás. Pero
estuvo (Pret) muy feo eso.   (L3,f23,1,ELA45)
'They say it *was* really tragic. I *didn't have a chance* to see the rest. But that
was real ugly.'

[16] [produced at the end of a narrative about the speaker's prom] Y *estaba* (Imp)
muy bonito el prom.   (R24,m20,2,ELA50)
'And the prom *was* real nice.'

[17] Researcher = R; Hector (22) = H
R: ¿Y la otra vez, qué *pasó* (Pret)?
H: *Era* (Imp) en el seventh grade, con un muchacho del sixth grade.   (H22,
m21,2,ELA11)
R: 'And the other time, what *happened?*'
H: 'It was in seventh grade, with a guy from sixth grade.'

---

[5] See Ch. 1, n. 7 for an explanation of the information given in parentheses, and of the symbols and
diacritics used in the examples.

(iv) Favourable discourse-pragmatic contexts for the occurrence of a form were identified in the speech of first-generation immigrants. If the same favouring contexts failed to elicit the expected forms in the speech of those in Groups 2 and 3, the forms in question were considered to be undergoing simplification or to be lost, depending on whether they did or did not appear in other contexts. This methodology is illustrated through a comparison of [18] and [19] from a speaker in Group 1 and in Group 3, respectively. Both passages are selected from conversations dealing with racial discrimination and prejudices.

[18] C: Sí, si viniera un día y te dijera, 'Mira, me voy a casar con un negro'.
  S: Con un negro, ah, bueno, yo pienso que yo sí *aceptaría* (Cond), porque claro mi hermana no va - no se va a casar con cualquier negro simplemente. Pues tomarlo como cualquier persona que *sea* (PS). . . . Y yo pienso que tan sólo por - por, cuando *vengan* (PS) los hijos, por ser hijo de mi hermana, pos yo lo *querría* (Cond) bastante también, aunque *sea* (PS) negrito, no le hace.   (S2,f25,1,ELA76)
  C: 'Yes, if one day she told you, "Look here, I'm going to marry a black".'
  S: 'A black, ah, well, I think that I *would accept* it, because of course my sister is not- is not going to marry just any black. So take him like if he were any other person. . . . And I think that just because - because - when children *came*, because he's my sister's son, well I *would love* him well, even if he *were* black, it doesn't matter.'

[19] C: . . . ¿Qué crees tú que dirías en este caso, qué, cuál reacción, cuál sería tu reacción, verdad, qué - ?
  D: Antes que me *dice* eso, yo *creo* que va a ir, *vamos a tener* mucho más oportunidades para yo conocer el hombre, de cualquier color, negro, blanco, café, y yo *puedo decir* algo de esa persona, si es bueno o no es bueno. Y mismo tiempo ella *va a hacer* que ella *quiere*.   (D36,m45,3, ELA90)
  C: '. . . . What do you think you'd say in this case, what, what reaction, what would your reaction be, right, what - ?'
  D: (Lit.) 'Before she *says* that to me, I *think* there's going to, we*'re going to have* much more opportunity for me to know the man, of any colour, black, white, brown, and I *can say* something about that person, if he's good or if he's not good. And at the same time she*'s going to do* what she *wants*.'

Note that [18–19] are samples of *hypothetical texts*, i.e. texts which convey imaginary, conjectural information, rather than facts stemming from perception and memory. In texts of this type, one would expect frequent use of weak assertive verb morphology, e.g. Cond and Sub. As expected, [18] (from Group 1) contains two Cond and three Sub forms. By contrast, every finite form in [19] (from Group 3) is either PI or PerFut. Given a situation of this sort, one may postulate that the speaker who produces [19] has failed to produce a Cond and/or a Sub form. Furthermore, if no favourable context (in 2–3 hours of transcribed conversation) prompts the use of these forms, it seems safe to conclude that they are nonexistent in this speaker's verbal system. This statement applies to Spanish language *production* only. Indeed, I have enough evidence to assume that most of the bilingual speakers at the lower levels of the Spanish proficiency continuum understand the meaning of these tense forms as used by their interlocutors.

(v) Finally, 'optional' contexts are defined as those where any of the variants involved may occur, with or without associated meaning differences (cf. Silva-Corvalán 1986: 605). For instance, the use of Ind or Sub in the example below is considered to be optional, with a slight meaning difference associated with the choice of either one.

[20] *Quizá vengo* (Pres)/*venga* (PS) mañana.
    'Maybe I*'ll come*/*would come* tomorrow.'

The qualitative analytical techniques employed in the analysis of the verb system used by the speakers allowed us to confirm both the existence of the proficiency continuum referred to in Chapter 1 (clearly represented in even a small sample of speakers, such as the one included here), as well as the presence of cross-overs and overlaps among the speakers in the three groups.

Indeed, three Group 1 speakers (M6, F5, M8, all male in the younger age group) appear to lack the PPS, a loss observable in most speakers in Group 2. This makes their system almost identical with that of three speakers in Group 2 (E30, M26, B27), US-born individuals in the older age group. Likewise, the system of three speakers in the special Group 3 (R35, A37, B33, US-born parents) is more fully developed than that of the three speakers at the lower end of the continuum in Group 2 (V21, E18, M25, younger age group, Mexico-born parents). These facts corroborate at least three of my impressionistic observations of the language situation in this community: (*a*) that first-generation male immigrants who have come to Los Angeles during their early teens are more prone than their female counterparts to start losing the language of their ancestors; (*b*) that Group 2 Mexican-Americans born in Los Angeles before the rapid population growth initiated in the 1950s have developed a higher level of proficiency in Spanish than those born in the 1960s or early 1970s; (*c*) that Group 3 speakers whose parents were born in rural areas of New Mexico, Texas, or Arizona (special Group 3) are closer in proficiency and fluency to speakers in Group 2 than to those in the 'regular' Group 3.

There are no clear-cut qualitative differences between first-generation immigrants and the rest of the speakers, as displayed in Table 2.2. However, while most of those in the former group use the verb system in the manner predicted for a basically monolingual variety of spoken Spanish, the majority of speakers in Groups 2 and 3 evidence a range of systems with more or less simplification and attrition.

TABLE 2.2. Stages of Loss of Tense–Mood–Aspect Morphemes

Group 1

	E1	S2	E12	P15	A9	L3	J16	R11	J14	M6	F5	M8
Inf	+	+	+	+	+	+	+	+	+	+	+	+
PresP	+	+	+	+	+	+	+	+	+	+	+	+
PastP	+	+	+	+	+	+	+	+	+	+	+	+
PI	+	+	+	+	+	+	+	+	+	+	+	+
PerFut	+	+	+	+	+	+	+	+	+	+	+	+
Pret	+	+	+	+	+	+	+	+	+	+	+	+
Imp	+	+	+	+	+	+	+	+	+	+	+	+
Imper	+	+	+	+	+	+	+	+	+	n	+	+
PS	+	+	+	+	+	+	+	+	+	+	+	+
PresPerf	+	+	+	+	+	+	+	+	+	+	+	+
IS	+	+	+	+	+	+	+	+	+	+	+	+
Cond-FutRef	+	+	+	+	+	+	+	+	+	+	+	+
Cond-PastRef	+	+	+	+	+	+	+	+	−	+	+	−
Pluperf	+	+	+	+	+	+	+	+	+	+	+	+
PluS	+	+	x	+	+	+	+	+	+	+	+	+
Perf Inf	+	+	+	+	+	+	+	+	+	+	−	−
Fut-PresRef	+	+	+	+	+	+	+	+	+	−	−	−
Fut-FutRef	+	+	+	+	o	o	−	o	−	o	o	−
PPS	+	+	+	+	+	+	+	x	+	−	n	n
Cond Perf	+	+	−	−	−	−	−	−	−	−	−	−

Group 2

	E30	M26	B27	L28	L19	A29	A20	R17	H22	V21	E18	M25
Inf	+	+	+	+	+	+	+	+	+	+	+	+
PresP	+	+	+	+	+	+	+	+	+	+	+	+
PastP	+	+	+	+	+	+	+	+	+	+	+	+
Pres	+	+	+	+	+	+	+	+	+	+	+	+
PerFut	+	+	+	+	+	+	+	+	+	+	+	+
Pret	+	+	+	+	*	*	*	*	*	*	*	*
Imp	+	+	+	+	+	+	@	@	@	+	@	@
Imper	+	+	+	+	+	+	+	n	+	o	+	+
PS	+	+	+	+	+	+	+	o	x	o	o	+
PresPerf	+	+	+	+	+	+	+	+	+	+	+	+
IS	+	+	+	+	x	x	x	o	o	o	o	o
Cond-FutRef	+	+	+	+	+	+	o	o	o	−	−	o
Cond-PastRef	+	+	+	−	+	+	+	−	−	−	−	−
Pluperf	+	+	+	+	x	−	x	+	+	−	−	−
PluS	+	+	+	+	x	+	x	−	−	−	o	−
Perf Inf	+	+	+	−	+	+	+	−	−	−	−	−

TABLE 2.2 (cont.)

Group 2

	E30	M26	B27	L28	L19	A29	A20	R17	H22	V21	E18	M25
Fut-PresRef	+	+	−	−	−	]	−	−	−	−	−	−
Fut-FutRef	]	−	−	−	−	−	−	o	]	−	−	−
PPS	−	−	−	−	+	+	−	n	−	n	n	n
Cond Perf	−	−	−	−	−	−	−	−	−	−	−	−

Group 3*

	R35	*A37*	*B33*	*A34*	R50	R49	M47	H48	S38	D39	J43	M41	*D36*	A46	R42	N40
Inf	+	+	+	+	+	+	+	+	+	+	+	+	+	+	+	+
PresP	+	+	+	+	+	+	+	+	+	+	+	+	+	+	+	+
PastP	+	+	+	+	+	+	−	−	+	+	+	−	+	+	−	−
PI	+	+	+	+	+	+	+	+	+	x	+	+	+	+	+	+
PerFut	+	+	+	+	+	+	+	+	+	+	+	+	+	+	−	+
Pret	x	+	*	+	*	*	*	*	*	*	*	*	*	*	x	*
Imp	+	+	x	+	x	@	o	@	@	@	@	@	@	@	@	+
Imper	+	+	+	n	+	+	+	+	o	+	−	+	o	]	−	n
PS	+	+	+	+	+	o	o	−	o	o	x	x	o	]	o	−
PresPerf	+	o	+	+	+	+	+	−	o	+	x	+	−	n	−	n
IS	+	o	+	+	x	+	o	−	−	−	x	−	−	−	−	−
Cond-FutRef	o	o	−	−	o	o	+	−	−	o	o	−	−	−	−	−
Cond-PastRef	+	+	−	−	−	−	−	−	−	−	−	−	−	−	−	−
Pluperf	−	o	+	−	−	−	−	+	−	o	x	−	−	−	o	n
PluS	o	+	−	−	−	−	−	−	−	−	n	n	−	n	n	n
Perf Inf	+	+	−	−	−	−	−	−	−	−	n	n	n	n	n	n
Fut-PresRef	−	−	−	−	−	−	−	−	−	−	−	−	−	−	−	−
Fut-FutRef	+	+	−	−	]	−	−	−	]	−	−	−	−	−	−	−
PPS	+	−	−	−	−	n	n	n	−	−	n	n	n	n	n	n
Cond Perf	−	−	−	−	−	−	−	−	−	−	n	n	n	n	n	n

* Italics indicate speakers in special Group 3.

These systems may be ordered according to how different they are from that of those in Group 1. Table 2.2 displays the variation characteristic of the continuum. The speakers are ordered from left to right according to the decreasing number of different tense forms attested in their data. On the vertical axis of the table, the ordering of the tense forms follows as closely as possible their sequence of loss and simplification in the sample of speakers.

The symbols in Table 2.2 mean the following: + stands for a tense form which is used according to the norms of general spoken Spanish, regardless of whether it has acquired expanded uses as other forms are simplified and lost; − indicates that the form is not part of the verb system underlying the speaker's spontaneous use of spoken Spanish; * indicates that the Pret/Imp opposition has become neutralized in a closed list of verbs which appear with imperfect morphology in both perfective and imperfective contexts; @ signals that a speaker has used a number of preterites instead of imperfects; x reflects that the form has failed to occur in a number of obligatory contexts; o signals that the form has failed to occur in a high number of obligatory contexts and appears to be non-productive, i.e. it is used with just one or two verbs;] indicates that the form occurs in one or a maximum of three different frozen expressions (e.g. *¡Que será, será!* 'What will be, will be!', *Te diré que* . . . 'I'll tell you that . . .'); n indicates that no pragmatic context for the use of a form has been identified in the data. The speakers in the table are identified with their name initial and number (see Appendix 1).

I should also point out that no occurrences of the Cond in its tense function (future in the past) are attested in the data. Cond FutRef and PastRef stand for modal uses of the Cond in future and past contexts. Fut PresRef stands for the modal use of the Fut to refer to hypothetical situations in the present; Fut FutRef corresponds to the tense use of the Fut. Note that the tense versus modal or aspectual function of tenses has been investigated exclusively for Fut and Cond. In all other cases, the term tense may subsume tense, mood, and aspect meanings.

The two extreme ends of the continuum, from most developed to most simplified, are represented by E1 and S2 (Group 1), and by N40 (Group 3). The most developed system used by Group 1 does not differ from the norms of general spoken Spanish.

With only three exceptions (L19, A29, R35), the absence of PPS clearly differentiates Groups 2 and 3 from most first-generation immigrants. The Fut, both as tense and as modal with present reference, is absent in the data from most of the speakers in these two groups as well. Further qualitative differences between Group 1, on the one hand, and Groups 2 and 3 on the other, are established by processes of simplification affecting all tenses from the Pret down on Table 2.2.[6] Of the compound tenses, only the PresPerf is used with some consistency down towards the lower stages of the continuum. Indeed, the Perf Inf and the PluS are used only by six of the twelve speakers in Group 2, and by two of the sixteen in Group 3. The Pluperf also undergoes early processes of simplification; note that only two speakers in Group 3 use it with some degree of consistency.

With only minor exceptions, the progression of simplification and loss falls into seven stages, implicationally ordered as shown in Table 2.3, such that if an individual uses the forms in (i), it may be assumed that the forms listed in (ii)–(vii) will form part of his verb system and will not be affected by processes of simplification.

---

[6] The Pret and the Imp undergo some interesting changes which I discuss later.

TABLE 2.3. Stages of Simplification (S) and Loss (L)

(i)	L:	Future Perfect	Group 1
		Conditional (tense function)	
(ii)	L:	Conditional Perfect	Groups 1, 2
		Present Perfect Subjunctive	
	S:	Future	
		Perfect Infinitive	
(iii)	L:	Future	Groups 2, 3
		Perfect Infinitive	
	S:	Pluperfect Subjunctive	
		Pluperfect Indicative	
		Imperfect Subjunctive	
		Preterite (with closed list of stative verbs)	
		Imperfect Indicative	
(iv)	L:	Pluperfect Subjunctive	Groups 2, 3
		Pluperfect Indicative	
	S:	Present Subjunctive	
(v)	L:	Imperfect Subjunctive	Group 3
		Conditional (modal function)	
	S:	Present Perfect Indicative	
(vi)	L:	Present Perfect Indicative	Group 3
	S:	Imperative	
(vii)	L:	Present Subjunctive	Group 3

Conversely, loss of PS (stage vii) implies as well the absence of the forms listed in (i)–(vi), and the simplification of the Pret Imp opposition, as indicated in (iii).

I have used a sort of 'apparent-time technique' in establishing these seven stages, assuming that the individual system most divergent from the norms of first-generation immigrants reflects the most advanced stage of simplification and loss, while intermediate degrees of divergence would reflect various intermediate stages of simplification and loss. As expected, given the existence of a proficiency continuum and the diverse social histories of the individuals in the sample, speakers in Groups 1–3 do not fall neatly into each stage. The relationship between the three groups and the different stages is as follows: two of the speakers in Group 1 are at stage (i) (E1, S2), and the three at the bottom of this Group (M6, F5, M8) are at stage (ii); four in Group 2 (E30, M26, B27, L28) are at stage (ii) as well; the other speakers in this group all share the loss of perfective marking on certain stative verbs, but only five (including L28) appear to be at stage (iii), just as two in Group 3 are (R35, A37, and possibly a third one: B33); the speaker with the lowest proficiency in Group 2 (M25) is at stage (iv), which would otherwise be characteristic of speakers in Group 3 only. Indeed, of the remaining speakers in Group 3, six are at stage (iv) (A34, R50, R49, M47, D39, J43), three at stage (v)

TABLE 2.4. Tense Systems across the Spanish Continuum

System			US born bilinguals		
	I	II	III	IV	V
Relative tenses					
Inf	+	+	+	+	+
PresP	+	+	+	+	+
PastP	+	+	+	+	−
Absolute tenses					
PI (present)	+	+	+	+	+
Pret (past)	+	+	+	+	+
Imp (past)	+	+	+	+	+
PerFut (future)	+	+	+	+	+
PresPerf (past with present relevance)	+	+	+	+	−
Fut (future)	+	+	−	−	−
Absolute-relative tenses					
PerCond (future in the past)	+	+	+	+	+
PS (future in the past/present)	+	+	+	+	−
IS (future in the past)	+	+	+	−	−
PluS (future perfect in the past)	+	+	+	−	−
Pluperf (past of past)	+	+	+	−	−
PPS (past of future in the present)	+	−	−	−	−
Cond Perf (future perfect in the past)	+	−	−	−	−
Cond (future in the past)	−	−	−	−	−
Fut Perf (past of future in future)	−	−	−	−	−

(H48, S38, M41), three at stage (vi) (D36, A46, R42), and one (N40) is at the lowest stage (vii).

What is remarkable about the manner in which the verb system appears to change is its regularity. Patterns of simplification and loss are never random, but at all stages conform to a predictable trend to develop a least grammaticalized system within the constraints of universal grammar possibilities and preferences (see Comrie 1985 for a discussion of these possibilities). Disregarding a few frozen expressions, a small residue of forms undergoing advanced simplification, and the neutralization of Pret and Imp with certain verbs (discussed later), it is possible to distinguish five different systems which represent a steady progression toward a less grammaticalized one. The least grammaticalized system in my data, system V in Table 2.4, consists of two relative tenses, Inf and PresP, and three morphological oppositions in the Ind: PI, Pret, and Imp. In addition to PerFut and PerCond, a number of periphrastic verbal constructions (discussed later in this chapter) as well as lexical expressions complement this system for the verbalization of tense, mood, and aspect meanings. The grammaticalized systems identified are shown in Table 2.4. Given in parentheses is the time meaning of the form, established with respect to the moment of speaking or present point of reference.

Systems I and II correspond to stages (i) and (ii), respectively, in Table 2.3, while systems III–V are 'purified' translations of stages (iii)–(vii), that is, they do not take into account stages of simplification. Table 2.4 incorporates PerFut and PerCond, given that these are by far the most frequently used forms in spoken Latin American Spanish, including Group 1 Mexican-American Spanish, for expressing future and future in the past time relations (see section 2.1.1).

Observe that system I has seven contrasting items in the past and only one in the future (Fut/PerFut),[7] 'in accordance with the general tendency of languages to have a better developed past than future system' (Comrie 1985: 85). System III, the most developed one attested among US-born bilinguals, has lost one of the past forms, the Cond Perf, and the Fut; system III retains five absolute-relative forms, two for future in the past (Per Cond and IS); one for future in the past or present (PS), one for future perfect in the past (PluS), and one for past of past (Pluperf). Of these, system IV retains the PS and the PerCond, and system V preserves only the PerCond for future in the past. The last items to disappear are past with present relevance (PresPerf) and future in the past/present (PS).

As displayed in Table 2.4, the grammaticalized system developed by English dominant bilinguals conforms to universal grammar constraints and preferences. It is not the case, for instance, that a past of past is lost in a system with past of future; the system also maintains the cross-linguistically more frequent future in the past (PerCond) rather than future perfect in the past (PluS). Moreover, systems III and IV have a grammaticalized future distinction (PerFut) not always present in non-contact languages, e.g. in German and Finnish (Comrie 1985: 45), and system III incorporates absolute-relative past distinctions not made in, for instance, Russian, which has only absolute tenses (Present, Past, and Future). It should in principle be possible, therefore, to find speakers at lower points along the bilingual-proficiency continuum who would use even further simplified verb systems. In addition, given widespread acceptance of the fact that simplified languages (e.g. child language, pidgins, early stages of second-language acquisition) rely heavily on context, it seems safe to assume that the most simplified tense system could consist of basically non-finite forms with perhaps a small number of auxiliary verbs, as is the case in many pidgins, but this stage is not attested in the data analysed here.

The question might arise whether the loss of compound tenses could simply derive from lack of the forms used in their composition. This is not the case, however, since speakers who appear to have systems IV and V use the forms *haber*, *había* (certainly with a different meaning, 'there to be', 'there was', respectively)

---

[7] These numbers do not include the Imp because this represents an exclusively aspectual opposition with the Pret, nor the PS because this form may refer to future in the past or in the present.

and PastPs (system IV only) in other types of construction. Note also that the composition *haber* + PastP is retained in the Pres Perf in system IV. Indeed, the different treatment of the PresPerf lends some support to Comrie's (1985: 78–82) argument that this tense is in fact radically different from the absolute-relative tenses, both conceptually and typologically. Some languages, for instance, have a distinct PresPerf but no other perfect forms, while others have the reverse. The former group is illustrated by Swahili and our bilingual system IV; Maltese exemplifies the latter.

One can further ask why languages in situations of linguistic stress develop these grammaticalized systems to the exclusion of other logical possibilities. The answer, it seems to me, must be sought in relation to all the four factors proposed as playing a role in the case of languages in contact: namely cognitive, social, intralinguistic, and interlinguistic. I return to the question of possible explanations later in this chapter.

2.1.2. *Non-spontaneous Use of Tense*

A fill-in-the-gap verb test (see Appendix 2) was administered orally to 37 of the 40 speakers included in Table 2.2 (M6, A46, and N40 did not complete this task). At the end of the second or third recording session with the speakers, I asked them to complete the examples in the verb test with any verb in any form that they considered appropriate. The speakers had the list of examples in front of them while I read them, and were allowed as much time as necessary to complete the task. They or I read some of the examples twice or more at their request.

The purpose of this questionnaire was to find out whether the absence of a form in the spontaneous recordings represented the total loss of that particular form or whether this form was still part of the speaker's verb system, available for use either in a more formal oral style or in the written mode. The test attempted to replicate a situation in which the speakers would have enough time to think and retrieve, presumably from their long-term memory, less frequently used forms. Furthermore, it provided syntactic contexts not attested in the data from some Group 2 and Group 3 speakers, which required a number of compound forms not used in the conversations.

Of the 37 speakers who answered the verb test, Table 2.5 comprises only those who provided a form which they had either not used at all or failed to use in some required contexts in the spontaneous recordings. Thus, a + in Table 2.5 corresponds to a form not used at all in the required contexts or not used at all in the spontaneous mode (cf. Table 2.2), while – x and o in Table 2.5 correspond to the same lack of or reduced use of a verb form as indicated by these symbols in Table 2.2. I assume that forms with pluses in Table 2.2 are in the speaker's verb system; therefore, no further information about these forms is included in Table 2.5 (i.e. the cells are left blank). Pluses in Table 2.5 are important; they allow us to

TABLE 2.5. Responses to the Fill-in-the-Gap Verb Test

	Group 1												
	E12	P15	A9	L3	J16	R11	J14	F5	M8	Q	A	S	C
PS										13	12/14	10/10	6/6
IS										18	12/14	9/10	4/6
Cond-FutRef										29	11/14	10/10	6/6
Cond-PastRef							−		−	15	2/14	2/10	2/6
Pluperf										27	10/14	10/10	6/6
PluS	+									28	11/14	3/10	0/6
Perf Inf								−	+	20	11/14	9/10	5/6
Fut-PresRef				++	+−		−	−		32	3/14	0/10	3/6
Fut-FutRef			++			++	−+	++	++	2, 17	19/28	11/20	6/6[a]
PPS						x	−	−	−	30	1/14	2/10	2/6
Cond Perf	−	+	−	−	−	−	−	−	−	5	3/14	6/10	6/6
Fut Perf[b]	−	−	−	−	−	−	−	−	−	9	2/14	8/10	5/6

TABLE 2.5 (cont.)

Group 2

	E30	M26	B27	L28	L19	A29	A20	R17	H22	V21	E18	M25	A
PS								+	+	−	+		3/12
IS					+		+	+	−	+	+	+	6/12
Cond-FutRef				−			+	−	+	−	−	−	2/12
Cond-PastRef								−	−	−	−	−	0/12
Pluperf					−		+	+	+	−	+	−	2/12
PluS					+			+	+	−	+	−	4/12
Perf Inf				−				+	+		+	−	3/12
Fut-PresRef			−	+	−	−	−	−	−	−	−	−	1/12
Fut-FutRef	++	−+	++	+−	++	—|	—|	—|	++	—|	+−	−+	13/12
PPS	−	−	−	−	−	−	−	−	−	−	−	−	0/12
Cond Perf	−	−	−	−	−	−	−	−	−	−	−	−	0/12
Fut Perf	−	−	−	−	−	−	−	−	−	−	−	−	0/12

TABLE 2.5 (cont.)

Group 3

	R35	A37	B33	A34	R50	R49	M47	H48	S38	D39	J43	M41	D36	R42	A
PS	–	–	–	–	–	+	+	+	+	+	+	+	–	–	7/14
PresPerf	–	+	–	–	–	–	–	–	–	–	+	–	–	–	2/14[c]
IS	–	+	–	–	–	–	–	–	+	–	–	–	–	–	2/14
Cond-FutRef	+	–	–	–	–	–	–	–	–	–	–	–	+	+	3/14
Cond-PastRef	–	–	–	–	–	–	–	–	–	–	–	–	–	–	0/14
Pluperf	+	+	–	–	–	–	+	–	–	+	–	–	–	–	4/14
PluS	+	–	+	+	–	–	–	–	+	–	+	–	–	–	5/14
Perf Inf	–	–	–	–	–	–	–	–	–	–	–	–	–	–	0/14
Fut-PresRef	–	–	–	+	–	–	+	–	–	–	+	–	–	–	3/14
Fut-FutRef	–	–	–	–	–	–	–	-+	–	–	–	–	–	-+	2/14
PPS	–	–	–	–	–	–	–	–	–	–	–	–	–	–	0/14
Cond Perf	–	–	–	–	–	–	–	–	–	–	–	–	–	–	0/14
Fut Perf	–	–	–	–	–	–	–	–	–	–	–	–	–	–	0/14

[a] [17] was not included in the test administered to the Chilean group.

[b] Recall that Fut Perf does not occur in the recorded conversations.

[c] Speakers A37 and J43 completed [9] in the verb test with a PresPerf form as an alternative to Fut Perf. This is an acceptable option, surprisingly not chosen by speakers in Groups 1 and 2, who tended to provide a Pret (a rather borderline alternative) even though the PresPerf is a productive form in their Spanish.

appreciate at a glance how many more verb forms are available to the speakers in the non-spontaneous mode.

The number in column Q corresponds to the number of the example to be completed in the verb test (see Appendix 2). Since the number of the example is the same for all Groups, column Q is included only in the results for Group 1. Note that two examples in the verb test (2, 17—see Appendix 2) created a context for the use of a Future form (PerFut, or Fut). I have included the responses to both examples in Table 2.5, because it is interesting to observe that the morphological Fut (Fut-FutRef), rare in spoken Latin American Spanish, is the form preferred by Groups 1 and 2 in a school-type test. This may indicate that the morphological Fut may also be preferred in a more formal oral register, or in writing.

The numbers in column A refer to the number of speakers in each Group who provided the relevant form in the example indicated in column Q, out of a total of fourteen speakers who completed the verb test in Group 1, twelve in Group 2, and fourteen in Group 3.

The same verb test was also administered to ten Spanish speakers from various countries (including Argentina, Colombia, Costa Rica, Spain, and Venezuela) living in Los Angeles at the time (column S), as well as to six Chilean speakers in Chile (column C). These sixteen people are all college-educated. Columns S and C are included in the table for Group 1.

One may wonder if there is any correlation between the number of pluses in the verb test that any individual has added to the number of forms used spontaneously and the level of schooling in Spanish or in general. The answer appears to be negative. Compare, for example, L19 and E18 with V21 and M25 in Group 2. The first two speakers have received no formal instruction in Spanish and their level of general education is in one case lower (L19) and in the other case the same or higher than that of the latter two speakers. Yet L19 and E18 add at least 50 per cent more verb forms in the test situation (4/7 and 6/12, respectively), while V21 only provides one of the twelve forms that she had not produced spontaneously, and M25 provides just two out of eleven forms not previously used.

Likewise in Group 3, the number of pluses added does not correlate with level of formal schooling in Spanish or in general. Other factors may be playing a role in the different behaviour observed in the two modes examined—spontaneous oral mode and test mode—one of which must certainly be level of proficiency in Spanish. One case where schooling may have had an effect concerns two speakers in Group 3, D36 and R42. These speakers had not used any Cond forms in the conversations, but completed an apodosis (Q 29), a modal non-past context, with this form. These speakers have received some instruction in Spanish as a second language (see Appendix 1), and question 29 is a typical school example for the elicitation of Cond.

With regard to the speakers' overall behaviour, the only notable difference in Group 1 corresponds to the Fut. It seems to me, therefore, that the absence or scarce occurrence of the morphological Fut in the conversations with speakers in Group 1 responds to its being stylistically marked rather than to loss. This observation may also apply to some speakers in Group 2 (eight out of twelve provided a Fut form in the completion task). As for the other tenses, absent in both modes, and especially in those examples which elicited the form expected from most of the other non-Mexican-American speakers tested (e.g. the Cond Perf and the Fut Perf), I feel more confident about asserting that they are either in an advanced stage of simplification or absent from the verb system of Group 1 speakers.

In addition to the Fut, Group 2 provides a number of Sub forms in the test. Indeed, the questionnaire further helped me confirm a diatopic difference between Mexican and Chilean Spanish in regard to the Cond Perf and the PluS. While Chilean Spanish (and some of the other varieties tested—see column S in Table 2.5) retains the Cond Perf in its modal function in the apodosis of conditional clauses (Q. 5 in the verb test), Mexican Spanish uses PluS instead. This modal function is extended to contexts where other varieties would use a modal in the Cond form plus a Perf Inf. Thus, Q. 28 in the verb test is completed with the PluS by eleven out of fourteen Group 1 speakers, by three of the speakers in column S, and by none of the Chileans. These different responses are illustrated in [21a], [21b], [22a], and [22b].

[21] Si hubieras ido con nosotros al estadio, (*a*) *habrías visto* (Cond Perf, Chileans) / (*b*) *hubieras visto* (PluS, Group 1) jugar a Fernando Valenzuela.
  'If you had gone to the stadium with us, you *would've seen* Fernando Valenzuela play.'

[22] Antes de haber ido tú a ese lugar horrible, (*a*) me *podrías haber* preguntado (Cond + Perf Inf, Chileans) / (*b*) *hubieras* preguntado (PluS, Group 1) cómo era.
  'Before going to that horrible place, you *could've* asked me what it was like.'

The PluS is in general much more frequently used by Group 1 speakers than, for instance, Chilean speakers. Frequency of exposure to this form, then, may explain the maintenance of this tense in at least half of the sample in Group 2, as well as its use in the test by five persons in Group 3. Most of the pluses for this Group in Table 2.5 correspond to forms which are undergoing simplification in the spontaneous mode, i.e. they are used only once in a while in contexts that require them. Therefore, the systems displayed in Table 2.4, which disregard forms undergoing advanced simplification, seem to be valid for both modes. The only exception is the Fut, as noted above, which would form part of system III if the answers given in the non-spontaneous mode were incorporated in Table 2.4.[8] There is a further reason to shy away from incorporating the results of the verb test: the kinds of knowledge tapped by a test of this sort may be quite different

---

[8] Note that no examples in the verb test required the use of Cond in its tense function.

from the one that underlies the spontaneous use of a language. For instance, in a test situation I could provide the second person plural form of verbs corresponding to informal *vosotros* 'you', but it is not quite clear to me what the status of this form is in the verb system of my variety of Spanish, which does not differentiate between formal and informal second person plural morphologically. I certainly know the forms, as I know many forms from other languages as well, but I would not consider them part of the system which underlies my productive use of Spanish.

At this point, it becomes necessary to consider the strategies that Mexican-American speakers are employing to compensate for the forms either lost or being simplified. I examine this matter in the following section.

2.2. Compensatory Strategies

As stated in Chapter 1, the general hypothesis investigated in this book is that in language-contact situations bilinguals develop strategies aimed at lightening the cognitive load of having to remember and use two different linguistic systems. This task of remembering and using two linguistic systems is not the same for all bilinguals. Although frequency of use of the receding language may facilitate the task, it is most likely heavier for those who have acquired two more complete systems. Neither English-dominant bilinguals at the lower stages of the Spanish proficiency continuum nor Spanish-dominant bilinguals with low English proficiency bear the same linguistic load as more competent bilinguals. However, the strategies they resort to when using Spanish include some of those utilized by bilinguals placed at higher levels along both continua (English and Spanish). In this section I discuss two of these strategies: semantic extensions of the verb tenses still available to bilinguals in the recessive language, and the development of periphrastic verbal constructions. As expected, both strategies occur with varying degrees of intensity across the Spanish continuum.

2.2.1. Patterns of Tense Extensions

Patterns of expansion appear to be as regular as patterns of loss. One may safely say that the general strategy is to use either a retained form with a meaning close to that of the one being simplified or lost, or the infinitive, a pure relative form.

In the data from Group 1, in addition to the standard patterns of form shifts (cf. Rojo 1974: 111–28) or expansions and the absence of some forms in the spontaneous mode, both characteristic of many Spanish varieties (listed in (a)–(d) in Table 2.6), we attest simplification of PluS, illustrated in [23], as well as loss of Perf Inf, and PPS ([24–5]). In Tables 2.6, 2.7, and 2.8 an asterisk indicates that the tense used is not an alternative option in any standard or non-standard monolingual Spanish variety that I know of; a question mark signals that it may be marginally acceptable in some non-standard varieties.

TABLE 2.6. Tense Extensions in Group 1

Tense expected	Tense used
(*a*) Fut	PerFut, PI
(*b*) Fut Perf	PerFut + Perf Inf
(*c*) Cond	Imp, PerCond
(*d*) Cond Perf	Pluperf, PluS
(*e*) PluS	Pluperf, ?PresPerf, ?IS
(*f*) Perf Inf	Inf
(*g*) PPS	?IS, ?PresPerf, ?Pret

[23–5] illustrate the extensions in (*e*), (*f*), and (*g*) respectively.

[23] Pero si, si me *he casado* (PresPerf) allá sabrá Dios cómo anduviera. (expected: *hubiera casado*, PluS)   (E12,f44,1,ELA92)
'But if, if I *had married* (lit. *have married*) over there God only knows what my life would have been like.'

[24] El podía *traerlo* (Inf), pero no quiso. (exp.: *haberlo traído*, Perf Inf)   (M8, m17,1,ELA59)
'He could *have brought* (lit.: *bring*) him, but he didn't want to.'

[25] No creo que *agarrara* (IS) mucho. (exp.: *haya agarrado*, PPS)   (M8,m17, 1,ELA59)
'I don't think that he could have *stolen* a lot.'[9]

An in-depth scrutiny and explanation of the semantic features shared by the tenses used and the substituted or expected tenses is beyond the scope of this book. I must note, however, that tenses are extended to substitute for others that I deem to be close in meaning because they have in common their time reference, their perfectivity, both time reference and perfectivity, or mood. Thus, in Group 1 the Perf Inf is substituted for by Inf and not by PI or Imp, for instance. Likewise, the PluS is replaced by Pluperf, PresPerf, or IS, and not by an entirely unmotivated Imp or PerFut. Continuing the cycle, once these expanding forms become lost, they are in turn replaced by a semantically close existing form.

Any given tense tends to be quite regularly replaced by the same other tense or tenses in the usage of speakers at the same or a similar stage in the continuum. However, this regular pattern of substitution is occasionally disrupted in the samples from speakers at the lower stages of the continuum in Groups 2 and 3. The occurrence of an unanticipated form is illustrated in [26], where a PS substitutes for a PI.

---

[9] I do not give a literal (lit.) translation into English of Spanish Subjunctive tenses given that this language lacks most of the forms corresponding to this mood.

TABLE 2.7. *Tense Extensions in Groups 2 and 3*

Tense expected	Tense used
(*a*) Cond-FutRef	IS, *PerCond
(*b*) PS	*PI
(*c*) IS	*Pret, *Imp
(*d*) Pluperf	*Pret
(*e*) PluS	*Imp, *Pret, *PI, *PerCond
(*f*) Cond Perf	*PerCond
(*g*) PresPerf	?PI, ?Pret
(*h*) Imp	*Pret

[26] Ella fue la que me habló, que 'Andale, Son, ¿por qué no te *metas* (PS) en este "contest"?' (exp.: *metes*, PI)[10]   (S38,f19,3,ELA31)
  'She was the one who told me, "Come on, Son, why don't you *enter* this 'contest'?" '

In addition to those of Group 1, Groups 2 and 3 display further tense extensions, summarized in Table 2.7. The asterisks and question marks refer to contexts where the expected form is required and it is not simply a pragmatic alternative as it may be the case with some verb tenses. For instance, if a PI is chosen over a PS in contexts where it could be interpreted to communicate a higher degree of assertiveness than the subjunctive (*Quizá vengo* (PI)/*venga* (PS) *mañana* 'Perhaps I will/may come tomorrow'), it is obviously considered an expected use of PI.

Given the early loss of Cond Perf, the lack of Pluperf in some individuals in Groups 2–3, and the later loss of PluS as well, the PerCond expands to substitute for both Conditionals and for PluS ([27–28B]), while the Pret takes over the functions of the Pluperf ([29]).

[27] No sé yo cuál tipo de vida *iríamos a tener* (PerCond).[11] Me imagino yo que hubiera sido - - bueno, no me puedo yo imaginar. (exp.: *habríamos/hubiéramos tenido*, Cond Perf/PluS)   (M26,f51,2,ELA85)
  'I don't know what type of life we *would've had* (lit.: *would go to have*). I imagine it would've been - - well, I can't imagine.'

[28] A: ¿Cómo ves tu vida en México si en vez de vivir aquí te hubiera tocado vivir allá?

---

[10] It might also be possible to analyse [26] as a case of mistaken type of conjugation, i.e. that the speaker has changed the verb *meter* 'put in, enter' from the -*er* to the more frequent -*ar* conjugation, in which case *metas* in [26] would be PI. I have no other evidence that the speaker may have changed the conjugation type, however.

[11] This form of the PerCond, with the verb *ir* 'go' in the Cond (*iríamos*) rather than in the Imp (*íbamos*), as in [28], is extremely rare.

B: Bueno, pues, *iba a tener que* (PerCond) acostumbrarme a las costumbres de allá. (exp.: *habría/hubiera tenido que*, CondPerf/PluS)   (A29,m60, 2,ELA73)

A: 'How do you see your life in Mexico if instead of living here you had had to have lived there?'

B: 'Well, I *would've had to have* (lit.: *was going to have to*) gotten used to the way things are over there.'

[29] Y estábamos esperando a mi 'amá - porque ella *fue* (Pret) a llevar mi hermano a la dentista. (exp.: *había ido*, Pluperf)[12]   (V21,f18,2,ELA17)
'And we were waiting for my mom - because she *had gone* (lit.: *went*) to take my brother to the dentist.'

Towards the lower stages of the continuum, Imp and PI may also substitute for PluS or Cond Perf ([30B]). In addition, PI and both Pret and Imp may replace the Imperfect Subjunctive in certain contexts ([31–2]).

[30] A: Eso era lo que yo te preguntaba antes. Si tú te podrías imaginar cómo, ¿verdad?. Si, si en vez de casarte aquí te hubieras casado allá [en México].

B: . . . no sé si *podía* (Imp), uhm, vivir allá. (exp.: *habría/hubiera podido*, CondPerf/PluS)   (M47,f33,3,ELA80)

A: 'That's what I was asking you before. If you could imagine how, right? If, if instead of having gotten married here you'd gotten married over there [in Mexico].'

B: . . . 'I don't know if I *could've* (lit.: *could*) lived over there.'

[31] Era antes que *compraron* (Pret) el trailer. (exp.: *compraran*, IS)   (S38,f19, 3,ELA31)
'It was before they *bought* the trailer.'

[32] Se comunicó con el POLICE DEPARTMENT a ver si tenían uno que *estaba* (Imp) interesado en ser TEACHER, so me llamaron a mí. (exp.: *estuviera*, IS)   (R50, m46,3,ELA36)
'He called the police department to see if they had anyone who *might be* (lit.: *was*) interested in being a teacher, so they called me.'

At the lower stages, PI expands to PS contexts ([33–4]), and it competes with the Pret in contexts where Group 1 speakers use a PresPerf form. Interestingly, the PresPerf (past with present relevance) tends to be substituted for by PI with stative verbs ([35]), and by Pret with verbs of activity ([36]). The speakers' differing way of treating stative and non-stative verbs is reflected as well in the changes which affect the Pret and Imp, an intriguing issue which I pursue later.

[33] I HOPE que no me *toca* (PI) la misma problema. (exp.: *toque*, PS)   (D39,f28, 3,ELA42)
'I hope I *don't run* into the same problem.'

---

[12] In English, these speakers use the Pluperf as expected (see s. 2.4).

[34] Yo estoy encargado en, en el taller. Nomás cuidando que *salen* (PI) los trabajos
en tiempo. (exp.: *salgan*, PS)   (H48,m39,3,ELA23)
'I'm in charge of, of the shop. Just supervising to make sure that the jobs *are
done* (lit.: come out) on time.'

[35] Esta fue la primera casa que compramos. *Estamos* (PI) como ғɪFTEEN YEARS aquí.
(exp.: *hemos estado*, PresPerf)   (R50,m46,3,ELA36)
'This was the first house we bought. We*'ve been* (lit.: *are*) for about fifteen
years here.'

[36] Si un castizo se casa otra vez con un español, ya nomás lo llaman español, ya
se *limpió* (Pret) su sangre. (exp.: *ha limpiado*, PresPerf)[13]   (D36,m45,3,
ELA43)
'If a "castizo" in turn marries a Spaniard, then they call him Spanish, because
his blood *has gotten clean* (lit.: *got clean*).'

Finally, the six speakers at the lowest points of the continuum (Group 3)
sometimes use the Inf in place of some of the forms lacking in their system,[14] as in
[37], or even more frequently simply switch to English, as in [38], which responds
to my question about imagining what the speaker's life would have been like in
Mexico.

[37] Y no quería que otras - personas - *hacer* (Inf) cosas por ella. (exp.: *hicieran*,
IS)   (A46,f31,3,ELA20)
'And she didn't want other people *to do* (required lit.: *that* other people *were
to do*) things for her.'

[38] Si crecí (Pret, exp.: PluS) en México, no creo que - uhm - - ɪ WOULD HAVE
GONE TO THE SAME SCHOOLS AS I DID HERE.   (M41,m18,3,ELA74)
'If I had grown up (lit.: *grew up*) in Mexico, I don't think that - uhm - - ɪ
would have gone to the same schools as I did here.'

It must be noted also that no required syntactic contexts are attested in these
speakers' samples for the use of a number of tenses (see Table 2.2). This is a clear
indication of the less fluent and simpler Spanish which they use.

The more tightly controlled situation provided by the verb test allowed me to
confirm most of the semantic extensions of the verb tenses still available to bilinguals
in the recessive language. This is seen by comparing Tables 2.6 and 2.7 with Table
2.8, which displays the most frequently used forms as alternatives to those expected
by the researcher in the verb test. A zero in Table 2.8 indicates that most of the
speakers in this group were unable to complete the example.

---

[13] Given the generic meaning of this utterance, this seems to me to be a clear context for the use of
a past with present relevance (as Spanish grammars note). On the other hand, the use of Pret, especially
if modified by the adverb *ya* 'already', is quite acceptable in specific situations (*Ya se fue* 'He's gone',
lit: already went).
[14] Dislocated uses of the Inf in standard varieties of Spanish include its use in apodoses (alternating
with Cond), and in direct commands (alternating with Pres Imperative).

TABLE 2.8. Tense Substitutions in the Verb Test

	Q	Group 1	Group 2	Group 3
PS	13	*PI	*PI	*PI
PresPerf	9	*Pret	*Pret	*Pret/*Inf
IS	18	*PS	*Imp/*PS	*Imp/*PS
Cond-FutRef	29	Imp	Imp	Imp/*PS
Cond-PastRef	15	Imp	Imp	Imp/PI/*Pret
Perf Inf	20	Inf	Inf	Inf/*Pret
PPS	30	IS/*PS	Cond/*PS	*PI/*Imp/*Inf
PluS	28	IS	IS	*ø/IS
Pluperf	27	*Pret	*Pret	*Pret
Fut-PresRef	32	PI	PI	*ø/PI
Fut-FutRef	2, 17	PerFut	PerFut	PerFut/PI
Cond Perf	5	PluS	PluS/*IS	PluS/*Imp
Fut Perf	9	*Pret	*Pret	*Pret/*Inf

Let us turn now to a somewhat more detailed look at the Pret and Imp forms. Superficial scanning of the data appears to indicate confusion in their use, as illustrated in [39–40].

[39] *Imp for Pret*:

Yo fui el único hombre que *tenían* (Imp).   (A29,m60,2,ELA2)

'I was the only son they *had*.'

[40] *Pret for Imp*:

En la casa - mi mamá era la única que *habló* (Pret) español, y las demás *hablaron* (Pret) en inglés.   (D36,m45,3,ELA43)

'At home - my mom was the only one who *spoke* Spanish, and the others *spoke* only English.' (required lit.: used to speak)

A closer examination of the simplification of Pret and Imp morphology along the proficiency continuum, however, reveals an interesting pattern of change. The shrinking of the Pret (at stage (iii) in Table 2.3), which clearly differentiates Group 1 from every one of the US-born speakers in the younger age groups, and from most in the older age groups, affects only a small number of verbs. These verbs, which are stative and occur more frequently in imperfective contexts in the data from Group 1, have neutralized the morphological perfective–imperfective distinction in favour of the Imp. The list includes *estaba* 'was' (Inf *estar*), *era* 'was' (Inf *ser*), *tenía* 'had' (Inf *tener*), and *sabía* 'knew' (Inf *saber*). Expectedly, speakers at higher points in the continuum in Groups 2 and 3 retain the Pret forms of these verbs and use them occasionally in perfective contexts. In contrast, four individuals in Group

2 (R17, V21, E18, M25), and the six speakers at the lowest end of the continuum in Group 3 never use these four verbs in their Pret form. On the other hand, five out of twelve speakers in Group 2, and nine out of sixteen in Group 3 wrongly use the Pret in imperfective contexts (@ in Table 2).

It might be argued that neutralization has been caused by the morphophonological irregularity of the Pret forms of the four stative verbs. This argument does not hold, however, because the same speakers use the irregular form *fue* with the meaning of 'went', which is homophonous with the Pret of *ser*. In addition, these speakers use other irregular Prets, *puse* 'put', *hice* 'did', *vine* 'came', *dije* 'said', *di* 'gave', etc. What these retained irregular Prets have in common is that they are non-stative verbs.

Thus, if restricted to a small number of verbs, prototypically stative and of frequent occurrence in the data, Pret simplification is allowed to occur. Its expansion, on the other hand, predictable on the basis of interactional (social) and interlingual considerations, affects a large number of verbs, including statives and non-statives (e.g. *cambiar* 'change', *dormir* 'sleep', *enojarse* 'get angry', *hablar* 'speak', *ir* 'go', *poner* 'put', *preocuparse* 'worry', *salir* 'go out', *usar* 'use').

The different patterns of expansion of Pret and Imp (Pret expands to imperfect contexts with stative and non-stative verbs, while Imp expands to perfective contexts with statives only) may be interpreted to indicate that the location of situations in the past, i.e. tense, is more crucial than signalling (at least by means of inflections) certain aspectual distinctions. This seems natural, given that the lexical meaning of the verb does not incorporate the notion of time, while all verbs have a certain inherent lexical aspect.

Further interesting changes are attested in the data which appear to be related to those affecting *fue*, the homophonous Pret of *ir* 'to go', and *ser* 'to be'. The majority of the bilinguals in Groups 2 and 3 use the Pret *fue* exclusively with the dynamic meaning of *went*. In addition, they use the Imp of *ser/estar*, *era/estaba* 'was', in both perfective and imperfective contexts, while the Imp form of *ir*, *iba* 'would go/was going/went', has lost its lexical meaning and is used only as an auxiliary in the *ir a* + Inf 'be going to + Inf' construction.

It is not possible for me to ascertain on the basis of the data studied whether all these changes occur independently of one another or whether one change has triggered some kind of chain reaction in the system. Whichever the case may be, the trend is, as in monolingual language changes, toward a one-to-one relationship between certain forms and their semantic content (*fue* = past of 'to go', *era* = past of 'to be', irrespective of aspect in both cases). The semantic content which remains is the one which is most frequently associated with the form in communication (interactional motivation). Further, when full lexical items (e.g. *iba*, Imp of 'to go') reduce semantically into grammatical forms, the lexical and paradigmatic gap left is filled in by a periphrastic construction. I examine these developments further in the next section.

TABLE 2.9. Changes Affecting *Ser* 'To Be', *Estar* 'To Be', *Ir* 'To Go'

	Ser	*Estar*	*Ir*
Group 1			
Imp	*era* 'was'	*estaba* 'was'	*iba* 'was going'
Pret	*fue* 'was'	*estuvo* 'was'	*fue* 'went'
Group 2, 3	⇓	⇓	⇓
Imp	*era*	*estaba*	*estaba* + *-ndo*
Pret			*fue*
Gr. 1, 2, 3	Auxiliary (past of future) ⇒		*Iba a* + Inf

2.2.2. *The Development of Verbal Periphrases*

With respect to the development of periphrastic and auxiliary constructions, the data give evidence of changes affecting *ser* 'be', *estar* 'be', and *ir* 'go'. As stated above, most of the bilinguals examined in Groups 2 and 3 use the Preterite *fue* 'went/was' exclusively with the dynamic meaning of 'went'. In addition, the Imps of *ser*/*estar* are used in both perfective (i.e. instead of *fue*/*estuvo* 'was') and imperfective contexts (see [12, 13, 41] below), while the Imp form of *ir*, *iba* 'would go/was going/ went', appears to have lost its lexical meaning of goal–oriented movement and is used only as an auxiliary in the *ir a* + Inf 'be going to + Inf' construction (see [28]).

[41] [Beginning of a narrative; perfective context]
      Ahhmm, pues una vez - a ver, *era* con un muchacho que pues a mí no me
      agradaba nada.   (H22,m21,2,ELA11)
      'Uhmm, well one time - let's see, it *was* with a guy that, well, I didn't like at
      all.'

   In turn, the lexical meaning of *iba* is expressed by *fue* 'went', or seemingly more frequently by means of the Imperfect Past Progressive (*estaba* + *-ndo* 'was + -ing', where the PresP form corresponds to a verb of movement), as shown in Table 2.9, and illustrated in [42]. In the sample from Group 1, the message communicated by *estaba caminando* 'was walking' in [42] would be expressed simply by *iba* 'went'- imperfective, or by the progressive form constructed with *iba*, *iba caminando* 'was walking' (lit.: went walking). Indeed, *estar* 'be' replaces a number of verbs of movement (e.g. *andar* 'go around', *venir* 'come') frequently used as semi–auxiliaries in progressive constructions in Spanish. [43] illustrates the replacement of *venir* 'come'.

[42] y después cuando estamos, yo *estaba caminando* a la casa con mi hermana - y
      su nombre era Baca [a classmate], entonces - y le grité, '¡Baca, tu madre es
      una "Baca"!'   (H22,m21,2,ELA11)

'and then when we were, I *was walking* home with my sister - and his name was Baca [a classmate whose name is homophonous with *vaca* 'cow'], then - and I shouted, 'Baca, your mother is a "Baca"!'

[43] Y como cuarto, cuarta milla alguien *estaba coming down* at me. Nadie lo, lo paró. Y me, me machucó.   (M41,m18,3,ELA34)
'And in about a quarter, a quarter of a mile someone *was coming* down at me. No one - stopped him. And he - hit me'.

My general hypothesis is supported by this preliminary analysis; *iba a* + Inf replaces the bound conditional morpheme *-ría* and achieves paradigmatic regularity, as follows: *va a* + Inf 'is going to + Inf' = future, *iba a* + Inf 'was going to + Inf' = past of future.

Another auxiliary-type construction attested in the data involves the use of a form of *hacer* 'to do/make' as a carrier of tense–mood–aspect, followed by a nominal which contributes the lexical meaning, as in [44] and [45].

[44] Lo *hicieron rape* a él.   (L28,f37,2,ELA23)
Lit.: to him *did rape* to him
'They raped him.'

[45] Ella estaba *haciendo disciplina* (a todos en casa).   (R50,m46,3,ELA36)
Lit.: she was *doing discipline*
'She was disciplining (everyone at home).'

These trends point in the direction of the following paradigm for past tenses, a stage which has not been categorically reached in the data examined, however:

	Imperfect	Preterite
Non-statives	Periphrastic Past Progressive with *estar* 'to be'	*hacer* + nominal
Statives	bound morpheme (*-ba*)	∅

The result is, then, that the perfective/imperfective opposition disappears with stative verbs, which mark past and irrealis with Imp morphology only. Non-statives, on the other hand, could develop an analytical paradigm which would retain the perfective/imperfective aspectual opposition.

2.2.3. Summary of Developments

Both spontaneous and non-spontaneous use of tense–mood–aspect morphology by the bilingual individuals studied in Los Angeles reveal an evident trend towards the development of a grammaticalized verb system which is simplified to comprise four synthetic and three periphrastic forms, corresponding to system V in Table 2.4. In addition, it is intriguing to observe that speakers show a clear inclination to split the verb lexicon in accordance with stative versus non-stative lexical aspect,

TABLE 2.10. Summary of Tense Changes

Complete system	Simplified morphological system with innovative periphrastic constructions
Inf	Inf
PresP	PresP
PastP	(retained as adjectives)
PI	PI
Pret	Pret/*hacer* + Inf (non-stative verbs)
Imp	Pret (non-stative verbs)
	Imp/*estar* + PresP (stative verbs)
Fut (tense)	PerFut/PI
Fut (modal)	PI (modal verbs)
Cond (tense)	PerCond/Imp
Cond (modal)	IS; Imp/Per Cond
PresPerf	PI (stative verbs)
	Pret (non-stative verbs)
Pluperf	Pret/Imp[a]
Fut Perf	PerFut; Pret
Cond Perf	PerCond/PluS; Imp
PS	PI
IS	PS; Pret/Imp
PPS	IS/Pret; Pret/Imp
PluS	Pluperf/IS; Imp

[a] Pret and Imp would coexist with their corresponding periphrastic constructions. Furthermore, these forms would contrast in modality: Pret would be realis, and Imp irrealis.

both at the level of bound morphology (Imp for statives, Pret for non–statives) and in the differing development of auxiliary constructions with *hacer* 'to make/do', and with *estar*.

If the variety of Spanish spoken by bilinguals in the mid-points of the continuum were to become stabilized—given such necessary sociolinguistic conditions as the continuous need to use this variety, normal transmission across generations, and a large enough community of speakers—the data examined provide evidence, it seems to me, to substantiate the proposal that the outcome could be the result of the changes summarized in Table 2.10.

2.3. Universality of the Processes

Regarding the question of the universality of the systems and processes identified in this study, we note certain parallels with simplification and loss in other languages in contact, such as those described by Dorian (1981) for East Sutherland

Gaelic, by Gal (1979; 1984) for Austrian Hungarian, by Mougeon and Beniak (1991) and Mougeon *et al.* (1985) for Canadian French, and by Trudgill (1976–7; 1983) and Tsitsipis (1981) for Arvanitika in Greece. For instance, the early loss of one of two 'same-meaning' structures (or 'stylistic shrinkage') has been documented in every one of these bilingual communities as well (cf. loss of Cond Perf, in competition with IS; loss of Fut and extension of PI and PerFut).

2.3.1. Emergence and Loss of Tense

Specifically in regard to tense in Gaelic, Dorian (1981: 141) notes early simplification of Fut and Cond in the larger part of the less proficient speakers of Gaelic and, even further, absence of these tenses in the lower levels of the proficiency continuum. Indeed, she further notes that 'only five out of ten SSs [semi-speakers] provided any recognizable conditionals at all, and only three consistently gave recognizable conditionals' (p. 140). Thus, the system of three morphophonologically marked tenses[15]—past, future, and conditional—is reduced to one, past. Similar observations are made by Trudgill regarding Arvanitika. The parallels with Mexican-American Spanish are striking.

With respect to creolization, Muysken (1981) claims that the emergence of tense, mood, and aspect categories in Creole languages is each governed by a theory of markedness. For the category *tense*, which we are interested in comparing with that in the bilingual continuum, a markedness index based on (*a*) association versus dissociation of three points (moment of speech, moment of the event, theoretical reference point) and (*b*) the anteriority or posteriority of the event with respect to the moment of speech justifies the hierarchy from least to most marked in Table 2.11 (cf. Muysken 1981: 191).

This markedness hierarchy, proposed to account for order of appearance of tense morphemes in Creole languages, predicts that the first feature to emerge as a tense category in early Creole systems would be *anterior*, which Muysken claims to be indeed the case. The hierarchy seems to be roughly valid also as a predictor of order of disappearance in the subordinate contact language that I have examined, such that the most marked tense disappears first (note that Fut Perf is not even attested in spontaneous production in Group 1), followed by past perfect (Pluperf) and simple future (Fut), and lastly by present perfect (PresPerf) and simple past (Pret). But clearly, it does not by itself make any predictions in the case of forms with the same index of markedness. For instance, it does not predict whether simple past or present perfect will emerge or disappear first; my research indicates that PresPerf is lost earlier when the ancestor of the receding language has a strong Pret. But I would expect the Pret to be lost first if the receding language were in an advanced process of losing this form in the spoken mode (as could happen if

---

[15] In Gaelic, only the verb for 'to be' has a present tense. The present of all other verbs, including the 'habitual' meaning, is formed with the present of 'to be' plus the corresponding gerund.

TABLE 2.11. Hierarchy of Markedness

Tense	Markedness index
Simple present	∅
Simple past	1
Present perfect	1
Simple future	2
Past perfect	2
Future perfect	3

contemporary French or Northern Italian, for instance, became restricted languages in a contact situation). That is, sociolinguistic evidence appears to be a better predictor of patterns of loss. Furthermore, this type of theory of markedness describes, but does not explain, the facts observed. Within a view of language as a system of human communication, to be explanatory, a markedness hierarchy needs to be justified with reference to factors which lie outside the linguistic system: cognitive and interactional factors.

One must be cautious in proposing parallels across languages and social situations, given that many scholars have agreed that simplification and other processes leading to change appear to be constrained to a large extent by both intralinguistic and social factors. In addition, as Dorian (1982: 36) warns us, 'Few if any languages which are now dying have been used for acquisition or aphasia studies in their earlier, more intact stages . . . Consequently, direct comparison of dissolution or reduction with acquisition is difficult or impossible.'

Nevertheless, it is arresting to note that some aspects of language loss appear to a certain extent to be the mirror image of development in creolization, and in first- and second-language acquisition. That is to say, in acquiring the verb system of Spanish, and indeed of various other languages (Brown 1974; Klein 1986; Slobin 1986), learners go through stages of development which are in some respects the reverse of the stages of loss identified in my data: the earlier tense forms to be acquired are present and past (both perfective and imperfective), while future, conditional, and compound tenses are acquired much in the same order in which they are lost across the proficiency continuum. However, it is possible that this correspondence may in fact reflect the freezing, at different levels of development of grammatical proficiency, of the bilingual's less dominant or subordinate language. The possibility of loss at the individual level, i.e. starting from an individual's more developed stage of Spanish in real time, is not documented in this study; but I could not dismiss a priori the possibility that those speakers placed at lower levels of Spanish proficiency at the time of this investigation had acquired the forms they now lack by the time they started using more and more English to the detriment of their mother tongue.

2.3.2. *Stative and Dynamic Lexical Aspect*

There is a large degree of correspondence not only regarding emergence and disappearance of tense–mood–aspect markers overall but also with respect to the development and loss of verbal inflections with different types of verb. In his study of Guyanese Creole, for instance, Bickerton (1975) gives evidence that stative and non-stative verbs are treated differently with respect to tense–mood–aspect marking. If unmarked, for instance, a non-stative verb is interpreted as referring to a past situation, while a stative verb would be non-past.

In the specific case of Spanish, there are intriguing similarities between the Mexican-American case and one particular instance of the acquisition of Spanish as a second language, as documented by Andersen (n.d.; 1991). Indeed, the development of some Pret and Imp forms in the Spanish as a second language of two English-speaking children (at ages 8–10 and 12–14) parallels in a number of interesting ways the facts observed in the Los Angeles data with respect to stative and dynamic verbs.

Sections 2.1 and 2.2 included discussions of the relationship between stativity and the simplification of Pret and Imp morphology on the one hand and the development of verbal periphrases on the other. It is striking to note that one of the children studied by Andersen, Anthony, at an earlier stage of Spanish acquisition than his sister Annette, uses Pret morphology *only with inherently punctual verbs*. All verbs in *past imperfective* contexts are *stative*, and appear with present-tense morphology. These include *vivir* 'to live', *ser* 'to be', *estar* 'to be', *saber* 'to know', *valer* 'to cost', and *poder* 'may'. Annette, on the other hand, uses these stative verbs in the Imp when required, but it is not known whether she would extend their use to perfective contexts, as Los Angeles speakers do. Regardless, there is sufficient coincidence between stages of acquisition and attrition to support the existence of a basic distinction between statives and other types of verb, and to suggest psychological and interactional explanations.

It is clear that speakers treat stative and non-stative verbs differently. What is not so clear is whether this is due to the innateness of this distinction (as proposed by Bickerton 1981 and Brown 1974, among others), or to the fact that statives occur much more frequently in imperfective form (cf. Andersen n.d.: 9–10) in everyday communication, or to both factors converging in the same direction. My study cannot throw any light upon the question of innateness, but it does suggest that the inherent imperfective meaning of certain verbs and their high frequency of occurrence in imperfective contexts favour the loss of the corresponding Prets, and thus a consequent change in the meaning of the 'new' Imp forms. At this stage, the loss of Pret morphology is lexically constrained to occur with 'prototypical' statives, but it is in theory possible for this loss to continue spreading through the verb lexicon in a manner which would reverse stages of development of Pret and Imp morphology.

There is one further parallel between Andersen's data and mine. It concerns the use of *fue*, the homophonous preterite of *ir* 'to go', and *ser* 'to be'. Just as many of the adult bilinguals in Table 2.2, Andersen's children in the earlier stages of acquisition use the Pret *fue* exclusively with the active meaning of 'went'. The trend appears to be towards a one-to-one relationship between certain forms and their semantic content, an observation made by many in relation to diverse language situations.

2.3.3. Analysis

The development and preferential use of periphrastic or analytical constructions is also well documented, both across situations of linguistic stress and in the historical progression of natural non-receding languages.[16] The replacement of most of the nominal case-marking by prepositions is a textbook example in the history of Latin, which may have been spurred on by intensive contact with other languages during the period of the Roman Empire. Speakers of Latin and the early Romance languages substituted several analytical verbal constructions (perfect tenses, *ser* 'to be' + PastP passive) for inflectionally marked ones (cf. Fleischman 1982; Vincent and Harris 1982).

In Mexican-American Spanish, existing periphrastic verbal constructions are either preferred over their semantically close synthetic ones (all Groups), or new ones are developed (see section 2.2.2) as a replacement strategy at the lower levels of the continuum (Groups 2 and 3). In this latter case, tense–mood–aspect distinctions are marked on one or two sorts of 'wild-card' verb (*hacer* 'to do/make', *estar* 'to be'). This strategy reduces the burden of having to keep verb-stem morphophonological variants under control, as well as having to maintain a productive command of tense-marking on the three conjugation types of Spanish— -*ar* verbs (*cantar* 'to sing'), -*er* verbs (*comer* 'to eat'), and -*ir* verbs (*sufrir* 'to suffer'). I do not concern myself with the changes which affect verb stems in Los Angeles Spanish. Suffice it to say that most of these changes involve either not making the morphophonological modifications which standard Spanish requires, thus keeping the stem regular throughout all tenses and persons (e.g. *hacieron* 'they did' for *hicieron*, from *hacer*), or making them in tenses where they are not required (as in *puedía* 'I could' for *podía*, from *poder*). Likewise, maintenance of a tense in this book means the use of any of the morphemes for that particular tense, regardless of whether it is correctly marked for person and number or whether it is the expected one for the conjugation to which the verb belongs.

---

[16] In the historical progression of natural non-receding languages analyticity and syntheticity appear to be a continuing cycle (see Ch. 7), as is well attested e.g. by the development of synthetical and analytical conditionals and futures in the Romance languages.

The 'wild-card' auxiliary-type verb as a compensatory tactic is reminiscent of that discussed by Dorian (1981: 150) for East Sutherland Gaelic semi-speakers. These individuals compensate for their lack of control over morpho(phono)logical tense-formation devices by relying more heavily on the progressive aspect, and all progressive tenses make use of one single conjugated verb, that corresponding to 'to be'. It is also similar, as Dorian (p. 150) notes, to the overuse of *müssen* 'must/ have to' among foreign workers in Germany, who use this modal as a substitute for morphological tense-markers of the verb.

The very interesting parallels revealed by a good number of diverse studies give evidence of the generality of the processes and phenomena which underlie changes and restructuring of verbal systems in situations of language contact (attrition or development) and acquisition. I will return to this topic in the last chapter. In the following section, I examine some of the explanations offered to account for these phenomena.

2.4. Explanations and Conclusions

With respect to the second research question motivating our study (see section 2.1), various explanations have been offered in the literature for the phenomena here observed. These explanations take into account certain factors of a different nature: on the one hand cognitive and social, on the other intra- and interlinguistic. Thus it is usually the case that more than one factor, or even all of them, may be motivating and constraining a specific process of change.

Regarding interlinguistic considerations, examination of the progression of simplification and loss in our data leads us to conclude that the impact of English is only indirect. That is, evidence does not seem to be sufficient to conclude that contact with a typologically different language would have resulted in a system different from system IV or V. Note, in addition, that direct influence from English does not justify the order in which the different tenses are lost: e.g. (*a*) the early loss of Cond Perf; (*b*) the early simplification and loss of Pluperf, as discussed below; (*c*) the loss of Perf Inf; (*d*) the retention of the PS down to system IV; (*e*) the loss of PresPerf; nor, finally, (*f*) the retention of the morphological Pret-Imp aspectual opposition down to very low points in the continuum.

In English, these speakers use the Pluperf as expected. Compare [46*a, b*] with the literal translations of the Spanish utterances in [47*a, b*]. These examples are from a narrative about a burglary told by V21 first in English [46*a, b*] and just a few minutes later in Spanish [47*a, b*].

[46] a.　We were waiting for my mom, 'cause she *had taken* my brother to the dentist.
　　　b.　I had this piggy-bank, I *had filled it up* and they *had broken* it.　　(V21, f18,2,ELA17)

[47] a.   Y estábamos esperando a mi 'amá - porque ella *fue a llevar* mi hermano a la dentista.

Lit.:   And (we) were waiting for my mom - because she *went to take* my brother to the dentist.

b.   Y yo tenía una alcancía que tenía mucho dinero adentro - y las personas la *agarraron*, ¡Y no tenía dinero!

Lit.:   And I had a piggy-bank which had a lot of money inside - and the persons *took* it, and it had no money inside! [i.e. the burglars had broken it and taken the money]   (V21,f18,2,ELA17)

Thus, as previous studies have shown (Dorian 1978; Silva-Corvalán 1986, among others), the effect of English is only indirect, inasmuch as it happens to be the superordinate language. Some changes occur rather as a result of reduction of both exposure to and use of a complete variety of a subordinate language in contact with a superordinate one. These changes affect closed inflectional paradigms. The more open lexical semantic fields appear to be more permeable to direct influence by a foreign system (see Chapter 6).

Earlier studies have given evidence that existing internal processes of change are accelerated in contact situations. This observation is supported in the Mexican-American data by the early loss of Cond/Perf and simple Fut. On the other hand, though one may identify both intra- and interlinguistic favouring factors, these *alone* predict neither the order nor the type of loss evidenced in the data examined.

Simplification and loss appear to be more appropriately accounted for by intra-linguistic, cognitive, and interactional considerations (as discussed by Ferguson 1982: 59). Note that the simplest system of grammaticalized tense, system V, appears to be cognitively less complex, and interactionally most justified in that the forms retained seem to be the most frequently used in conversation and, one may surmise, the most useful ones for the speakers' communicative purposes.

I use the term cognitive complexity in relation to semantic transparency and to the number of temporal anchoring points involved in a tense form. Indeed, there seems to be widespread agreement that grammaticalized distinctions marked by bound morphology are disfavoured in situations of linguistic stress (e.g. language acquisition, pidginization; cf. Givón 1979) because of their low semantic transparency and thus higher processing complexity, as compared with more or less corresponding lexical and periphrastic constructions. In addition, with respect to the number of temporal anchoring points, absolute-relative tenses are cognitively more complex. They are like secondary constructions in that their meaning combines two points of reference. Observe that no morphologically marked absolute-relative tense is retained in system V, and the only one still present in system IV, the PS, is undergoing advanced simplification at this stage.

Notice that interactional factors do not favour the retention of absolute-relative tenses in a contact situation where the domains to which the subordinate language is restricted call much more frequently for reference to immediate concrete worlds.

In contrast, such factors favour the retention of Pret-Imp morphology, an opposition which plays a crucial communicative role in reference to past situations (Silva-Corvalán 1983*a*), which in turn constitute a favourite topic of conversation.

Finally, intralinguistic motivations also favour the maintenance of bound Pret and Imp morphemes as handy markers of realis versus irrealis, and dynamic versus stative aspect, respectively. In contrast, intralinguistic preferences, i.e. those existing in Group 1, as well as in Mexican varieties (according to the frequencies of verbal forms provided by Moreno de Alba 1978: 196–216), favouring periphrastic constructions over synthetic or compound ones account for the early loss of Cond (as tense), Fut, Fut Perf, and PPS.

All four factors, then, contribute in complex and interactive ways to the simplification and loss of forms in the various stages of restructuring of the verb system of a language under stress, in ways similar to those observed in the development of non-receding languages.

3

The Effect of Tense–Mood–Aspect Simplification on Narrative and Hypothetical Discourse

3.1. Introduction

THE PRECEDING chapter has documented the simplification and loss of verbal inflections in the Spanish of Los Angeles bilinguals. This chapter proposes to examine the effect simplification and loss may have on the expression of *meaning complexes* (Klein and von Stutterheim n.d.) in hypothetical and narrative discourse. Klein and von Stutterheim define a meaning complex (p. 1) as the set of temporally, spatially, logically, etc. ordered information expressed in such texts as route descriptions, narratives, and reports. I explore the question of what it is that cannot be said at the lower stages of the bilingual continuum or, at least, that cannot be said with the same degree of stylistic flexibility or semantic subtlety as a result of attrition of the verb system. In order to provide some answers, albeit far from definitive, to this general question, I analyse and compare narratives and samples of hypothetical discourse about hypothetical situations produced by Spanish- as well as by English-dominant bilinguals.

In regard to narratives, the discussion in Chapter 2 allows us to predict that the retention of Pret forms may permit speakers to communicate at least so-called foregrounded information, while the loss of absolute-relative tenses as well as simplification of Imp predict difficulties with the explicit establishment, by means of verb morphology, of certain temporal sequences. With respect to hypothetical discourse, simplification and loss of Cond and of Sub forms could have rather drastic consequences in reference to hypothetical situations, which might be misinterpreted as factual by an out-group individual.

3.2. Oral Narrative

3.2.1. Analysis

Conversational narratives have been chosen as a source of data because they constitute clearly identifiable meaning complexes whose internal organization correlates with some specific linguistic phenomena, e.g. the distribution of tenses in the various parts of the narrative.[1] In addition, this organization lends itself to an analysis in terms of *adjunct*, *auxiliary*, and *necessary* information in relation to these various parts. This section focuses, therefore, on both the linguistic and content structures of the narratives in order to explore the effect that the attrition of certain elements of the Spanish language system may have on the semantic-pragmatic level. In the analysis, I use a slightly modified version of the framework proposed by Labov (1972*b*) and Labov and Waletsky (1967). There has been much work on oral narrative since these publications, some of which has pointed out weaknesses in the analytical model put forth in them and in its applicability to the study of narratives produced within different cultures. Despite this criticism, I decided to use Labov's framework, with a few modifications, because it had proved to be appropriate to explain different time and aspectual interpretations of verb morphology in an earlier study of Spanish oral narrative that I had conducted (Silva-Corvalán 1983*a*).

Labov (1972*b*: 359–60) has defined narrative as 'one method of recapitulating past experience by matching a verbal sequence of clauses to the sequence of events which (it is inferred) actually occurred'. The verbal sequence consists of independent clauses which are temporally ordered, i.e. they have *temporal juncture* and cannot be reshuffled without changing the semantic interpretation of the order of the events. Labov posits that a fully developed narrative may show the following elements: abstract, orientation, complicating action, evaluation, result or resolution, and coda. To these, I propose to add three more elements which occur fairly frequently in conversational narratives: pre-narrative, preface, and elaboration. Let us consider them in example 1 from Group 1:

[1] *A*: A9,f62,1,ELA3; *B*: A29,m60,2,ELA3[2]
1. A: Entonces, yo jugando con ella, jugando con ella, todo el tiempo.
2. Entonces, volvió en otra ocasión
3. y dice, '¿Pues, sabes qué?' dice 'No le hace lo que tú pienses, tú te vas a casar con mi hijo.'
4. B: Otra vez le volvió a repitir [*sic*] la misma cosa.
5. A: Y le dije yo, 'Bueno, ándele pues.'
6. Yo iba a llevarle la corriente, le llevaba la corriente;
7. todos los días salíamos a comprar verdura o alguna cosa;
8. 'tonces nos encontrábamos, 'Buenos días, ¿cómo está?' Y, y todo esto, y así, ¿verdad?
9. Todavía no le conocía, OK?
10. Pasó.
11. Entonces en una, en una tarde había terminado . . . habíamos terminado mi hermana y yo de la cena.

[1] See Tsitsipis (1988) for an interesting ethnographic study of narrative performance by speakers of Arvanitika, a receding language.
[2] See Ch. 1, n. 7 for an explanation of the abbreviations and symbols used in the examples.

12.   Y *lavé* los trastes y todo eso;

13.   entonces el, los botes de los desperdicios estaban afuera.

14.   Entonces, *llevaba* yo el, el traste de los desperdicios, iba . . . ya en la tarde como . . . cosa de las seis de la tarde,

15.   *y salí* afuera allá a tirar los desperdicios al bote.

16.   Y *abrí* la puerta y el

17.   . . . *salí.*

18.   Pero así, al salir la puerta había ramas, ¿verdad? Y ento -

19.   había una banqueta que era la que xxx hasta los últimos xxx atrás.

20.   Y en eso que *voy saliendo*

21.   y *va pasando* una persona así,

22.   ya mero que le *echo* los desperdicios,

23.   '¡Ay, perdone!'

24.   Y ya me, me *detuve.*

25.   'Oh, no tenga cuidado', *dice.*

26.   Luego la persona *siguió caminando.*

27.   Entonces ya *fui* yo

28.   y *tiré* los desperdicios.

29.   ¿Quién era esa persona? [speaker laughs and looks at her husband]

30. B: Y, y, yo cuando llegué a la casa me quedé pensando. Dije, '¿Quién era esa señorita que está ahí, que vive enfrente?' Yo nunca la había visto aquí.

    A: Yo no me di cuenta porque ya estaba oscuro.

    B: Y yo le pregunté a mi mamá.

    A: Yo no me di cuenta. Yo no más vi que era un hombre, pero no me di cuenta quién era, ni sabía tampoco quién era, no lo conocía.

1. A: So, me, just kidding with her, kidding with her, always.

2.   So, once she said again

3.   she says, 'You know what?' she says, 'It doesn't matter what you think, you're going to marry my son.'

4. B: She said the same thing to her again.

5. A: And I said, 'Well, okay.'

6.   I just wanted to agree with her, I agreed with her;

7.   every day we went to buy vegetables or something;

8.   so we met 'Good morning, how are you?' And this and that, you see?

9.   I hadn't met him yet, OK?

10.   and so it went.

11.   So one, one evening I had finished, my sister and I had finished having dinner.

12.   And I *did* the dishes and all that;

13.   and the, the garbage cans were outside,

14.   And, I *was carrying* the, the garbage cans, I was . . . in the evening like, at . . . about six in the evening,

15.   and I *went out* there to throw away the garbage.

16.   And I *opened* the door and the
17.   . . . I *went out.*
18.   But, outside by the door there were branches, right? And the-
19.   there was a sidewalk that was the xxx to the end xxx in the back.
20.   And as I *am going out*
21.   someone*'s going by* like this,
22.   I almost *throw* the garbage on him,
23.   'Oh, excuse me!'
24.   And so I, I *stopped.*
25.   'Oh, don't worry', he *says.*
26.   And then the person *kept walking.*
27.   So then I *went*
28.   and *threw away* the garbage.
29.   Who was that person? [speaker laughs and looks at her husband]
30. B: And, and me, when I got home I thought. I said, 'Who was that lady who was there, who lives across from us?' I had never seen her here.
    A: I didn't see very well because it was dark.
    B: And I asked my mother.
    A: I didn't see very well. I just saw that it was a man, but I didn't see who it was, nor did I know who it was. I hadn't met him.

Example [1] does not have an abstract. Indeed, I have noted before (Silva-Corvalán, 1983a) that *abstracts*, which summarize the story and occur toward the beginning, frequently are either absent in conversational narratives or created interactively by the participants. This section may be unnecessary in [1], given that the narrative is part of a longer conversational passage about the events which led to the speaker's meeting and marrying her husband. Clause 11 in [1] illustrates what I call the *preface*, a statement which announces that the ensuing speech event is a narrative. Thus, the preface creates the *frame* within which the speaker expects the listener to interpret the linguistic material. A number of expressions may serve as the preface: *entonces una tarde* 'then one afternoon', *fíjate que un día* 'you know, one day', *te voy a contar algo*, 'I'm going to tell you something', *me acuerdo de una vez* 'I remember one time', etc.

The *pre-narrative*, illustrated by clauses 1–10 in [1], precedes the narrative proper. It consists of a *minimal narrative* or *sub-narrative* (notice the sequence of events with temporal juncture in clauses 2, 3, and 5), which may provide orientation but whose main function is evaluative: the pre-narrative builds up interest and curiosity in the listener. This is what differentiates it from the abstract, which may be considered to be a summarized pre-narrative with no evaluation function. In [1], which narrates the speaker's first encounter with her husband, the pre-narrative emphasizes the feeling of the inevitability or predetermination of certain events (*tú te vas a casar con mi hijo* 'You are going to marry my son'). Indeed, shortly before, the speaker had said, *Porque como te digo, ya estábamos en el plan de Dios que así tenían que ser las cosas* 'Because like I'm telling you, we were already in God's plan that that's the way things had to be'.

The counterpart of the pre-narrative is the *elaboration*, a passage which follows the narrative proper. As its name indicates, in this section the speaker elaborates on the events, makes comments, clarifies, and expands the narrative with further details. Its main function appears to be evaluative: the narrator's purpose is to highlight the fact that the events were important and unusual. Example [1], which ends with an elaboration section (30), is illustrative.

The evaluation is an important component of a narrative. It conveys the information that the story is worth reporting because the events were dangerous, wonderful, hilarious, weird, amusing, or unusual (Labov 1972*b*: 371). The evaluation may *be internal*, or it may be *external*, that is to say, in clauses which are not included in the narrative event structure. Example [1] uses both types of evaluation. Notice the use of direct speech in (25) as part of a narrative clause, the skilful switch to the historical present (HP) in (20), both internal evaluation devices which highlight the most climactic moments (cf. Silva-Corvalán 1983*a*), and the use of a rhetorical question as an external evaluation mechanism in (29). (29) (plus the speaker's gesture toward her husband) also functions as the *coda*, since it brings the participants back to the moment of speaking. The *resolution*, which answers the question *What finally happened?*, occurs in (24–8). These lines tell us how the series of events narrated in [1], which occurred *en una tarde* 'one evening' (11), conclude.

The *orientation* element provides information about the time, place, participants in the event, and situation in separate orientation sections (11, 13, 18, and 19), or as part of the narrative clauses (14). The sequence of narrative clauses, which are independent clauses with verbs in the Pret, the Imp, or the HP, in the simple or progressive form, constitutes the *complicating action*. In [1], this sequence includes (12), (14), (15–17), and (20–8), which illustrate all possible tense forms except the Imp Progressive.

In sum, despite being fairly short, narrative [1] is complete in that it includes all possible narrative elements but one (an abstract), and it provides *auxiliary information* (i.e. orientation and evaluation material), *adjunct information* (i.e. distinct reference to entities and events not central to the comprehension of the sequence of narrative events proper), and *necessary information* (i.e. information needed to comprehend unequivocally the sequence of narrative events). For instance, although in [1] the information that it was dark is necessary, it is given explicitly only later in the elaboration section; but at the crucial points the listener may infer that it was difficult to see and perhaps also dark thanks to the auxiliary information given in clauses 11, 14, and 18.

The well-formed semantic and rhetorical structure of the narrative in [1] is matched by the variety and well-formedness of the morphosyntactic structures. For the purposes of this study, it is of particular interest to note that progressive constructions are formed with semi-auxiliary verbs other than *estar*, namely *ir* 'to go' (20–1) and *seguir* 'to keep' (26), since one of the changes discussed in Chapter

2 pertains to the almost exclusive use of *estar* in progressives by speakers in Groups 2 and 3.

Similar analyses may be proposed for a number of narratives from Group 1 speakers, as [2] further illustrates. Narrative structures are complete; they include preface (1 in [2]), evaluation, orientation, complicating action, resolution, and elaboration ((19–24) in [2]). In sum, they provide necessary information, adjunct information, and a wealth of auxiliary information with orienting and evaluative function.

[2] L: L3,f23,1,ELA45

1. L: Fíjate que ahorita, con esto de que estamos hablando, me acuerdo de una vez, no sé si mi papá te contó;

2. Este, llegaron unos, unos negros allí; en la casa,

3. tocaron, ¿verdad?

4. y este, le dijeron a mi papá que saliera, que traían unas, unas televisiones robadas, que si querían comprar o no sé qué cosa, no sé,

5. (*a*) no sé, ahorita no me acuerdo si dijeron que eran robadas o no, no sé. (*b*) Pero el caso, yo, yo no estaba en la casa.

6. Y sí, llegaron,

7. tocaron

8. y le dijeron a mi papá que saliera, que muy baratas.

9. Pues mira, salió.

10. Las, las televisiones estaban como, o sea, estaban en un, ¿cómo te podría decir?, en cartón, como si fueran nuevecitas y nada más les podías mirar el puro frente, el puro frente, o sea la pantalla, es todo, y pues limpiecitas y todo. Y se miraban así bien empacaditas, así como nuevecitas, como sacadas de la fábrica, ¿me entiendes?

11. Entonces le pidieron a mi papá como cincuenta- no, cien dólares por dos.

12. Pues dijo mi papá, 'Pues esto es rápido, rápido'.

13. Pasó rápido la cosa,

14. que porque los andaban siguiendo, no sé qué, ¿verdad?, que rápido.

15. Pues fíjate, (*a*) ¿ino les suelta los cien dólares mi papá!? (*b*) Y, y fue y, y dándoselos.

16. Desaparecieron.

17. Y que empieza a sacarlas, este, a desempacarlas.

18. (*a*) ¡No eran televis - , no eran ni televisiones! (*b*) ¡Eran la pura pantalla! /laughter/

19. Y le pusieron, no sé qué le pondrían, pues sí, una sí tenía la pa- sí creo una de esas televisiones sí tenía la parte, una parte, pero viejísima.

20. ¿Tú crees? /laughter/ ¿Tú crees? ¡Híjole!

21. Llegué a la casa y todos serios. Y dije yo, '¿Qué pasó?'

22. Y yo miré esos mugreros allá afuera. /laughter/ 'Y este, ¿pa' qué? Tienen aquí, ya tenemos bastante, bastante junk [yonk] aquí' - - Y este, mi papá

muy serio ¿verdad?, pues jamás le había pasado una cosa así. Y este, y todos
serios – –

23.   Y me contaron. Y yo me di una enojada.

24.   Dije, '¡Ay, y pues cómo se ponen a comprar eso!' Y parece, y era cuando
       más necesitaba el dinero uno. ¡Imagínate que, que fueron y los soltaron! Y
       yo dije, '¡Dios mío, pero cómo!'

25.   Pero sí, fíjate. Le pasan a uno cosas así, exactamente.

1. L: You know now, because of what we're talking about, I remember once, I
       don't know if my dad told you about it;

2.   Some, some blacks went there; to the house,

3.   they knocked, right?

4.   and, they asked my dad to come out, that they had some, some stolen
       television sets, would he be interested in buying or something, I don't
       know,

5.   (*a*) I don't know, now I don't remember if they said that they were stolen
       or what, I don't know. (*b*) But anyway, I, I wasn't home.

6.   And so, they came,

7.   and knocked

8.   and they asked my dad to come out, that they were very cheap . . .

9.   So, he went out.

10.   The, the television sets were like, they were in a – how can I tell you? – in
       a box, as if they were brand new, and you could only see the front, only the
       front, the screen, that's all, and really clean and all. And they looked really
       well packed, like really brand new, factory new, you understand?

11.   So they asked my dad fifty – no, one hundred dollars for two.

12.   So my dad said, 'Well this is fast, fast.'

13.   Everything happened very fast,

14.   that they were after them, and so on, I don't know, right?, that it had to be
       fast.

15.   So, can you believe that my dad gives them the one hundred dollars!? He
       went, and he gives them to them.

16.   They vanished.

17.   And he starts to take them out, uh, to unpack them.

18.   (*a*) They weren't telev – they weren't even television sets! (*b*) They were
       just the screen! /laughter/

19.   And they put them, I don't know what they had put them, well one, one
       did have the scr – I think one of those sets did have the part, one part, but
       very, very old.

20.   Can you believe it? /laughter/ Can you believe it? Gee!

21.   I came home and everyone was very serious. And I said, 'I wonder what's
       happened.'

22.   And I saw those thieves outside. /laughter/ And, 'Why? You have here,
       we have here enough, enough junk.' – – And uh, my dad was very serious,

right?, because nothing like that had ever happened to him. And, everyone was very serious - -

23. So they told me. And I got really angry.
24. I said, 'Ay! how can you buy such a thing!' And it seems, and it was when we most needed the money. Imagine! They just went and gave them the money! And I said, 'My God! How could you!'
25. But you see. These things happen to you, exactly like this.

None of the linguistic structures in the narratives from Group 1 deviate from general standard spoken Spanish. Furthermore, they illustrate a variety of independent and subordinate clauses, Ind and Sub verbal forms—including, among others, the Pluperf, the Cond, and the IS—and progressive constructions with verbs other than *estar*. This variety of tenses and syntactic structures is incorporated in an abundance of evaluation devices which include the following, among others:

(*a*) Phatic expressions which stimulate listener involvement and interest, namely imperative forms (e.g. *fíjate* 'note', *pues mira* 'well, look', *imagínate* 'imagine'), and rhetorical questions (e.g. *¿Me entiendes?* 'You follow me?', *¿Tú crees?* 'Can you believe it?', *¿Cómo te podría decir?* 'How could I put it to you?').

(*b*) Comparative clauses and superlatives (e.g. *Tenía mucho más dinero que ella* 'He had a lot more money than her', *Una de esas televisiones tenía una parte, pero viejísima* 'One of those television sets had a part that was a very, very old part').

(*c*) Hypothetical manner clauses (e.g. *Las televisiones estaban como . . . como si fueran nuevecitas* 'The television sets looked as if . . . as if they were new').

(*d*) Adjectives qualified by adverbs of degree (e.g. *muy baratas* 'very cheap', *bien empacaditas* 'very well packed').

(*e*) The HP, which frequently co-occurs with climactic events (see [1], clauses 20–2, and [2], clauses 15*a* and 17).

(*f*) Exclamations (e.g. *¡Dios mío, pero cómo!* 'My God, how could you!').

(*g*) Negative constructions which call the interlocutor's attention to a state of affairs which appears to be contrary to what is expected (e.g. [2], clauses 5*b* and 18*a*).

(*h*) Direct reported speech (e.g. [1], clauses 5, 23, 25; [2], clauses 12 and 21–4).

An examination of ten narratives by speakers in Groups 2 and 3 reveals some interesting differences from those told by Group 1 speakers. These differences concern mode of delivery, code-switching, evaluative techniques, clause complexity, the establishment of referents and topic reference continuity, the verb system, and others which I do not discuss here (e.g. lexical differences, prepositions).

(*a*) *Mode of delivery*. The most striking difference in this respect refers to the fact that Group 1 narratives are delivered smoothly, with few self-corrections or false starts, while the rest of the narratives contain numerous pauses, false starts, self-corrections, and hesitation markers. In addition, these narratives have fewer of the prosodic and kinesic features which characterize a *performed narrative*, namely expressive sounds, sound effects (e.g. lengthening of phonetic segments, imitation of noises made by entities involved in the narrative), motions, and gestures (cf. Wolfson 1982: 24–9).

(*b*) *Code-switching.* Code-switching from Spanish to English does not occur in the narratives examined from Group 1, although some of the speakers in this Group code-switch once in a while during the recording sessions. In contrast, code-switching characterizes nine of the ten narratives from Groups 2 and 3. Switching to English appears to have two functions in these narratives: to fill in lexical gaps in Spanish, and to serve as an evaluative mechanism (cf. Koike 1987; Silva-Corvalán 1983*b*). Observe the switches (italicized) in [3] from Group 2. Note that (1) is not italicized because I may have prompted B's switch to English by introducing the word 'surfing', for which, to my knowledge, there is no Spanish equivalent.

[3] B: A29,m60,2,ELA 2; I: researcher; E: B's son, m34
    I: Sí. Pero decían que estaba peligroso para hacer surfing.
1. B: Even for the surfers también. /Sí, sí./ Vi uno que se subió en una, una ola de esas.
2. Y luego quebró - *it broke* - arriba así,
3. y él estaba así co - , casi mero arriba - ,
4. y, y lo agarró
5. y, y lo, y lo voltió así
6. y se lo, se lo llevó *all the way in.*
    (E: Uh, I got a friend of mine at work, he -)
7. B: Yo en San Pedro me agarró una de esas - *long time ago when I was younger.*
8. Me 'garró allí en-
9. *You know where the breaker is in San Pedro?* [addressed to the researcher]
    I: ¿Haciendo surfing o nadando?
10. B: No, nadando.
11. *I used to like to ride, ride the waves in.*
    (E: You know those guys that -)
12. B: Me agarró una de ésas
13. y me voltió así, y - todo el cuerpo.
14. y me llevó así -
15. y iba yo tragando hasta agua.
16. Y - , me, me 'garró
17. y me raspó todas las piernas.
18. *I was bleeding up on my leg,*
19. porque me, me 'garró abajo
20. y me llevó hasta abajo, *all the way down* -
21. y - me raspó las, las piedras o conchas,
22. yo no sé qué sería lo que había abajo.
    (E: You know those guys that follow a boat on a parachute?)

23. B: *My legs were all bleeding.*
    (E: You know those guys - sometimes in Acapulco?)
    I: ¿Que tienen como unas alas - así grandes no más? [Researcher addresses E]
    E: Yeah, it's a parachute - they got a rope.
24. B: Oh, that pulls you when you go up in the air.
    I: Oh, sí, sí.
    E: And then you release yourself.
25.   I got a friend of mine - parachute dragged him - - [E tells his story in English][3]

    I: Yes. But they were saying that it was dangerous for surfing.
1. B: [Even for the surfers] also. /Yes, yes./ I saw one who got on one of those waves.
2.   And then it broke - [*it broke*] - above like this,
3.   and he was like this li- almost on top-,
4.   and, and it got him,
5.   and, and it, it turned him over like this
6.   and it dragged, it dragged him [*all the way in*].
    (E: Uh, I got a friend of mine at work, he -)
7. B: Me in San Pedro one of those got me - [*long time ago when I was younger*].
8.   It got me there in-
9.   [*You know where the breaker is in San Pedro?*] [addressed to the researcher]
    I: Surfing or swimming?
10. B: No, swimming.
11.   [*I used to like to ride, ride the waves in.*]
    (E: You know those guys that -)
12. B: One of those got me
13.   and turned me over like this, and - my whole body.
14.   and it dragged me like this -
15.   and I was even swallowing water.
16.   And - it, it got me
17.   and it scratched all my legs.
18.   [*I was bleeding up on my leg*],
19.   because it got me down
20.   it dragged me down, [*all the way down*] -
21.   and - they scratched me, the, the rocks or shells,
22.   I don't know what was down below.
    (E: You know those guys that follow a boat on a parachute?)

---

[3] Note that E illustrates the typical phenomenon I referred to in ch. 1: this young man (approx. 34 years old) understands the conversation I am having with his father in Spanish, but his participation is in English.

23. B: [*My legs were all bleeding*].
    (E: You know those guys - sometimes in Acapulco?)
    I: Those who have like wings - like these big ones? [Researcher addresses E]
    E: Yeah, it's a parachute - they got a rope.
24. B: Oh, that pulls you when you go up in the air.
    I: Oh, yeah, yeah.
    E: And then you release yourself.
25.   I got a friend of mine—parachute dragged him——[E tells his story in English][3]

   In [3] the speaker switches to English only to provide auxiliary information with orientation and evaluative function, as in (7), (9), (11), (18), (20), and (23), i.e. no complicating action clauses contain switches. As we move down the proficiency continuum, however, speakers do not appear to code-switch to provide auxiliary information only, but in addition they switch to English in narrative clauses proper. This is most likely done to compensate for gaps in their knowledge of the Spanish lexicon. These lexical gaps may have also prompted some of the switches in [3], specifically those that relate to surfing. Indeed, the switches in (2), (9), and (11) appear to indicate that in this speaker's linguistic experience, aquatic sports are talked about in English, thus causing either the non-acquisition or the loss of Spanish lexical items in this semantic field.

   [4–6] are illustrative of switches that occur in narrative clauses in the complicating action. [4] occurs in the narrative presented in [7], which I discuss later in relation to evaluation.

[4] Y luego, *all of a sudden* fue *tumbling down*.   (V21,f18,2,ELA17)
    'And then, *all of a sudden*, it went *tumbling down*'.

[5] . . . en cinco minutos me dijeron que podía *go ahead*, y so pues me fui. Y como cuarta milla alguien estaba *coming down at me*. Nadie lo paró y me, me machucó de frente.   (M41,m18,3,ELA34)
    '. . . in five minutes they told me that I could *go ahead*, and so I went. And in about a quarter of a mile someone was *coming down at me*. No one stopped him and he, he hit me head on.'

[6] Yo me puse ahí, a - - peliar con ellos, y eso es cuando me - - *they tore me up*.   (D36,m45,3,ELA43)
    'I started fighting with, ah, with them, and that's when *they tore me up*.'

   (*c*) *Evaluative techniques*. Several authors have shown (e.g. Schiffrin 1981; Silva-Corvalán 1983*a*) that the HP co-occurs with the most climactic or dramatic events in an oral narrative and, therefore, that it is an internal evaluation mechanism. Likewise, it has been argued that direct speech is a kind of play-acting (Haiman and Thompson 1984) serving to make the narrative more vivid and interesting. Furthermore, rhetorical questions and phatic expressions have the effect of involving the listener more forcefully with the various elements of the story. Narratives from Group 1 incorporate these and other evaluation techniques (listed in (a)–(h) above), as [1–2] show. In contrast, *none* of the ten narratives from Groups 2 and 3 include rhetorical questions, nor phatic expressions (see [3]); reported direct speech occurs only in two of these narratives, and the HP in only one ([7], clauses 2 and 3), but note that these HP forms are not used in the climactic part of the complicating action, as they would be in a narrative from Group 1 (see [1], clauses 20–2). These differences are also suitably illustrated by comparing English dominant bilinguals' narratives in both languages. [7] and [8] provide an appropriate case; they correspond to a narrative told first in Spanish and immediately afterwards in English, at my request, by one of the speakers in Group 2 (V21).

[7] V: V21,f18,2,ELA17; I: researcher

    I: Ajá. Total que nos, nos interrumpimos cuando me 'stabas contando de - A ver si me acuerdo, cuando tenías - - como cinco o seis años, me de -

    V: Como tres, cuatro años.

1. Lego con - hermano nos 'stá - tirando la - nos 'staba tirando cosas de allá arriba del álblo, árblo, - whatever.

2. Gara - un - un clock y lo tiró -

3. y yo digo, no más estaba viendo qué 'staban tirando.

4. Y lo vi que tiró - el, el relol. Luego lo vi y luego,

5. *all of a sudden* fue - tumbling down, y me cayó aquí,

6. ¡y saló mucha sangre! Y pa, parecía que 'staba - salendo de mi ojos, pero era de aquí.

    I: De la nariz.

7. V: Sí, pero muchos, tanto. Me 'cuerdo que - que 'gararon un - como una taza muy grande, y - y allí estaba, ¡allí 'staba toda la sangre!

8. Mi mami me agarró, me - me 'cuerdo que - 'staba las - perlas de mi mamá ahí - y - y me llevaron al hospital. Y me recuerdo del doctor.

9. Me, no más vi una - *big machine* de, de abajo mi - you know off - /Claro./ I was laying on the hospital bed. I just saw a big -

10. *I don't know, I was scared.*

11. Pero después de eso I got un lollipop; remember the lollipop? Y luego - como a couple of days after, tenía - como stitches pero parecía como una - roach, una cucaracha - aquí.

12. To'vía tengo la cosa poquito, no puede ver porque - *I have a lot of, you know, other scars from the, athletes and like that.* /I: Claro/

13. Me 'cuerdo d'eso; también mi hermano se 'cuerda d'eso. /I: ¿No se acuerda?/ Todavía se 'cuerda. /I: Todavía se acuerda, claro./ Todos nos recuerdamos d'eso, también mi mami. Porque se, se 'sustaron mucho, también mi hermano.

14. Mi hermano creí - *thought that I was dying or something like that.* Y - pos todo eso. To'vía me acuerdio de eso.

15. Era más mie- *It was scary*.

   I: Aha. So we- we got interrupted when you were telling me- Let's see if I can remember, when you were - about five or six years old, you we-

   V: About three, four years old.

1. Then with - brother was - throwing - he was throwing things at us from up a tlee, ree [she self-corrects her pronunciation of the Spanish word for *tree*], - whatever.

2. Grabs - a - a clock and he threw it -

3. and I say, I was just looking to see what he was throwing.

4. And I saw him throw - the, the clock. Then I saw him and then,

5. *all of a sudden* it went - tumbling down, and it fell on me here,

6. and I bled a lot! And it lo, it looked as if my eyes were bleeding, but it was from here.

   I: From the nose.

7. V: Yes, but a lot, so much. I remember that - that they grabbed a - like a very big cup, and - and there, there was all the blood!

8. My mom grabbed me, I - I remember that - - the pearls - my mom's pearls were there - - and - and they took me to the hospital. And I remember the doctor.

9. Me, I just saw a - - *big machine* from, from under the - - you know off - /Yeah./ I was laying on the hospital bed. I just saw a big -

10. *I don't know, I was scared*.

11. But after that I got a lollipop; remember the lollipop? And then - like a couple of days after, I had - like stitches but it looked like a - roach, a roach - here.   .

12. I still have that thing, you can't see because - *I have a lot of, you know, other scars from the, athletes and like that*. /I: Sure/

13. I remember that; my brother also remembers that. /I: He doesn't re-member?/ He still remembers. /I: He still remembers, of course./ We all remember that, my mom also. Because the-, they got very scared, my brother also.

14. My brother thin - *thought that I was dying or something like that*. And - all that. I still remember that.

15. It was more sca - *It was scary*.

[8]

   I: Yeah. Could, could you tell me the whole thing in English?

   V: In English? /Yes./ Let's see - since the beginning? /Yes./

1. V: When I was young I used to live in El Monte and over there in the front yard we had *this really big humungus tree*.

2. And my brother when he was small he, you know, he had a couple of friends over, and he was playing with the ball, and it got stuck on top of the tree. And m, and I was under the tree playing Barbies with my friends - -

3. and ah, he kept throwing stuff, you know, *objects, different kind, you know, big, small*
4. and - he finally thought of getting this clock, you know, *a bright idea of his.* And he threw it while I was just, you know, I myself was just there sitting and looking at him throwing stuff, you know, *I was very curious.* And then, when he threw the clock I also watched him - do that.
5. And all of a sudden, *before I knew it*, it fell on my face.
6. And, you know, before I knew it, I wa-, in front of me there was a big bowl of blood and everything, and, and then I had - ma, I remember being in my mom's arms in the car, you know, with her. Something ma, I know she had something in my ma-, face. I don't know what it was. I think it was a *trapo.* /Right./
7. And I got to the hosp-, I arrived at the hospital -
8. and I remember being at the hospital table - and a big machine over my head overlooking- I was overlooking it. And then after, I guess, the operation - I got a candy, a lollipop. /Yeah./
9. And after a couple of weeks - oh, not a couple of weeks, a couple of days - the scar or whatever I had - looked like a *big*, you know, *cockroach*, that had, you know, just standing there. I used to look in the mirror and used to say. *Oh, I used to hate it!* And my brothers and sisters used to make fun of me and everything. I remember looking at the mirror and I was going like this [gesture]. /Yeah/

Note that in [7] evaluative statements occur almost exclusively in English switches (italicized; see in particular (10), (14), and (15)). Switches to English occur also to compensate for either lack of knowledge or memory lapses in Spanish (see (2), (9), (11), (12)). By contrast, the speaker's English version (in [8]) contains only a one-word switch to Spanish (*trapo* 'rag', (6)), and a number of evaluative statements which do not occur in the Spanish version (italicized in [8]), such as 'this really big humungus tree' (1), 'a bright idea of his' (4), 'I was very curious' (4), 'Oh, I used to hate it!' (9). In addition to switching, the speaker employs other evaluative techniques in the Spanish version of the narrative which are also present in the English version, namely adjectives, intensifiers (e.g. (6), (7) in [7], and (1), (3), (8), (9) in [8]), and repetition. It appears that the speaker uses repetition in Spanish to achieve rhetorical effect. Note that in [7], (13) she states, although almost as if reading a list in terms of prosody, that she, her brother, everyone, and her mom remember those events. This series of statements highlights the fact that the experience was indeed scary (as she explicitly points out in an *English* switch in [7], (15)).

Furthermore, orientation is much more detailed in [8]: compare (1–3) with the bare-bone orientation given in [7], (1). There is necessary and adjunct information in the Spanish version in [7], but the auxiliary information is quite scant, and prosodic effects (e.g. steep changes in pitch which accompany exclamations in

Spanish) are missing. Thus, the narrative loses liveliness as compared to its corresponding English version, despite the fact that the English version constituted a
retelling of the story. As such, one would not expect it to be as lively and interesting as a spontaneous narrative.

(d) *Clause complexity.* I refer here exclusively to the use of subordination. A
variety of types of subordinate clause occurs in all levels of the proficiency continuum (as illustrated in [3], [7], [9], and [12]). However, the frequency of use of
these constructions diminishes towards the lower end. Support for this observation
is provided by a more extensive quantitative study of the same speakers examined
in this book conducted by Gutiérrez (1990). This author includes nominal, adjectival, and adverbial subordinate clauses and shows a decreasing use of subordination, from 46 per cent to 29 per cent to 24 per cent in Groups 1, 2, and 3 in the
sections which provide auxiliary information, i.e. where one would expect orienting and evaluative subordinate constructions to occur. This seems to be an indication of syntactic simplification, especially so in the case of decreasing use and, in
some narratives, absence of relative clauses, given that these are considered to be
'the prototypical exemplar' of subordination (Haiman and Thompson 1984). Relative clauses, for instance, do not occur at all in four of the ten narratives from
Groups 2 and ·3, while three of four narratives examined for this specific purpose
in Group 1[4] contain this type of clause.[5]

(e) *The establishment of referents and topic reference continuity.* It is well-known
that Spanish allows the non-expression of subjects and maintains subject reference
continuity by means of verb morphology. In most cases of subject switch reference, however, the subject tends to be expressed, and indeed must be expressed if
the context does not clarify any possible ambiguities between competing referents
(see Chapter 5, and Silva-Corvalán 1982). These discourse/pragmatic rules are
broken only at the very low stages of the Spanish proficiency continuum.

Note that in Spanish only third-person plural verb forms may have a zero non-
referential subject, unless it is an impersonal construction marked with *se* (*Se vive
bien aquí* '(one) lives well here') or a construction with a 'weather verb' (*Llueve mucho
aquí* '(it) rains a lot here') Thus, while [9] below is well formed and acceptable as
a discourse-initiating statement, [10] is not because non-third-person plural verb
morphology requires previous establishment of a subject referent.

---

[4] Since one of the narratives included from this Group had relative clauses and the other had none,
I randomly chose two additional ones (from S2,f24,1,ELA37 and from C13,m45,1,ELA4). They both
happened to include relative clauses.
[5] On the basis of an examination of rates of relativization in two Uto-Aztecan languages, Hill (1989)
suggests a different interpretation. She acknowledges that reduced rates of relativization in substratum
languages in language shift may perhaps be due to 'the failure of speakers to evaluate narrative in a
stigmatized language' (p. 162), but feels much more strongly that, at least in Mexicano, this reduction
is not a reflection of language attrition but may be associated with the role of the substratum in coding
solidarity with Mexicano (as opposed to Spanish) by the speakers in her group of 'narrow-honorific
men'. I have not studied the functions of relative clauses in my data; therefore, at this time I can only
evaluate their diminishing occurrence as one further indication of the overall decrease in the frequency
of use of subordinate constructions, as noted in Gutiérrez (1990).

[9] ¿Sabes? ø entr*aron* a robar a la casa de al lado.
'You know? [They] broke into the house next door'.

[10] *¿Sabes? ø entr*ó* a robar a la casa de al lado.
'You know? [He] broke into the house next door.'

The discourse or intersentential rule that requires the previous establishment of the subject referent of a non-third-person plural verb is violated in the following narrative by a seventeen-year-old young man from Group 3, but examples of this sort are rare in the general data and only this case is illustrated in the ten narratives studied from Groups 2 and 3.

[11] J: J43,m17,3,ELA 57; I: researcher
 1. I: Y la pelea, a ver si me la cuentas.
 2. J: Era un día, ea - era en Cal State.
 3. I: ¿Cal State LA.?
 4. J: Cal State LA. /I: ¡Ah, mira!/ Pero ahí no, no me gusta pelear ahí. No me gu, - porque a era xxx era bad luck para ir pelear ahí. /I: ¡Fíjate!/
 5.   So esa era lo que - fui a pelear ahí,
 6.   pos la primera vez que pel-, pelé ahí me, me patiaron la cara y sangré de la boca. Yo fui a limpiar y - y so - se - la segunda vez pelé ahí - - me patiaron en el ojo - y me dejaron black eye. /I: ¡Ah!/ En la tercer vez eso es cuando me quebraron la nariz. So ahí, ahí, - ahí no me gusta pelear. Ahí no iba a las peleas.
 7.   Bueno pues, a - ese día fui a peliar y *peliamos*.
 8.   Patiaron ahí y,
 9.   y me salí de la pelea
10.   y me quité mi nombre de la lista. /I: Aahh./
11.   Es que es la - process of elimination, OK? /I: Sí/ Pelea - dos pelean. El que pierde se va pa' rear, hasta que llegan así un - un ladder.
12. I: Claro como una escalerilla así, sí.
13. J: Aha, yeah. Y me *'ruinó*.
 1. I: And the fight, let's see if you tell it to me.
 2. J: It was a day, i- it was at Cal State.
 3. I: Cal State LA.?
 4. J: Cal State LA. /I: Oh, I see./ But not there, I don't like to fight there. No I don't li- because it was - it was bad luck to go to fight there. /I: Imagine that./
 5.   So that was what - I went to fight there.
 6.   Well the first time that I fou-, fought there, they kicked my face and I bled from the mouth. I went to clean and- and so- se - the second time I fought there - they kicked me in the eye - and they gave me a black eye. The third time that's when they broke my nose. So there, there, - I don't like to fight there. I didn't go to the fights there.

7.   Well then, that day I went to fight and [we] *fought*.
8.   They kicked there and,
9.   and I withdrew from the fight.
10.   and I removed my name from the list. /I: Aah!/
11.   It's that it's the - process of elimination, okay? /I: Yeah./ Fight - two fight. The one that loses goes down, until they get like this a - a ladder.
12. I: Right, like a ladder.
13. J: Yeah. And [he] *ruined* me.

Observe now that in [11], a story about a certain type of boxing competition, lines 7 and 13 contain verb forms (∅ *peliamos* '[we] fought', ∅ *me 'ruinó* [he] ruined me') whose referents have been either only partly introduced (in the case of '[we] fought', the speaker ('I') has been introduced, but not the opponent) or not previously introduced in the narrative. It is obviously possible to infer that the speaker fought against someone (in (7)) and that someone 'ruined him' (in (13)). However, since the hearer (I was the hearer, and later also the analyst) expects the explicit introduction of subject referents in this structural and discourse context, the violation of this rule causes a certain degree of puzzlement, i.e. there is loss of what I call adjunct information.

(f) *The verb system.* I have shown elsewhere (Silva-Corvalán 1983a) that different tense forms correlate with the various sections of an oral narrative, such that the specific narrative context in which the verb form occurs in large part determines its tense and aspect meaning. In addition, our interpretation of the order in which narrative events take place relative to one another depends to a large extent on the verb form used to codify such events.

One of the most striking results of the present study is the observation that there are no deviations from this established pattern in the tense forms of the complicating action sequence in eleven of the twelve narratives analysed. Only one narrative, which represents a very low point in the continuum (the position of speaker A46 with regard to loss of tense–mood–aspect morphology—Table 2.2—is third from the bottom), demonstrates one case of deviation which makes it difficult to understand the order in which two of the events took place. I refer to the italicized sentences, (7) and (13), in [12].

[12] A: A46,f31,3, ELA20; I: researcher
1. A: . . . Y, y me llamaron. Mi mamá me llamó. Y from East LA to Pico Rivera, I made it- [gesture to indicate she was really fast]
2.   She called the paramedics first, then she called me.
3. I: ¿Ella- cuando ella llamó a los paramedics, tu abu-, tu nana ya estaba - con el nivel de azúcar alto?
4. A: No, no. /I: ¿No?/ No estaba en coma.
5. I: ¿Estaba en coma?
6. A: No que-, no, no quería despertar. /I: Claro./
7.   Okay. *Cuando llegaron los paramedics - - yo llegué.* /I: Claro/

8.   Ellos entraron y le, le dieron un, un sugar shot. /I: Claro./
9. I: ¿Y tú no estabas ahí, o ya estabas ahí?
10. A: No, no - no /I: Oh, no./
11.   Llegué - como el mismo tiempo. /I: Ah, ya./
12.   Pero hablé con, con un señora que sí, que estaba afuera. Un, un neighbor /I: vecino/, ve, vecina.
13.   Y - *cuando entré ya, ya le pusieron el sugar shot.* /I: Oh./
14.   Y, y estaba 'ciendo, así twitches, /I: convulsiones/, con, convulsions.

1. A: And, and they called me. My mom called me. And from East LA to Pico Rivera, I made it- [gesture to indicate she was really fast]
2.   She called the paramedics first, then she called me.
3. I: She, when she called the paramedics, your gra-, your grandmother already had a high sugar level?
4. A: No, no. /I: ¿No?/ No, she wasn't in a coma.
5. I: She was in a coma?
6. A: No, no, she didn't want to wake up. /I: Of course./
7.   Okay. *When the paramedics arrived I arrived.* /I: Yes./
8.   They entered, and they gave her a, a sugar shot. /I: Yes./
9. I: And you weren't there, or were you already there?
10. A: No, no - no. /I: Oh, no./
11.   I arrived - at about the same time. /I: Oh, OK./
12.   But I spoke with, with a lady that was outside. A, a neighbour. /I: Neighbour./ Neighbour.
13.   And *when I entered already, already they gave her the sugar shot.* /I: Oh./
14.   And, and she was already twitching, like this. /I: Convulsions/ Con-convulsions.

(7), with a Pret form in both the main clause (*llegué* 'I arrived') and the temporal subordinate one (*llegaron* 'they arrived'), indicates that the two events were simultaneous. However, the speaker explains later (note the verbal exchange in (9–11) in [12]) that she arrived *after* the paramedics. Therefore, the relative order of this sequence of events would have been clearer coded either as in [13] (i.e. with the order indicated by an adverb), or as in [14] (i.e. with the order signalled by the verbal forms).

[13] Llegaron los paramedics *y luego/después* llegué yo.
      'The paramedics arrived, and *then/after that* I arrived.'
[14] Yo llegué cuando los paramedics (recién) *habían llegado.*
      'I arrived when the paramedics *had* (just) *arrived*.'

With respect to (13) in [12], it is necessary to note that in Group 1, as in general standard Spanish, *cuando . . . ya* with the meaning of 'when . . . already' requires Pluperf with activity verbs in the clause which contains *ya* 'already', as in [15].

[15] Cuando llamé ya se había ido.
   'When I called he had already left.'

   The occurrence of Pret instead of Pluperf prompts a preferred interpretation
(perhaps even the only one) of the sequence *cuando . . . ya* as '*when . . . then finally*',
as in [16]:

[16] Cuando llamé ya se fue.
   'When I called then he finally left.'

   This is, therefore, the preferred interpretation of (13) in [12]: 'And when I
entered then finally they gave her the sugar shot'.[6] However, the correct temporal
sequence is precisely the reverse. The use of *ya* 'already' among speakers at the
lower ends of the continuum needs to be investigated further. It is quite likely, for
instance, that *ya* may be developing into a tense-marker meaning 'past', just as in
some creole languages (e.g. Zamboangueño, which indicates past by preposing *ya*
to the verbal lexeme, as in *yakome* '(I) ate' versus *takome* '(I)'m eating' (Frake 1977)),
such that, if it occurs with a verb marked for past, this verb would be interpreted
to refer to a 'past of past' situation. If this were the case, (13) in [12] would not be
misinterpreted by those who share these new norms.

   In other elements of the narrative, however, tense-form deviations start occurring at very high points in the continuum. Notice, for instance, the use of the Imp
for Pret in the orientation in [11], (2) (*era* 'it was' for *fue* 'it was'), in the coda in
[17] (*había* for *hubo* 'there was'), and in an abstract in [18] (*tenía* for *tuvo* 'I had').

[17] Y vino y empezamos a pelear, pero ni él ganó ni yo. Y después de eso no *había*
   problemas.   (H22,m21,2,ELA11)
   'And he came and we started fighting, but neither he nor I won. And after
   that *there was* never any problem.'

[18] *Tenía* un accidente en mi, en mi carro hace como, hace año, el treinta de abril
   va a ser el año.   (M41,m18,3,ELA34)
   'I *had* an accident in my, in my car about, about a year ago, it'll be a year on
   the thirtieth of April.'

   The speakers in Group 1, on the other hand, never fail to use the Pret in these
types of examples. Here, the Pret is required because the examples occur within a
narrative frame, a complex event which is presented as a unit and must be referred
to as a single whole by means of a perfective form. It is interesting to note that
verbs which occur in the Imp instead of the Pret form are not event verbs. Indeed,
these verbs include *ser* 'to be', *tener* 'to have', and *haber* 'there to be', that is to say,
the simplification appears to be limited to stative verbs (cf. section 2.2); it does not

---

[6] This was, by the way, the translation given by a graduate student assistant, member of the
Mexican-American community. This student was born in the USA but, perhaps because of her
university specialization in Spanish, has a high level of proficiency in this language. She helped me
translate a number of narratives into English.

affect action verbs which are on the time line of the temporally sequenced events in the complicating action.

In the preceding chapter I have shown that the IS and all compound forms start to be replaced, variably at first, by simple Ind forms in the speech of some speakers in Group 2. At the low levels of the continuum, both IS and all compound forms disappear. This type of attrition is illustrated in the narratives studied here. Pret replaces Pluperf, and it also replaces PluS in the auxiliary information of a narrative from Group 2 ([19] and [20], respectively).

[19] Y el chofer nomás se paró y dijo si tenía el dinero para pagar su moto. Yo mientras estaba todo asustado en medio de la calle con mi carro que se - me *apagó.* (M25,m19,2,ELA55).
'And the driver got up and asked me if I had the money to pay for his motorcycle. In the meantime I was all scared in the middle of the street with my car which *stopped* on me.'

[20] I: ¿Y, y el carro se - golpeó o algo, o casi nada?
    M: Oh, muy poquito, casi nada, nada casi, ahm, como - si alguien se *puso* arriba de mi carro, y le *hizo* poquito - un - un golpe.   (M25,m19,2,ELA55)
    I: 'And the car got hit or something, or almost nothing?'
    M: 'Oh, just a little, almost nothing, almost nothing, ahm, as - if someone *had stood* (lit.: stood) on my car, and *had done* (lit.: did) a little - a - a little damage.'

3.2.2. Conclusions

Let us return to one of our starting questions: what effect does language attrition have both on the structure and the semantics of oral narratives? Or, what differentiates the narratives of a Spanish-dominant speaker from those of a non-Spanish dominant speaker?

On the one hand, it seems fairly clear that linguistic simplification does not affect the level of *necessary information* in the *complicating action* section. This is because the Pret form of verbs is retained down to the lowest stages of the continuum, at least in our sample, and this is precisely the form used to code the pivotal events in the time line of the narrative. In addition, the content structure of the narratives (preface, orientation, resolution, etc.) is not significantly reduced. On the other hand, adjunct information, i.e. information which is in turn part of auxiliary (evaluative and orienting) information, is lost to some extent, but it is only at the low end of the Spanish proficiency continuum that instances of this loss create some small degree of puzzlement in the analyst/interlocutor.

By contrast, there is some significant loss of internal and external evaluation devices. We may conclude, then, that the narrative provides a frame within which bilinguals of varying degrees of proficiency can successfully make a number of statements about past events which may be fairly easily comprehended by an interlocutor. However, if 'the point' of telling a narrative lies in its evaluation, it is likely that language attrition may result in the hearer's failure to infer some significant messages. Assuming that bilingual speakers are aware of this possible loss, I would predict that in more natural communicative situations, non-Spanish dominant speakers will narrate their stories entirely in English or will switch to English to provide auxiliary information as B does in [3], and V in [7]. Obviously, switching would be possible only if the audience had the necessary competence to understand spoken English, a type of competence which is fairly extended in the Mexican-American community of East Los Angeles.

3.3. Discourse about Hypothetical Situations

I proceed now to consider the effect that simplification and loss of verbal morphology may have on the expression of meaning complexes in *hypothetical oral discourse*, i.e. discourse which conveys imaginary, conjectural information, rather than facts stemming from perception and memory (Klein and von Stutterheim, n.d.: 31). In passages of this type, one would expect frequent use of weak assertive verb morphology, e.g. Cond and Sub, alongside the more assertive or factual PI and Pret tenses. Indeed, the use of verb morphology is closely related to the various manners in which speakers choose to express their attitude towards the possibility that the contents of a proposition or a number of propositions constituting a discourse unit may be true in a present or future world, or could have been true in a past world given certain conditions. The choice among two or more semantically similar ways of communicating a piece of information determines a specific style of communication, which in the case of the expression of possibility characterizes it along a scale of assertiveness. Thus, depending upon the linguistic choices made by a speaker, and the manner in which he structures discourse about hypothetical situations, his communicative style may appear to be assertive, categorical, assured, defensive, committed, uncommitted, doubtful, or sceptical.

The analysis of hypothetical reference requires topics which elicit both past and non-past time reference, as well as the expression of various degrees of possibility and assertiveness. These necessary data were obtained during the recording sessions in the Mexican-American community by introducing such topics as (*a*) for past reference: life in Mexico if X had not come to the US, life in the US if X had chosen a different career, job, or school; and (*b*) for non-past reference: speaker's response to (i) the possibility of X dating or marrying someone from a different race, religion, or cultural background, (ii) situations which would justify abortion, (iii) the possibility of having a lot of money. Two or more of these topics were discussed with every speaker included in the study. This section is based on an analysis of samples from fourteen speakers, six in Group 1 (E1, L3, F5, C13, J14, R11), and four each in Groups 2 and 3 (A20, V21, R24, A29, A34, D36, S38, R50).

Apparently not much attention has been paid to conversational discourse which refers to hypothetical situations nor to argumentation in studies of language attrition. Although hypothesizing is part of argumentation, especially so in essays and debates dealing with social sciences and humanities topics, not every hypothetical discourse is necessarily argumentative. The linguistic strategies which play a role in the creation of discourse of this type include, on the one hand, the structure of the hypothetical oral text[7] itself and, on the other, such language devices as verb morphology, the modal verbs *poder* 'can/may', *deber* 'must', etc. First, I shall discuss verb morphology in relation to hypotheticality.

3.3.1. The Language of Hypothetical Discourse

To examine hypothetical discourse it becomes necessary to discuss, even if only briefly, the modal value of verb morphology, in addition to the specific contribution of modal verbs and expressions. In this regard, I have proposed (Silva-Corvalán 1990*b*) that a crucial function of verb morphology is to contribute to the proposition the meaning of 'more or less assertiveness', where *assertiveness* is defined as speaker belief or confidence in the probability that the proposition may be true. Degrees of assertiveness are pragmatically inferred to convey degrees of hypotheticality. These two notions are in an inverse relation, such that more assertiveness is inferred to convey stronger likelihood that the proposition is true, i.e. less hypotheticality. Assertiveness and hypotheticality correlate with verb morphology roughly as in the scale in Table 3.1, which is suggested to apply in reference to non-counterfactual situations in the data examined. A similar scale has been argued for in the context of studies of conditional clauses by Klein-Andreu (1986*b*). She presents a well-justified six-place scale along two axes, *assertiveness* and *actuality*, which I incorporate in Table 3.1. In addition, counterfactuality in the past is expressed by the PluS and by the Cond Perfect.

Both the discourse topic and verb morphology contribute to creating a hypothetical world, along with lexis, syntax, and prosody. The use of verbs which either weaken the degree of assertiveness of the proposition (e.g. *creer* 'to think/to believe', *pensar* 'to think', the modal verbs), or refer to wishes (e.g. *querer* 'to want/ to wish', *tener ganas* 'to want'), as well as the use of such related adverbial and adjectival items as *posible* 'possible', *probable* 'probable', *quizás* 'maybe', *puede que* 'maybe' serve to confirm the non-actuality of the situation referred to. Finally, hypothetical worlds are created by syntactic means, e.g. conditional clauses, and temporal clauses which establish a future time frame.

3.3.2. The Structure of Hypothetical Discourse

The fact that these oral texts refer to situations which speakers have not previously experienced, and which do not necessarily have an iconic time or spatial line of

---

[7] 'Oral text' and 'discourse' are here used synonymously.

TABLE 3.1. Scale of Assertiveness Conveyed by Verb
Morphology in Reference to Non-past Situations

	Most assertiveness
Factual	Present Indicative
	Preterite
Least hypothetical	Future
	Imperfect Indicative
	Present Subjunctive
Most hypothetical	Conditional
	Imperfect Subjunctive
	Least assertiveness

reference and development (as in narratives and descriptions, for instance, where the order in which utterances are produced is said to mirror the order of events/ spaces in the real world) accounts for their rather loose structure both in terms of the necessary sections which must compose them and with respect to the relative order of these sections in the creation of the discourse.

I have examined eighteen samples of hypothetical discourse produced by the six speakers in Group 1 referred to above. The analysis indicates that there are at least two types of hypothetical discourse: *strictly hypothetical*, and *hypothetical with supportive argumentation*. In the data examined, strictly hypothetical passages have a future time perspective and typically occur when the speaker does not seem to envision any cause for disagreement with his statements; rather, speakers are speculating about their possible actions given a certain condition (e.g. having a lot of money, having more free time, becoming ill, retiring). As one would expect in conversational discourse, argumentation may be embedded in the development of a strictly hypothetical text, but I will show that it is not part of its main or central structure. Furthermore, although not attested in the data examined, strictly hypo-thetical discourse could also have a past time orientation; for instance, given a topic dealing with what a speaker could have done when visiting a certain place, but did not.

Hypothetical passages which refer to past counterfactual situations usually in-corporate argumentation in their central structure, as do passages where certain specific issues are being discussed, either within a present or a future time perspec-tive. These oral texts involve the speaker in trying to justify a certain action or line of reasoning, or weighing the positive or negative consequences of a situation. In hypothetical texts with supportive argumentation it is always possible to infer that the speaker expects some degree of disagreement with his stance.

A complete hypothetical discourse with supportive argumentation may comprise the following elements: hypothetical macro-frame, hypothetical statement, argu-mentation, anchoring, qualification, disclaimer, and coda. Of these, the first two define what I call *a minimal hypothetical passage*. Strictly hypothetical discourse, on the other hand, does not include argumentation nor anchoring as part of its central structure. In what follows, I define and illustrate the various elements contained in hypothetical discourse.

3.3.2.1. Establishment of a hypothetical macro-frame

A *macro-frame* is a body of knowledge that is evoked in order to provide an inferential base for the production and understanding of discourse.[8] In the data examined, this is in every case done through a question such as *¿Te imaginas cómo habría sido tu vida si te hubieras quedado en México?* 'Can you imagine what your life would have been like if you had stayed in Mexico?', or through a statement followed by a short prompting question, *Mucha gente está en contra del aborto, pero yo lo aceptaría en algunos casos, ¿Y tú?* 'Many people are against abortion, but I would accept it in some cases, wouldn't you?'[9]

Establishing a macro-frame, then, necessarily also means establishing a discourse topic. This defines the sequence of utterances included in what we refer to as the hypothetical discourse passage. In this sense, a macro-frame shares some definitional characteristics with what Van Dijk (1980: 332–44) discusses in terms of macro-speech acts and macro-structures.

3.3.2.2. Hypothetical statements

These consist of one or a series of utterances which present the speaker's statements about his possible actions, attitudes, and beliefs given a certain state of affairs. The most frequent construction used to encode hypothetical statements is, expectedly, the conditional clause of the type 'if p then q'. If the state of affairs or condition 'if p' has been established in the hypothetical frame, the speaker's statements contain in nearly every case only the second part of the conditional period, 'then q', i.e. the assumed consequence of p. However, throughout the discourse speakers put forth a number of hypothetical statements dependent on certain conditions presented by the speakers themselves, the content of which is related to the hypothetical macro-frame.

---

[8] This definition is based on the one given for *frame* by Levinson (1983: 281): 'A frame . . . is a body of knowledge that is evoked in order to provide an inferential base for the understanding of an utterance.'

[9] All hypothetical macro-frames were created by the researcher. This may perhaps be due to the nature of our data-collection procedure, the sociolinguistic recorded dyadic conversation. However, it seems to me that it may also reflect, if not some reluctance on the part of speakers to engage spontaneously in conversation about hypothetical situations (even when they are not being recorded), at least a marked preference for topics concerning factual situations.

3.3.2.3. *Argumentation*

These discourse passages consist of an utterance or a series of utterances which present reasons offered in proof, rebuttal of, or as the motivation for a hypothesis, statement, or position with respect to an issue.

3.3.2.4. *Anchoring*

Anchoring refers to the strategy of linking the hypothetical statements to the real world by means of illustrative narratives or exposition of relevant facts of which the speaker has direct knowledge. It appears that anchoring has a double function: communicative and cognitive. Its communicative function is argumentative and entreating, inasmuch as it supports the speaker's hypothesis and aims at convincing the listener of the possibility that the speaker is correct in its assumptions. Cognitively, anchoring hypothetical texts to experienced facts makes production and processing easier. Indeed, we have already mentioned that hypothetical discourse does not stem from perception and memory. This makes the problem of linearization, conceptualization, and linguistic encoding a harder task as compared with that of encoding narrative texts, for example (cf. Levelt 1979; 1982). Thus, speakers frequently illustrate their hypothetical statements with anecdotes about people they know to be in the sort of world which they imagine for themselves, and either state explicitly or imply that this is what they would do, would have to do, or would perhaps have done.

3.3.2.5. *Qualifications*

Qualifications consist of an utterance or a series of utterances which moderate or restrict the hypothetical statements, making them less strong. Given a hypothetical statement of the form 'if *p* then *q*' (*Si regresamos a México estaremos mejor* 'If we return to Mexico we'll be better off'), qualifications take the form 'but if *p* then possibly also −*q*' (*Pero si regresamos a México quizá no estaremos mejor* 'But if we return to Mexico perhaps we won't be better off'), or even a contrary hypothesis 'though if −*p* then possibly also *q*' (*Aunque si no regresamos a México quizá también estaremos mejor* 'Though if we don't return to Mexico perhaps we'll also be better off'), or are encoded as a proviso of the form '*q*, provided that *x*'. Qualifications are also conveyed by such verbs as *creer* 'think, believe' and *pensar* 'think', and they may be reinforced by means of lexical expressions of the type of *puede que* 'maybe', *probablemente* 'probably', etc.

3.3.2.6. *Disclaimers*

These are utterances which convey the speaker's reluctance or refusal to accept responsibility for the certainty of his conjectures about counterfactual and possible situations. Examples of disclaimers are such utterances as *No puedo yo saber/asegurar* 'I can't tell/be sure', *No sé, es difícil saber* 'I don't know, it's difficult to tell', *Así me lo imagino, ¿no?, pero no sé* 'This is how I imagine it, right?, but I don't know'.

3.3.2.7. Coda

As in oral narrative, the end of a hypothetical text may be overtly marked by means of expressions like *Eso es lo que yo pienso* 'That's what I think', *Así es como habría sido* 'This is how it would've been', *Y todo eso habría hecho* 'And I would've done all that'. However, as we have noted in the case of conversational narratives, codas are quite infrequent in conversational hypothetical texts as well.

At this point, let us consider the analysis of the structure and language of hypothetical discourse proposed through an examination of two examples from Group 1. Example [21] is a case of hypothetical discourse with supportive argumentation. The issue is abortion.

[21] B: C13,m54,1,ELA85; I: researcher

I: (*a*) . . . ¿Pero en qué situaciones, por ejemplo, crees que aceptarías el aborto? ¿Le aconsejarías a alguien que se hiciera un aborto, en cualquier caso, un aborto?   (*Hy/Fr*)

B: (*b*) Bueno, no, no aceptaría eso   (*Hy/St*)

(*c*) porque me sentiría yo como, como un asesino quitarle la vida a un niño.   (*Argu*)

(*d*) Ni en caso de que, digo yo,   (*Qual*)

(*e*) muchos padres, pues si ven a sus hijos en problemas así, no los dejan discurrir por ellos mismos,   (*Hy/St*)

(*f*) pero creo yo que   (*Qual*)

(*g*) no sería capaz de quitarle a un hijo, a uno de mis hijos o, o, a cualquiera de, a mis herma - a mi hermana, o a los - en caso que hubiera alguna vez pasado ese detalle, verdad?   (*Hy/St*)

(*h*) Porque yo creo que   (*Qual*)

(*i*) la vida, se la da a uno Dios. Y el ser que nace tiene que nacer.   (*Argu*)

(*j*) Pero, bueno, eso yo no sé   (*Discl*)

(*k*) si alguna vez en caso de, de que se vaya a morir la persona, ¿verdad?   (*Hy/St*)

(*l*) Probablemente, eso yo creo que   (*Qual*)

(*m*) ni Dios, ni Dios le permitiría a nadie, ¿verdad?, dejar morir a la madre por, por el niño, ¿verdad?   (*Hy/St*)

(*n*) Pero está dificil también porque son dos, son dos seres que se quieren.   (*Discl*)

I: Sí, pero la madre ya está aquí ya y el -

B: (*o*) Sí. Y luego le hace más falta a los demás hijos, especialmente si tiene familia, ¿verdad?   (*Argu*) (*p*) En ese caso, pues, todavía   (*Qual*)

(*q*) podría yo, a, como le dicen los, los gringos, ¿verdad?, *bend* poquito.   (*Hy/St*)

I: (*a*) . . . But in what situations, for instance, do you think you could accept abortion? Would you advise someone to have an abortion, in all cases, abortion?   (*Hy/Fr*)

B: (*b*) No, I wouldn't accept that   (*Hy/St*)

(*c*) because I would feel like, like a murderer, taking the life of a child,   (*Argu*)

(*d*) And in the case of, I think,   (*Qual*)

(*e*) many parents, well, if they see that their children are in this kind of trouble, they don't let them decide by themselves,   (*Hy/St*)

(*f*) but I think   (*Qual*)

(*g*) I wouldn't be able to take the child of one of my children, or, or any of, of my sister, or of - in case something like that had ever happened, right?   (*Hy/St*)

(*h*) Because I think that   (*Qual*)

(*i*) life, God gives it to you. And the being who is born has to be born.   (*Argu*)

(*j*) But, well, I don't know,   (*Discl*)

(*k*) if in a given case, if the person's going to die, right?   (*Hy/St*)

(*l*) probably, that I think that   (*Qual*)

(*m*) not even God, not even God would allow that to happen to anyone, right?, to let the mother die for, for the child, right?   (*Hy/St*)

(*n*) But it's difficult also because they are two, they are two people one loves.   (*Discl*)

I: Yes, but the mother is already here and the -

B: (*o*) Yes. And then she's needed more by the rest of the children, especially if she has a family, right?   (*Argu*)

(*p*) In that case, well maybe   (*Qual*)

(*q*) I could, as the, the gringos say, right?, *bend* a little.   (*Hy/St*)

The structure of the hypothetical discourse in [21] illustrates the following elements in its development:

(*a*)   Hypothetical macro-frame
(*b*)   Hypothetical statement 1
(*c*)   Argumentation
(*d*)   Qualification
(*e*)   Hypothetical statement 2
(*f*)   Qualification
(*g*)   Hypothetical statement 3
(*h*)   Qualification
(*i*)   Argumentation
(*j*)   Disclaimer
(*k,m*) Hypothetical statement 4

(*l*)   Qualification
(*n*)   Disclaimer
(*o*)   Argumentation
(*p*)   Qualification
(*q*)   Hypothetical statement 5

Note that [21] contains five hypothetical statements, three supported by argumentation, and no anchoring. It also incorporates five qualifications, and two disclaimers. It might be possible to develop a sophisticated method of quantification of the proportional number of the various elements, also taking verb morphology and lexicon into account as an index of degree of assertiveness. This complex and time-consuming task is not attempted here, however, because it is beyond the specific purpose of this chapter. At this point, based on the larger number of qualifications and disclaimers over hypothetical statements and argumentation, plus the absence of anchoring, I interpret the style of [21] as relatively less assertive than a hypothetical text containing anchoring, and fewer disclaimers and qualifications ([22] incorporates anchoring, for instance, and illustrates a more assertive style). Thus, my interpretation of the pragmatics of [21] is that the speaker views the issue of abortion as quite complex and is not prepared to commit himself to a categorical position. Even though he acknowledges the fact that there may be attenuating circumstances which could justify abortion (*k*), he qualifies the related hypothetical statement (*l,m*), and proceeds to disclaim responsibility in (*n*). However, his attitude changes slightly in response to the researcher's implication that the mother is more important than the baby, so that he ends the passage allowing for the possibility that he 'could bend a little' (*q*).

The language used in [21] supports my interpretation: four of the five hypothetical statements have Cond rather than PI tense morphology; two of the five qualifications are reinforced (*probablemente* 'probably' (*l*), and *todavía* 'maybe' (*p*)). Note, furthermore, that hypothetical statement (*q*) is modalized (*podría* 'could'), while hypothetical statement (*b*) is not (*no aceptaría* 'would not accept'). This indicates that it is more difficult for this speaker to justify abortion than to disapprove of it, an attitude which is valued in his social group.

Example [22] presents a hypothetical discourse with anchoring. This passage deals with the possibility of having to think about what one would do if a son or a daughter wanted to marry someone from a different cultural and ethnic group.

[22] R: R11,f43,1,ELA77; C: researcher
C: (*a*) ¿Qué harías si una de tus hijas o un hijo viniera un día y te dijera 'Me voy a casar con un, alguien que es musulmán, o budista, o con un japonés, o un iraní', ¿verdad?, pues -   (*Hy/Fr*)
R: (*b*) Pues no, no he pensado,   (*Discl*)
   (*c*) (*Anchoring*: illustrative narrative)   (*Ancho*)
   tengo la experiencia de una, una supervisora que tenía antes.

(*c*1) Ella es de religión también católica y, y hace como unos dos años, salió la hija con un judío.   (*Frame*)

Me dice exactamente así que, 'Parece, pero,

(*c*2) no creo que llegue a ninguna seriedad, no creo, no.'   (*Hy/St*)

Y sí, yo le digo a fulanita, me acuerdo que es la única mujer que tiene, tiene tres hombres, es mayor que R, como dos años yo creo. Y hace unos tres, cuatro meses volvió a la oficina a saludarme. Y le pregunté, le preguntaron por su familia. Me dice,

(*c*3) 'Pues, fíjate que B., B. está haciendo planes ya de casarse.'   (*Qual*)

(*c*4) Y le digo, '¿Y cómo aceptan a este güero?'   (*Frame*)

(*c*5) Dice, 'No sé, dice, yo creo que voy a tener que empezar a hacer a, a convertirlo al catolicismo.   (*Hy/St*)

(*c*6) No sé cómo lo voy a hacer.   (*Discl*)

(*c*7) Yo le digo a B. que va a ser un, un amigo muy difícil,   (*Hy/St*)

(*c*8) porque él es un judío, judío, de religión bien, bien fundada, bien sedimentada, como la de nosotros.'   (*Argu*)

(*c*9) Decía, 'No sé, voy a tener que, se, se son-, se rió, bromeó, voy a tener que, hacerlo, hacerlo católico.'   (*Hy/St*)

(*c*10) De allí si no lo logra es que,   (*Qual*)

(*c*11) bueno, no sé, no sé, pero ya es cuestión de B, pero yo no he pensado tampoco en eso.   (*Discl*)

. . .[10]

C: (*d*) ¿Pero tú crees que podrías aceptarlo? Tú te, imagínate que un día venga uno [de tus hijos][11] y te diga -   (*Hy/Fr*)

R: (*e*) Yo pienso, Carmen, que,   (*Qual*)

     (*f*) yo tendría que [aceptarlo].   (*Hy/St*)

C: (*a*) What would you do if one of your daughters or a son came to you one day and said: 'I'm going to marry a, someone who is Muslim, or Buddhist, or a Japanese, or an Iranian', right?, well -   (*Hy/Fr*)

R: (*b*) Well no, I haven't thought about it,   (*Discl*)

     (*c*) (*Anchoring*: illustrative narrative)   (*Ancho*)

     I know the case of a, a supervisor I had before.

     (*c*1) She is also Catholic and, and about two years ago, her daughter started going out with a Jew   (*Frame*)

     She says exactly this to me: 'It looks as if, but,

     (*c*2) I don't think this will become serious, I don't think so, I don't.'   (*Hy/St*)

     And yes, I tell this woman, I remember she is the only daughter she has, she has three sons, she's older than R, about two years I think. And about three,

---

[10] The passage omitted here deals with the topic of how couples from even the same ethnic and cultural group find it extremely difficult to achieve a successful marriage.

[11] Language material within square brackets does not have phonetic realization, but is inferrable from the context.

four months ago she came by my office to say hello. And I asked her, they asked her about her family. She says,

(*c*3) 'Well, I tell you, B, B's making plans to get married.'   (*Qual*)

(*c*4) And I say to her: 'And how come you accept this "güero" (anglo)?' (*Frame*)

(*c*5) She says: 'I don't know, she says, I think I'm going to have to start, start converting him to Catholicism.   (*Hy/St*)

(*c*6) I don't know how I'm going to do it.   (*Discl*)

(*c*7) I tell B he's going to be a, a very difficult friend,   (*Hy/St*)

(*c*8) because he's Jewish, Jewish, with a very strong religious background, very strong, like us.'   (*Argu*)

(*c*9) She said: 'I don't know, I'll have to, to, she smi -, she laughed, kidding, I'll have to, make him, make him Catholic.'   (*Hy/St*)

(*c*10) And then if she doesn't succeed it's because,   (*Qual*)

(*c*11) well, I don't know, I don't know, but it's now in B's hands, but I haven't thought about that either.   (*Discl*)
      [10]
. . .

C: (*d*) But do you think you could accept it? Do you, imagine that one day one of [your children][11] came to you
      and said -   (*Hy/Fr*)

R: (*e*) I think, Carmen, that   (*Qual*)
      (*f*) I would have to [accept it].   (*Hy/St*)

The structure of 22 is as follows:

(*a*)   Hypothetical macro-frame
(*b*)   Disclaimer
(*c*)   Anchoring
(*c*1)   'Real world' frame
(*c*2)   Hypothetical statement
(*c*3)   Qualification (mixed marriages do occur)
(*c*4)   Hypothetical frame reworded
(*c*5)   Hypothetical statement
(*c*6)   Disclaimer
(*c*7)   Hypothetical statement
(*c*8)   Argumentation
(*c*9)   Repetition of hypothetical statement in *c*5
(*c*10)   Qualification
(*c*11)   Disclaimer
(*d*)   Hypothetical frame (recreated)
(*e*)   Qualification
(*f*)   Hypothetical statement 1

In [22] the speaker restates the researcher's hypothetical frame in real world terms in (*c*1). Having established that mixed relationships do occur and may in fact lead to mixed marriages (*c*3), the speaker anchors the researcher's hypothetical frame (*c*4) and her own hypothetical statement (*c*5) to the comparable factual events with which she seems to identify herself at the moment of the conversation. The speaker's answer to the hypothetical frame recreated in (*d*) supports my proposal that anchoring does indeed fulfil the communicative function of presenting, through real facts, the speaker's own hypothetical statements, and supportive argumentation. In the illustrative narrative, though realizing that mixed marriages cause difficulties, the mother accepts her daughter's decision. Likewise, R's final hypothetical statement (*f*) about her own possible actions is that she would have to accept a mixed marriage as well.

Anchoring as well as verb morphology create a more assured communicative style than that of [21].[12] Note that the elements in the anchoring passage are never coded with Cond morphology. All these factors, then, lead me to propose that in [22] the speaker intends to assert quite positively that a son or daughter cannot be prevented from marrying whoever they choose. But the speaker's attitude towards mixed marriages is one of forced acceptance. This is made clear in the final hypothetical statement, which the speaker has chosen to modalize with *tener que* 'to have to' in the Cond. The alternative without the modal, *yo lo aceptaría* 'I would accept it', would not convey the same implication of resignation to outside forces compelling her to assent to a situation which might not be approved by her immediate community or perhaps even by her interlocutor (whom the speaker may have judged to be Catholic because of her Hispanic background). Furthermore, despite the inclusion of anchoring and the more assertive verb morphology used in [22] as compared to [21], the use of Cond and the occurrence of disclaimers and qualifications make the style of communication somewhat doubtful, i.e. appropriately non-assertive.

It seems correct to say, then, that the hypothetical discourse produced by Group 1 speakers characteristically ranges, as expected by its very nature, from weakly assertive to least assertive, i.e. the situations described are inferred to range from least to most hypothetical.

3.3.3. *Reference to Hypothetical Situations in Groups 2 and 3*

By contrast with Group 1, those speakers in Groups 2 and 3 who show loss of some lexical units related to modality and loss of least assertive verb morphology give the impression of having an invariably assertive and assured style of communication in reference to hypothetical situations. Furthermore, the structure of this type of discourse appears to be simpler, in that there are fewer disclaimers and qualifications. And these speakers produce much less language material (i.e. fewer words) than those in Group 1, in response to the researcher's establishment of a hypothetical macro-frame. For instance, in a variety of samples of hypothetical

---

[12] This comparison would perhaps be more reliable if both discourse passages dealt with the same issue.

discourse from eight speakers in Groups 2 and 3, there is only one example of anchoring,[13] there is little or no argumentation, and qualifications are conveyed lexically rather than syntactically (e.g. *creer* 'to believe' is used to qualify hypothetical statements, not conditional constructions of the type 'but if *p* then possibly also *–q*', or '*q*, provided that *x*'). Consider [23], from the same speaker who told me the narrative in [7].

[23] V: V21,f18,2,ELA67; C: researcher

C: Y, y, pero tú, tú piensas casarte un día, ¿no es cierto?

V: Sí.

C: Y, e, ponte si conoces a alguien de México.

V: ¿Mero, mero México?

C: Sí.

V: Yo creo que no me caso con una persona así [*Hy/St*]. Porque yo, e, los hombres de mero México creen que las señoras, muchachas deben estar en la casa [*Argu*]. Tienen en xxx mismo pensamiento de viejos, tú sabes, que, como señoras están la casa y niños y no hacen nada, que no pueden hacer nada, no deben hacer nada - afuera de la casa [*Argu*]. Y, um, yo no creo que [interrupted *Qual*] - No quiero casarme con una persona así [*factual statement*].

C: And, and, but you, you plan to marry one day, don't you?

V: Yes.

C: And, uh, what if you meet someone from Mexico.

V: From Mexico itself?

C: Yes.

V: I think that I don't marry a person like that [*Hy/St*]. Because I, eh, men from Mexico think that ladies, girls ought to be at home [*Argu*]. They have xxx the same ideas as the old, you know, that, how ladies are at home, and children, and they don't do anything, that they can't do anything, that they shouldn't do anything - outside the home [*Argu*]. And, uh, I don't think that [interrupted *Qual*] - I don't want to marry a person like that [*factual statement*].

Note one interrupted qualification, no disclaimers, and in fact a closing factual statement in [23]. The style of communication appears assertive, categorical, decidedly against the possibility of marrying a Mexican man. The outright rejection of this idea, however, may not have been what speaker V21 wanted to convey. Yet the absence of qualifications, disclaimers, and of weak assertive verb morphology contribute to creating this effect.

Thus, the reduction in the amount of language material and consequent absence of some of the elements of a hypothetical discourse, as well as the loss of Cond and Sub morphology, block speakers in Groups 2 and 3 from expressing a high degree of hypotheticality.

---

[13] This example is produced by speaker A34 (f40,3,ELA83) when imagining her life had she lived in Mexico.

Despite these losses, however, which result in a reduced range of styles of communication (e.g. the more doubtful or sceptical style is absent), misinterpretation rarely occurs. In the data examined, only once does the researcher give signs of confusion about the factual status of the situation referred to. This is because the speaker (S38, [24]) talks for a relatively long time in reaction to the question whether being married to an Anglo male would be more or less difficult than, or very different from, being married to a Mexican-American. Thus, after a while the hypothetical frame is no longer obvious, given that the speaker uses mostly PI forms. At this point, the researcher needs to ask for clarification:

[24] S: S38,f19,3,ELA66; C: researcher

S: . . . Y es todo diferente, y siempre tengo que estar al pendiente que qué es lo que él quiere, qué es lo que él está acostumbrado, o qué le gusta a él. Y todo va a ser diferente, todo, todo. Como tengo que pensar en dos maneras en el mismo tiempo, lo que yo quiero y lo que él quiere.

C: Así te imaginas, claro. [clarifying]

S: . . . And everything is different, and I always have to be worrying about what it is that he wants, what it is that he is used to, or what he likes. And everything is going to be different, everything, everything. Like I have to think in two ways at the same time, what I want and what he wants.

C: That's how you imagine it, isn't it? [clarifying]

The relative successful communication of hypotheticality is achieved basically because participants share a macro-point of reference or macro-frame for the interpretation of the utterances as referring to non-factual situations. This frame is usually created by an explicit or implicit question suggested by the researcher. Given the assumption that speakers understand this question, their immediate response is interpreted as referring to a hypothetical world, regardless of the factuality conveyed by the verb forms used.

In this vein, compare [25] with [26], and [27] with [28]. Note that in [25–8] one would expect frequent use of weak assertive verb morphology, e.g. Cond and Sub. As expected, [25] and [27] (from Group 1) contain these forms. By contrast, every finite form in [26] and [28] (from Group 3) are either in the PI or in the PerFut.

[25] *Future, open possibility*; A: A9,f62,1,ELA73; C: researcher

C: A ver, vamos a, a, vamos. Si tuvieras pero tanta plata ¿qué vas a hacer, Ali, con tanta plata? ¿Qué has pensado?

A: *Si tuviera tanta plata* - No necesito plata para ser feliz.

C: Verdad que no, pero si la tuvieras ¿qué?

A: Mhm. ¡*Si la tuviera*, Carmen! /C: ¿O qué sueños tienes?/ Bueno, primeramente *lo que hacía, adoptaba* - ese es mi sueño, *si yo tuviera ahorita, si tuviera ese dinero, adoptaba seminaristas* - - - Eso *sería* mi ilusión y allí *pondría* todo mi dinero.

C: Let's see. Now, if you had so, so much money, what are you going to do, Ali, with so much money? Have you thought - ?

A: *If I had so much money* - I don't need money to be happy.

C: Right, but if you had it, then what?

A: Mhm. *If I had it*, Carmen! /C: Or what dreams do you have?/ Well, firstly, *what I would do, I would adopt* - - that's my dream - - *if I had, right now, if I had that money, I would adopt seminarians* - - - that *would be* my ideal and I *would put* all my money there.

[26] R: R24,m20,2,ELA50

R: Pues, ya que *pago* los taxes, me *llevo* mi dinero, verdad? /um, hmm/ Y me *compro* una casa y si ya *tengo*, pues, me *compro* otro. /um, hmm./ Entonces, *busco* a mis hermanos o mi papá, ¿okay?, y si él *tiene* biles [pagos] muy grandes, como para esta casa, pues, le *ayudo*. Y un carro nuevo para todos hasta que ya no *tengo* dinero.

R: Well, after I *pay* taxes, I *take* my money, right? /uhm, uhm/ And I *buy* a house, and if I *have* one, well, I *buy* another. /uhm, uhm/ Then, I *look for* my brothers or my father, okay? and if he *has* big bills, like for this house, well, I *help* him. And a new car for everyone until I *have* no money.

[27] *Past, counterfactual*; A: A9,f62,1,ELA73; C: researcher

C: . . . ¿Cómo te imaginas tu vida en México, si en vez de venirte para acá te hubieras quedado en México?

A: Bueno, yo como mujer, mi ilusión era el hogar, porque no tuve escuela. No tuve, e, la educación, ¿verdad?, para- *Tal vez que si hubiera tenido la oportunidad sí me hubiera preparado*, pero la pobreza no lo permitió.

C: . . . How do you imagine your life in Mexico, uh, if instead of coming over here you had stayed in Mexico?

A: Well, me being a woman, my ideal was the home, because I had no schooling- *Maybe if I had had the opportunity, then I would have prepared myself*, but poverty didn't permit it.

[28] D: D36,m45,3,ELA90; C: researcher

C: Entonces si tú por ejemplo en vez de vivir aquí hubieras vivido en México, ¿cómo te imaginas tu vida allá, de qué manera diferente crees tú?

D: Mi primer cosa, que *pude hablar* el español mejor. Y también *voy a sacar* con - a tener diferentes valores de México en ideal del hombre y de mujer, el machismo, ideas.

C: ¿Cómo, cómo te imaginas diferente, que hubiera sido así?

D: *Yo creo que vivo, yo creía* que como hombres de ahí, salir con la idea que las mujeres son majas y son - mocionale - mocionale. /Sí, emocionales/.

C: Then if you for instance instead of living here had lived in Mexico, how do you imagine your life there, in what way different do you think?

D: My first thing, I *was able to speak* Spanish better. And I'm also *going to get* - *have* different values in Mexico about ideas of man and woman, machismo, ideas.

C: How, how different do you imagine it would have been?

D: *I think I live, I thought* like the men there, get the idea that women are pretty and are – 'motional – 'motional. /Yes, emotional./

The hypothetical frame created in [25] and [26] is one of open possibility in the future: 'imagine what you would do if you won a lot of money'. Within this context, in [25] speaker A9 conveys different degrees of assertiveness by means of PI, Imp, IS, and Cond morphology. By contrast, every verb in R24's passage ([26]) appears in the PI. Thus, though his text is distinctly hypothetical, he conveys a high level of self-assurance which may be far from the message he really intended to communicate.

Examples [27–8] illustrate a past counterfactual hypothetical frame: 'imagine what your life would have been like in Mexico'. Expectedly for a speaker in Group 1, A9 uses PluS in [27], while D36's (Group 3) weakest assertive form is *creía* (Imp) 'I would think'. There is no doubt that D36 intends to convey hypotheticality in [28]. However, his failure to use PluS makes it difficult to maintain the past counterfactual frame, and leaves open the possibility that he may be presenting the situation as possible in a future world. This speaker's use of the Pret of *poder* 'can/be able to' (*que pude hablar el español mejor* 'that I was able to speak Spanish better') in answer to the researcher's first question is an indication, on the other hand, that he understands that the frame created is past counterfactual.

3.3.4. Conclusion

The analysis shows that, in regard to the discourse communicative level, quantity of expression is reduced toward the lower points in the proficiency continuum, in that speakers in Groups 2 and 3 offer an ever-diminishing range of possibilities as they speculate either about the past or about the non-past. This fact, however, may not be related exclusively to the loss of verb morphology; it may also relate to lack of lexical choices, and perhaps also to speakers' reluctance to discuss hypothetical situations. In turn, this reluctance may be rooted in cultural and cognitive factors. Although cultural factors should not be dismissed a priori, it seems to me that, if relevant, they would be so across the continuum, and would not be responsible for the differences encountered across the three groups. Regarding cognitive factors, I have already mentioned the problem of linearization, conceptualization, and linguistic encoding of situations not stemming from perception and memory. In this respect, it is clear that narration of past events is a cognitively simpler task than hypothesizing, as explained by Levelt (1979; 1982). Support for this observation comes from the fact that when hypothesizing, even Group 1 speakers continually anchor their text to factuality by illustrating their statements with anecdotes about people they know to be in the sort of world which they have been asked to imagine for themselves.

Group 1 speakers have available to them a system of verb morphology which allows them to convey different degrees of possibility, assertiveness, predictive certainty, etc. A further outcome of this study has been to show that reduction of this system restricts the number of possible choices in the field of modality, such that at the lower levels of the continuum the use of almost exclusively PI morphology conveys a strong degree of assertiveness and predictive certainty, without differentiating between more or less possible situations in the hypothetical world created.

3.4. Summary

The form of an oral text is determined by a number of complex elements of the environment in which the discourse takes place (e.g. speakers' interrelationships, degree of formality), by the topic of the discourse, and by the speakers' belief systems and the effect they intend to have on their interlocutors. The speaker's assessment of these factors leads him to make a number of choices from those made available to him by two systems: a system of principles of discourse organization, and the language system. These choices, paradigmatically and syntagmatically consistent, concern all language levels (phonetics, prosody, lexicon, morphology, syntax) and the manner in which a given oral text may be structured and developed.

These two types of element have constituted an objective reference point for my comparison of narrative and hypothetical discourse across the Spanish proficiency continuum. I have noted that language attrition rarely leads to misunderstanding in these two types of discourse genre. Almost obviously, mutual comprehension may be facilitated in the data–collection situations by the interlocutors' high degree of communicative co-operation. In situations of spontaneous verbal interaction, speakers with low levels of proficiency in Spanish refrain from communicating in this language at any length. They intersperse their discourse in English with Spanish words, phrases, or sentences which they feel confident will be clearly understood. When there arises the uncommon need to communicate in Spanish with monolingual Spanish-speakers who have not yet developed the ability to understand English (almost exclusively very recent immigrants), they will most likely be required to produce relatively simple meaning complexes: route directions, greetings, exposition of factual situations. In this respect, I have shown that all speakers in the sample examined manage to convey the main events of a past experience in Spanish. On the other hand, it is clear that language attrition affects the encoding of auxiliary information in narratives, and leaves almost no stylistic choices available to Group 2 and 3 speakers in reference to degrees of hypotheticality in future and counterfactual situations.

4

Exploring Internal Motivation for Change

4.1. Introduction

CHAPTER 2 explored some of the changes that have affected the verb system of
Spanish as speakers within a number of family nuclei shift to English, the majority
language. In this respect, I showed that simplification and loss of tenses did not
appear to be the result of transfer from the superordinate language. On the other
hand, those tenses already undergoing simplification in the oral Spanish of first-
generation immigrants were lost even in the speech of US-born bilinguals with
high levels of Spanish proficiency. This observation lends support to the hypothesis that in language contact situations a number of changes have an internal
motivation, in that (a) they are in progress in the 'model' monolingual variety
before intensive contact occurs and/or (b) they may be spurred by such features as
the semantic opaqueness of certain language specific forms or the relative complexity
of a given paradigm. When shown to be of one of these types, these changes have
been considered to be autonomous developments explicable in terms of the linguistic system involved, and quite probably responsive to such cognitive require-
ments as the need to simplify and generalize rules, perhaps to make oral production
quicker and more automatic.

Chapter 4 deals with two independent changes that are internally motivated in
the sense of (a) and (b) above: the generalization of *estar* 'to be' and the placement
of verbal clitic pronouns. I hope to demonstrate that language contact has the
effect of speeding up the diffusion of these changes despite their autonomous or
language-internal source. This chapter also examines a related question: the omission
of required clitic pronouns across the Spanish proficiency continuum.

4.2. The Extension of *Estar*

4.2.1. The Ser/Estar Opposition

The particular change discussed here is the extension of the copula *estar* 'to be' to
contexts previously limited to *ser*, also translated as 'to be'.[1] This type of study

---

[1] One of the characteristics of both Rumanian and the Iberian Romance languages (Catalan, Galician,
Spanish, and Portuguese) is the existence of two copulative forms: Rum. *a fi* and *a sta*, Cat. *ésser* and
estar, Gal., Sp., and Port. *ser* and *estar*, which originate from Latin *esse(re)/sedēre* and *stāre*, respectively.
Stāre disappeared in French (except as part of the paradigms of être 'to be', a suppletive verb); it has
been retained in Italian with an expanded range of lexical meanings and some copular and auxiliary
functions.

differs from most previous research on the effects of bilingualism insofar as it examines a semantic change and its syntactic consequences in the grammar of the minority language. That is, while trying to throw light on the issues raised by language contact, I explore the complex question of semantic-syntactic variation and change.

Two specific questions, raised by the linguistic problem at hand and by the sociolinguistic situation, are investigated: (*a*) How does the extension of *estar* proceed, i.e. what linguistic and social contexts are more or less favourable to the innovation? (*b*) What effect does language contact have on the actuation of the change?

The study of *estar* is based on language samples from thirty-three of the Mexican-American bilinguals. They are all conversationally fluent in Spanish, but the range of topics in which fluency is achieved is gradually more and more reduced towards the lower end of the proficiency continuum. I focus exclusively on predicate adjective constructions of the type illustrated in [1–3]:

[1] [Mi abuelita] es blanca. Ni es gorda ni es delgada. Está bien.   (M8,m17,1, ELA59)
   [My grandmother] is (*ser*) fair-skinned. She's (*ser*) neither fat nor slim. She's (*estar*) okay.

[2] (*a*) El es blanco y - (*b*) no está, ni está; gordo ni está flaco. Está en medio. (H22, m21,2,ELA11)
   (*a*) 'He's (*ser*) fair-skinned and - (*b*) he's not, he's (*estar*) neither fat nor skinny. He's medium.

[3] Y yo le dije p'atrás: (*a*) 'Pero yo estoy inteligente y muy guapo y no te puedo tener todo.'   (D36,m45,3,ELA43)
   And I answered back to him: (*a*) 'But I'm (*estar*) intelligent and very handsome and I can't have everything.'

Examples [1–3] are produced by three speakers from the three different groups studied. [2*b*] and [3*a*] illustrate the diffusion of *estar* to contexts in which standard varieties of modern Spanish allow only *ser*. The extension to new contexts represents a more advanced stage in a continuous process of syntactic-semantic extension of the copula *estar* throughout the history of Spanish. I will show here that the more recent development in the context of predicate adjectives involves the elimination of some selectional restrictions which apply to the choice of *estar* in this environment. The ultimate result would be the loss of a semantic distinction in the system of two contrasting copulas. At the stage of development characterized here, the system is undergoing simplification, i.e. the progressive generalization of a form X (*estar*) to a larger number of contexts, which in turn implies the loss or reduction of the use of a competing form Y (*ser*).

As illustrated in [4–7], modern Spanish predicate adjective constructions fall into three groups: (*a*) those which allow both *ser* and *estar* ([4–5]); (*b*) those which allow only *estar* ([6]); (*c*) those which allow only *ser* ([7]).

[4] Juan es/está alto.
John is (*ser/estar*) tall.

[5] La luna es/está redonda.
The moon is (*ser/estar*) round.

[6] La taza está/*es vacía.
The cup is (*estar/*ser*) empty.

[7] El discurso es/*está breve.
The speech is (*ser/*estar*) brief.

The distribution of the copulas, especially in the context of predicate adjectives, has been one of the most thoroughly studied and most debated issues in Spanish linguistics. (Useful monographs on this subject are Falk 1979; Navas Ruiz 1963, Vañó-Cerdá 1982.) Indeed, the syntactic and semantic complexity of the question is due in part to the fact that in Spanish the Latin meaning of *estar* (from Lat. *stare*) 'to stand' has undergone a series of modifications and has become more general,[2] leading to the occurrence of *estar* with an increasing number of adjectives. This process of change may be observed through comparison of some examples from the *Poema de Mio Cid* in two versions: the original version, in Old Spanish (OS), and a translation into Modern Spanish (MS). (The examples are taken from Copçeag and Escudero, 1966: 342–3.)

[8] (*a*) OS: non se abre la puerta, - ca bien era cerrada
(*b*) MS: mas no cede la puerta, - que estaba bien cerrada.
but the door doesn't open, - because it was well locked.

[9] (*a*) OS: Armado es mio Cid - con quantos qu'el ha.
(*b*) MS: Armado está el Cid - y cuantos con él están.
the Cid is armed - and (so) are all those who are with him.

[10] (*a*) OS: Dios, ¡qué alegre era - tod cristianismo!
(*b*) MS: Dios, ¡qué alegre estaba - todo el cristianismo!
God, how content Christians were!

In the (*a*) versions of [8–10], the copula employed is *ser*; in the (*b*) versions it is *estar*. In Modern Spanish, *estar* is required in the contexts illustrated in [8] and [9]. On the other hand, the syntactic structure of [10] allows both *ser* and *estar*—although, as is well known, with different semantic interpretations: in MS, [10*a*], with *ser*, would describe the nature of Christianity as happy, while [10*b*], with *estar*, would refer to a state of happiness, implying that Christianity may not be happy at all

---

[2] As pointed out by Pountain (1982), the weakening of *stāre* to a point in which it is little more than a copula, and its encroaching on some of the functions originally fulfilled by **esse(re)*, have happened, though to different extents, in all the Ibero-Romance languages. Copçeag and Escudero (1966) suggest that Rumanian may be following a development similar to that of Spanish.

TABLE 4.1. Parameters Explicative of the Choice between *Ser* and *Estar* in Contrasting Contexts

Ser	Estar
Inherent or essential	Accidental or circumstantial
Imperfective	Perfective
Permanent	Temporary
Defining, abstract, and independent of immediate experience	Dependent on concrete and/or immediate experience
Not susceptible to change	Susceptible to change
Presented within a class frame of reference	Presented within an individual frame of reference

times. It is clear, then, that throughout the history of Spanish the contexts of use of *estar* have increased to the detriment of those of *ser*. At the same time, the forms contrast semantically and pragmatically in a number of syntactic contexts, with more or less clear meaning differences according to the nature of the subject referent and of the attribute assigned to it. Thus, with a large number of adjectives both copulas are accepted (see [4–5]); but some adjectives co-occur only with *estar* (e.g. *lleno* 'full', *contento* 'content'), and some under normal conditions co-occur only with *ser* (e.g. *inodoro* 'odourless', *ambicioso* 'ambitious', *inteligente* 'intelligent', see also [7]). Significantly, this is so 'under normal conditions'; in exclamatory or sarcastic comments, when the speaker wishes to convey the message that the characteristic attributed to the referent of the subject is somehow surprising or unexpected, the copula employed is *estar*, as in *¡Qué inteligente estás!* 'How clever you are (today)!' v. *Eres inteligente* 'You are intelligent'. Indeed, Querido (cited in Luján 1981: 172) suggests that it is always possible to find a context for the use of *estar* with an adjective which normally co-occurs with *ser*, but not vice versa.

Various parameters have been proposed to account for the choice between *ser* and *estar* in contexts where either may occur; some of them are presented in Table 4.1. (See both Falk and Navas Ruíz for detailed evaluations of the parameters included in this table.)

For the purposes of this study, it seemed to me that the concepts of 'class' v. 'individual' frame of reference (based on Falk 1979),[3] and 'susceptibility' v. 'non-susceptibility' to change, proved the most adequate to explain the choice between *ser* and *estar* and the tilt toward *estar* in contexts where more conservative varieties of Spanish choose *ser* either categorically or more frequently. The use of *estar* in newer contexts implies a semantic change concerning the parameters that motivate the choice of copula. This raises the interesting question of the meaning that these

---

[3] Falk discusses at length the applicability of these concepts, referred to by him as 'class norm' and 'individual norm', to the distribution of *ser* and *estar*.

copulas may have such that these meanings allow for changes in the uses of the forms and possibly also for changes of meaning. However, providing a definitive answer to this question is beyond the scope of this chapter.

The parameter of 'class' v. 'individual' frame of reference accounts for constructions like [4] and [5] as follows. The proposition *Juan es alto* attributes to Juan the characteristic of being 'tall' on the basis of a frame of reference which the speaker has for a set of entities (masculine human beings) of which Juan is a member; conversely, Juan *está alto* credits Juan with tallness within an individual frame of reference, which the speaker has established on the basis of his previous knowledge of this specific human being. In [5], the attribute with *ser* predicates that the moon is round in regard to the set of entities of which roundness may be predicated; with *estar*, the attribute assigns roundness within an individual frame of reference implying that it is not always so. Accordingly, it may be possible to imagine a situation in which [5] with *estar* is not acceptable—one when a speaker sees the moon for the first time, during a full moon. In this specific (though rare) situation, example [11] (with *ser*) is acceptable, whereas [12] (with *estar*) is not:

[11] ¡Mira! La luna es redonda.

[12] ¡Mira! *La luna está redonda.
       Look! The moon is round.

The 'individual' frame of reference includes some of the other parameters in Table 4.1. Indeed, the establishment of such a frame requires a concrete previous experience of the referent to which the given attribute is assigned, and implies that the relationship between referent and attribute is susceptible to change. Thus, [12] is acceptable in the real world (since it may be safely assumed that speakers have indeed seen the moon in its various changing shapes), but while [13*a*] is also acceptable, the choice of *estar* in [13*b*] is not. In fact, under a set of normal conditions the entity 'building' does not allow for the establishment of any individual frame of reference with respect to the attribute roundness, given its exemption from change in regard to that attribute.

[13] (*a*) El edificio es redondo.
      (*b*) *El edificio está redondo.
             The building is round.

Perfectivity, temporariness, and circumstantiality may also be subsumed under the 'individual' frame of reference. Indeed, these three parameters imply susceptibility to change. In turn, the establishment that a given attribute is susceptible to change requires knowledge of the entity to which it is being assigned so that it may be compared with itself at different points in time. Note that the cases so often quoted as counterexamples to the concepts of perfectivity, temporality, and circumstantiality (*Está viejo/calvo/muerto* 'He's (*estar*) old/bald/dead') are nicely accounted for by the notion of 'individual' frame, which allows for change but does not specify that the new state be perfective or temporary.

Without entering into any detailed discussion of the explanations proposed for the *ser/estar* opposition, I hope to have suggested the complexity of the question before presenting the study undertaken in Los Angeles. Clearly, the choice between *ser* and *estar* does not depend only on syntactic or lexical constraints. Indeed, the acceptability of either copula may not be determined by the researcher on the basis of the relevant sentence alone; the extended discourse and shared knowledge among the interlocutors must be considered.

The data for this specific study were obtained through recordings of conversations between the author and 33 of the Mexican-Americans under examination, including men and women of different ages from the three basic groups established. Approximately fifty hours of transcribed materials were analysed.[4]

4.2.2. Analysis and results

Let us look at [1–3] this time in the pertinent discourse passages [14–16].

[14] Mi abuelita es - (*a*) no es alta ni es baja. Es como la mitad, como - cinco pies, algo así. Y es - de pelo negro. Lo tenía largo, creo que se lo cortó. Lo tiene como hasta la cintura - ella. Y - usa lentes mi abuelita. Tiene - - (*b*) es blanca. (*c*) Ni es gorda ni es delgada. Está bien.   (M8,m17,1,ELA59)
My grandmother is - (*a*) She's (*ser*) neither tall nor short. She's like average, like - five feet, something like that. And she's - black-haired. She used to have it long, I think she had it cut. It goes down to her waist. And - she wears eyeglasses, my grandmother. She has - - (*b*) she's (*ser*) white-skinned. (*c*) She's (*ser*) neither fat nor slim. She's just right.

[15] El es como cinco pies y - - diez pulgadas de altura. Ahmm, está un poco calvo - - y su cabello es negro y así chino. Ahmm, tiene los ojos verdes. Está - - (*a*) él es blanco y - - no está, (*b*) ni está gordo ni está flaco. Está en medio, así, no sé cómo decirlo. /I: ¿Mediano?/ Mediano, sí, (*c*) está mediano. (H22,m21,2,ELA11)
He's about five foot and - - ten inches tall. Uhmm, he's a little bald - and his hair is black and very curly. Uhmm, he has green eyes. He's - (*a*) he's (*ser*) white-skinned and - he's not, (*b*) he's (*estar*) neither fat nor skinny. He's medium, I don't know how to put it. /I: Average?/ Average, yes, (*c*) he's (*estar*) [of] average [build].

[16] Mi papá era un hombre - muy alto. (*a*) 'Todos los Campas son altos, - como me dijo mi tío - menos usted, Daniel.' /I: ¿Te dijo?/ ¡El cabrón! Y yo le dije

---

[4] In an earlier study (Silva-Corvalán 1986), I examined *estar* in a smaller sample of 27 speakers. Another difference concerns the fact that the 1986 article quantified innovative uses of *estar* as opposed to conservative uses of the same copula. More appropriately, the present chapter quantifies these innovative cases of *estar* in predicate adjective constructions as opposed to tokens of *ser*, all conservative uses, given that the former are encroaching into the realm of *ser*, and not of *estar*. I would like to thank Elvira Behrend (cf. Behrend 1986) for bringing this crucial fact to my attention.

p'atrás: (*b*) 'Pero yo estoy inteligente y muy guapo y no te puedo tener todo.'   (D36,m45,3,ELA43)

My father was a very tall man. (*a*) 'All the Campas are (*ser*) tall, - as my uncle once told me - except you, Daniel.' /I: He really told you so?/ The son of a bitch! And I answered back to him: (*b*) 'But I'm (*estar*) intelligent and very handsome and I can't have everything.'

These passages illustrate descriptive discourse, dealing here with people *unknown* to the interlocutor. Having observed that *estar* appeared to be used innovatively in the community under study, I tried to elicit examples with *ser* and *estar* in the flow of conversation by leading the speakers toward describing people and places *unknown* to me. By the discourse/pragmatic norms of standard general Spanish,[5] this type of description is carried out within a class frame. Even if the relationship between referent and attribute is susceptible to change, the copula used is *ser*, unless an individual frame has been explicitly established (e.g. through lexical means such as the time adverbs *now* and *before*) Interesting exceptions in this respect are such adjectives as *calvo* 'bald' and *viejo* 'old', which in descriptions are far more frequently introduced with *estar*. (Note its use in [15]: *está un poco calvo* 'he's a little bald'.) The motivation appears to be pragmatic. In our society, being bald or old is no asset; therefore, speakers tend to treat these not as defining features but as circumstantial states.

In agreement with speakers of standard general Spanish, a member of Group 1 produces examples [14*a–c*], with *ser*. In the same communicative discourse context, a speaker in Group 2 extends the use of *estar* to introduce the adjectives *gordo* 'fat', *flaco* 'skinny', and *mediano* '[of] average [build]' in examples [15*a–c*]. In [16*b*], a speaker in Group 3 goes so far as to combine *estar* with the adjective *inteligente* 'intelligent', even though intelligence is considered to be an inherent quality that is not susceptible to change, and the proposition is clearly presented in a class frame. These facts appear to indicate that the innovative uses of *estar* follow a path of lexico-semantic diffusion within the linguistic system, and that in regard to social factors, speakers whose families have been residing in the US longer are at the most advanced stage. Similarly, Fernández (1964: 277) observes that *estar* has gradually become accepted with an increasing number of adjectives throughout the historical development of Spanish. He points out that it extended to *lleno* 'full' earlier than it did to *contento* 'content', finally became obligatory with both, and 'it has now timidly started to be used with *feliz* "happy" ' (my translation). I must add that my impression is that Latin Americans are far from timid in this respect, i.e. we attribute the quality of being *feliz* more frequently with *estar* than with *ser*.

With respect to the important question of the meaning of *estar*, one could make

[5] Standard general Spanish here serves to refer to the Spanish spoken by college-educated native Spanish speakers from different countries in the Hispanic world, e.g. Argentina, Chile, Colombia, Mexico, Spain, Venezuela. Various speakers from these countries were consulted; they all agreed with my analysis of a required class frame in the description of people and places unknown to the interlocutor.

the strong claim that a single invariant meaning pervades all its uses, including its occurrence in locative predicates (*Juan está en casa* 'John is at home') and progressive constructions (*Juan está leyendo* 'John is reading'). Indeed, one can argue that this abstract invariant meaning could be something like 'state of being'. This general meaning, however, would not account for the choice between *ser* and *estar* in all cases.[6] In this study I operate with a somewhat weaker claim: I assume that linguistic forms may have a prototypical meaning which accounts for the core of their uses; this prototypical meaning may include a composite of defining features which, as Coleman and Kay (1981: 43) have argued in regard to the meaning of Eng. *lie*, 'are not necessary conditions, and the evaluative logic according to which these conditions are found to be satisfied, or not, is in general one of degree rather than of simple truth and falsity'. This notion of fuzzy boundaries and non-discreteness may allow us to understand the diachronic process of ever-extending contexts in which *estar* has come to be used in Spanish. Indeed, the long disagreement on the meaning of the opposition *ser/estar* may in large part be due to the discussant's insistence on proposing a clear-cut dichotomy and, in many cases, one explanatory parameter (e.g. imperfective v. perfective aspect) to the exclusion of others (e.g. the pragmatic norm illustrated by [14]). Actually, it seems possible that all or, at least, some of the features proposed (see Table 4.2) are contained in the prototypical meaning of *ser* and *estar*. Furthermore, the semantics of the attribute and its relationship with the subject referent may also have fuzzy edges and lend themselves to various degrees of acceptability with one or the other copula, as illustrated by the various judgements of the following:

[17] Su niña está alta. 'Her girl is tall.'

[18] Su niña está bonita. 'Her girl is pretty.'

[19] ?Su nariz está grande. 'Her nose is big.'

[20] ?Sus pestañas están lacias. 'Her eyelashes are straight'.

[21] ??Su piel está clara. 'Her skin is white.'

[22] *Su niña está inteligente. 'Her girl is intelligent.'

Outside a communicative context, where words seem to be associated with their prototypical meanings, [17, 18] are acceptable; [19, 20] are slightly more acceptable than [21]; and [22] is clearly unacceptable. But the prototype view suggests that, in actual communication, speakers may choose to focus on one or another of the elements contained in the prototype, thus opening the door to a semantic change. Changes in the semantics of nouns and attributes may bring about changes in the manner of conceptualizing their relationship and, consequently, in the selection of a copula. However, I have no evidence that the adjectives used innovatively with

---

[6] Strictly, it would not account for the unacceptability of *está* in example (*b*) below, for instance: (*a*) El jarrón está sucio 'The vase is (*estar*) dirty'; (*b*) El jarrón es/*está grande. 'The vase is (*ser*/*estar*) big'; (*c*) Juanito está grande. 'Johnny's (*estar*) big'. Interestingly, however, (*b*)-type sentences with *estar* constitute a high percentage of the innovative tokens found in the data examined.

estar (e.g. *gordo* 'fat', *joven* 'young', *inteligente* 'intelligent', *interesante* 'interesting') have undergone semantic changes relevant to the problem at hand. Rather, it appears that the innovative uses reflect a process of loss of certain selectional restrictions on *estar*.

The question of the meaning of nouns and adjectives is different from that of copulas like *ser* and *estar*. By definition, a copula is a link, a connector, and carries little or no lexical meaning. However, the fact that there exists an opposition between *ser* and *estar* suggests that these forms do carry some semantic load. I wish to propose that in the more conservative varieties of Spanish, the meaning of *estar* in opposition to *ser* includes a composite of at least two elements: 'state of being' and 'perfectivity'. This permits the selection of *estar* in three pragmatic contexts: individual frame of reference, susceptibility to change, and circumstantiality. As concerns change, I would like to suggest that the nature of everyday communication (subject referents are normally known to the interlocutors and attributes are therefore assigned within an individual frame) blurs the distinction between class and individual frame and leads speakers to focus away from this parameter. At this stage, the focus is on the use of *estar* to introduce attributes which are circumstantial and/or susceptible to change. Thus, within the linguistic system, one might identify three stages. At Stage I the meaning of *estar* involves both 'state of being' and 'perfectivity'; its selection is constrained by (*a*) a discourse/pragmatic norm which requires that in certain contexts the attribute be presented within an individual frame and (*b*) the nature of the subject referent and of the attribute assigned to it, such that the latter must be susceptible to change, and/or it must be circumstantial. At Stage II, the individual frame restriction has been lost, and the nature of the subject referent with respect to change and circumstantiality may or may not be relevant.[7] At Stage III, the only constraint on the selection of *estar* is that it should introduce an attribute; the meaning of the copula is 'state of being', i.e. the element of perfectivity is lost. At this stage, then, *ser* and *estar* would no longer contrast in predicate adjectives. The occurrence of *ser* would be lexically limited to a small group of homonymous adjectives of the type of *listo*: *Juan es listo* 'Juan is (*ser*) smart', *Juan está listo* 'Juan is (*estar*) ready'. All this is summarized in Table 4.2.

In reality, the speech of individuals is characterized by a certain amount of variation between a more restricted selection of *estar*, as in Stage I, and a less restricted one, as in Stage III. The placement of speakers in any one of these three stages would not depend, therefore, on the presence or absence of a more or less restricted selectional rule in their grammar, but on the frequency of use of *estar* in constructions where the conditions of susceptibility to change and individual frame are unfulfilled. Note, however, that Tables 4.5 and 4.7 below show that two further linguistic factors appear to play a role in the diffusion of the change:

---

[7] These possibilities are suggested by putting subject (S) in parentheses in Stage II in Table 4.3. A stands for 'attribute'.

TABLE 4.2. Stages in the Extension of *Estar*

Stage I	Stage II	Stage III
S *estar* A	(S) *estar* A	*estar* A
Meaning		
'State of being'	'State of being'	'State of being'
'Perfectivity'	'Perfectivity'	
Pragmatics		
Individual frame		
Susceptible to change	Susceptible to change	
Circumstantial attribute	Circumstantial attribute	Attribute

S = subject; A = attribute.

semantic transparency of the choice between *ser* and *estar*, and type of adjective. The effect that these two factors may have on the stages proposed in Table 4.2 has not been studied quantitatively. Table 4.2 is based on my qualitative analysis of the data, which indicates that only speakers in Group 3 variably reach Stage III, i.e. they use *estar* with adjectives which under no conditions appear to refer to attributes either circumstantial or susceptible to change. The amount of data is insufficient to quantify the stages displayed in Table 4.2 for each speaker, while at the same time controlling for individual frame, susceptibility to change, and circumstantiality. One would expect this quantitative analysis to show that speakers with lower levels of Spanish proficiency evidence more frequent uses of *estar* corresponding to Stage III.

At this synchronic state of the language, one would have to postulate that the speakers' grammar includes a variable rule of copula selection in contexts where *ser* and *estar* seem synonymous. Indeed, this synonymy must be demonstrated for every token of *estar* coded 'innovative'. The variation is illustrated with the speech of the group 3 speaker who produces [16a], with the required copula *ser*, and [16b], which presupposes the elimination of all constraints on the selection of *estar* except that of introducing an attribute. Likewise, first- and second-group speakers evidence variable systems, as flows from the descriptive passages in [23–6]:

[23] Lo único que tiene que (*a*) es chaparrita. Te -, tiene pelo corto. (*b*) No es muy gorda ni flaca ni - De cara pues no se me hace fea. (*c*) Está bonita. (*d*) Pa' mí tiene que estar bonita.   (M6,m27,1,ELA51)
   The only thing is that (*a*) she's (*ser*) short. Sh -, she has short hair. (*b*) She's (*ser*) neither fat nor skinny nor - Her face, you see, I don't think she's ugly. (*c*) She's (*estar*) pretty. (*d*) Well, in my opinion, she's (*estar*) pretty.

[24] ¿Rasgos de ella? Mira, (*a*) la nariz de ella no es como la mía; está un poco grande, pero - anchita. (*b*) Ah, sus ojos son chicos como los míos. Su cara, tú sabes, es - bueno, (*c*) era muy bonita mi madre.   (E12,f44,1,ELA27)

Her features? Well, (*a*) her nose is not like mine; it's (*estar*) a little big, but
- wide. (*b*) Ah, her eyes are (*ser*) small like mine. Her face, you know, it's -
well, (*c*) she was very pretty, my mother.

[25] E: Tiene las pestañas - /A: chinas/ Sí, chinitas. No las tiene muy tupidas,
        ¿verdad?, como hay veces unas personas tienen -

    A: Sí. Hay gente que ¡Ay, y qué chulas se les ven!, ¿verdad?

    E: Mm - no las, tiene - sí. No las tiene así de 'tejaván', como dicen, ¿verdad?

    A: 'De becerro'. (*a*) Así he oído yo la forma cuando [las pestañas] están
        lacias, lacias - -

    A: No, no, no, no. (*b*) Yo digo que la mía [la nariz] está chistosa. /E: ¡No!/
        Nunca me ha gustado mucho mi nariz.   (A20, f19, 2, ELA29)

    E: His eyelashes are - /A: curly/ Yeah, curly. They're not thick, right?, like
        some people sometimes have -

    A: Yeah. There are people who - Gee, and they look real pretty!, right?

    E: Uhm - He doesn't - yeah. He doesn't have them like 'eaves', as they say,
        right?

    A: Like a calf's. (*a*) That's how I've heard they call them when they [the
        eye-lashes] are (*estar*) straight, straight - -

    A: No, no, no, no. (b) I say that mine [the nose] is (*estar*) funny. /E: No!/
        I've never liked my nose much.

[26] R: (*a*) Está alta. Mide seis diez. (*b*) Está muy alta la muchacha.

    C: ¿Cuánto mides tú?

    R: Seis uno.

    C: ¡Ella es más alta que tú!

    R: No. Yo estoy seis uno y ella cinco; quiero decir cinco diez, no seis.

    R: (*c*) Y está muy grande la, la muchacha; muy durita.

    C: ¿Y sus colores así?

    R: (*d*) Está muy clara, como mi papá.   (R24,m20,2,ELA50)

    R: (*a*) She's (*estar*) tall. She's six ten. (*b*) She's (*estar*) very tall, that girl.

    C: How tall are you?

    R: Six one.

    C: She's (*ser*) taller than you!

    R: No. I'm six one and she's five; I mean five ten, not six.

    R: (*c*) And she's (*estar*) very big, this girl; very strong.

    C: And her colour?

    R: (*d*) She's (*estar*) very fair, like my dad.

Examples [23-4] are from speakers in Group 1. [23*a*-*b*] follow the norms of
general Spanish; but [23*c*-*d*] are innovative because no individual frame has been
established for the use of *estar*. Observe that in [24*c*], in a similar context, the speaker
selects the more conservative copula *ser*, but in [24*a*] she uses *estar* to attribute a
non-circumstantial quality to her mother's nose. Examples [25-6] are from

speakers of Group 2; they illustrate similar cases of *estar* used innovatively in discourse which requires a class frame, and with attributes of a non-circumstantial nature. These examples give clear indication that the linguistic system of speakers in all groups varies between Stages I, II, and III. Indeed, viewed without the constraint imposed by an individual or class frame context, the relationship between a person and the attribute 'tall' or 'pretty' is susceptible to change, so [23c] and [26a–c] appear to be at Stage II. However, susceptibility to change is slightly more difficult to justify (though certainly not impossible) when the attributes 'big' and 'funny' are predicated of a nose, 'straight' of eyelashes, and 'fair' of someone's skin.

It would, of course, be possible to ask whether the very use of *estar* might not create an individual frame of reference, with no need for a supporting context. In contrast, I have adopted here the view that 'supporting context' is required in order for the speaker to be able to choose *estar*. To confirm this judgement, which is crucial in my evaluation of *estar* as innovative in the various contexts, I prepared a 'fill-in-the-gap' questionnaire with examples presented in isolation: one could not assume shared experience of the imagined subject referents, since sentences were presented outside any continuous discourse context. Thus presented, the examples conveyed defining descriptive statements.

I gave the questionnaires to three different groups: six graduate students (from various Latin American countries and from Spain) in the Department of Spanish and Portuguese at USC; six college-educated Chileans in Chile; and thirty-one of the thirty-three Mexican-American speakers included in the copula study (representing the three Groups). The assumption was that, if the context were not required to create an individual frame of reference, speakers in all groups would use *ser* and *estar* randomly to complete the sentences, without any clear discrete differences between the various groups. The examples to complete, slightly adapted from examples produced by the speakers under study during the recordings, contained the following sentences:

1. Mi hija ____ buena para pelear.
   My daughter ____ good at fighting.
2. Cuando los niños ____ chiquitos hablaban más español.
   When the children ____ small they spoke more Spanish.
3. Las orientales ____ chaparritas, ¿verdad? No ____ altas.
   Orientals ____ short, right? They ____ not tall.
4. Sí, ____ fácil hablar español. [*Not included in Chile*]
   Yes, it ____ easy to speak Spanish.
5. ¡Qué curiositos se ven cuando ____ chiquitos!
   How pretty they look when they ____ little!
6. Quería ver qué tan alto ____ para poder llevar sus tacones altos.
   She wanted to see how tall he ____ to see if she could wear her high heels.
7. Bueno, Juan me podía ganar a correr, porque yo ____ más chica que él.
   Well, John beat me when we used to run, because I ____ smaller than him.

Exploring Internal Motivation for Change

TABLE 4.3. Responses to the *Ser* (*S*)/*Estar* (*E*) Questionnaire

Example	G		C		Gr. 1		Gr. 2		Gr. 3	
	S	E	S	E	S	E	S	E	S	E
1	5	1	5	1	10	1	8	1	10	1
2	6	0	6	0	3	8	4	5	2	9
3a	6	0	6	0	11	0	9	0	5	6
3b	6	0	6	0	10	1	9	0	5	6
4	6	0	–	–	11	0	9	0	10	1
5	6	0	5	1	3	8	3	6	1	10
6	6	0	4	2	7	4	7	2	2	9
7	6	0	6	0	8	3	6	3	4	7
8	6	0	6	0	11	0	9	0	8	3
9	6	0	6	0	11	0	9	0	11	0
10a	6	0	6	0	8	3	6	3	7	4
10b	6	0	6	0	8	3	8	1	6	5
11	6	0	6	0	10	1	7	2	7	4
12	6	0	6	0	9	2	8	1	6	5
No. of different examples completed with *estar*		1		3		10		9		13

Note: G = 6 graduate students; C = 6 Chileans; Gr. 1 = 11 speakers; Gr. 2 = 9 speakers; Gr. 3 = 11 speakers.

8. A mí me gusta María; ____ simpática.
   I like Mary; she ____ nice.
9. El niño de mi sobrina ____ inteligente.
   My niece's child ____ intelligent.
10. La casa de mi hijo ____ grande y también ____ bonita.
    My son's house ____ big, and it ____ also pretty.
11. Me gusta tu hermana. ____ chaparrita, pero tiene bonito cuerpo.
    I like your sister. She ____ short, but well-formed.
12. Yo tenía un amigo suizo. No ____ delgado ni gordo; pesaba unas 170 libras.
    I had a Swiss friend. He ____ neither slim nor fat; he weighed about 170 pounds.

The responses given by the Mexican-Americans, especially when compared with their linguistic behaviour in conversation (note that the adjective *inteligente* 'intelligent' appears only with *ser* in the elicitation task), invite further study (cf. s. 2. 1.2). For the purposes of this chapter, however, I limit myself to presenting, in Table 4.3, the figures obtained with respect to the choice between *ser* (*S*) and *estar* (*E*).

TABLE 4.4. Percentage of Innovative *Estar* (*a*) over All Tokens of *Estar* and (*b*) over All Tokens of Innovative *Estar* plus All Tokens of *Ser*

	Conservative use		Innovative use		Total no.
	No.	%	No.	%	
Ser	833	100	0	0	833
(*a*) *Estar/estar*	431/853	51	422/853	49	853
(*b*) *Estar/estar + ser*			422/1255	34	

The responses to the 'fill-in-the-gap' task, which visibly divide speakers into conservative and innovative groups, confirm my analysis of the naturalistic data collected in the Mexican-American community of East Los Angeles. *Estar* is being used innovatively in this community: the message conveyed by *estar* in certain contexts is the same as would have been conveyed by *ser*. Note that, in more conservative dialects (G and C), *ser* is used almost categorically. In more advanced dialects, although we find some variation, a clear trend exists toward obliteration of the class individual frame opposition, with an increase in the use of *estar* and a consequent reduction in the uses of *ser* by speakers with a longer history of family bilingualism (Group 3).

Innovative *estar* is not restricted to Mexican-American Spanish, however. Its extended use is attested in the materials for the study of Mexico City Spanish published by the Universidad Nacional Autónoma de México (UNAM 1971; 1976), and it has been examined in some detail in the Spanish spoken in Michoacán (Mexico) by Gutiérrez (1989). Furthermore, I have noticed innovative *estar*, especially with evaluative adjectives, in spoken Madrid Spanish, and de Jonge (1987) observes that it is quite frequent in Caracas Spanish in the context of expressions of age.

For the purpose of identifying the linguistic and social contexts more or less favourable to the innovative uses of *estar*, the data from the 33 Mexican-Americans were analysed quantitatively by using the crosstabs program of SPSS (Nie *et al.* 1975). A total of 1,686 tokens of *ser* and *estar* were coded. As Table 4.4 illustrates, only *estar* constructions represent innovations with predicate adjectives, with a high frequency of 49 per cent of all uses of *estar*. This table also indicates that *estar* has extended to 34 per cent of the cases where more conservative varieties of Spanish would use *ser*.

The 422 cases of innovative use of *estar* were so classified on the well-tested assumption that the speaker did not intend to convey any meaning difference by choosing *estar* rather than *ser*. Thus the data analysis allowed me to assume that [26*a*], *Está alta*, means the same as *Es alta* 'She's tall' (obviously in that specific context); so [26*a*] was codified as 'innovative'. Had the same example occurred with *ser*, it would have been codified as 'conservative'.[8] A total of 402 (95 per cent) of the innovative cases correspond to constructions where *estar* functions in what the discourse passage indicated should have been a class frame context. The copula *ser*, on the other hand, occurs most frequently in a class frame context (690/833 cases, i.e. 83 per cent), or in contexts not codified with regard to frame of reference.[9] Examples [27–8] illustrate individual frame contexts where the selection of *estar* is not innovative:

[27] B: (*a*) Edward estaba muy gordo, ¿verdad?
　　　A: Como que engordó un poco, ¿verdad?　　(B33,f18,3,ELA29)
　　　B: (*a*) Edward was (*estar*) very fat, wasn't he?
　　　A: He did gain a little weight, didn't he?

[28] (*a*) [Mi hija] es un poquito gordita, (*b*) aunque ya no está muy gordita ahora. Especialmente, (*c*) ya está un poquito más delgada.　　(R11,f42,1,ELA18)
　　　(*a*) [My daughter] is (*ser*) a little fat, (*b*) though she's (*estar*) not very fat right now. Especially, (*c*) now she's (*estar*) a little slimmer.

Note that in [27] the subject referent is known to both speakers, who share an individual frame of reference for Edward in regard to how fat he has been at various stages of his life. Conversely, in [28*a*] the subject referent (the speaker's daughter) is unknown to the interlocutor. Thus, *estar* is conservative in [27*a*], while *ser* (*es* 'is') is so in [28*a*]. In [28*b*–*c*], however, the speaker explicitly creates an individual frame of reference through lexical means (the adverbs *ya* 'presently', and *ahora* 'now') and contrasts her daughter's present physique with an earlier state. Accordingly, the copula *estar* selected in [28*b*–*c*] is conservative.

Of various internal and external factors included in my quantitative analysis, only those which show interesting correlations will be discussed here.[10] One of these factors is *type of adjective*, included to test the hypothesis of lexical diffusion. Indeed, certain adjectives, amenable to classification into different semantic groups, appeared to favour the use of innovative *estar*. The results of the cross-tabulation of innovative use by type of adjective are presented in Table 4.5. (Three adjectives of time, all used with *ser*, are not included in this table.)

'Age', 'size', and 'colour' include adjectives which refer to features of both

---

[8] I cross-checked my codification of innovative/conservative *estar* for most of the 422 cases with codifications done by 3 of my graduate students. There was total agreement. I would like to thank Manuel Gutiérrez (Chilean), and Alicia and Francisco Ocampo (Argentinians) for their help in this respect.

[9] Three types of example were not codified with respect to frame of reference, being instead included as 'other cases' in this factor group: (i) Subjectless constructions (*Ya estaba/era oscuro* 'It was (*estar/ser*) dark already'); (ii) constructions which, given a normal state of affairs, do not allow *ser* in standard general Spanish (*Los tomates están podridos* 'The tomatoes are rotten'); (iii) Constructions with sentential subjects, incompatible with the establishment of an individual frame (*Hablar bien es importante* 'To speak well is important').

[10] Quantified but omitted from discussion are the following factors: animacy of the subject, adjective grading (comparative, superlative), level of proficiency in English, level of schooling in English and in Spanish.

TABLE 4.5. Cross-tabulation of Innovative Use by Type of Adjective

Type of adjective	Innovative use	
	No.	%
Age	136/174	78
Size	101/191	53
Sensory character	8/17	47
Physical appearance (animate)	43/138	31
Description (non-animate)	12/48	25
Evaluation	90/394	23
Miscellany	10/56	18
Moral value	15/118	13
Colour	4/38	11
Class	3/78	4
Total no.	422/1,252	

Note: $p = <.00$. Statistical Significance is given as a value of p, where any value above .05 is considered to reflect a non-significant correlation.

animate and inanimate subject referents (e.g. *alto* 'tall', *grande* 'big', *joven* 'young', *mayor* 'old', *amarillo* 'yellow'); 'physical appearance' and 'description' refer to non-measurable descriptive features of animate and inanimate referents, respectively (e.g. *curiosito* 'cute', *tosco* 'coarse', *liso* 'smooth', *sucio* 'dirty'); 'evaluation', 'sensory', and 'miscellany' may predicate features of both animates and inanimates. Evaluative adjectives judge both animate and inanimate entities (e.g. *interesante* 'interesting', *bueno* 'good', *fácil* 'easy'); moral adjectives judge only animate referents (e.g. *honesto* 'honest', *respetable* 'respectable', *noble* 'noble'). Social status or class is predicated only of animates (e.g. *pobre* 'poor', *católico* 'catholic', *mexicano* 'Mexican'). Sensory adjectives comprise attributes which may be perceived by tasting, smelling, or hearing (e.g. *dulce* 'sweet', *caliente* 'hot', *silencioso* 'quiet'). 'Miscellany' includes various types of adjectives: of physical state (e.g. *borracho* 'drunk', *sano* 'healthy'), mental state (e.g. *porfiado* 'stubborn', *celoso* 'jealous'), and others not easily classifiable into any of the preceding types (e.g. *inocente* 'innocent/naive', *femenina* 'feminine', *alérgico* 'allergic', *soñador* 'dreamer').

Interestingly, adjectives differ with respect to the innovation: age and size favour it in over 50 per cent of the tokens; sensory adjectives also appear to favour it but the number of tokens is rather low (17 in the samples from the 33 speakers). Next come adjectives of physical appearance, with 31 per cent of innovative cases; description, evaluation, and miscellany with 25, 23, and 18 per cent of innovation. Included in the first four groups are adjectives which, independently of the communicative context, refer to qualities which may be conceptualized as susceptible to change, especially so when they are assigned to animate beings. Animacy of the subject appeared to me at first to be an entirely valid correlation. Indeed, note that adjectives which describe non-animate entities do not favour the change (25 per cent) as much as those which describe animate entities (31 per cent). However, size (53 per cent) and age (78 per cent), highly favourable as well, include a good number of adjectives which relate to inanimate entities, as illustrated in the excerpts from house descriptions in [29–30],[11] so the question of the subject's animacy was not further pursued.

[29] Una de esas recá -, recámaras es el master bedroom, el más grande. Y el otro está pequeñito.   (H22,m21,2,ELA50)
One of those bed -, bedrooms is the master bedroom, the larger one. And the other one is (*estar*) small.

[30] Teníamos otro cabanete [*sic*] allá arriba - pero estaba muy largo, y no cabía la hielera, y no estaba, no estaba ancho.   (M47,f33,3,ELA52)
We had another cupboard up there - but it was (*estar*) too long, and the refrigerator wouldn't fit, and it wasn't (*estar*), it wasn't (*estar*) wide.

Evaluative adjectives, including examples with such attributes as *barato* 'cheap', *caro* 'expensive', *difícil* 'difficult', occur very frequently when judging entities found in the immediate context and in expressions of subjective reactions in which *estar* is the accepted copula (e.g. *¡Qué difícil está esto!* 'How difficult this is (*estar*)!', *Está buena esta sopa* 'This soup is (*estar*) good'). Absolute frequency of occurrence of *estar* with certain individual attributes may be promoting its extension to less frequent class frame contexts in which the same attributes are used. After all, frequency, as Anttila (1972: 187) points out, is not 'a mere mechanistic concept, as it has repercussions in association formation and memory'.

The correlation between the remaining four groups of adjectives and innovative *estar* is, interestingly, relatively much weaker. Clearly, the theory of lexical diffusion of phonological change (Wang 1969) may be extended to syntactic-semantic changes, as the process of diffusion of *estar* within a speaker's vocabulary appears selectively to affect certain lexical items or groups of lexical items which together constitute a semantic field (size, physical appearance, age, etc.).

Table 4.6 presents some of the quantitative results by group, by speaker, and by type of adjective. Under this last factor I have listed the three most favourable types that occurred more than ten times in the data from all the speakers, age, size and physical appearance, and the three least favourable types to the innovation, colour, moral value, and class. Observe that the totals for each group do not correspond to the sum of the cases for the speakers. This is because Table 4.6 does not list those speakers who had fewer than ten tokens of innovative *estar* in their speech sample. Percentages are given only if there are more than five tokens in a cell. Otherwise, raw numbers are given in parentheses.

---

[11] House descriptions are also subject to the class frame of reference pragmatic constraint.

TABLE 4.6. Percentage of Innovative Uses of *Estar*

Speaker	Total N	Innovations N	Innovations %	Age N	Age %	Size N	Size %	Phys N	Phys %	Colour N	Colour %	Moral N	Moral %	Class N	Class %
Group 1	*575*		*27*	*79*	*84*	*81*	*42*	*89*	*21*	*21*	*5*	*44*	*0*	*31*	*0*
E1: FY	62		40	15	93	14	64	(0/3)		(0/2)		11	0	0	0
S2: FY	70		31	18	72	(1/4)		18	17	(0/1)		0		(0/3)	
F5: MY	37		27	(1/3)		(4/4)		10	20	(1/2)		0		(0/2)	
M6: MY	28		54	5	100	(1/2)		(3/5)		(0/2)		0		0	
M8: MY	38		8	(3/3)		6	0	(0/3)		10	0	0		(0/1)	
A9: FO	29		41	6	100	5	100	(1/3)		0		9	0	0	
E12: FO	34		44	8	63	6	67	7	57	0		8	0	0	
C13: MO	94		14	(2/2)		7	43	24	8	0		0		16	0
J14: MO	52		25	10	90	(0/2)		6	17	0		7	0	(0/2)	
P15: MO	45		27	(2/2)		6	0	(3/4)		0		5	0	(0/2)	
Group 2	*357*		*45*	*52*	*71*	*65*	*65*	*29*	*59*	*11*	*18*	*44*	*23*	*11*	*9*
R17: FY	26		42	(4/4)		6	83	0	0	0	0	8	0	0	0
A20: FY	102		63	17	94	19	74	14	79	(1/3)		10	20	0	0
V21: FY	27		67	8	75	5	60	0		(1/2)		0		0	
H22: MY	41		51	0		13	85	(1/4)		(0/3)		6	17	0	
R24: MY	39		67	(4/4)		12	67	(2/2)		(0/1)		9	67	(1/1)	
Group 3	*323*		*33*	*43*	*77*	*45*	*56*	*20*	*35*	*6*	*17*	*30*	*17*	*17*	*6*
B33: FY	16		81	(1/1)		(4/4)		(1/1)		(1/3)		(0/1)		0	
S38: FY	21		52	(2/2)		10	70	0		(0/2)		(0/1)		0	
M47: FO	34		41	(3/4)		9	67	(1/1)		(0/1)		(0/4)		(0/1)	
D36: MO	39		26	6	83	(0/3)		(1/1)		0		8	25	5	0
H48: MO	42		26	5	80	(0/1)		(0/1)		0		0		(0/2)	
R50: MO	64		28	8	75	10	50	(0/1)		0		0		6	0
Significance			*p* = <.00	*p* = <.23		*p* = <.02		*p* = <.00		*p* = <.43		*p* = <.00		*p* = <.28	

Note: F = female; M = male; Y = 15–29 yrs. old; O = 30–65 yrs. old; N = total no. of tokens; % = % of innovative tokens. Phys = physical appearance; Moral = moral value.

Assuming that the results of Group 1 reflect the path followed by the extension of *estar* by adjective type, and noting also that the innovation is favoured by those speakers who have acquired English from birth (see below, Table 4.8) and whose speech diverges the most (impressionistically and by speaker's own evaluation) from Group 1 Spanish, it appears safe to suggest that those speakers who present some innovative uses with colour, moral, or class adjectives represent more advanced stages of the change, and seem more affected by the contact situation. A serious problem, however, is raised by the scarcity of the data in a number of cells. I feel that conclusions about Group 1 are safer, though, because despite individual differences and empty cells for colour, moral, and class adjectives, what stands out is that *estar* is never used innovatively with moral or with class adjectives, and only once is employed in this way with a colour adjective, by F5. Interestingly, F5's social history is one of intensive interaction with Group 2 type youngsters in El Monte, the barrio where he lives (cf. Milroy and Milroy 1985 on social network theory in relation to language variation and change).

A more serious problem is raised by the empty cells in Groups 2 and 3. For instance, lack of data in some crucial cells makes the behaviour of R17, S38, M47, H48, and R50 similar to that of speakers in Group 1. Thus, we may compare only six of the speakers in these two groups with respect to their distance from those in Group 1, and on the basis of just a few tokens for each (bold numerals in Table 4.6). As compared to Group 1, then, the number of types of adjective affected by the extension of *estar* in Groups 2 and 3 divide the speakers as follows:

One further type of adjective affected (colour or moral value): V21, H22, B33, and D36.

Two more types affected (moral value and colour or class): A20, and R24.

Note that A29 (Group 2) and R42 (Group 3) are not included in Table 4.6 because there are fewer than ten innovative tokens of *estar* in their speech samples. One of six innovative tokens used by A29 corresponds to a moral value adjective; three of four innovative tokens used by R42 correspond to moral and class type adjectives. This is further indication of the extension of *estar* to a larger number of adjective types in these two groups.

In sum, group totals indicate more regularly the increase in innovation from Group 1 to Groups 2 and 3. But, as with many other studies of syntactic variables, we are faced with difficulties as soon as we set individuals apart, because of deviations from the norm of the group but mostly because of lack of sufficient spontaneously produced data. Although the interpretation of results for these speakers must be tentative, the addition of new adjective-type contexts for the use of *estar* seems reasonable proof of acceleration of this change in Mexican-American Spanish (see definition of acceleration in Chapter 1).

Let us now examine the results of Table 4.7, which correlates innovative use with the semantic transparency of the choice between *ser* and *estar*.

TABLE 4.7. Cross-tabulation of Innovative Use by the Semantic Transparency of the Choice between *Ser* and *Estar*

Semantic transparency	Innovative use							
	Total		Group 1		Group 2		Group 3	
	No.	%	No.	%	No.	%	No.	%
Different modality	367/846	43	126/362	35	147/262	56	94/222	42
Apparent synonymy	28/171	16	16/79	20	6/50	12	6/42	14
Choice not allowed in standard language	19/174	11	11/102	11	2/24	8	6/48	12
Clear difference	8/64	13	3/32	9	4/21	19	1/11	9
Significance	$p = <.00$		$p = <.00$		$p = <.00$		$p = <.00$	

These results also support the hypothesis of gradual diffusion. In this case, the process appears to be controlled by what I have called the 'semantic transparency' of the choice between *ser* and *estar* to introduce an adjective in a given sentence. The motivation for including this factor is provided by the observation, made in historical linguistics, that complex systems are more likely to change than simple ones; i.e. when the rules underlying an aspect of the grammar are opaque, we have a potential source for re-interpretation.

As already explained, the coding of *estar* as conservative or innovative for every token takes the sentence and the discourse/pragmatic context into account. The decision as to whether the choice between *ser* and *estar* is transparent, however, depends exclusively on an evaluation of how transparently or unquestionably one or more of the parameters listed in Table 4.1 may account for the relationship between subject referent and attribute in terms of meaning *at the sentence level*. Thus, [23c–d] are coded 'innovative' because they violate the class frame pragmatic norm, and they are also coded 'different modality' because the two alternatives (presented in [31a] with *estar* and in [31b] with *ser*) may be accounted for by all the parameters in Table 4.1. This context is the most favourable to the innovation in every group.

[31] (a) [Ella] está bonita. '[She] is (*estar*) pretty.'
   (b) [Ella] es bonita.

The contrast between *ser* and *estar* is transparent ('clear difference' in Table 4.7) with a group of adjectives which have different meanings associated with the choice of copula, as shown in the translation of [32–3]:

[32] (a) Esta radio es buena. 'This radio is (*ser*) of good quality.'
   (b) Esta radio está buena. 'This radio is (*estar*) functioning well.'

[33] (*a*) Pedro es callado/vivo. 'Peter is (*ser*) shy/smart.'
     (*b*) Pedro está callado/vivo. 'Peter is (*estar*) silent/alive.'

This context, as expected, is not favourable to diffusion (13 per cent total average). Interestingly, the three innovative tokens in Group 1 are produced by C13, who is married to M26, who is in turn responsible for three of the four innovative tokens in Group 2 (see Milroy and Milroy 1985 on social network theory in relation to language variation and change). The remaining two tokens occur in the sample from R24 (Group 2) and R50 (Group 3).

In the same vein, the innovation is disfavoured (11 per cent in Group 1 and total average) by adjectives which in the standard language categorically require one or the other copula, as in [34].

[34] (*a*) Eso es preferible. 'That is (*ser*) preferable.'
     (*b*) *Eso está preferible. *'That is (*estar*) preferable.'

Contexts in which the *ser/estar* opposition is not associated with a semantic difference in the adjective, and in which the choice of one or the other copula represents what I have termed 'different modality', i.e. different and more or less subtle ways of conceptualizing the relationship between the attribute and the subject referent, correlate favourably with the innovative use of *estar*. Indeed, in such contexts, illustrated by [35], innovative *estar* is used more frequently than *ser* in Group 2 (56 per cent of the cases), and it is also quite frequent in the other two groups. Also favourable (16 per cent total in the three groups) are a number of cases quantified separately and included in the group labelled 'apparent synonymy'. In these examples, the opposition *ser/estar* appears to have almost no semantic load: while it may be possible to propose a fairly undisputed explanation for the alternatives in [35], it is much more difficult to do so for those in [36]:

[35] El mole poblano {(*a*) está/(*b*) es} bueno ahí.
     'Puebla mole [a Mexican dish] is good there.'

[36] Si el hombre {(*a*) está/(*b*) es} soltero, puede hacer lo que quiera.
     'If the man is unmarried he can do whatever he pleases.'

Alternative (*a*), with *estar*, is considered to be innovative in a discourse context which does not support the establishment of susceptibility to change and/or an individual frame of reference. Furthermore, while [35*a–b*] represent 'different modality', [36*a–b*] qualify as 'apparent synonymy'. Indeed, in conservative varieties of Spanish the choice of *ser* or *estar* to link the attribute 'good' with *Puebla mole* is explained by the fact that the alternative with *ser* is defining, independent of immediate experience, and presented within a class frame; but the alternative with *estar* is dependent on immediate experience, and implies susceptibility to change. Note that to qualify [35*a*] with the time adverb *ahora* 'now', thus implying change with respect to another time, would make the use of *estar* conservative. In [36], the choice of *ser* or *estar* to link the attribute 'unmarried' to 'man' does not seem clearly linked to any of the parameters discussed. Example [36*a*] is coded 'innovative' in order to be methodologically consistent with the discourse/pragmatic requirement of class frame of reference; at the sentence level, however, it does not appear possible to maintain that alternatives (*a*) and (*b*) unquestionably contrast with respect to any other explanatory parameter, namely 'circumstantiality', 'dependency on concrete experience', or 'susceptibility to change'. Note, for instance, that neither alternative would become more or less acceptable if the examples were qualified with *ahora*.

The preceding discussion indicates that we should expect apparent synonymy to be more favourable to the extension of *estar* than different modality. This expectation is not fulfilled, as the percentages in Table 4.7 show. None the less, it is of even more interest to see that diffusion of *estar* is least favoured both when the opposition *ser/estar* is associated with clear semantic differences and when the opposition is not allowed in the standard language, i.e. when use of *estar* would result in blatant unacceptability.

Let us now examine the results of the cross-tabulation between innovative use and both (*a*) level of proficiency in Spanish, and (*b*) age of acquisition of English. Levels of proficiency in English and Spanish were established on the basis of the speaker's self-evaluation and the author's global and impressionistic assessment of the speaker's competence in each language. The speakers were evaluated relative to one another; this assessment took into account at least the following elements: pauses, hesitation, self-corrections, switches into the other language, questions requiring information about how to say something, phonetic transfer, lexical transfer, and violations of rules of tense–mood–aspect, person, number, and gender agreement. The three levels of Spanish proficiency do not necessarily correspond to membership in Groups 1, 2, or 3, but all those in Group 1 are included in the 'native proficiency' level. Likewise, all speakers in Group 3 started acquiring English from birth, and all those in Group 1 started acquiring it at age twelve or older; although all speakers in Group 2 are born in the USA, some of them started acquiring English between the ages of five and seven. Table 4.8 presents the results.

The results displayed in Table 4.8 show that the level of oral proficiency in Spanish does not establish differences with respect to the innovative uses of *estar*. By contrast, it is arresting to note that, if the speaker acquires English before the age of six (no speakers in the sample started acquiring English between the ages of six and eleven), his speech will show a noticeably higher percentage of innovative uses as compared to one who has acquired this language after the age of eleven. This correlation may be interpreted in at least three ways: (*a*) early contact with a linguistic system in which a single form, *be*, may correspond to two forms, *ser* and *estar*, favours the evolution toward the use of a single form in contexts which allow both (albeit contrastively); (*b*) early contact between two linguistic systems speeds up processes of change in the system of the less used language; (*c*) lack of formal education in a language speeds up processes of change. My study does not discriminate among these three hypotheses: all three may be correct.

TABLE 4.8. Innovative *Estar* by Spanish Proficiency and by Age of English Acquisition

	No.	%
Spanish proficiency		
Native	241/717	34%
Good	156/463	34%
Lower	25/75	33%
Significance	$p = <.99$	
English acquisition		
From birth	75/116	37%
3–5 years	164/265	40%
12–20	79/195	29%
21+	26/47	25%
Significance	$p = <.00$	

The hypothesis in (*a*), which acknowledges the possibility of influence from the dominant language, could be explored by replicating this study in a situation of language contact between two languages with dual systems of copulas. The results of Table 4.8 support the possibilities in (*b*)–(*c*). Note, however, that in my subject sample, acquisition of English before age six necessarily implies lack of formal instruction in Spanish as a native, official language. I have not answered, therefore, the question of what effect language contact *per se* has on the diffusion of innovative *estar*; i.e. at this point, one could argue that the change is accelerated by lack of formal instruction, regardless of the situation of contact. To examine this further, it would be necessary to study a population of illiterate Spanish monolingual families. This rather difficult task has not been attempted. A comparison with the extension of *estar* in Mexico, however, allows me to propose that one of the consequences of language contact has been the acceleration of this change.

4.2.3. Acceleration of Change

A comparison of the status of *estar* in Mexican-American Spanish with the results of a similar study conducted by Gutiérrez (1989) in Morelia (Michoacán, Mexico) indicates that the diffusion of *estar* is at a more advanced stage in the USA, and that other factors, in addition to lack of formal education, must be at work in change acceleration. Gutiérrez collected conversational Spanish data in Michoacán, and attested the same type of diffusion of *estar* discussed in this chapter. Examples [37–8] are taken from his doctoral dissertation:

[37] . . . y ahora vivimos allí en Prados Verdes en las casas de Infonavit, *están chiquitas*, pero *están bonitas*.

... and now we live in Prados Verdes in the Infonavit houses, *they are small* (*estar*), but they *are pretty* (*estar*).

[38] ... dicen que allá [en USA] crecen mucho y aquí *estamos muy enanos.*
    ... they say that over there [in the USA] they grow a lot and here we *are* (*estar*) *extremely short.*

Gutiérrez's (1989: 116) results show that, as in Los Angeles, the adjective types most favourable to the innovation are age (43 per cent), size (34 per cent), physical description (33 per cent), and evaluation (12 per cent); no innovative uses occur with moral value, colour, or class type adjectives (cf. Table 4.5 above).

As regards the social variables that may correlate positively with innovative *estar*, Gutiérrez observes that women appear more innovative than men; he also notes that higher education correlates with lower percentages of innovation (6 per cent and 21 per cent for university education and elementary education, respectively). The low number of total cases does not permit him to establish correlations with the social variables while at the same time controlling for type of adjective; necessarily, then, his results must be interpreted with caution, since it is in principle possible that education skewing may be a consequence of the types of adjective used in each education group.

Acceleration of change seems to me to be supported by a comparison of both the overall frequencies and the increase in linguistic contexts for the diffusion of *estar* in Los Angeles with those of Morelia. Whether this speeding up is due specifically to the situation of language contact remains to be explored further; the existing evidence suggests multiple causation, i.e. language contact and lack of formal instruction both contribute to the propagation of a change in the secondary language. Language contact manifests itself not exclusively as transfer from the contact language, but in such phenomena as simplification of alternatives, selective acquisition, or freezing of the competence reached at a certain age. All these strategies converge in the direction of alleviating the load of having to remember and use two different linguistic systems.

Table 4.9 presents a few general comparative percentages.

Compared to Morelia speakers, percentages of innovation are higher even in Group 1. For the three groups in Los Angeles, the overall percentage of innovative *estar* is 34 per cent; it is only 16 per cent in Morelia. Furthermore, in each of the three Groups studied in Los Angeles, the younger speakers were shown to have a higher percentage of innovative uses of *estar*. Table 4.9 shows that this generational difference does not seem to exist in Morelia: innovative uses of *estar* remain the same across age groups (7 per cent/7 per cent; 26 per cent/27 per cent). Percentages increase along the education factor (from 7 per cent to 26–7 per cent), although not regularly; they are lower in the 'elementary education' group than in the 'secondary education' group.

Let us observe, furthermore, that the hypothesis regarding acceleration of internal changes also receives support from the results shown in Table 4.10. For the

TABLE 4.9. Proportion of Innovative Uses of *Estar* in Los Angeles and Morelia

	Los Angeles						Morelia (Michoacán) Total	
	Group 1		Group 2		Group 3			
	No.	%	No.	%	No.	%	No.	%
F	282	32	258	42	113	48	96	19
M	293	23	99	53	210	25	43	12

Age	Education					
	Tertiary		Secondary		Elementary	
	No.	%	No.	%	No.	%
30–50	9	7	12	26	3	19
13–29	15	7	70	27		

TOTAL   422/1,255 (34%)   139/886 (16%)

Note: The results for Morelia are also broken down by age and by level of education.

TABLE 4.10. Cross-tabulation of Innovative Use of *Estar* by Group and by Age (Los Angeles)

	15–29 years		30–65 years	
	No.	%	No.	%
Group 1	7 speakers 82/295	28	6 speakers 74/280	26
Group 2	5 speakers 140/234	60	4 (3) speakers 19/123 (18/80)	15 (23)
Group 3	5 speakers 39/99	39	6 speakers 68/224	30
Significance	$p = <.00$		$p = <.00$	

older Group 2 speakers I have given results including and excluding L28 (latter result in parentheses), who is quite exceptional with respect to *estar*; she has a very low 2 per cent of innovation (1/43).

In each group, the younger speakers show a higher percentage of innovative uses. Observe, however, that in Group 1 the difference between the younger and the older speakers is only of 2 percentage points, similar to the situation reported above for Morelia. That is, within a family of first-generation immigrant speakers, we may assume that the speech of the older and the younger members will not differ much in the use of *estar*.

Conversely, in a mixed family, the younger second- or third-group members will show marked differences in regard to this feature when compared with older first- or second-group members of this family. Note that the gap between the older and the younger speakers in Group 2 widens to 45 percentage points. The difference is not as steep within Group 3. Indeed, in terms of overall percentages of use of a given linguistic form, my research demonstrates that in some cases Group 3 speakers may not be very distant from Group 1 (cf. quantification of preverbal clitics, Table 4.17). Overall percentages in Group 3 must be interpreted with caution, however. I have noted that speakers who are at the lower levels of the Spanish proficiency continuum use a smaller lexicon, especially so in regard to adjectives. This may account for their producing fewer innovative forms, while at the same time extending the diffusion to new adjective-type contexts, as shown above in Table 4.6.

Some of the tables show performance in terms of group behaviour; but there is actually a certain range of variation within each group (cf. Table 4.6). Among those in Group 1, place of origin in Mexico appeared to be a determining factor: impressionistically, innovative *estar* seemed more frequent among speakers from the northernmost regions of Mexico such as Tijuana, and Ciudad Juárez. To examine the possible effect of diatopical differences on those speakers whose parents have come from different places, I have compared overall percentages in three families, as shown in Table 4.11. Tijuana borders California, Ciudad Juárez borders Texas; Zacatecas, Jalisco, and Michoacán are neighbour states located further south (see Fig. 1.2; Morelia is in the north-east of Michoacán).

It is clear that, despite differences in parents' places of origin, those in the younger age group have a uniformly higher percentage of innovation, characterized by an increase of 7–42 percentage points from the older to the younger generation within each family. The lowest difference corresponds to Family 1. Interestingly, the mother (E12), who evidences the highest percentage of innovative *estar* in Group 1, came to the USA when she was about eighteen years old from Tijuana, a border city characterized by intensive interaction with US residents. The same degree of interaction, however, characterizes Ciudad Juárez, yet R11 (the mother) evidences 33 per cent of innovative uses, only 7 percentage points higher than Morelia speakers with secondary education, and her husband (J14) shows a slightly lower percentage than both Jalisco/Zacatecas and Morelia speakers.

TABLE 4.11. Innovative *Estar* in Three Families

Parents' origin		No.	%	Offspring	No.	%
GROUP 1						
Family 1:						
E12	Tijuana	34	44	H22 (son)	41	51
P15	Jalisco/Zacatecas	45	27	R24 (nephew)	39	67
Family 2:						
R11	C. Juárez	27	33	R17 (daughter)	26	42
J14	C. Juárez	52	25	V21 (daughter)	27	67
GROUPS 2–3						
Family 3ᵃ: (mixed)						
(L,f43,2, Tijuana)				S38 (daughter)	21	52
R50	Los Angeles	64	28	R42 (son)	24	17

ᵃ The mother's samples of speech (L,f43) have not been analysed.

There is one exception in Family 3, R42. As I have pointed out in the preceding chapters, R42 represents an interesting case. He did not develop productive competence in Spanish as a child, but was exposed to this language from birth both at home and in the community. At the time of the data collection, he had completed three semesters of Spanish in high school. He was able to converse with me with quite a good degree of fluency and showed a very high level of oral comprehension. It seems to me that, had he not had at least a fairly well-developed receptive proficiency in Spanish, he would not have reached the degree of productive proficiency he now demonstrates. However, his Spanish does appear to show the effect of schooling, and this sets him apart from other youngsters who have acquired this language in natural settings. Of these youngsters, four of the five included in Table 4.11 use innovative *estar* in more than 50 per cent of all cases. The uniform speech behaviour of these younger speakers suggests that the change affecting *estar* has become a stable feature of Mexican-American Spanish in Los Angeles.

4.2.4. Conclusions

Numerous linguists (Meillet 1926, Bloomfield 1933, Tauli 1956, Benveniste 1968, among many) have noted that semantic bleaching (i.e. the loss of lexical meaning) goes hand in hand with an emphasis on grammatical function (or grammaticalization). This phenomenon is characteristic of the development of modal and auxiliary verbs, of determiners, prepositions, conjunctions, and of a number of bound grammatical morphemes in natural languages. Spanish is no exception to this form of growth. The development of *estar* from its original meaning of 'to stand' to its present rank as an 'auxiliary verb' in progressive constructions, and as a copula with predicate locatives and predicate adjectives, is a further illustration of this universal tendency. In the specific context of predicate adjectives, as I have shown in this chapter, the continuous extension of *estar* at the expense of *ser* is intensified and diffused more rapidly in a stable and prolonged situation of bilingualism. This observation offers a response to one of the questions which motivated the study in the first place: what is the effect of language contact on language change? The innovation examined here represents part of an evolutionary trend in Spanish and other Romance languages. Given such a situation, the result of language contact will be acceleration of the change.

It may be argued that at least one further condition is necessary for this rapid diffusion: reduced access or lack of access to formal varieties of the language, as well as to those institutions which maintain conservative and prescriptive language norms, conditions that are present in Los Angeles Spanish. To examine the relative impact of these and other factors which often coincide with intensive societal bilingualism (e.g. reduction in domains of use, diminished concern for the acquisition and/or maintenance of a standard variety of the secondary language, lack of formal instruction in this language), one could investigate internally motivated changes in the superordinate language, English in our case. It seems to me that if the hastening of changes in the direction of regularization of paradigms, and the loss of one or more 'competing' structures with closely related meanings is in any way motivated by the bilingual's need to lessen his cognitive load when having to communicate rather frequently in two or more languages, then we should expect to find that internally motivated changes which involve the generalization of a form X to a larger number of contexts are also accelerated in a situation of extended language contact in the system of the superordinate language. Future research will need to examine superordinate language variables to contribute to the examination of this hypothesis.

With respect to specific influence from English on the fate of the competing forms *ser* and *estar*, it appears reasonable to suggest that the extension of *estar* in progressives (cf. Ch. 2) and its frequent association with *be* in these constructions may be a factor favourable to the rapid diffusion of *estar* in the context of predicate adjectives, where Spanish anyway evidences a slow process of change independently from any language-specific influence. For instance, de Jonge (1987) shows that *estar* is replacing *ser* in the context of adjectives of age (e.g. *grande* 'old/older', *pequeño* 'small/young') in the standard varieties spoken in Caracas (Venezuela), and in Mexico City.

There is nevertheless no evidence in Los Angeles that the dual system of copulas is heading toward imminent collapse, despite contact with a linguistic system in which *ser* and *estar* correspond to a single form, 'be', and despite the aggressive behaviour of *estar*. There is a noticeable movement toward steady functional specialization, but the continuous 'renovation' of Spanish through the arrival of new waves of immigrants secures the necessary input to keep Los Angeles Spanish from drifting away entirely from other Spanish dialects. The possibility of continuous contact with complete and monolingual varieties of Spanish distinguishes the Mexican–American community from other communities which have undergone or are undergoing language shift and possible eventual language death (such as those, among others, investigated by Dorian 1981, Gal 1979, and Hill 1989). Language shift occurs at the individual and family level in Los Angeles, but it is far from obvious at the community level.

Clearly, although the *ser/estar* opposition with attributes is lost to a large extent among speakers in Groups 2 and 3, the system described here does retain some degree of meaningful opposition. Furthermore, in other syntactic contexts (nominal and prepositional predicates) the distribution of *ser* and *estar* persists as in the standard norms. I have demonstrated also that it seems correct to assume the occasional existence of 'semantically meaningless' variation; that is, *ser* and *estar* alternate in certain contexts without conveying meaning differences. Indeed, to account for the possibility of change or for change in progress, variation theory must assume that at a given stage the variants involved—phonological, syntactic, or lexical—are referentially and pragmatically synonymous, either in all or in a subset of possible contexts. The present study further supports the hypothesis that change-related variation observed in apparent time (i.e. across generations) reflects stages of diffusion in *real time* (cf. Labov 1972a: ch. 7).

Within the framework of variation theory, one further question raised here concerns the path followed by innovation in the linguistic and social systems. One important and stimulating outcome of this study, I hope, has been showing, both qualitatively and quantitatively, the step-by-step movement of the process.[12] Within the linguistic system, the change is not abrupt; that is, it does not occur in all possible contexts at once. Rather, the diffusion is gradual and context-selective; it appears to depend on factors related to the semantic transparency of the choice between *ser* and *estar*, as well as to changes in the manner of conceptualizing the relationship between the subject referent and the attribute ascribed to it. These changes, which become apparent in the skewed diffusion according to type of adjective, trigger the loss of certain constraints imposed by such parameters as susceptibility to change, and the class/individual frame. From this state of affairs, one is free to draw the conclusion that the theory of lexical diffusion made explicit by Wang (1969) may be extended to, and indeed finds support in, syntactic-semantic changes.

[12] Both Fernández's observations and Vañó-Cerdá's revealing synchronic and diachronic study of *ser* and *estar* with adjectives imply the idea of lexical diffusion. Vañó-Cerdá explains that his classification of adjectives into three groups (of extrinsic, intrinsic, and active sense) is motivated both by his 'synchronic study of the uses of "*ser*" and "*estar*", and by the behaviour . . . of the two verbs with respect to the different classes of adjectives throughout the historical evolution of the language' (p. 314, my translation). Neither linguist (nor anyone else as far as I know) has examined the process quantitatively or established any parallel with the lexical diffusion of phonetic changes.

Finally, the external factors which accelerate innovation have been shown to be related to the situation of language contact and shift in which Spanish happens to be the less favoured language. The diffusion of *estar* is most advanced among the younger speakers in Group 2. This is interesting because this is the US-born group which, if any, is likely to pass on Spanish to their descendants. Thus, it is possible that *estar* may continue its expansion to all types of predicate adjective.

4.3. Verbal Clitic Pronouns

4.3.1. Verbal Clitics Along the Continuum

This section discusses verbal clitic pronouns (Cls),[13] in small capitals in [39–40], an area of the grammar of Spanish which appears to lend itself to the investigation of the processes characteristic of a situation of language contact: simplification, transfer, and overgeneralization.

[39] LA *vi ayer*
       HER saw-1sg yesterday
       I saw her yesterday

[40] SE *cortó*
       HIMSELF cut-3sg
       He cut himself

For this specific study I have analysed data from twenty of the speakers, who represent the various degrees of Spanish and English proficiency characteristic of the total sample under investigation. Fifteen of these speakers belong to four different families; the remaining five are not related to anybody else in the sample. The analysis allows me to conclude that this particular aspect of the morphosyntax of Spanish is fairly impermeable to interlinguistic influence.

Even though it is not entirely clear to me how comparable Spanish clitics may be to oblique pronouns in English, I assume cross-linguistic equivalence when, in a given English sentence, the oblique pronoun translates the Spanish verbal clitic.[14] Accordingly, *lo* is considered to be equivalent to *him*, unstressed, in [41–42]:

[41] LO *conocí en la fiesta de Pepe*
       HIM met-1sg in the party of Pepe
       I met HIM at Pepe's party

---

[13] This section is based on work started in collaboration with Manuel Gutiérrez while he was a graduate student at USC (cf. Silva-Corvalán and Gutiérrez, 1995). I would like to thank Manuel for his contribution.

[14] Note, however, that stressed oblique pronouns in English must be translated with non-verbal stressed pronouns in Spanish in addition to the Cl, as in the following example. (See García *et al.* (1987) for an illuminating analysis of the question of inter-translatability and cross-linguistic equivalence.) I saw *him* at the store (not *her*); *Lo$_i$ vi a él$_i$* en la tienda (no A ELLA).

[42] *Quería ver*LO *temprano*
    wanted-1sg see HIM early
    I wanted to see *him* early

Overgeneralization, simplification, and transfer allow us to advance certain hypotheses with respect to the behaviour of Cls along the continuum.

Simplification accounts for the extension of one of two or more structures which have the same or similar meaning. This justifies expecting a trend towards the categorical occurrence of one of the two possible alternative positions for Cls in constructions with verbal periphrases, either preverbal ([43*a*]) or postverbal ([43*b*]). Overgeneralization, on the other hand, might result in the extension of so-called 'lexical reflexive' or 'obligatory reflexive' constructions, as in [44*b*]. This overgeneralization of reflexive-type constructions is in fact a trend which appears to characterize the diachronic development of many verbs in Spanish.[15]

[43] (a) LO *puedo hacer mañana*   (b) *Puedo hacer*LO *mañana*
       IT can-1sg do tomorrow   can-1sg do IT tomorrow
       I can do IT tomorrow

[44] (a) *¡Mi hermano no - - creció hasta cuando tenía cuarenta!*   (Group 1: standard non-reflexive form)
    (b) *¡Mi hermano no* SE *creció hasta cuando tenía cuarenta!*   (Group 3: non-standard reflexive form)
       My brother didn't (SE) grow up until he got to be forty!

Furthermore, if transfer from English affected this area of the grammar of Spanish, the bilingual's propensity to make both languages structurally more similar should result in omission of the Cl when the corresponding English construction does not require an oblique pronoun, as in [45] (examples of this type are further discussed in Chapter 5, which deals with the issue of syntactic transfer).

[45] . . . *y me dieron en la cara, y* ∅ *quebraron mi, mi* jaw (Gr. 3)
       and me hit-3pl in the face, and ∅ broke-3pl my, my jaw
    . . . *y me dieron en la cara, y* ME *quebraron la, la mandíbula* (Gr. 1)
                                  TO ME broke-3pl the, the jaw
    . . . and they hit me in the face, and broke my, my jaw

---

[15] My evidence for this statement, anecdotal and impressionistic, is based on the fact that native speakers of Latin American Spanish find it very difficult to explain the semantic difference between certain pairs of non-reflexive/reflexive verbs in a number of examples (e.g. *morir/morirse* 'to die', *ir/irse* 'to go'), and use the reflexive form in cases which according to prescriptive grammars should be constructed with the non-reflexive one (e.g. *Juan se murió en un accidente* 'John *se* died in an accident', *Juan se fue en auto a la escuela hoy* 'John *se* went to school by car today'). Furthermore, my father used to tell me that it was not 'necessary' to use such verbs as *demorar* 'to take long', or *comunicar* 'to communicate' in the reflexive form, as in *Juan se demoró mucho* 'John *se* took too long', or *Juan se comunicó con María* 'John *se* communicated with Mary'; but I, like most of my Chilean peers, use them exclusively in the reflexive form.

Transfer should also result in the preference for postverbal placement of the Cl ([43*b*]). This type of transfer, which at first evidences itself not in ungrammaticality but in an increased frequency of use of parallel structures, is proposed by Klein-Andreu (1986a: 7) as the most likely to occur, as well as the most likely to become part of the community language norms. Furthermore, though previous research has shown that, as compared to free morphemes, bound morphology is more resistant to change (cf. Meisel 1983*b*, Pfaff and Portz 1979, Poplack's 1978 'free morpheme constraint', Weinreich 1974),[16] the presence or absence of inflectional markings in one language is also cited as one of the possible features to be affected by the presence or absence of corresponding inflections in the contact language (cf. Meisel, Weinreich). Thus, as inflections, Cls may be a plausible site for transfer from English to affect at least both the position and the actual occurrence of Cls.

4.3.1.1. Omission of Cls

For the examination of Cl omission, in every sentence where a Cl occurred or should have occurred the Cl was classified according to its functional relation to the verb. Nine different groups or contexts were established, listed in [46–54]:

[46] **Accusative**: LO *va a grabar* 'She's going to record HIM'

[47] **Dative**: LE *mostré el libro a Rod* 'I showed (HIM) the book to Rod'

[48] **Obligatory reflexive**: SE *salió del equipo* 'He (SE) left the team'

[49] **True reflexive**: SE *cortó* 'He cut HIMSELF'

[50] **Indirect reflexive**: SE *cortó el dedo* 'He (SE) cut his finger'

[51] **Reflexive with inanimate subject**: SE *quemó el pan* 'The bread (SE) got burnt'

[52] **Reciprocal**: NOS *veíamos a menudo* 'We (NOS) often saw each other'

[53] **Impersonal 'se'**: *ahí* SE *come bien* 'One (SE) eats well there'

[54] **Affective**: *yo* TE *corro 3 millas todos los días* 'I run (YOU) 3 miles every day'.

Examples of the type of [54] are characteristically used in a colloquial or informal style in Spanish.

Observe that in these nine contexts English may or may not be equivalent to Spanish with respect to requiring a pronoun. The correspondences seem to be as follows:

(*a*) Equivalent in English and Spanish: [46], [47], [49], and possibly also [52] and [54].

(*b*) Non–equivalent contexts: (i) A reflexive verb form in Spanish corresponds to a non-reflexive intransitive verb in English: [48], [51]. (ii) A so-called indirect reflexive construction, in which the Cl in Spanish has the same referent as the

---

[16] In agreement with a number of researchers (Givón 1976, Meisel 1983*b*), I view Cls as verbal inflections, i.e. as bound morphology (cf. Silva-Corvalán 1981).

TABLE 4.12. Clitics Omitted in Required Contexts

Group 1				Group 2			Group 3		
S2,	f24	0/308		R17, f21	2/277	0.7%	S38, f19	1/184	0.5%
A9,	f62	0/317		V21, f18	6/148	4%	D39, f28	3/295	1%
R11,	f42	0/296		H22, m21	0/320		A46, f31	0/77	
E12,	f44	0/296		R24, m20	0/207		R42, m15	24/45	53%
M8,	m17	3/298	1%	A29, m60	2/263	0.8%	J43, m17	7/257	2.7%
J14,	m41	0/247					H48, m39	0/131	
P15,	m54	0/298					D36, m45	23/255	9%
							R50, m46	3/292	1%
TOTALS		3/2063	0.1%		10/1225	0.8%		61/1597	3.8%

possessor in the direct object of a corresponding non-reflexive construction in English: [50]. (iii) An 'impersonal' use of *se*, marking the absence of any subject, which may correspond to a construction with an impersonal subject pronoun (*one*, *you*) in English: [53].

Regarding the possible omission of Cls, it is interesting to note that in a subset sample of thirteen speakers in Groups 2 and 3, of a total of over 2,822 contexts for the occurrence of an obligatory Cl (contexts [46–53]), only 71 are missing (2.5 per cent). Seven speakers in Group 1 were also examined. Only one of these failed to provide an obligatory Cl, three times in 298 cases. Examples [55–6] illustrate omissions; Table 4.12 displays the quantitative results by speaker:

[55] ... *tenemos una$_i$ y nosotros ø$_i$ llevamos* [*la moto$_i$*] [*la$_i$*] have-1pl one$_i$ and we ø$_i$ take-1pl [the bike$_i$]
     We have one$_i$ and we take it$_i$ (S38,f19,3,ELA30)

[56] ... *muy amarradas las tenían - - y ellas$_i$ ø$_i$ rebelaron, ø$_i$ rebelaron* [*se$_i$*]
     ... very controlled them had-3pl - - and they ø rebelled, ø rebelled
     ... they had them very controlled - - and they rebelled, they rebelled
     (D36,m45,3,ELA43)

Observe in Table 4.12 that it is in Group 3 where omission is somewhat more noticeable, and that R42 has an exceptionally high frequency of omission (53 per cent). Of the other speakers in Group 3, the second highest percentage of omission corresponds to D36: 9 per cent of a total of 255 contexts of occurrence. In Group 2, the highest percentage corresponds to V21: 4 per cent.

Excepting R42, these results show a very low percentage of omissions. Expressed Cls, however, are not always marked correctly for gender, number, and/ or case, as illustrated in [57–9]; but this is a different question, i.e. it concerns processes of loss of gender, number, and case rather than of whatever type of loss the absence of a Cl represents.

TABLE 4.13. Clitics Omitted in Required Contexts, by Clitic Type and by Group

Clitic type	Group 1 (1 speaker)		Group 2 (5 speakers)			Group 3 (8 speakers)		
[46] Accusative		0%	2/262	0.8%	} 0.8%	15/433	3.4%	} 2.7%
[47] Dative	2/119	1.6%	4/487	0.8%		11/521	2%	
[48] Obligatory reflexive	1/100	1%	2/278	0.7%		13/355	3.6%	
[49] True reflexive		0%	2/39	5%		6/54	11%	
[50] Indirect reflexive		0%		0%	} 1.26%	10/77	13%	} 6.6%
[51] Reflexive with Inanimate Subject		0%		0%		4/26	15.4%	
[52] Reciprocal		0%		0%		2/15	13.3%	
[53] Impersonal		0%	–			–		
[54] Affective	–		–			–		

[57] *Pero la misa$_i$, el padre* LO$_i$ *dijo muy pronto.*
but the mass-fem$_i$, the father IT-masc$_i$ said too soon
But the mass, the father celebrated IT too soon   (V21,f18,2,ELA67)

[58] *Yo creo que no* LO *(los libros) usan.*
I believe that not IT-sg (the books) use
I believe they don't use THEM   (J43,m17,3,ELA57)

[59] LE$_i$ *iban a mandar a él$_i$.*
HIM-dat$_i$ went to send 'a' him-acc$_i$
They were going to send HIM   (J43,m17,3,ELA57)

Table 4.13 displays the percentages of omitted Cls by group according to type of Cl. Table 4.13 indicates that in Groups 2 and 3 omission occurs more frequently when it concerns a reflexive or reciprocal clitic, with a total omission of 1.26 per cent and 6.6 per cent in Groups 2 and 3, respectively. By contrast, under 1 per cent of dative and accusative Cls are omitted in Group 2, and only 2.7 per cent of these Cls are omitted in Group 3. If we eliminate R42 from Group 3 (for the reasons explained in section 4.2.3), the results still show higher omission with reflexives and reciprocals, as flows from Table 4.14. Speaker R42 appears to show the effect of schooling in his use of Spanish. Thus, even though another young man in Group 3, J43—who acquired this language in natural settings—and R42 appear to have a similar overall level of proficiency in Spanish in terms of fluency, a closer examination of their speech shows that R42's use of Cls is further removed from the norms of Group 1 despite the fact that this speaker, but not J43, has received formal instruction in Spanish in high school. This difference with respect to omission of Cls (2.7 per cent omitted by J43; 53 per cent by R42) is also apparent in regard to Cl position, as I show later.

TABLE 4.14. Quantification of Clitic Omission for Seven Speakers in Group 3

Type of clitic	No.	%
Accusative	6/408	1.5%
Dative	9/518	1.7%
Reflexive and reciprocal	22/510	4.3%

With respect to the omission of dative and accusative Cls, it may be concluded that transfer from English does not play any role (if it did, we should have obtained a higher percentage of omission of datives and accusatives when the coreferential element is expressed; but this is not the case). As for reflexives, note that omission is relatively high even in equivalent contexts ([49] true reflexives). Furthermore, in most cases the factors which determine which verbs have a reflexive form in Spanish are opaque. Here, then, we may have at least two motivations leading to the same result: the complexity of the system in Spanish, and transfer of the subcategorization of non-reflexive verbs in English to a number of verbs which are 'obligatory reflexives' in Spanish, as in [56]. This type of transfer, which may have syntactic consequences, is explored in Chapter 6. The quantitative evidence, however, does not support wholesale syntactic transfer. Furthermore, clitic omission is almost non-existent in Group 2, which includes the US-born bilinguals who might pass on their modified Spanish variety to younger generations.

4.3.1.2. *Clitic position in verbal periphrases*

The position of Cls in contemporary spoken Spanish may be either categorically or variably pre- or postverbal depending on the type of verbal phrase, as explained in (a)–(c). Examples [60–3] illustrate.

(*a*) Cls are *categorically preverbal* with finite verbal forms:

[60] LO *compró*/LO *ha comprado ya*
    She bought IT/has bought IT already

(*b*) Cls are *categorically postverbal* with Infs, PresPs, and gerunds in complement clauses:

[61] *Vine para ver*TE
    came-1sg for see-YOU
    I came so as to see YOU

[62] *Viéndo*LA *te acordarás de ella*
    seeing-HER you-refl remember-fut-2sg of her
    Seeing her you'll remember her

(*c*) When Cls refer to an argument of an Inf or a PresP in a verbal periphrasis with a finite 'semi-auxiliary' verb, they may *variably* occur *before the finite verb*. The appearance of the Cl in front of the finite verb has been proposed as the consequence of clause union by Aissen and Perlmutter (1976), and of restructuring by Rizzi (1978). This, then, is the *only variable context* for clitic placement in Spanish (cf. Myhill 1988; 1989):

[63] *Viene a ver*TE/TE *viene a ver*
      comes-3sg to see-YOU/YOU comes-3sg to see
      He's coming to see YOU

It is interesting to note that none of the twenty speakers studied violates the categorical pre- or postverbal placement constraints illustrated in [60-2]. In regard to those utterances which allow one of two positions for Cls ([63]), on the other hand, our study indicates that, contrary to what a naive view of transfer might predict, postverbal placement is less frequent in the speech of bilinguals. Furthermore, the variables which simply *favour* preverbal placement in Spanish dominant bilinguals (and in monolinguals—cf. Landa 1989, Myhill 1988) appear as *almost* categorical contexts for this order: the Spanish of bilinguals moves in the direction of strengthening Spanish internal trends rather than English patterns (cf. the extension of *estar* 'to be').

In his study of Cl placement in written Spanish, Myhill (1988) proves quantitatively that this phenomenon is constrained by at least two factors: the semantic properties of the matrix or 'semi-auxiliary' verb, and the relative topicality of the subject and the Cl. The former factor favours restructuring (or clause union, i.e. matrix plus Inf as one simple clause) more strongly than the latter. Thus preverbal placement is strongly favoured when this verb retains little or none of its basic meaning, and functions rather as a marker of tense, modality, or aspect, as illustrated by a comparison of [64-5]. In [65] the verbal periphrasis resembles a single finite verb, and thus favours the preverbal placement of the Cl.

[64] *Matrix verb*: *venir* 'to come' (basic meaning)
      Pepe *viene* a entrevistar*me* hoy.
      Pete's coming to interview *me* today

[65] *Matrix verb*: *venir* 'keep' (grammaticalized meaning)
      Pepe *me viene* molestando por años ya.
      Pete's *been/kept* bothering *me* for years

In [64-5] the Cl could have been placed in pre- or postverbal position. However, the preverbal position is preferred when the matrix verb conveys epistemic meanings, progressive aspect, and future tense, three meanings which Bybee (1985) has shown to be expressed most frequently by means of bound morphology in natural languages. The quantification of this preference for preverbal position in

TABLE 4.15. Cross-tabulation of Clitic Position by the Semantics of the Matrix Verb

	Total		Epistemic	Deontic	Progressive	Future	Basic meaning
	N	%	(%)	(%)	(%)	(%)	(%)
Chile	232	70	85	15	89	91	33
Spain	327	70	79	60	91	94	41
Mexico	210	77	75	63	80	92	41
Venezuela	302	62	75	56	75	74	32

Notes: Percentages correspond to preverbal position. N = number of variable contexts for clitic placement. $p = <.00$.

data from four Spanish-speaking countries (Chile, Spain, Mexico, Venezuela) is summarized in Table 4.15.[17]

The fact that Cls are a Romance creation, and that their position with respect to the verb did not become fixed in Spanish before the fifteenth century, justifies considering their variable position in verbal periphrases a syntactic-semantic change in progress, which involves the gradual grammaticalization of a number of verbs.[18] The trend to place the Cl in front of the matrix verb is, therefore, internally motivated and related to the semantics of this verb.

The existence of the same tendency in bilingual Spanish is confirmed by our study of Cl placement. Table 4.16 displays the quantification of preverbal v. post-verbal placement of Cls in verbal periphrases with those verbs which occurred at least ten times in the sample of speech from the twenty speakers. Despite the existence of a parallel construction with a postverbal pronoun in English, the internally motivated opposite trend in the direction of preverbal placement appears stronger in Los Angeles, as displayed in Table 4.16. No percentage is given when there are fewer than five cases in a cell; the 'matrix' or 'semi-auxiliary' verbs are ordered according to decreasing frequency of occurrence in Group 1. This ordering roughly corresponds as well to decreasing frequency of preverbal placement.

The results indicate that future (*ir a* 'go to'), progressive (*estar* 'be'), and epistemic (*poder* 'may') meanings clearly favour preverbal position, even more strongly than in other varieties of Spanish (see Table 4.17). This preference for preverbal position applies as well to the less favouring root modality (*deber (de)* 'must', *tener que* 'have

---

[17] The data (taken from Esgueva and Cantarero 1981; Instituto de Filología Andrés Bello 1979; Rabanales and Contreras 1979; UNAM 1971) were coded by a group of my graduate students as part of a research methods course. I am grateful to these students for allowing me to use the coded data. Some of the matrix verbs examined are listed in Table 4.16.

[18] Both in Spain and in Chile, speakers with a high level of education have told me that, when they were students in the 1960s, their instructors corrected them if they placed Cls preverbally in verbal periphrases. This preverbal position was allowed only with 'pronominal main verbs' (e.g. *asustarse* 'to get scared': *Se va a asustar* '(He)'s *se* going to get scared'). This prescriptive attitude supports an analysis of preverbal placement with other types of verbs as a change in progress.

TABLE 4.16. Preverbal Clitic Placement in Verbal Periphrases

Matrix verb	Group 1 (7 speakers)		Group 2 (5 speakers)		Group 3 (8 speakers)	
	No.	%	No.	%	No.	%
Ir a 'go to'	85/92	92	35/36	97	61/66	92
Estar 'be'	30/33	91	19/20	95	31/35	89
Poder 'may'/'can'	23/38	60	18/19	95	36/47	83
Tener que 'have to'	17/30	57	12/16	75	8/13	65
Empezar a 'begin'	8/11	73	0/1		2/2	
Querer 'want to'	6/19	32	6/11	55	12/23	52
Deber (de) 'must'	1/6	17	3/5	60	1/2	

to'), and to the inceptive class (*empezar a* 'begin'). This trend increases among second-generation bilinguals. Speakers in Group 3, on the other hand, though still behaving according to this general tendency, have slightly lower percentages of preverbal Cls than those in Group 2. This general result is not too surprising, however. A comparison of other features of Group 3 Spanish with Group 2, namely verb morphology and the extension of *estar* 'to be', reveals that, as a group, third-generation immigrants do not seem to continue along the lines of a 'natural' historical development of their ancestors' language. There is a break at this point: the language of this group moves qualitatively further away from the norms of Group 1 speakers, and also shows signs of convergence with the dominant contact language.

There is, as we have seen, a certain amount of individual variation within each group, but the only speaker who clearly departs from the strong general tendency to place the Cl preverbally is R42 (Group 3). In only one of ten possible contexts is the Cl preverbal in his data; i.e. R42 strongly favours postverbal position (90 per cent) when this is a grammatical alternative in Spanish. I suggest that this is a further consequence, in addition to Cl omission, of his formal learning of Spanish, an experience which sets him apart from other members of his community, and which appears to have made him more vulnerable to transfer from English. Assuming that formal learning increases the speaker's awareness of form, this result would support Meisel's (1983*b*) observation that speakers who focus on form are more likely to use transfer strategies than those who focus mostly on the messages they wish to convey.

4.3.1.3. Acceleration of change

As in the case of the extension of *estar*, the internally motivated trend to place Cls preverbally in verbal periphrases, to a large extent as a consequence of a process of

TABLE 4.17. Percentage of Preverbal Clitics in Verbal Periphrases in Los Angeles, in
Four Spanish-Speaking Countries (Chile, Spain, Mexico, Venezuela),
and in Written Spanish

Matrix verb	Group			Chile, Spain, Mexico, Venezuela	Written Spanish	
	1 (%)	2 (%)	3 (%)	(%)	No.	(%)
Ir a	92	97	92	89	136/181	75
Estar	91	95	89	83	75/84	89
Poder	60	95	83	76	33/178	19
Tener que	57	75	65	45	7/46	15
Querer	32	55	52	61	12/90	13
Empezar a	73	–	–	46	3/32	9
Deber (de)	17	60	–	34	7/62	11

grammaticalization of a number of matrix verbs, is accelerated in a situation of intensive language contact. This acceleration is clearly observed in Table 4.17, which compares total percentages of preverbal Cls in Los Angeles with the cumulative percentages for four Latin American countries. Table 4.17 also includes some of the results obtained for written Spanish by Myhill (1989), who examined prose from five contemporary Latin American writers: Benedetti, Fuentes, Márquez, Quiroga, and Rulfo.

As pointed out above, Group 2 has a higher percentage of preverbal Cls with every semantic class of matrix verb. Indeed, with *ir a* 'go to', *estar* 'be', and *poder* 'may', preverbal placement is almost categorical. In the other classes, the proportions in Groups 2 and 3 are in every case over 50 per cent. Note, furthermore, that written Spanish displays much lower percentages of preverbal Cls with every verb but *estar*. This difference is not unexpected: in general, the written mode proves to be more conservative with respect to innovative language features. The various quantitative data indicate, therefore, that this aspect of the grammar of Spanish reflects an ongoing change which is more advanced, i.e. which has accelerated, in a language-contact situation.

4.4. Conclusions

Section 4.3 offers evidence that some aspects of the morphosyntax of a language (verbal clitics) are fairly impermeable to interlinguistic influence in a context of societal bilingualism. A similar conclusion is reached by King (1989: 144–5), who shows that Newfoundland French does not exhibit convergence with English, the dominant language, with respect to either the omission or the placement of object Cls. Furthermore, based on a study of Warlpiri–English bilinguals, Bavin (1989: 285) concludes that changes affecting the pronominal system of Warlpiri (including object Cls) cannot be attributed to direct influence from English, but rather to 'a move towards semantic transparency, which is generally internally motivated change'. This coincidence of results in three different language-contact situations certainly strengthens the conclusion reached in the present study.

Indeed, the preverbal slot for Cls in Spanish appears to be as firmly imprinted in speakers' minds as tense–mood–aspect inflections are shown to be. Furthermore, so-called reflexive Cls seem tightly associated with their verbal lexemes in the case of 'obligatory reflexive' verbs; in addition, there are a number of examples which offer evidence of overgeneralization of this lexical pattern (as in [44b]). Further evidence of the 'reality' of Cl morphemes is provided by utterances where the Cl appears in Spanish and the verb in English, as in [66–8].

[66] *Mi* mom *quiere que* LOS keep - my grades up
my mom wants that THEM keep - my grades up
My mom wants me to keep my grades up   (J43,m17,3,ELA57)

[67] *y lo que*$_i$ *queda* - LO$_i$ invest in stock o *algo así*
and what$_i$ remains - IT$_i$-acc invest in stock or something like that
And whatever remains you invest it in stock or something like that
(J43,m17,3,ELA57)

[68] *No, uno - no* SE *quieren* tie down
no, some - not SE want tie down
No, some don't want to get tied down [get tied down = amarrar*se*]
(J43,m17,3,ELA57)

In the case of naturally developed bilingualism, this study does not offer evidence in favour of an overall transfer of parallel structures from the dominant language. Regarding Klein-Andreu's (1980; 1986a) hypothesis, then, my study suggests that it should be modified to incorporate a condition on the type of parallel structure likely to be transferred or preferred, as follows: in situations of intensive bilingualism, the higher frequency of use in a subordinate language S of morphological and/or syntactic parallel structures in a superordinate language F will occur only if the parallel structure in F corresponds to a preferred structure (i.e. more widely used variant) in S prior to the initiation of contact with F.

It should be clear that this condition on parallel structure transfer corresponds to what has been discussed in terms both of acceleration of change and of overgeneralization. Therefore, it seems that a theory of simplification, motivated by interactional, cognitive, and intralinguistic factors (see Chs. 1 and 7), which predicts the loss of certain morphosyntactic variables in subordinate contact languages, accounts more appropriately than transfer for the preferred preverbal placement of Cls, as well as for the preference for progressive over simple forms observed by Klein-Andreu in the Spanish of Puerto Ricans in New York, and the preference for the prepositional phrase *à la maison* (*de*) over the 'simple' prepositions *chez*, *sur*, and *à* verified by Mougeon *et al.* (1985) in Canadian French.

Accounts based on simplification and transfer must consider both the structures of the languages involved and the type of contact situation. For instance, an analytical construction in language F (generally regarded as cognitively simpler than a corresponding synthetic one) which is rare or nonexistent in language G may indeed be more complex for speakers of language G to acquire when learning language F as a foreign language, or to transfer into language G from F. An example is offered by Dorian (personal communication), who notes that imperfect speakers of East Sutherland Gaelic generalize the more widely used synthetic possessive construction rather than the free-standing possessive pronouns, even though the latter structure finds a parallel in English, the contact language.

As for the role of the superordinate language in the shaping of the extension of *estar* as well as the patterns of use of Cls, my conclusion approaches that of Dorian (1978) in her study of East Sutherland Gaelic. We have dealt with different areas of the grammar; yet in both studies direct influence from English, though possible, is difficult to identify. This does not altogether preclude the possibility of transfer; the convergence of certain grammatical features is certainly evident elsewhere (see Chs. 5 and 6). In most cases, however, direct transfer seems to involve lexical items, frozen/idiomatic expressions, and verb subcategorizations. This last type of transfer motivates some omissions of Cls. None the less, ungrammaticality due to *estar* and Cl usage is far from being widespread in Groups 2 and 3. Typically, modifications regarding *estar* and Cls in these groups are for the most part more appropriately described as more advanced stages of 'natural' internal trends in the ancestor variety.[19] Conspicuous ungrammatical cases are very rare, and unlikely to become norms, given that they occur in the speech of individuals who will probably refrain from passing Spanish on to their descendants.

[19] With respect to Cls, this statement could even apply to simplification of case-, gender-, and number-marking. Indeed, although this type of simplification is not attested in Group 1, case-, gender-, and number-marking of Cls is lost to various degrees in different varieties of Spanish. For example, case-marking with human object referents is lost to a large extent in spoken Madrid Spanish; gender is not marked in the dative case in standard Spanish; plural marking with dative clitics is to a large extent lost in many varieties of Latin American Spanish (e.g. *Ya le$_i$ entregué el libro a los alumnos$_i$* 'I already gave (*le$_i$*-3sg) the book to the students$_i$').

5

Exploring External Motivation for Change

5.1. Introduction: On the Permeability of Grammar[1]

I NOTED in Chapter 1 that the transfer of features from one language into another is one of the strategies used by bilinguals to cope with having to communicate in two different linguistic systems. Throughout this book, I have examined the possibility that a number of changes affecting Spanish in Los Angeles may be the result of (among others) specific processes of transfer of features from English, that is, processes that imply what Martinet (in his Preface to Weinreich's *Languages in Contact*) calls 'the permeability of linguistic cells'.

Weinreich (1974: 4) states that the study of 'purely linguistic problems about bilingualism' may allow the linguist to 'see the cause of the susceptibility of a language to foreign influence *in its structural weaknesses*' (my emphasis), i.e. in the existence of structural spaces and incomplete or unbalanced correlations within the system. Weinreich (p. 44) further observes that foreign grammatical elements may permeate the speech of a bilingual but are only very rarely incorporated in the language as a code. Thus, he concurs with Meillet, Jakobson, and Sapir (all three cited on p. 25) in supporting the impermeability of a grammatical system to foreign structural elements except when they correspond to the system's internal tendencies of development, an observation which has been shown to be dangerously circular.

More recently, Thomason and Kaufman (1988) note that linguists have challenged the view that a grammatical system is impermeable to direct transfer of foreign elements. On the basis of evidence provided by a number of studies, they argue that purely linguistic constraints 'on contact-induced change will not work' (p. 16), and go as far as to say that 'any linguistic feature can be transferred from any language to any other language' (p. 14). However, their conclusion that 'it is the social context, not the structure of the languages involved, that determines the direction and the degree of interference' (p. 19) is not entirely in disagreement with Weinreich's (1974: 4–5) proposal that 'the extent, direction, and nature of interference of one language with another can be explained even more thoroughly in terms of the speech behavior of bilingual individuals, which in turn is conditioned by social relations in the community in which they live'.

[1] I would like to thank Enric Vallduví for helpful comments on an earlier version of this chapter, and Francisco Ocampo for his help with word-order questions. I would also like to thank some of my graduate students for contributing in various manners to the progress of this chapter: Alazne Landa, Loli Martínez-Moya, Luis Candia, and Gorka Elordieta.·

The controversy concerns which specific factor associated with intensive language contact actually motivates change: transfer of elements from the contact language, perhaps under pressure to make more similar the structures of the languages involved? Lack of formal education in one of the languages? Reduced use of one of the languages and consequent incomplete acquisition of this language? Transfer is undoubtedly a controversial notion, as I pointed out in Chapter 1. Some of the more obvious cases of transfer, usually at the lexical, morphological, and phonetic levels of analysis, may be more easily identified and evaluated as to their stability in the borrowing language in terms of frequency of occurrence and numbers of users (cf. Poplack *et al.* 1988; Mougeon and Beniak 1991). By contrast, at the syntactic level it is more difficult to identify transfer and to prove that there has been permeability of a grammatical system to influence from a different one. More often than not, this difficulty arises from the fact that a given phenomenon may be considered to be syntactic by some analysts, but lexical (e.g. verb subcategorization) or morphological (e.g. clitic pronoun usage, gender agreement) by others. Thus, uncontroversially syntactic phenomena appear to be reduced to such questions as word order, the possibility of null arguments, and patterns of subordination.

In this chapter I examine four different phenomena which I hope will offer further evidence that Weinreich's proposals appear to be correct, at least in a sociolinguistic situation of intensive and extensive bilingualism in which two languages with unequal social and functional status are in contact. Indeed, in agreement with Meillet, Jakobson, Weinreich, and more recently Bickerton (1981), and Givón (1979), the research considered in this chapter indicates that, even under conditions of intense contact and strong cultural pressure, speakers of a secondary language do not introduce elements which cause radical changes in the syntactic system of this language under normal conditions of transmission (cf. Thomason and Kaufman 1988). It may be possible that any linguistic feature can be transferred from any language to any other language as a 'nonce-borrowing' in the speech of bilinguals (cf. Weinreich 1974), but only those that are compatible (in the sense proposed in the conclusion to this chapter) with the structure of the borrowing language at any given stage will be adopted, disseminated, and passed on to new generations.

It must be kept in mind, however, that Spanish and English have been in contact in the USA for under 200 years, and that US Spanish has enjoyed the uninterrupted presence of monolingual or near-monolingual Spanish-speaking immigrants. It is possible, that, given enough time depth and favourable socio-political conditions, the changes allowed, which occur gradually, may lead to the development of a language fundamentally different from non-contact standard Spanish. At this stage in history, the evidence favours the hypothesis proposed in section 1.1 above, that the structure of the languages in contact governs the introduction and diffusion of innovative elements in the linguistic systems; while the sociolinguistic history of the speakers is the primary determinant of the language direction and degree of diffusion of the innovations, as well as of the more distant or remote linguistic outcome of language contact.

In opposition to Weinreich, on the other hand, my research indicates that the permeability of a grammar to foreign influence does not depend on *its structural weaknesses* but rather on the existence of superficially (in terms of string order; cf. Prince 1992) parallel structures in the languages in contact. Given a primary language A and a secondary language B, the permeability of B will not be evident in the incorporation of new syntactic structures on the model of A, but first and foremost in the following: (*a*) the extension of the discourse-pragmatic functions of a structure in B according to the model of the functions of the parallel structure in A (cf. Weinreich's notion of 'modelling' at the lexical level; this extension of pragmatic functions of structures already existing in the 'borrowing' language may have motivated the statement that a language would change only in agreement with its internal tendencies of development); (*b*) the preferential use or increase in the frequency of use in B of an existing structure parallel to one in A to the detriment of variants in B (which may or may not convey different discourse-pragmatic meanings); and (*c*) the loss of semantic-pragmatic constraints governing the use of the variants of a syntactic variable in B when the corresponding structure in A is not sensitive to such constraints. (*a*), (*b*), (*c*) are instances of the types of transfer (2), (3), (4) discussed in Chapter 1 (p. 4).

The grammatical phenomena studied here do not allow me to provide a definitive answer to whether (*c*) occurs independently of (*b*), or whether (*c*) is a consequence of (*b*). However, the tendency to overgeneralize reflexive-type verbs (see Ch. 4), thus losing the semantic content conveyed by the opposition reflexive/non-reflexive, an opposition which finds no parallel in English, appears to indicate that (*c*) is not necessarily dependent upon (*b*). Reduction of the range of social domains for the use of a language appears to be a stronger cause of loss of semantic-pragmatic variants than preferential choice of a structure that is parallel with one in the contact language.

Within this wider definition of permeability (as compared to a narrower definition in terms of introduction of new syntactic structures), let us consider four possible cases of permeation of the syntax of Spanish by English grammatical rules: (1) non-expression of the complementizer or relative pronoun *que* 'that'; (2) omission of an obligatory Cl when the corresponding English construction does not require an oblique pronoun; (3) obligatory Subject–Verb–X order; and (4) obligatory expression of a lexical subject. These cases may illustrate permeability of the type of (*b*) and (*c*) above.

An example of permeability of type (*a*), the extension of the discourse-pragmatic functions of a structure in B according to the model of the functions of the parallel structure in A, is offered in Los Angeles Spanish by the extension of the discourse-pragmatic functions of the deictic *este/esta* 'this' (masc./fem.) in the speech of a few bilinguals. *Este/esta* 'this' appears to replicate the function of 'new-*this*' in

English, a term proposed by Wald (1983) to refer to the use of unstressed *this/these* to introduce into discourse indefinite specific referents which are being foregrounded for extended attention. This type of construction with new-*este* 'this' is not attested, to my knowledge, in Mexican Spanish, but it occurs in the data from East Los Angeles (ELA), albeit infrequently. [1] and [2] are illustrative.

[1] *Yo ahorita, yo terminé un caso que, este negrito mató a cuatro hombres y a una mujer. Y vivían muy, - como animales.*
I recently, I finished with a case that, *this* black man killed four men and a woman. They lived very, - like animals   (R50,m46,3,ELA36)

[2] *... había dejado mi papá el carro ahí y había dejado las mulas, ah, irse, ¿ves? Pero esta mula tenía la, la idea de que si no comía algo en la casa, no se iba.*
... my dad had left the cart there and he had let the mules, uhm, go, you see? But *this* mule had the, the idea that if it didn't eat something in the house, it wouldn't leave   (A37,m57,3,ELA22)

In [1], a brand-new referent which is not present in the situation where the communication takes place, *negrito* 'black man', is introduced in subject position and modified by the deictic *este* 'this'. In general spoken Spanish, however, deictics are not used to modify nouns referring to brand-new entities, nor are brand-new referents introduced in subject position (see discussion in section 5.5). The passage that follows [1] concerns *este negrito* 'this black man'. I must conclude, therefore, that [1] illustrates transfer into Spanish of the pragmatic function of 'new-*this*': the introduction into discourse of an indefinite specific referent which is being foregrounded for extended attention. A similar analysis in terms of transfer applies to [2], the beginning of a narrative in which 'this mule' plays an important role. In this case the speaker has introduced all the mules (in object position), but the first mention of one specific mule would require the use of the quantifier *una* 'one' before it could be referred to as *esta mula* 'this mule' in the ensuing discourse.

5.2. Non-expression of a Complementizer or Relative Pronoun *Que* 'That'

At first glance the non-expression of a complementizer in Spanish constitutes an obvious candidate for an explanation based on direct transfer from English of the possibility of a null complementizer in relative clauses and in complement clauses. This section shows, however, that examples such as [3] correspond to permeability of type (*b*), increase in the frequency of use of a parallel structure, rather than to introduction of a new rule allowing the non-expression of the complementizer.

[3] *Yo creo ∅ inventaron el nombre.*
I believe (that) they invented the name   (A20,f19,2,ELA46)

Note that the non-expression of *que* 'that' is not attested in relative clauses in LA Spanish, but only in complement clauses, i.e. no examples of the type of [4] are found in the speech samples from any of the bilinguals studied.

[4] **El nombre ∅ (ellos) inventaron era extraño.*
The name (that) they invented was strange

Interestingly, in the particular context of complement clauses the non-expression of *que* 'that' is not a case of incorporation of a feature or rule foreign to the Spanish system. Indeed, *que* is allowed to be unexpressed in verb complements in formal and in written registers of Spanish, as shown in [5–6] (cf. Subirats-Rüggeberg 1987: 168–73). The same phenomenon is not allowed in relative clauses, however, as seen in [7].

[5] *Te ruego ∅ me lo envíes pronto*
I pray (that) you send it to me promptly

[6] *Deberían tomarse precauciones pues se cree ∅ podrían ir armados.*
Precautions should be taken because it is believed (that) they could be armed

[7] **Te agradezco el regalo ∅ me enviaste*
Thank you for the present (that) you sent me

In LA Spanish, zero *que* appears almost exclusively with complements of the *estimative* verb *creer* 'to believe/to think' (estimative verbs are defined in section 5.5), and in the first person singular, *yo creo* 'I believe/think'. This may be a reflection of the data, however, in which *creer* is by far the most frequent estimative verb. Other verbs of this type, such as *pensar* 'to think', used quite sporadically, may also occur with a null complementizer ([10]). Furthermore, the speaker who is at the most extreme end of Spanish language attrition in the sample, N40, produces an example of zero complementizer with a non-estimative verb in English contained in a Spanish sentence with no prosodic breaks: *Esa noche* we found out ∅ *ella se fue* 'That night we found out ∅ she'd left'. Examples [8–13] further illustrate the variation between expressed and zero complement:

[8] '*No la hallo muy entusiasmada', yo pensé entre mí. Yo creo ∅ no la quiere ver* [la película] *como yo.*
'I don't think she's very interested', I thought for myself. I believe ∅ she doesn't want to see it [the movie] as much as I   (A20,f19,2,ELA29)

[9] . . . *no muy chiquito, pero yo creo ∅ ha crecido como - unas seis pulgadas.*
. . . not very small, but I believe ∅ he has grown about - about six inches   (L19,f22,2,ELA54)

[10] *Mi mamá no quiere que hago eso. Ella piensa ∅ si, si no voy full-time no voy a terminar*
My mom doesn't want me to do that. She thinks ∅ if, if I don't go full-time I won't finish   (S38,f19,3,ELA66)

[11] *Sí, creo que no más esa vez fuimos.*
     Yes, I think that only that time we went   (A20,f19,2,ELA29)

[12] *Yo creo que son robadas* [las radios]
     I think that [the radios] are stolen goods   (B33,f19,3,ELA29)

[13] *. . . pero no sé cómo, pues, no sé cómo, pero pienso que eso va a ser.*
     . . . but I don't know how, well, I don't know how, but I think that that's
     going to happen   (S38,f19,3,ELA66)

Zero *que* occurs fairly frequently in the speech of 19 of 35 speakers examined.
These 19 speakers are distributed as follows. Group 1: two younger women and
two older women (4 of a group of 13 speakers comprising 8 females and 5 males);
Group 2: four younger women and two older women (6/11: 7f, 4m); Group 3:
three younger women, two older women, two younger men, and two older men
(9/11: 6f, 5m).

The sex correlation is intriguing: 10 of 15 women show zero *que* in Groups 1
and 2, but none of the 9 men examined in these groups. Only the men in Group
3 (4/5) leave the complementizer unexpressed. I have not systematically examined
sex as a possible predictor of degree of language maintenance or loss. Impressionistically, however, it seems to me that women maintain the language of their
ancestors with a higher degree of proficiency than their brothers in any given
family; so I would not expect the women in my sample to show the effect of
English more strongly than men. The fact that only women are using null
complementizers in Groups 1 and 2, therefore, appears to be further evidence that
zero complementizer in English may have had only a favouring effect in the
diffusion of zero *que* in the LA bilingual community. The phenomenon has firm
roots in Spanish itself, and its extension to the oral mode may have had its origins
in ancestor Mexican varieties. The linguistic distributional restriction to a type of
complement clause where other Spanish registers also allow zero *que* argues in favour
of permeability as defined above, i.e. limited to already existing structures in the
language. It is possible that explanations based on the vague concept of 'latent
internal tendencies' (Weinreich 1974: 25) may have been motivated by change that
has affected structures severely restricted according to register or style in any given
language.

5.3. Omission of Obligatory Verbal Clitics

Consider at this point another candidate for syntactic transfer: the omission of an
obligatory Cl, specifically in constructions where the Cl is said to function as a
marker of possession of the entity referred to by the direct object (Solé and Solé
1977: 30). This is illustrated in [14a] (the standard form), and in [14b], where the
first-person singular Cl *me* 'me-dative' has been omitted and possession is marked
by a possessive determiner in the direct object nominal. I argue in this section that

[14*b*], which replicates its English translation, corresponds to permeability of types (*b*) and (*c*).

[14] (*a*) . . . *y me dieron en la cara, y me quebraron la mandíbula*
                   and me hit-3pl in the face, and me broke-3pl the jaw
        (*b*) . . . *y me dieron en la cara, y ∅ quebraron mi, mi jaw*
                   and me hit-3pl in the face, and ∅ broke-3pl my, my jaw
                   . . . and they hit me in the face, and broke my, my jaw   (D36,m45,3,
        ELA43)

Examples of the type of [14*b*], though not frequent (these examples do not always involve a switch to English), occur in the speech of many of the US-born bilinguals in the sample, but do they represent a new syntactic construction? It seems to me that the answer is negative. The structure of [14*b*] exists in Spanish, with a variant that does not have a parallel in English, as illustrated by [15*a, b*], and their single English translation.

[15] (*a*) *Tiraron una piedra y quebraron mi portalápices (*a mí).*
        (*b*) *Tiraron una piedra y me quebraron el portalápices (a mí).*
                 They threw a stone and broke my pencil-holder

Constructions of the type of [15*a, b*] are characteristic of a number of verbs subcategorized for a direct object and, under certain conditions, an indirect object whose referent has the semantic role of beneficiary, as shown in [16]:

[16] *quebrar:* [__ NP$_x$ (*a* NP$_y$)],[2] where x = theme, y = beneficiary
        Other verbs in this class include: *agarrar* 'to grab', *aplastar* 'to crush', *arreglar* 'to fix', *dibujar* 'to draw', *lavar* 'to wash', *limpiar* 'to clean', *peinar* 'to comb', *quemar* 'to burn'.

The condition requiring an indirect object is of a semantic-pragmatic nature: it concerns the degree of detachment or inalienability viewed as existing between the referents of the direct object and the indirect object, such that the more closely related they are the higher the degree of active participation the 'beneficiary' has in the situation, and consequently the higher the likelihood of being coded as an indirect object rather than simply as a possessor (see García 1975, esp. ch. 4, on the meanings of case roles). This is exemplified in [17, 18]:

[17] (*a*) *Le arreglé la corbata a Juan;* (*no hizo bien el nudo*)
                 I fixed John's tie; (he didn't tie a good knot)
        (*b*) *Arreglé la corbata de Juan/ su corbata;* (**no hizo bien el nudo*)
                 I fixed John's tie/his tie; (he didn't tie a good knot)
[18] (*a*) *Me lavó el pelo (a mí)* (**mientras yo limpiaba la casa*)
                 He washed my hair (while I cleaned the house)

---

[2] By convention, square brackets represent the subcategorization of a lexical item, NP stands for noun phrase, and parentheses indicate optional elements.

(b) *Lavó mi pelo* (mientras yo limpiaba la casa).
He washed my hair (while I cleaned the house)

Note that the interpretation of [17a, 18a] is that the indirect object referent is a relatively active participant in the situation (cf. García 1975: ch. 4) and therefore closely related to the affected entity (the direct object; for instance, Juan was wearing the tie in [17a]. By contrast, in [17b, 18b], by virtue of the passive role of the possessor, which is coded in the direct object, the affected entity must be interpreted as being detached from its possessor. Thus, in [18b], *mi pelo* 'my hair' must refer to hair which is not attached to the speaker; for instance, hair that the speaker has had cut and washed to make a wig.

The English translations given in [15, 17, 18] show that the two Spanish variants correspond to one in English (although the distinction can be clarified in English by other means). This interlinguistic difference is further indicated by the fact that the Spanish sentences in [17, 18] may or may not be appropriately continued by the language material given in parentheses, which highlights the closeness of the affected entity to the beneficiary, while the English translation accepts it in every case.

Indeed, the English verbs corresponding to those listed in [16] do not allow an indirect object in this language, as exemplified in [19, 20].

[19] *I grabbed the arm to John/*I grabbed John his/the arm

[20] *He washed the hair to me/*He washed me the hair

Bilinguals who use examples like [14b] (*quebraron mi, mi jaw* 'They broke my, my jaw') appear to be violating a semantic-pragmatic constraint. A lexical explanation is also possible: the subcategorization of verbs as those listed in [16] is changing along the English model such that they do not allow an indirect object. This explanation, if correct, is compatible with the semantic-pragmatic one. In fact, the semantic-pragmatic constraint is needed to characterize this particular set of verbs undergoing change in LA Spanish. As [21] illustrates, other types of verb, subcategorized for an optional indirect object with a semantic role other than beneficiary, do not appear to be changing.

[21] (*Le$_i$*) *entregó la pistola (al policia)$_i$* i = goal
He handed in the pistol (to the policeman)$_i$ (R50,m46,3,ELA38)

On the other hand, some speakers in Groups 2 and 3 redundantly mark possession in Spanish constructions where the equivalent English construction would not require it, as shown in [22], an indication that changes in the Spanish pattern may be occurring independently of direct English influence. [22] contains three separate markers of possession, the Cl *me* 'me', the stressed object pronoun in the indirect object *a mí* 'to me', and the possessive determiner *mi* 'my'. Possessive determiners do occur with body parts in standard Spanish when the sentence does not include an indirect object or dative Cl referring to the possessor (e.g. *Ponlo debajo de* TUS *pies* 'Put it under *your* feet'.

[22] ... *y me pegó a mí en mi brazo*
      and me hit to me on my arm
      ... and he hit me on the arm   (R24,m20,2,ELA50)

In conclusion, Spanish has not been permeated by a foreign syntactic structure, i.e. a verb phrase with a direct object containing a possessor and a possessed entity and no Cl correferential with the possessor, [[∅ V] [possessive det. N]] (see [17*b*, 18*b*). Rather, there seems to be a process of lexical change affecting the occurrence of one of the possible arguments of a set of verbs. This occurrence is controlled by a semantic-pragmatic constraint concerning the degree of closeness between the entities involved and their degree of active participation in the situation. The loss of this constraint is probably triggered by the bilinguals' preference for equivalent structures in the two languages (cf. Klein-Andreu 1986*a*) and by the fact that the parallel structure in English is not subject to the same semantic-pragmatic constraint. These modifications correspond to the types of possible grammatical permeability presented in (*b*) and (*c*) above, which involve neither incorporation nor necessarily loss of syntactic structures.

5.4. Obligatory SVX Order

The order of major arguments in Spanish, sensitive to semantic-pragmatic rules, may also offer a ground for possible modifications of the type of (*b*) and (*c*). For instance, it is well known that Spanish allows both SV and VS order with single-valency verbs (cf. Silva-Corvalán 1977; Ocampo 1989). Ocampo (pp. 171–2) has shown that VS is the strategy selected to introduce new subject referents into discourse. English, by contrast, does not have an exactly parallel VS option. In this respect, compare the word order of [23*a*], produced by a Spanish monolingual, with its English translation:

[23] ... *estuve una hora ahí* [a clinic] *tocando timbre, (a) salió el médico* [VS]
      (From Ocampo 1990: 97, ex. 14)
      ... I was there [a clinic] for an hour, ringing the bell, (*a*) the doctor came
      out   [SV]

In [23*a*], the new NP subject referent *el médico* 'the doctor' is introduced in postverbal position in Spanish, while the English version maintains its more rigid SV order regardless of the informational status of the subject. Consider now [24], produced by a Spanish-English bilingual:

[24] *Una vez estaba en una gasolinera aquí (a) y una señora llegó ahí* [SV]. *Yo estaba ahí esperando, estaban trabajando en el carro. (b) Una señora entró* [SV] *y me preguntó si conocía* ...
      Once (I) was at a gas station here (*a*) and a lady got there. (I) was waiting there, (they) were fixing my car. (*b*) A lady came in and asked me if (I) knew ...   (H48,m39,3,ELA24)

In [24a], the new NP subject referent *una señora* 'a lady' is introduced in preverbal position; it occurs in this same position in [24b], apparently reintroduced after a parenthetical explanation. Both [24a] and [24b] replicate the English versions. This constitutes further illustration of the bilingual's choice of a structure which parallels one in his dominant language, thus violating not a syntactic rule but a semantic-pragmatic constraint in Spanish, his secondary language.

It appears that modifications of semantic-pragmatic rules which lead to both loss or overgeneralization of syntactic variants are frequent in language-contact situations (see e.g. Dorian 1980; Landa 1995; Silva-Corvalán 1991a). But how likely are modifications that affect word order in LA Spanish to spread and become stable? An analysis of data from 15 speakers indicates that pragmatically controlled word-order variation is still quite strong. Consider, among many found in the data, [25a], produced by the same speaker as [24], where the new subject referent, *mi papá* 'my dad', is introduced in postverbal position, as expected in Spanish. Further illustration of SV/VS variation is offered in [26, 27].

[25] [Eso] *pasó el otro día.* (a) *Vino mi papá* [VS], *'Mira, aquí esta - necesitan un precio aquí en estas formas'*
That happened the other day. (a) My dad went, 'Look here, this - they need a price on these forms'   (H48,m39,3,ELA24)

[26] *Pero yo me levanto a ver qué se va a hacer ese día.* (a) *Si el niño necesita esto* [SVO], (b) *si la niña necesita lo otro* [SVO] (c) *y así va la rutina* [VS] . . . (d) *Y los niños realmente nos tienen jóvenes* [SVX]. *Porque H. dice de* (e) *cuando tenía él dieciséis* [VSX], *diecisiete* (f) *y llegaba el mes de marzo* [VS], *le gustaba subirse a una loma y volar papalotes.*
But I get up to see what we're going to do that day. (a) If the boy needs this, (b) if the girl needs that (c) and the routine goes on like this . . . (d) And the children really keep us young. Because H. says that (e) when he was sixteen, seventeen (f) and March came, he liked to climb up a small hill to fly kites.   (L28,f37,2,ELA23)

[27] A: *¿Nació en Colorado* [tu papá], *me dijiste?*
D: *No. Yo creo que* (a) *su papá nació en Colorado* [SVPP]. *Mi, mi abuelo.*
A: Was he [your dad] born in Colorado, did you say?
D: No. I think (a) his dad was born in Colorado. My, my grandfather (D36,m45,3,ELA43)

Examples [26, 27] illustrate the expected variation in word order: [SVO/X] with evoked or given NP subjects ([26a, b, d]); [VS] order with new NP subjects ([26c, f]); [VSX] with non-contrastive subject pronouns ([26e]); and [SVPP] with a new but contrastive NP subject ([27a]), where the speaker's father is being contrasted with his father's father.

I have conducted a fairly rough quantitative analysis of word-order patterns in data from 15 speakers (see Table 5.1), marking the preverbal/postverbal placement

TABLE 5.1. Speakers Included in the Study of Word Order and Subject Expression

Group 1			Group 2			Group 3		
	Sex	Age		Sex	Age		Sex	Age
E1	F	20	V21	F	18	S38	F	19
S2	F	24	A20	F	19	A46	F	31
A9	F	62	L19	F	22	M47	F	33
			L28	F	37	R42	M	15
			R24	M	20	H48	M	39
						D36	M	45
						R50	M	46

of the subject without considering differences in types of verb (e.g. transitives, intransitives), the informational status of the subject (new or evoked information), or the number of expressed constituents in the sentence. The results show higher percentages of preverbal subjects in English dominant bilinguals (see Table 5.2), which could be interpreted to reflect a trend towards a more fixed SVX order. However, this possible outcome is still distant. Similar observations about the resilience of word order under pressure from a different word-order system are made by Mithun (1989: 245–6) in regard to Oklahoma Cayuga word order, in a situation of contact in which English is also the dominant language.

The distribution of the speakers included in the quantitative analysis of word order and in the study of subject expression in section 5.5 below is summarized in Table 5.1: three speakers from Group 1; five from Group 2; and seven from Group 3.

A total of 643 sentences with expressed subjects were quantified. Overall results for the 15 speakers indicate that 499/643 expressed subjects were placed preverbally, i.e. 78 per cent. The percentages by group show a steady, though not large, increase of preverbal subjects: Group 1, 74 per cent (99/133); Group 2, 77 per cent (177/230); Group 3, 80 per cent (223/280).

The subjects were classified into three types: personal pronouns, NPs, and 'other pronouns' (e.g. demonstrative and indefinite pronouns like *esos* 'those', *alguien* 'someone'). The informational status of these three types of constituent, as well as the observed correlation between word order and informational weight, seemed to justify considering them separately: personal pronouns tend to refer to already activated, given information, NPs tend to introduce new information into discourse. The status of the 'other pronouns' in this respect was not investigated; thus, in principle, it appeared prudent to separate them from the other two categories. The results, displayed in Table 5.2, confirmed the advisability of the separation into these three classes. With respect to word order, speakers in Groups 1 and 2 treat

TABLE 5.2. Cross-tabulation of Subject Placement by Type of Subject and by
Speaker Group

| | Preverbal subjects | | | | | | |
| | Personal pronouns | | Noun phrases | | Other pronouns | | |
	No.	%	No.	%	No.	%	p
Group 1	71/84	85	22/39	56	6/10	60	<.00
Group 2	98/108	91	59/90	66	20/32	63	<.00
Group 3	135/144	94	73/118	62	15/18	83	<.00

'other pronouns' in a manner similar to NPs. In Group 3, however, other pronouns favour preverbal position rather strongly.

With every type of subject, Groups 2 and 3 increase the percentage of preverbal
placement. This percentage is quite high with personal pronouns in Group 1, 85
per cent; and even higher in Groups 2 and 3, 91 per cent and 94 per cent. As
expected, NPs and other pronouns occur less frequently than personal pronouns in
preverbal position in the three groups of speakers; but the trend in favour of
preverbal position by speakers in Groups 2 and 3 is also apparent with these types
of subjects: from 56 per cent and 60 per cent in Group 1 to 66 per cent and 63 per
cent in Group 2; in Group 3, NPs have a slightly lower percentage of preverbal
position, 62 per cent, in comparison with Group 2, but a high 83 per cent of preverbal 'other pronouns'.

Assuming that differences in communicative needs may be neutralized by the
amount of data and similarity of discourse topics, the attested increase of preverbal
subjects in Groups 2 and 3 may be interpreted, however, as the consequence of
processes of loss of semantic-pragmatic constraints on preverbal subject placement, as illustrated in [21]. Once again, this process of loss may be favoured by
contact with a more rigid SV-order language but does not constitute a radical
change in the system of Spanish.

Indeed, preverbal placement of personal-pronoun subjects is the most frequent
variant in monolingual varieties. Furthermore, Ocampo (1989) shows that in spoken Argentinian Spanish (from the Rio de La Plata region), NP subjects are almost
categorically preverbal in pragmatically unmarked SVX constructions (95 per cent,
see Table 5.3). With single-valency non-state verbs, on the other hand, SV is less
frequent than VS (40 per cent v. 60 per cent), but the subject can be predicted to
be almost categorically preverbal (96 per cent) when it conveys evoked information
in pragmatically unmarked constructions. These figures, adapted by me from
Ocampo (pers. comm.; see also Ocampo 1989), are summarized in Table 5.3.

As Table 5.3 clearly indicates, NP subjects are much more frequently placed

TABLE 5.3. Subject Noun Phrase Placement in Pragmatically Unmarked Sentences in Rio Platense Spanish

SVX (S mostly evoked)		SV (S = evoked)		VS (S = new)	
252/264	95%	23/24	96%	33/34	97%
Totals		SV/SV+VS	23/58	40%	
		SV(X)	275/322	85%	

preverbally in Rio Platense Spanish, a variety not in intensive contact with English, than in any of the samples of LA Spanish included in this study. The higher percentages of preverbal subjects in English dominant bilinguals, as compared to the Spanish dominant group, on the other hand, may perhaps be interpreted as reflecting an incipient movement in the direction of the SV(X) order of the dominant language.

5.5. Obligatory Expression of Subjects

5.5.1. Analysis

The fourth potential case of permeation concerns the possibility that the expression of subjects in the Spanish of bilinguals may be becoming obligatory, as one might surmise on the basis of such examples as [28]. Note that in this example the speaker repeats the subject of [28*a*], *un mexicano* 'a Mexican', in [28*b*], where one would normally expect a non-expressed subject (see [29*b*] below).

[28]   *En tiempos antiguos - (a) un mexicano case* [se casaba] *con un*[a] *mexicana y (b)*
   UN MEXICANO *no puede* [podía] *hablar con - otros - nacionales* [grupos étnicos]
   In the past - (*a*) a Mexican married a Mexican and (*b*) A MEXICAN couldn't talk
   with other ethnic groups   (R42,m15,3,ELA30)

In this section I will focus on the question of subject expression in some detail, and will address two specific questions: (1) Does the almost categorical expression of subjects in English favour a higher percentage of expression of subjects in bilingual Spanish as compared to monolingual dialects, i.e. is there evidence of transfer of type (*b*)? (2) What accounts for the variable expression of lexical subjects at the various stages of Spanish-language attrition?

Most Romance languages, e.g. Spanish, Catalan, Italian, Portuguese, allow both filled and empty subject syntactic positions, as shown in [29*a*, *b*] respectively.

[29] (a) *Cuando Juana~i~ vivía aquí, ella~i/t~ siempre nos invitaba a su casa*
          When Juana~i~ lived here she~i/t~ always invited us to her home

     (b) *Cuando Juana~i~ vivía aquí, ∅~i/t~ siempre nos invitaba a su casa*
          When Juana~i~ lived here *∅/she~i/t~ always invited us to her home

The phenomenon illustrated here, to which I refer as the *variable expression of the subject*, lends itself to the investigation of permeability of type (*b*), i.e. increased preference for subject expression, given that English requires the subject position to be filled in contexts where Spanish does not, as the translations in [29] show.

Note that, with respect to this phenomenon, the incorporation of elements foreign to the structure of the language would have to involve the occurrence of non-referential, 'dummy' subjects, as in [30, 31].

[30] *EL *está lloviendo*
     IT is raining

[31] *ELLOS *me robaron el auto* [said without knowing who stole the car]
     THEY've stolen my car

Not surprisingly, there is not a single case of such non-referential, dummy subjects in the Spanish data examined.

If a higher percentage of expression of subjects is attested in bilingual Spanish, this would be the result, then, of a rather insidious type of permeability; given that it does not violate sentence-based grammatical rules, it is less salient and could spread with relative ease. This type of transfer obviously requires a quantitative examination of subject expression in the data.

It is not entirely clear how comparable subjects may be in English and Spanish. Indeed, if the role of the subject pronoun in English is to indicate person and number, then it is quite plausible that bilingual speakers may associate subject pronouns in English with Spanish verb inflections. If this is the case, we would expect a lower rather than higher overall frequency of pronoun expression, as well as a higher frequency of expression with morphologically neutralized verb forms (e.g. *cantaba* 'I/he, she sang')[3] in bilingual Spanish as compared to monolingual or Spanish dominant varieties. By contrast, if bilinguals establish cross-linguistic equivalence at a surface level, and if they truly tend to make both languages structurally more similar (cf. Gumperz and Wilson 1977), then we would expect a much higher frequency of subject pronouns as a result of intensive contact with English.

I have argued, furthermore (Silva-Corvalán 1986; 1990*c*; and in Chapter 4 above), that bilinguals tend to follow internal language preferences when simplifying variables. This hypothesis does not predict which variant will be favoured by bilinguals in the case of a stable linguistic variable such as subject expression seems

---

[3] A morphologically neutralized verb form is any of the undifferentiated forms for 1st and 3rd person singular in all the tenses of the subjunctive mood, in the imperfect of the indicative, and in the conditional (see Table 2.1).

to be. If we consider the issue of analysis versus bound morphology, however, we may conclude that overt subjects will be preferred over verb inflections as markers of person and number.

On the other hand, many linguists (e.g. Dorian 1980; Landa 1995; Silva-Corvalán 1986; 1991*a*) have documented the loss of semantically close alternatives correlated with different pragmatic functions in processes of simplification. Assuming this type of loss and the pragmatic functions of subject expression (see below) in a pro-drop language (i.e. a language that allows null lexical subjects), we may expect a trend towards fewer subjects. We are faced, then, with 'competing motivations' (cf. DuBois 1985): contact with a non-pro-drop language and analysis favouring categorical subject expression; and loss of (marked) pragmatic options favouring zero subjects.

It is certainly also possible to look at the issue at hand within the framework of parametric syntax and its associated theory of markedness. In accordance with traditional linguistic thought, some parametric studies (e.g. Roeper and Williams 1987, cited in Romaine 1992) make use of markedness theory to predict stages of language acquisition, such that unmarked settings of parameters are said to be acquired earlier than marked ones. In regard to the so-called pro-drop and non-pro-drop phenomena, however, there is some controversy both over which of the two settings is the marked one[4] and over which is the possible interrelationship between markedness theory and ease of acquisition (cf. Romaine 1992).

Despite evident disagreements, the parametric model of syntax has been applied to the study of pidgins, creoles, and second-language acquisition. But here again one finds contradictory evidence and claims, compounded by the unresolved questions posed by transfer theory and by the hypothesis that L2 acquisition replicates the stages of L1 acquisition.

One could pursue this line of thinking and examine subject expression in a pro-drop language in contact with a dominant non-pro-drop language, as illustrated by Spanish and English in Los Angeles, adopting the structural analysis proposed by Adams (1987) in her study of the loss of pro-drop in French. Note, however, that her theory forces her to assume a VOS underlying word order for pro-drop Romance languages, and an SVO word order for non-pro-drop languages such as French and English. Her well-argued analysis, however, leaves her at a loss to explain why Yiddish is not pro-drop while Chinese languages are, and why Italian requires the expression of the second-person singular subject pronoun with subjunctives.

Having found no agreement on, or satisfactory answer to, the question of subject expression, I have chosen to disregard the autonomous syntax option. Relying on a view of language as a system of human communication whose structural features will best be explained with reference to cognitive and social factors, I continue to

---

[4] According to Romaine (1989: 39–41), Hyams proposes that pro-drop is the unmarked case for first-language acquisition, while White argues that pro-drop is the marked setting.

adhere to a semantic-pragmatic approach to syntactic variation, and incorporate semantic-pragmatic variables as possible factors determining the expression or non-expression of subjects.

Structurally, the observation that Spanish has the option of expressing or not expressing a subject pronoun appears to be valid for most sentential contexts in a discourse vacuum. Examined in the normal flow of speech, however, the complexity of the question of variable subject expression becomes clear. It is evident on the one hand that the phenomenon is not optional in every possible environment and, on the other, that speakers may also have the option of expressing or not express-ing an NP subject, as illustrated in [32, 33]. Methodologically, then, it appeared appropriate to me to consider NPs in at least some of the quantitative analyses of this question.

[32] Pepe llegó temprano hoy a la oficina; *Pepe/?él/∅ se vino en taxi.
      Pepe arrived at the office early today; *Pepe/he/*∅ came by taxi

[33] Me vine con Pepe hoy a la oficina; Pepe/él/∅ vive cerca de mi casa
      I came to the office with Pepe today; Pepe/he/*∅ lives near my home

Note that if the subject is coreferential with the subject of the preceding sen-tence, as in [32], a full subject NP is not acceptable in Spanish (assuming an informational intonation pattern, i.e. the pragmatic function is to communicate information with no further connotations or implicatures). However, if the subject is coreferential with the referent of an oblique constituent in the preceding sen-tence, the three alternatives are allowed: full NP, pronoun, or null subject.

Studies during the past decade have shown (cf. Bentivoglio 1987; Enríquez 1984; Silva-Corvalán 1982) that the variable expression of subjects is controlled by discourse-sensitive factors, namely the establishment of an entity as the topic of more than one sentence (a sentential topic is a referent 'about which new information is being added in the proposition'; Lambrecht 1987: 222) ([34]); the need to express focal information ([35, 36]); the need to identify subject referents clearly ([37]).

Establishment of topic

[34] S = S2,f24,1,ELA37; C = researcher
S: creo que si él lo hiciera - el sacrificio [studying in the evenings] - o yo lo hiciera, sería algo bueno.
C: Sí. Para ayudarle al niño.
S: Al niño, sí. /C: Um, hmm, sí./ A veces sí (a) yo me pongo a pensar y digo, 'Bueno, (b) yo no estoy tan mayor todavía'. Porque para la edad que ∅ tengo - son veinticuatro años. /C: Claro./ Entonces, (c) ∅ me pongo a pensar que apenas sería una edad como para - Yo todavía, este, pudiera ser una mujer soltera. /C: Um, hmm./ Y - ∅ sé que ∅ tengo mi niño, entonces, con más razón decir uno, (d) '∅ tengo el, el tiempo perdido, bah, ∅ puedo aprovecharlo'.

S: 'I think that if he made it - the sacrifice [studying in the evenings] - or I made it, it'd be good.

C: Yes. To help the boy.

S: The boy, yes. /C: Um, hmm, yes./ Sometimes (*a*) *I* start thinking and say, 'Well, (*b*) *I*'m not that old yet'. Because for my age - I'm only twenty four. /C: Yeah./ So, (*c*) (*I*) start to think that it would be hardly the age to - I still, eh, could be a single woman. /C: Um, hmm./ And - (*I*) know (*I*) have my son, so, there's even a better reason for one to say, (*d*) '(*I*) have, have wasted time, bah, (*I*) can use it well.'

Focal information

[35] ø dije entre mí, ø dije, 'Oye, Alb., ¿eras *tú* (*ø) el que estabas hablando allá arriba? *Yo* (*ø) mismo - estuve, a, sorprendido de mí. - ¿*Yo* (*ø) era el que estaba hablando allá arriba? Primero ø me encomendé a Dios.　(A29,m60,2, ELA2)

I (ø) said to myself, I (ø) said, 'Listen, Alb., Were *you* (*ø) the one speaking up there?' *I* (*ø) myself - was surprised at myself. - *I* (*ø) was the one speaking up there? First I (ø) entrusted myself to God.

Contrast

[36] Y *yo* me fuí a trabajar y *él* se quedó ahí un rato. Le hizo el reporte a la policía y todo　(R11,f42,1,ELA18)

*Y ø me fuí a trabajar pero ø se quedó ahí un rato. Le hizo el reporte a la policía y todo

And I (*ø) went to work and he (*ø) stayed a while longer. (He) gave the report to the police and all

Clarification of subject referent

[37] S = S2,f24,1,ELA37; C = researcher

S: Pues, se me grabó tanto en la mente que cuando la sepultaron, yo de noche miraba visiones, pero era la realidad. Porque yo despertaba gritando y mi hermana tenía que levantarse a verme. /C: Ah, fíjate./ Y (*a*) ella iba a mi lado y (*b*) yo estaba temblando, que hasta los dientes se oían que pegaban.

S: Well, it got so fixed in my mind that when they buried her, I saw visions at night, but it was real. Because I would wake up screaming and my sister had to get up to see what was happening to me. /C: Oh, gee!/ And (*a*) she'd come up to my bedside and *I* was trembling, you could even hear my teeth striking together.

Thus, although the subject is not required in the second conjunct of [32, 33], nor in any of the sentences in [34], it is required in the italicized positions in [35, 36,[5] 37]. Intralanguage analyses and cross-language comparisons must take these facts into account, therefore, when examining the issue of pro-drop and of possible interlinguistic transfer. Note that the English translations in [29, 32–7] require a subject pronoun in every case.[6]

Clearly, then, discourse-related factors should be taken into consideration in cross-group comparisons. Accordingly, this study adheres to the methodology used in previous discourse-based studies. Basically, this consists in coding each subject, expressed or not, of a finite verb by a number of factors hypothesized as having some bearing on subject expression (cf. Bentivoglio 1987; Cifuentes 1980–1; Morales 1986: ch. 5; Silva-Corvalán 1977; 1982). (Excluded from quantification are fixed phrases, e.g. *tú sabes* 'you know', *eso es* 'that's it', as well as other categorical contexts such as impersonal constructions.) For this chapter, a total of 2,176 cases were examined and coded in the data from the three groups of speakers.

Building upon previous investigations, the internal variables listed below were included in the analysis (see Appendix 3 for a list of all the factors included in each independent variable group):

(i) Coreferentiality index. The subject in question is coded according to whether it is coreferential with the subject of the preceding finite verb ([34 *a*, *b*] illustrate coreferential subjects), with another argument of the preceding finite verb, or with none of the preceding clause arguments (see [44–7]). Unless otherwise stated, coreferentiality between subjects is opposed to switch reference between subjects in the tables below, i.e. patterns of coreferentiality with other syntactic constituents are disregarded in the columns labelled 'switch' in the tables.

(ii) Morphological ambiguity of the verbal form. The morphologically ambiguous forms include the first and third person singular of the Imp and the Cond, as well as of the two Sub tenses ([37 *a*, *b*] illustrate 'ambiguous' Imp forms).

(iii) Communicative value of the subject, with respect both (*a*) to its status as focal or part of the focal information in its sentence ([35]), and (*b*) to its status as a focus of contrast ([36]). Evidently, every contrastive subject is also focal information in its sentence, but not vice versa. Furthermore, I differentiated contrast from focal information on the basis that their correlation with subject placement/word order would not necessarily be the same, and word order was also being examined.

A subject is considered to convey focal information when it represents the most

[5] Note that the requirement that a contrastive subject be expressed cannot be captured on the basis of just the structural description; it must be specified that the subjects are non-coreferential. If they are coreferential, the contrastive situation does not obtain, regardless of the structural description, and expressing the subjects becomes 'optional': *ø/yo hablo bien español y/pero el inglés ø/yo lo hablo muy quebrado* 'I speak good Spanish and/but English I speak poorly'.

[6] English allows null subjects in strings of co-ordinated sentences with a coreferential subject when these sentences present sequential situations as illustrated in (i) and (iii) (cf. [32]): (i) *Pete came by taxi and ø arrived early at the office today*; (ii) *Pete came by taxi.* *ø arrived early at the office today.* (iii) *Pete got up at six, ø came by taxi, and ø arrived early at the office today.*

crucial piece of information in its sentence at the purely informational level. Note that a subject may carry intonational prominence for pragmatic purposes other than the communication of the newest or most crucial information; for instance, to call the listener's attention towards the referent of the subject in relation to some unusual or unexpected situation, as in [38]. In these cases of marked pragmatic functions, the subject is not coded as focal (Rodrigo 1991). Indeed, the speaker can make a communicative choice in examples of the type of [38]: to highlight the subject referent or not (Ba or B*b*); this choice is associated with the possibility of expressing or not expressing the subject, respectively. In the case of informationally focal subject referents, this choice is not available, as the unacceptability of [39, B (*b*)] indicates:

[38] A: *Juan no puede ayudarnos mañana.*
　　 B: (*a*) ESE/JUAN *no ayuda nunca*/(*b*) ∅ *no ayuda nunca*
　　 A: Juan can't help us tomorrow
　　 B: (*a*) THAT ONE/JUAN never helps/(*b*) *(He) never helps

[39] A: *¿Quién no puede ayudarnos mañana?*
　　 B: (*a*) JUAN *no puede*/(*b*) *∅ *no puede*
　　 A: Who can't help us tomorrow?
　　 B: (*a*) JUAN can't/(*b*) *(He) can't

(iv) Semantics of the verb.[7] It was hypothesized that some types of verb would favour subject expression: estimative and verbs of the type *gustar* 'to like' were therefore coded separately from other verbs.

Estimative verbs are those verbs that tend to present the speaker's point of view as implicitly opposed to that of others (e.g. *to think, to believe, to assume, to agree with*; cf. Enríquez 1984: 152, 235–45). This implicit idea of contrast may explain their positive correlation with subject expression. As observed before, explicit contrast is a categorical context for subject expression.

Verbs of the type *gustar* 'to like' in Spanish are those that subcategorize a subject with the semantic role of *theme*, and an indirect object with the role of *experiencer*, as in [40].

[40] *A Pepe le gustó/le encantó/se le olvidó/se le perdió el vino*
　　 to Pete to–him liked/lacked/forgot/lost the wine
　　 Pete liked/loved/forgot/lost the wine

With these types of verb the subject is frequently inanimate and conveys the new information in the sentence; I considered it necessary, therefore, to code them separately.

---

[7] I also examined the effect that the reflexive/non-reflexive form of the verb might have on subject expression based on the hypothesis (suggested to me by Flora Klein-Andreu a few years ago) that reflexive forms might favour non-expression given the 'disambiguating effect' of the reflexive pronoun. Cross-tabulations showed that the correlation was random; i.e. given a reflexive/non-reflexive verb one could expect a 50/50 chance of an expressed subject.

(v) Type of subject. Every subject was coded according to its category (e.g. pronoun, noun phrase) and the person and number of its referent.

(vi) Subjects were also coded to indicate if they occurred within the same turn of speech, or at a new turn. New turns were considered those points at which a different speaker initiated a turn, as well as those at which the speaker either quoted himself or someone else within the same turn of speech.

(vii) Finally, I also investigated the possibility of a correlation between subject expression and clause type: main or subordinate on the one hand and declarative, interrogative, exclamative, and imperative on the other. However, only declarative sentences were examined quantitatively due to the very few cases of interrogatives, exclamatives, and imperatives attested in the data.

Of these independent variables, quantitative evidence provided by the cross-tabulations performed (with the statistical program *crosstabs* in SPSSX) indicated that change in turn of speech and clause type (independent v. subordinate) did not appear relevant. By contrast, coreferentiality, morphological ambiguity, verb semantics, type of subject, and communicative value (i.e. contrast and focus) showed statistically valid correlations with subject expression. Contrast and focal information, as expected, proved to be categorical contexts for the expression of a nominal or pronominal subject. Thus, although examples of the type of [41], with a non-expressed contrastive subject, and [42], with a non-expressed focal subject, are in principle possible 'errors', they are not attested in the data. That is to say, no examples were found of non-expressed focal or contrastive subjects, even where the verb inflection unmistakably identified the subject referent (as in [41, 42]).

[41] *Mi hermano estudió en USC, *y/pero ∅ estudié-1sg en Indiana*
     Lit.: My brother studied at USC, *and/but ∅ studied-1sg at Indiana

[42] *¿Quién trajo los libros? *∅ los traje-1sg.*
     Lit.: Who brought the books? *∅ them brought-1sg

For the purpose of establishing whether English-dominant bilinguals show any preference for pronoun expression, it may be sufficient to compare their linguistic behaviour with that of Spanish-dominant bilinguals in the community. A stronger case would be made, however, if the results were compared with Spanish varieties not in intensive contact with English. This comparison is rendered difficult by the fact that every study of this variable has incorporated slightly different constraints in regard to what is to be included in the quantitative analysis. On the whole, however, there are similar trends in the results obtained. Including NPs and categorical contexts of occurrence (i.e. contrast, focus), the overall percentage of subject expression in the three groups in East Los Angeles (ELA) is 41 per cent (892/2176), remarkably close to the 43 per cent (457/795) attested in my study of subject expression in West Los Angeles Spanish (Silva-Corvalán 1977).

To compare with non Mexican-American Spanish varieties, the results shown in Table 5.4 exclude NPs, but they do retain focal and contrastive pronouns.

TABLE 5.4. Cross-tabulation of Subject Pronouns by Speaker Group in ELA and Comparison with Madrid (Spain), Boston (Puerto Rico Spanish), Santiago (Chile), and Caracas (Venezuela)

	Expressed pronouns/ total no. of verbs	%	Yo 'I'		Nosotros 'we'	
			No.	%	No.	%
Group 1	118/360	33	58/137	42	6/39	15
Group 2	163/586	28	57/197	29	11/76	15
Group 3	198/758	26	78/222	35	4/61	7
Madrid	4,857/23,717	21	3,249/10,185	32	253/2,431	10
PRS (Boston)	–	37[a]	573/1,333	43	35/208	17
Caracas	–		329/721	46	28/171	16
Santiago	1,587/4,182	38	752/2,238	34	99/571	17

[a] This percentage has been adapted from Hochberg (1986) so as not to include the fixed phrase *tú sabes* 'you know'. Bentivoglio's (1987) and my studies do not include fixed phrases.

Subsequent cross-tabulations examining the effect of coreferentiality and verb ambiguity were performed both including and excluding these categorical contexts.

The percentages of expressed subject pronouns do not indicate any striking differences overall among the three ELA groups, but there is a gradual decrease of the frequency of expression in Groups 2 and 3 as compared to Group 1. ELA percentages for all pronominal subjects are intermediate between those reported for Madrid, 21 per cent (Enríquez 1984), and for Chilean, 38 per cent (Cifuentes 1980–1), and Puerto Rican Spanish (PRS) in Boston, 37 per cent (Hochberg 1986: 613). In regard to expression of the first-person pronouns *yo* 'I' and *nosotros* 'we' only, the percentages of expression are lower than the frequency reported for PRS and for Venezuela (Bentivoglio 1987: 36).

Note that Group 3 speakers, expected to show the effect of contact more than any other group, have the lowest global percentage of subject expression in East Los Angeles. Further, the percentage of usage in Madrid and among Groups 2 and 3 speakers is almost the same for *yo* (and fairly close for *nosotros* in Group 3), while the highest percentages correspond to Caracas, a variety which is not in intensive contact with English. Should it be concluded from these overall results that evidence is sufficient to bury the 'transfer from English' hypothesis once and for all?[8] Certainly not without controlling subject expression in its relation to semantic-pragmatic factors, a methodology which should be incorporated in any comparison across groups or individuals.[9]

[8] See Morales (1986: 89–100) for a brief reference to arguments in favour of this hypothesis, and for her own counter-argument based on a study of subject expression in a sample of Puerto Rican bilinguals.

[9] Hochberg (1986) does not use this control, thus weakening the strength of the cross-dialectal evidence she discusses in support of her functional hypothesis.

Though overall group results in East Los Angeles show some decreasing frequency of expression in Group 3, cross-tabulation by each speaker indicates clear crossovers between groups, as seen in Table 5.5, which orders the speakers from highest to lowest percentage of expressed subjects (column 1). In addition to speaker's name and group membership, Table 5.5 includes the following: (*a*) In column 1, the number and percentage of occurrences of all types of subject (pronouns and NPs) over total number of finite verbs for each speaker. (*b*) In column 2, the percentages for pronouns only. (Unless specified, all tables include personal and 'other' types of pronoun.) In the 'other' group (see Appendix 3, factor 9: Subject type) I have included such deictic pronominals as *éste* 'this one' and *eso* 'that'. (*c*) In column 3, number, rounded-off percentages, and statistical significance for all types of subject cross-tabulated by coreference. (*d*) In column 4, number, rounded-off percentages, and significance for all types of subject cross-tabulated by ambiguity of the verb form. Statistically significant correlations are italicized in columns 3 and 4.

The results displayed in Table 5.5 show a wide range of different frequencies of subject expression, but these may be motivated by diverse communicative needs. More importantly, this table shows that the coreferentiality index has a stronger correlation than ambiguity with the subject expression variable. While coreferentiality is statistically valid for 13 of the 15 speakers, the morphological constraint is valid for only 5: 2 of the 3 speakers in Group 1, and 3 of the 5 speakers in Group 2.

Combining speakers into groups, the correlation between ambiguity of the verbal form and higher subject expression, shown to be valid in previous studies (Cameron 1990; Hochberg 1986; Silva-Corvalán 1982), turns out to be statistically valid in Groups 1 and 2, but non-existent in Group 3. The results are displayed in Table 5.6.

Tables 5.4–6 include focal and contrastive subjects, which are obligatorily expressed, and NPs. The exclusion of these types of subject obviously reduces total percentages, but it does not alter the relative frequency patterns of expression across groups or the correlation with the ambiguity variable, as illustrated in Table 5.7.

With regard to morphological ambiguity, then, it must be concluded (*a*) that it exists as a weak constraint on subject expression among some speakers in Groups 1 (A9), and 2 (L28, A20), and (*b*) that it no longer exists in Group 3. In spite of this loss, there are very few cases of confusion in the data; and most of them are clarified almost immediately by the ensuing discourse (cf. Ranson 1991). Speakers in Group 3 may be relying much more on contextual clues, therefore, to disambiguate the subject referent, as in the following passage, in which the speaker is talking about an aunt who had been burnt.

[43] Toda la cara - pelo - todo el pelo, eyebrows. Cuando fuimos, fuimos mi mamá
      y yo - a verla, ∅ estaba hinchada, ∅ parece [parecía] pumpkin, ∅ estaba muy
      hinchada de los ojos. (*a*) ∅ no tenía los ojos claros, estaban - pi - dark brown.

TABLE 5.5. Cross-tabulation of Subject Expression by Speaker, by Coreferentiality, and by Ambiguity of the Verb Form

Name (Group)	1 Pronouns and NPs/total verbs		2 Pronouns	3 Pronouns and NPs					4 Pronouns and NPs					
				Coreferential		Switch			Ambiguous		Non-ambiguous			
	No.	%	%	No.	%	No.	%	$p = <$	No.	%	No.	%	$p = <$	
L28 (2)	76/133	57	42	10/39	26	64/91	70	.00	15/20	75	59/110	54	.12	
H48 (3)	79/162	49	38	19/57	33	59/101	58	.00	20/47	42	58/111	52	.29	
S2(1)	79/169	47	39	26/73	36	49/92	53	.02	36/60	60	39/105	37	.00	
D36 (3)	81/180	45	32	16/87	18	64/91	70	.00	22/49	45	58/129	45	1.00	
R50 (3)	60/134	45	30	9/54	17	51/78	65	.00	13/26	50	47/107	44	.73	
A20 (2)	70/158	44	27	9/41	22	58/105	55	.00	21/37	57	46/109	42	.17	
A9(1)	56/138	41	32	10/48	21	40/80	50	.00	16/32	50	34/96	35	.14	
E1(1)	54/136	40	26	5/44	11	22/59	37	.00	16/23	70	35/105	33	.00	
S38 (3)	52/131	40	28	11/40	28	39/84	46	.06	16/29	55	34/95	36	.09	
R42 (3)	43/111	39	21	15/54	28	28/55	51	.02	5/14	36	38/95	40	.98	
L19 (2)	57/148	39	26	7/62	11	50/86	58	.00	21/30	70	36/118	31	.00	
R24 (2)	73/196	37	26	13/84	16	58/108	54	.00	14/23	61	57/169	34	.02	
V21 (2)	50/140	36	22	11/64	17	38/69	55	.00	15/23	65	34/110	31	.00	
M47 (3)	40/123	33	16	10/46	22	30/76	40	.06	14/37	38	26/85	31	.56	
A46 (3)	22/117	19	8	2/64	3	20/50	40	.00	9/60	15	13/55	24	.34	

TABLE 5.6. Cross-tabulation of Subject Expression by Ambiguity of the Verb form[a]

| | Ambiguous | | Non-ambiguous | | |
	No.	%	No.	%	$p = <$
Group 1	65/111	59	101/297	34	.00
Group 2	83/129	64	221/598	37	.00
Group 3	95/256	37	271/670	40	.39

[a] Pronouns and NPs included.

TABLE 5.7. Cross-tabulation of Subject Pronoun Expression by Ambiguity of the Verb Form[a]

| | Pronouns/total verbs | | Ambiguous | | Non-ambiguous | | |
	No.	%	No.	%	No.	%	$p = <$
Group 1	88/330	27	37/83	45	51/247	21	.00
Group 2	109/531	21	23/69	33	86/462	19	.00
Group 3	154/712	22	42/202	21	112/510	22	.80

[a] Focal and contrastive pronouns excluded.

> I don't know what color her eyes were, pero – with the fire – ø tenía como un film over it, and they were light, almost light blue or light grey. /C: Oh!/ They were so light! Y – y estaban – tenían morphine /C: Claro/ para el pain /C: Para el dolor/ dolor. Y – hablamos con ella y ø quería agua. Y, y ø me dijo que ø quería agua, ø quería agua. Pero – no pudíamos – darle nada.   (A46, f31,3,ELA20)

> Her whole face – hair – all her hair, eyebrows. When (we) went, my mom and I went – to see her, (she) was swollen, (she) looked like a pumpkin, (she) was very swollen, her eyes. (a) (She) didn't have light-coloured eyes, (they) were – – pi – dark brown. I don't know what colour her eyes were, but – with the fire – (she) had like a film over it, and they were light, almost light blue or light grey. /C: Oh!/ They were so light! And – and (they) were – (they) had morphine /C: Yeah/ for the pain /C: For the pain/ pain. And– (we) spoke with her and (she) wanted water. And, and (she) said that (she) wanted water, (she) wanted water. But – (we) couldn't – give her anything.

In [43], nine singular verb forms occur without an expressed subject. The seven morphologically ambiguous Imp forms have three possible grammatical subjects: the speaker, her mother, and her aunt. The mother and the aunt are also possible

TABLE 5.8. Percentage of Subject Expression by Syntactic Function of the Coreferential Argument in the Preceding Sentence[a]

	No.	%
'Sentential subject'	30/42	63
Switch reference with all arguments	624/1,080	57
Coreference with oblique argument	18/36	50
Coreference with direct object	28/86	33
Coreference with indirect object	14/48	29
Coreference with subject	176/873	20

[a] All types of subject included. The subjects of 7 sentences which occurred after a short pause in the conversation were excluded from the quantification of coreferentiality because their status in this respect was not quite clear to me.

subjects of the two non-ambiguous third-person singular forms (one Pres and one Pret) in the passage. However, the content of the passage plainly indicates that the subject referent of these nine verbs is the aunt. No subject needs to be expressed given the unbroken topic chain, yet six Spanish speakers consulted agreed that they would have tended to express the pronoun *ella* 'she' in [43*a*] (*Ella no tenía los ojos claros* 'she didn't have light-coloured eyes').

Previous studies of subject expression indicate that the most significant internal variable determining variable subject expression is coreferentiality, such that if the subject is coreferential with the subject of the preceding finite verb it is expressed in only 20–5 per cent of cases, as opposed to 50–60 per cent subject expression in cases of switch reference (cf. Bentivoglio 1987; Hochberg 1986; Silva-Corvalán 1982).

This coreferentiality constraint applies differently when the subject is coreferential with a complement of the preceding sentence, or when it refers to the preceding proposition or propositions. Expression will be highest in this latter case ([44]),[10] second highest when there is switch reference with all the arguments of the preceding verb ([45]), lowest when the subjects are coreferential; and at least in the sample from ELA speakers included here, coreferentiality with an indirect object ([46]), a direct object, and an oblique argument ([47]) correlates with a gradual increase in subject expression, as shown in Table 5.8. Let us first consider some examples.

[44] Coreference with preceding proposition or propositions:
De vez en cuando pasa *eso*   (L19,f22,2,ELA54)
Sometimes *that* happens

[10] This group also includes sentential subjects, as in '*Lo que tú quieres* puede causar problemas. ø puede agravar las cosas' ('*What you want* may cause problems. It (ø) may make things worse').

TABLE 5.9. Cross-tabulation of Subject Expression by Coreferentiality[a]

	Coreferential		Switch		
	No.	%	No.	%	$p = <$
Group 1	41/165	25	125/243	51	.00
Group 2	50/290	17	254/437	58	.00
Group 3	82/402	20	284/524	54	.00

[a] Pronouns and NPs included.

[45] Switch reference with all arguments of the preceding verb:
Agarran los recibos y con ese dinero (ø-3pl) empiezan el día. Y cada vez que *él* trabajaba les hacía falta cinco o diez dólares.   (L19,f22,2,ELA54)
They get the receipts and they start the day with that money. And whenever *he* worked, they were missing five or ten dollars.

[46] Switch reference with subject - coreference with indirect object:
Le dijo *al manejador*ᵢ que si (ø)ᵢ le permitía abrir el cuarto porque tenía miedo   (R50,m46,3,ELA36)
He asked *the driver*ᵢ if heᵢ would let him open the room because he was scared.

[47] Switch reference with subject - coreference with oblique object:
Me estacioné a cinco minutos de mi oficina. *Mi oficina* es pequeña.
(L19,f22,2,ELA54)
I parked five minutes away from my office. *My office* is small.

These correlations are very interesting because they appear to support hypotheses which explain other phenomena (e.g. Cl duplication, Cl omission, relativization; see e.g. Franco 1991; Givón 1976; Keenan and Comrie 1977; Landa 1995; Silva-Corvalán 1981) on the basis of hierarchies of topicality. Furthermore, they bury once and for all the idea that old/new information as an opposition between information that the speaker assumes to be present/not present in the interlocutor's consciousness is a factor with strong correlations with the subject expression variable. If presence in the interlocutor's consciousness were the determining factor, it would predict similar percentages in all cases of coreferentiality. Rather, what appears to be crucial is whether the entity referred to by the subject has been established as a discourse topic. If it has not, mentioning it in a complement does not appear to be sufficient. Therefore, it tends to be referred to lexically in the subject position before it can be left unexpressed in an ensuing sentence.

The quantitative results displayed in Table 5.9 oppose coreferentiality to switch reference with the subject, regardless of possible coreferentiality with another argument of the preceding finite verb, and include categorical factors, i.e. focal and contrastive subjects. The results support the validity of the coreferentiality constraint when the speakers are assembled into the three groups.

To examine coreferentiality and ambiguity further, Table 5.10 excludes categorical factors and considers pronouns only in rows (*a*) and pronouns and NPs in rows (*b*).

When the speakers are grouped as in Table 5.10, the results show that, while only Groups 1 and 2 are still sensitive to the ambiguity of the verbal form (cf. Table 5.7), the three groups maintain the constraint on the expression of coreferential subjects. Methodologically it seems appropriate to include NPs in the cross-tabulation, since speakers may be using them to code switch-reference subjects or to disambiguate referents, as well as to exclude subjects that are obligatorily expressed (i.e. focal and contrastive). Table 5.10 shows that the percentages obviously change when NPs are included, but the significance of the correlations is not much altered.

When individual results are examined excluding categorical factors, the results remain quite similar to those of Table 5.5 in terms of relative frequencies and statistical significance; therefore, I do not present them here.

Some speakers show a higher percentage of expressed coreferential subjects as compared to E1 (Group 1) and L19 (Group 2), who have the lowest percentage (excepting A46, a speaker at the bottom of the continuum who has an exceptionally low percentage of expressed subject pronouns; see Table 5.5), and they are not expressing as many switch-reference subjects. At the same time, they are not expressing many pronouns when the verb form is ambiguous, as much as E1 or L19 (70 per cent each), and they are expressing too many with non-ambiguous forms (e.g. L28, H48, D36, R50, R42 in Table 5.5). What could explain this differential degree of relevance between coreferentiality and identity of verbal form in the first- and third-person singular?

Both factors, expression of subject with ambiguous verbal forms and in cases of switch reference, converge towards a disambiguating function. In the case of ambiguous verbal forms, many speakers, but especially those in Group 3 (see Tables 5.5 and 5.10), seem to be relying on context for the disambiguation of subject referents. The differential stages of loss of these constraints may reflect a certain degree of direct transfer from English, inasmuch as English speakers may not be as sensitive to person and number verb inflections as they would be to matters of coreferentiality. This could favour the retention of the coreferentiality constraint as compared to ambiguity.

Note that English allows coreferential subjects of independent sentences to remain unexpressed even if there is an intervening subordinate clause with a switch subject in cases of VP conjunction, as in [48], but requires the expression of a coreferential subject in subordinate clauses, as in [49]. Spanish, by contrast, does not favour an expressed subject in utterances like [49], as I indicate in the translation.

TABLE 5.10. Cross-tabulation of Subject Expression by Group, by Coreferentiality, and by Ambiguity of Verb Form[a]

	Coreferentiality (%)	Difference	Switch (%)	p = <	Ambiguity (%)	Difference	Non-ambiguity (%)	p = <
Group 1:								
(a)	21	11	32	.03	45	24	21	.00
(b)	21	19	40	.00	50	25	25	.00
Group 2:								
(a)	10	21	31	.00	33	14	19	.00
(b)	13	30	43	.00	44	18	26	.00
Group 3:								
(a)	15	14	29	.00	21	–	22	.80
(b)	16	28	44	.00	30	2	32	.59

[a] Focal and contrastive subjects excluded: (a) pronouns only; (b) NPs included.

TABLE 5.11. Cross-tabulation of Coreferential Subjects by Type of Subject and by Speaker Group[a]

| | Coreferential subjects | | | |
| | Personal pronouns | | Noun phrases | |
	No.	%	No.	%
Group 1	33/88	38	0/23	0
Group 2	26/109	24	8/60	13
Group 3	56/154	36	5/98	5
	$p = <.05$		$p = <.03$	

[a] Focal and contrastive subjects excluded.

[48] My mom opened the door carefully when I told her the light was on, ø pushed a chair that was in the way, and suddenly ø saw the thief

[49] My mom always pays cash when *she/*ø* goes shopping
Mi mamá siempre paga al contado cuando *ø/?ella* va de compras

Further support for the sensitivity of English speakers to questions of coreferentiality is provided by the Hudson-Edwards' (1986) study of the grammaticality judgements offered by 303 college students on such complex sentences as those in [50–3].

[50] Joe saw Jane while taking his break

[51] Bob saw Sue while taking her break

[52] Arnold saw Grace while making a fool of himself

[53] Herb saw Susan while making a fool of herself

These authors conclude that three of four principles found to be operative in judging the grammaticality of sixteen complex sentences of the type of [50–3] relate to conditions of coreference between the subject of the subordinate clause and the subject or another argument of the main clause.

I examined the possibility of direct transfer by cross-tabulating only coreferential and non-focal subjects by type of clause, main or subordinate. Unfortunately, the scarcity of the data does not allow valid quantification, but I did not observe any trend towards expressing a higher percentage of subjects in subordinate clauses. There is a trend, albeit weak, towards losing the coreferentiality restriction overall (see S38 and M47 in Table 5.5), regardless of type of clause.

Further support for this analysis, that there is a gradual loss of the coreferentiality restriction, is provided by cross-tabulating expressed coreferential personal pronouns and NPs by speaker group. Table 5.11 presents the results.

Table 5.11 indicates that pronouns and NPs behave quite differently in regard to the coreferentiality constraint. While Group 1 speakers may use a fairly high percentage of coreferential as opposed to switch-reference subjects, they do not produce a single coreferential, non-focal subject NP (0/23). By contrast, these noun phrase subjects do occur in Groups 2 and 3 (13 per cent and 5 per cent).

Although it cannot be denied that knowledge of English may favour the retention of the coreferentiality constraint and the loss of the ambiguity constraint, internal Spanish-language factors must be contemplated as well. Indeed, I am not aware of any study of subject expression that has challenged the validity of the coreferentiality constraint in the Spanish variety studied. By contrast, while the Real Academia (1973: 422), Gili y Gaya (1970: 228), and research by Cameron (1990), Cantero Sandoval (1976), Hochberg (1986), and Silva-Corvalán (1982) argue for a correlation between higher subject expression and verb-form ambiguity, two studies of spoken Spanish, Barrenechea and Alonso (1977) in Buenos Aires and Enríquez (1984) in Madrid find no statistical support for this correlation. Thus there may be grounds for arguing that the ambiguity restriction is lost in a language-contact situation because internal language factors do not strictly require it (note that it is not statistically valid for A9 in Group 1—see Table 5.5).

5.5.2. Discussion

With respect to frequency of subject expression, then, English-dominant bilinguals do not express a higher percentage of subjects overall. Crucially, however, when they express these subjects they do not seem to follow some of the constraints that Spanish dominant bilinguals adhere to.

As for the factors that account for the variable expression of subjects, only two speakers in Group 3 appear to violate the coreferentiality restriction. Other factors, though not discussed in detail in this chapter, remain significant as well. For instance, both focal and contrastive subjects occur in Groups 2 and 3. Furthermore, the semantics of the verb reveals statistically significant correlations in each one of the three groups ($p = <.00$). In all three groups the highest percentage of subject expression correlates with estimative verbs (67 per cent, 53 per cent, 66 per cent, mostly *creer* 'to believe' and *pensar* 'to think'), and with verbs of the type *gustar* 'to like' (56 per cent, 91 per cent, 80 per cent). These types of verb were hypothesized to correlate with higher subject expression because of the implied contrastive situation associated with estimative verbs and, in the case of *gustar* verbs, because of their correlation with new information non-animate subjects.

It is also the case that across groups non-personal pronouns are much more frequently expressed than any personal pronoun, and that plural personal pronouns are expressed quite infrequently (the 2pl form *ustedes* 'you' was not quantified because it occurred only five times in the nearly thirty hours of speech examined), as displayed in Table 5.12. This table includes focal and contrastive subject pronouns, as well as all types of sentence and clause (factors 11 and 12 in Appendix 3).

TABLE 5.12. Cross-tabulation of Type of Subject by Speaker Group

	Group 1		Group 2		Group 3	
	No.	%	No.	%	No.	%
1 sg	58/139	42	58/204	28	78/229	34
2 sg (*tú* + *usted*)	9/32	28	3/12	25	3/30	10
3 sg	24/101	24	35/112	31	60/251	24
1 pl	6/39	15	12/79	15	4/63	6
3 pl	9/36	25	20/126	16	16/123	13
Other pronouns	19/32	59	46/90	51	36/81	44
	$p = <.00$		$p = <.00$		$p = <.00$	

The first-person singular pronoun *yo* 'I' has a much higher percentage of expression than any other pronoun in Group 1, a result which agrees with those shown for other Spanish varieties (cf. Table 5.4). This higher percentage of occurrences of *yo* 'I' has been explained as a consequence of the egocentric nature of verbal communication: by explicitly referring to himself, the speaker fulfils the pragmatic need to keep himself overtly present in the verbal interaction (cf. Morales 1986: ch. 5; egocentricity would not apply in the case of *nosotros* 'we' because in the first person plural the speaker's reference to himself is diffused). If the expression of *yo* 'I' has this pragmatic function, the much lower percentage occurrence of this pronoun in Groups 2 and 3 would constitute evidence of the gradual loss of semantic-pragmatic functions in language-contact situations.

Overall, then, it appears that the restrictions on subject expression shown to be valid for other Spanish varieties remain to a large extent intact in Groups 2 and 3, except for the loss of the morphological ambiguity factor. Otherwise, there is a decrease in the strength of the coreferentiality restriction, and to a certain extent also a weakening of the pragmatic need to refer explicitly to oneself and to the interlocutor. Given the pragmatic functions of expressed subjects in Spanish, the overall lower frequency of subjects in Groups 2 and 3, and the loss of the ambiguity constraint in Group 3, converge to offer some evidence in favour of the hypothesis that predicts the loss of semantic-pragmatic options in secondary languages.

By contrast, the possibility of an association of subject pronouns in English with Spanish verb inflection is not supported (or we would find more subjects expressed with neutralized verb inflections). This is also evidence against an across-the-board type of transfer in a drive for structural parallelism. This specific study has examined a syntactic variable which is pragmatically controlled in Spanish. Pragmatic constraints which do not have contextual alternatives are maintained in East Los Angeles, namely the effect of verb semantics, focality, and contrast. Such constraints as switch reference, the foregrounding of self, and morphological ambiguity, which may be compensated for by means other than subject expression (for instance by the larger linguistic or extra-linguistic context), tend to be lost.

Is there evidence, then, of syntactic permeability in the data examined? The answer is negative if permeability is defined narrowly as *acts of syntactic reception*, i.e. changes which involve not loss but additions to the grammar of a language resulting from the external linguistic influence of a dominant language (Campbell and Muntzel 1989: 190–1). On the other hand, a wider definition of syntactic permeability would include the gradual loss of discourse-pragmatic restrictions, which does produce structures with a slight 'foreign accent', comparable to what happens at the phonetic level:

[54] Una noche me quedé de acuerdo con una amiga. Me iba a ir a quedar a su casa. (*a*) Yo no tenía deseos de salir, (*b*) yo no tenía nada que buscar en la calle. Dejé el niño encargado con una prima y (*c*) yo me salí [to go to her friend's].   (L19,f22,2,ELA82)

One night I agreed to go over to a friend's. I was going to stay at her place. (*a*) I didn't want to go out, (*b*) I had nothing to find in the street. I left my son with a cousin and (*c*) I went [over to her friend's].

According to my own intuitions and those of six Spanish-speaking graduate students whom I consulted, the subject *yo* 'I' is necessary to clarify the subject referent in [54*a*]; it is unnecesary in [54*b*], and unexpected in [54*c*]. [54] contains a series of coreferential subjects. The situations are not explicitly contrastive, nor is there evidence of any other pragmatic function which might justify the occurrences of *yo* in [54*b*, *c*]. Thus, [54] seems to illustrate a less constrained use of subject pronouns, a development which might ultimately lead to subjects becoming basically markers of person and number.

The trend towards a more fixed SVX word order, and at the same time towards a lower frequency of subject expression, two opposing trends if English is taken as the measure for comparison, is further proof that secondary languages do not blindly calque the structures of a superordinate language. Rather, the explanation for these opposing trends is more adequately found in the loss of semantic-pragmatic constraints.

The scenario for the change would involve loss of pragmatic constraints leading to a syntactic change. This may be comparable to phonological changes, which may start with the spread or overgeneralization of one allophonic variant causing the disappearance or loss of another, and eventual restructuring of the phonological system. Weinreich (1974: 14) stated: 'Interference arises when a bilingual identifies a phoneme of the secondary system with one in the primary system and, in reproducing it, subjects it to the phonetic rules of the primary language.' It seems to me that my study offers evidence to extend this statement to the level of syntax, as follows: *Transfer arises when a bilingual (unconsciously) identifies a lexical or syntactic structure of the secondary system with one in the primary system and, in reproducing it, subjects it to the semantic-pragmatic rules of the primary language.*

Consider one further example:

[55] Viajamos nosotros por tren y conocimos en el viaje bastante gente. (*a*) *Y una señora que - nos pusimos a platicar ella tenía un bebé.* Y entonces el niño estaba enfermo. Ya no me acuerdo exactamente. Se desmayaba y ella estaba preocupada y lo tenía con medicinas.   (L28,f37,2,ELA23)

We travelled by train and met a lot of people. *And a lady that - we started talking with she had a baby.* And then the child was sick. I don't remember exactly. He fainted and she was worried and was giving him medicines.

Is the italicized structure in [55] a case of syntactic transfer? Is it a violation of a constraint on subject pronoun expression? Note that two coreferential constituents, an NP, *una señora* 'a lady', and a pronoun, *ella* 'she', may both qualify as subjects of *tenía* 'had' in [55a]. This would certainly be a *new* construction in Spanish. This language allows NPs that are prosodically clearly left dislocated to be coreferential with the subject, but not two (as it were) subjects in the same sentence, French style: *Mon père il est venu* 'My dad he has arrived'.

Note as well that Spanish does not introduce new referents into discourse in subject position. The strategy consists in using *haber* 'there to be':

[56] *Y había una señora que nos pusimos a platicar;* (y) *ella* tenía un . . .

And there was a lady we started talking with; (and) she had a . . .

Indeed, Ocampo (1989: 171–2) has shown that brand-new and brand-new anchored referents are introduced as postverbal NP arguments of the single-valency verbs *haber* 'there to be', *estar* 'to be', and *existir* 'to exist', a fact which, according to Ocampo, responds to the maxim proposed by Lambrecht (cited in Ocampo, p. 172): 'do not introduce a new referent and talk about it in the same clause'.

On the other hand, colloquial non-standard English has a similar 'French-style' construction:

[57] . . . and *this lady she* had a baby. And the baby was sick . . .

Based on the existence of examples like [57], could [55] be considered a case of syntactic transfer, or is it rather an instance of discourse-function transfer, the introduction of a non-salient new referent in the subject position? It appears to be both: a new structure and its related function. Yet, what is the frequency of this particular 'act of syntactic reception'? In approximately twenty hours of speech from fifteen speakers examined for this study, there are only two examples, both produced by the same speaker (L28,f37,2; see [53] in Chapter 6). This is most probably a nonce borrowing with no immediate consequences for the syntactic system of Spanish.

5.6. Conclusion

I summarize my observations about syntactic permeability as follows:

(i) Transfer may occur when bilinguals (unconsciously) identify a surface string in the secondary system with one in the primary system and, in using it, subject it to the discourse-pragmatic rules of the primary language. This shows that languages are permeable at the discourse-pragmatic level. A similar conclusion is reached by Prince (1992) based on a study of *dos*-sentences in Yiddish. According to Prince, this Yiddish construction does not alter Germanic syntax but replicates the discourse function of Slavic *eto*-sentences, i.e. the structuring of the proposition into two parts, focus followed by presupposition (cf. *it-cleft* constructions in English).

(ii) The intensity of discourse-pragmatic transfer may be primarily determined by socio-cultural parameters rather than by language structure. This observation is based on the attested fact that longer duration of family residence in the USA and reduced domains of use of Spanish correlate positively with a higher degree of simplification or loss of discourse-pragmatic rules.

(iii) Transfer may occur at the lexico-syntactic level when bilinguals (unconsciously) identify a lexical item in the secondary language with one in the primary language and subject it to the subcategorization of the item in the primary language. I consider this an instance of lexico-syntactic permeability, and discuss it in Chapter 6.

(iv) The syntactic permeability of grammars is at first evident only in nonce syntactic borrowings, i.e. impermanent and occasional instances of immediate disturbances of the surface syntactic structures/strings of a language. Given sufficient time depth and the appropriate socio-cultural conditions surrounding contact, nonce syntactic borrowings may become incorporated in the system of the borrowing language. An instance of this type of outcome may be illustrated by the grammatical convergence exhibited by four languages in contact in Kupwar (India), two Dravidian languages (Kannada and Telugu), and two Indo-Aryan languages (Urdu and Marathi) (Gumperz and Wilson 1977).

(v) Under conditions of normal transmission (Thomason and Kaufman 1988), nonce syntactic transfer will spread with enormous difficulty in the language system and across speakers (if at all; see my brief discussion of Gumperz and Wilson's study below and also Chapter 7). The syntactic system of grammars is remarkably impermeable to foreign influence.

Considering the fact that I have dealt with two European languages which have many surface similarities, and that the contact situation is uniquely favourable to the 'immigrant' language (the uninterrupted flow of large numbers of Spanish-speaking immigrants, for instance), my conclusions would appear rather bold. Indeed, in order to reach conclusions of convincing generality, it would be necessary to carry out close studies of dissimilar as well as similar languages in comparable contact situations. One such study has been conducted by Mougeon and Beniak (1991); they also note that direct ('overt' in their terminology) grammatical transfer is rare, but the situation they examine also involves two European languages, English and French in Ontario.

My observations find some encouraging support, furthermore, in Weinreich's remark, based on a survey of a considerable number of unrelated bilingual and multilingual situations, that foreign grammatical elements are only very rarely incorporated in the language as a code (1974: 44).

On the other hand, Gumperz and Wilson (1977: 151) argue that their study of Indo-Aryan/Dravidian language contact in India offers evidence 'that borrowing extends to all aspects of the grammatical systems'. Note, however, that these authors study the outcome of contact that has existed for more than six centuries in the case of Kannada and Marathi, and that Urdu-speakers have been in the region of Kupwar for more than three centuries. In addition, Gumperz and Wilson conclude that 'almost all the changes can be interpreted as *reductions* or *generalizations* that *simplify* surface structure in relation to underlying categories and relationships' (164; my emphasis) It appears, then, that 'the creole-like' present varieties of Kannada, Marathi, Urdu, and Telugu spoken in Kupwar have not really borrowed or introduced new syntactic rules into their systems, but rather essentially lost existing variants and retained or extended those that paralleled structures in the other languages. If this were so, the Kupwar contact situation would offer strong evidence from dissimilar languages in support of my observations. If, on the other hand, the grammar of the 'creole-like' varieties is radically different from that of the corresponding standard varieties, it would be necessary to investigate at what point in the centuries of development of these varieties these radical changes were introduced.

In sum, it seems to me that, if Thomason and Kaufman's (1988: 14) statement that 'any linguistic feature can be transferred from any language to any other language' refers to the introduction of foreign elements into a language code, it needs to be qualified with respect to syntactic features as follows: under conditions of normal transmission, any linguistic feature from language S may end up being present in language F after a long process of step-by-step changes in language F such that at any given step the change involved will not constitute a radical modification of the system of F but rather the extension of an already existing syntactic variant (i.e. the modification is compatible with the structure of the borrowing language). It seems to me that this chain-like process may advance when a syntactic variant loses its status of 'marked' (in terms of frequency and/or pragmatic function), thus opening the door for further structural changes to take place. I must note, however, that I have examined a rather narrow range of syntactic phenomena—the possibility of null arguments and word order—and that I consider verb subcategorization a lexico-semantic question, albeit with syntactic consequences (see Chapter 6).

6

Conflicting Loyalties

6.1. Introduction

WEINREICH (1974: 68) proposes a definition of language shift as the change from the everyday, traditional use of one language to that of another. He also proposes the term 'language loyalty' to describe a state of mind in which a language, in opposition to other languages, is assigned a high value by its speakers, who are driven to defend this language from foreign interference and/or from an imminent language shift. Language loyalty is defined 'as a principle . . . in the name of which people will rally themselves and their fellow speakers consciously and explicitly to resist changes in either the functions of their language (as a result of a language shift) or in the structure or vocabulary (as a consequence of interference)' (99).

I have no evidence (as could have been provided by extended observation or direct questioning, for instance) that the speakers included in this study consciously or explicitly resist transfer from English or shift to English. Most of them have expressed, however, spontaneously in conversation or in response to direct questions, positive attitudes towards Spanish as well as willingness to maintain it and pass it on to their descendants. I refer to these expressions as 'acts of loyalty' and examine them in this chapter. This scrutiny shows that acts of loyalty are in conflict with uncommitted behaviour (i.e. lack of commitment to turn positive attitudes into action) in most of the speakers in Groups 2 and 3. In addition, the preceding chapters have offered evidence of transfer, although mainly of the indirect type. In this chapter, I present and briefly discuss uses of lexical items by bilinguals in Groups 2 and 3 which deviate from the norms of Group 1 speakers. I apply the phrase 'acts of shifting' to these uses because they appear to be the consequence of direct transfer of forms and/or form meanings from English. Acts of shifting are apparently in conflict with acts of loyalty, but in fact they seem to me to represent a successful strategy for the maintenance of Spanish among second- and third-generation immigrants in Los Angeles.

In Chapter 1 (p. 4) I listed four types of phenomenon as illustrations of potential transfer, not all of which are necessarily present in every case of contact. Briefly, these include: (1) The replacement of a form in language S with a form from language F, or the incorporation from language F into language S of a form previously absent in S. This constitutes an instance of direct transfer. (2) The incorporation of the meaning of a form R from language F, which may be part of the meaning of a form P in S, into another form, structurally or semantically similar to R, in system S. This is an instance of direct semantic transfer. (3) The higher frequency of use of a form in language S, determined on the basis of a comparison with more conservative internal community norms, in contexts where a partially corresponding form in language F is used either categorically or pre-ferentially. (4) The loss of a category or a form in language S which does not have a parallel category or form in the system of F. (3) and (4) are instances of indirect transfer.

The preceding chapters, however, have shown evidence against direct influence from English on a number of aspects of Spanish grammar: patterns of simplification of the tense–mood–aspect system, omission and simplification of verbal clitic pro-nouns, non-expression of the complementizer *que*, extension of *estar*, expression of subjects, subject position relative to the verb. None of these phenomena constitute a clear illustration of transfer of types (1) or (4), i.e. no replacement or incorpor-ation of forms and no loss of categories are explainable as the result of contact specifically with the English language. Rather, these modifications, when they occur, seem to be the consequence of processes of simplification constrained by the grammar as well as by the social environment and reduced communicative functions of the affected language.

The extension of discourse-pragmatic functions discussed in Chapter 5 (syntac-tic permeability of type a, p. 135), on the other hand, corresponds to the type of transfer (2) that I describe as the incorporation of the meaning of a form R from language F into a structurally or semantically similar form in system S. At the syntactic level, this type of transfer does not appear to be frequent. By contrast, the loss of semantic and pragmatic constraints (which in some cases may be argued to be of type 4) is evident in the linguistic phenomena examined, but the motivation for this loss cannot be definitely ascribed to direct influence from English. Indirect transfer, apparent in the higher frequency of use of parallel forms (3), is the only type decidedly supported by the data examined in the previous chapters.

Where, then, do we find evidence of direct transfer of types 1 and 2? As already suggested in Chapter 1, evidence of direct transfer abounds at the level of the lexicon, which is affected in various manners. In sections 6.2 and 6.3, I discuss the different types of replacement and incorporation of lexical forms and/or meanings and their occurrence across the Spanish proficiency continuum. Sections 6.4 and 6.5 discuss 'acts of conflicting loyalties', i.e. both spontaneous and elicited attitudes towards Spanish.

6.2. Acts of Shifting: Modelling

Weinreich (1974: 47) identifies three types of lexical interference: transfer of form (presumably with their corresponding meaning), transfer of meaning only, and transfer of form and meaning in the case of compound lexical items. He further subdivides this third type (pp. 50–3) into three more groups, one of which he refers to as *semantic extensions* or *loan translations*, defined as 'reproduction in terms of equivalent native words [which] can be carried out with compounds, phrases, and even larger units such as proverbs' (p. 50). Both Otheguy (1993), and Otheguy *et al.* (1989) (OGF) show the terminological and conceptual problems involved in Weinreich's classification. Furthermore, Otheguy (1993) forcibly argues that Weinreich's notion of loan translation was not properly developed to account for modelling of compound lexical items: 'by defining loan translations as unusual combinations of words, Weinreich created a theoretical impasse in which it became impossible to distinguish between unusual things to say and unusual linguistic means with which to say them' (p. 36).

In view of the difficulties posed in particular by Weinreich's analysis of possible cases of multiple-word modelling, OGF propose to set these aside, and to deal with individual words only. Single-word transfers must further be differentiated from *switches* to English. OGF do this by applying a simpler version of the model developed for this purpose by Poplack (1987) and Poplack *et al.* (1989). These authors have established a set of criteria to distinguish switches from borrowings, e.g. level of phonological assimilation, level of social integration, discourse function, frequency of occurrence. Of these, OGF take into account the phonological factor only (they state that the investigation of the other criteria is beyond the scope of their paper), and count all phonologically integrated single-word items as cases of transferring.

Thus, their classification distinguishes between items that preserve English phonology (single-word switches), and those that have been adapted to Spanish phonology (single-word borrowings). In this latter group, they differentiate between *loans*, the transferring of forms with their meanings (e.g. *puchar*, which replaces *empujar* 'to push'), and *calques*, the transferring of meanings only (e.g. *grados* 'degrees' extends its meaning to incorporate one of the meanings of English *grades* 'marks showing a student's level of achievement').

OGF's is a well thought-out and useful taxonomy of borrowings that allows them to quantify the rate of increase of 'anglicisms' between two generations of Cuban-Americans (residing in the town of West New York, New Jersey), as well as to conclude that second-generation Cubans use numerous 'duplicating calquewords that displace existing, traditional Spanish message formulations' (*grados* displaces *notas*, for instance), an indication that their command of the Spanish lexicon is diminishing. OGF's classification into loans and calques corresponds to Otheguy's (1993) distinction in terms of transferring and modelling, and it corresponds also to the possible types of transfer phenomenon that I describe under types 1 and 2 above (see also Chapter 1). Therefore, I adopt the distinction between additions to the inventory of the impacted variety (i.e. loans, transferring, type 1 transfer) and (semantic) modifications of the existing inventory (calques, modelling, type 2 transfer) in my discussion of lexical transfer, and extend it, with some adjustments, to apply to multiple-word cases of loans and calques. My main interest is to identify and discuss some types of single or multiple-word calque that are attested at different points in the bilingual proficiency continuum.

Otheguy (1993) correctly notes that the 'unusual combinations of words' that are generally considered loan translations form a heterogeneous set including (*a*) items that do not constitute a linguistic innovation of any kind, but rather combinations which at most represent a cultural or pragmatic innovation (e.g. *El día de dar gracias* 'Thanksgiving Day' and *máquina de contestar* 'answering machine', instead of *contestador automático*, lit.: automatic answerer), as well as (*b*) items in which the innovation results from the establishment of novel metaphorical conceptualizations. An example of this last group is *llamar para atrás* 'to call back', where *atrás* 'behind/to the back/backwards' is claimed to have been metaphorically extended to incorporate the concept of repetition. Nevertheless, Otheguy admits that the English construction (to go/pay/send/ back, etc.) may have motivated the metaphorical extension of the concept of behindness to the temporal notion of repetition in Spanish. I return to this example later.

Based on an analysis of the Los Angeles data, I distinguish the following types of what are generally considered to be borrowings:

6.2.1. Single-Word Loans

This category consists of the transferring of forms with their meanings (e.g. *bil* from 'bill', in the sense of payment owed, *mapear* or *mopear* from 'to mop', *puchar* from 'to push', *sinque* from 'sink', *so* from 'so' (*so* is a loan that replaces the Spanish conjunction *así que* even in the speech of Group 1 speakers. It is a stable, widespread loan in LA Spanish), *suiche* from 'switch', *troca* or *troque* from 'truck', all attested in Groups 1, 2, and 3).

6.2.2. Single-Word Calques

This category consists of the transferring of meanings into an already existing lexical item (e.g. *parientes* 'relatives' extends its meaning to incorporate the meaning of English *parents*, attested in Group 3). Many other single-word calques are attested in the three groups, for instance *aplicación* 'application', including making a request (Span.[1] *solicitud* 'application', in the sense of making a request), *grados* 'grades' (marks showing a student's level of achievement) (Span. *notas*), *papel* '(news)paper' (Span. *diario/periódico*), *moverse* 'to move [to another house]' (Span. *cambiarse/mudarse de casa*), *carpeta* 'carpet' (Span. *alfombra/moqueta*), etc.

6.2.3. Multiple-Word Calques that Do Not Alter Semantic and/or Grammatical Features

Examples are *días de semana* 'weekdays' (Span. *días de trabajo*), *máquina de contestar* 'answering machine' (Span. *contestador automático*), *patio de juegos* 'playground'

---

[1] The abbreviation Span. used in the examples stands for general standard or popular Latin American Spanish.

(Span. *patio (de escuela)*), *tarjeta de plástico* 'plastic' (i.e. credit card, Span. *tarjeta/ tarjeta de crédito*).

In what follows, I have chosen to disregard single-word borrowings and the types of 'unusual combination' that do not alter the semantic and syntactic resources of Spanish (cf. Otheguy, 1993), except to note here that they are attested in the speech samples from all the speakers under study. Instead, I focus on two types of calque: calques of bound collocations, idioms, and proverbs, and lexico-syntactic calques (defined in Sections 6.2, 4–5 below), that is, on multiple-word calques that have lexico-semantic and grammatical consequences on the replica (or borrowing) language.

It will be obvious to the reader that some of the combinations included as lexico-syntactic calques could perhaps have been considered a bound collocation or at times even an idiom. Indeed, the borderline between all these forms of collocations is often rather tenuous, as is also the type of transfer and the effect that it may have on the replica language.[2] This section is, therefore, more an approximation to the difficult question of multiple-word modelling than a definitive proposal for its solution.

6.2.4. *Calques of Bound Collocations, Idioms, and Proverbs*

A bound collocation, idiom, or proverb from the source language is reproduced exactly with lexical units from the replica language. The calque may alter semantic and/or collocational features of the replica language, but these modifications remain restricted to the phrase in question. (This section does not discuss proverbs, which are not attested in the Los Angeles data.)

I am acutely aware of the difficulties involved in the definition and identification of collocations and idioms (see e.g. lengthy discussions in Cruse 1986; Jackson 1988; Ruhl 1989). Cruse defines the term 'idiom' as 'a lexical complex which is semantically simplex' (p. 37), and illustrates it with *to kick the bucket, to pull someone's leg, to spill the beans.* The term *collocation*, on the other hand, is semantically transparent (i.e. divisible into semantic constituents) and it refers to strings of lexical items which regularly co-occur. Bound collocations, like *foot the bill* and *curry favour*, are idiom-like in that their 'constituents do not like to be separated' (Cruse 1986: 41), yet they are not idioms because they are, like collocations, semantically transparent. However, the semantic transparency of 'foot' or 'curry' is debatable, since it seems that neither is otherwise used in the way in which they are in the collocations 'foot the bill' or 'curry favour'.

Many word combinations may not be classified neatly into one or another type, but the question of precise classification does not concern me, since the borderline between a bound collocation and an idiom seems to me difficult to resolve. What I consider important about the calquing of either bound collocations or idioms

---

[2] Similar difficulties have probably stopped Otheguy *et al.* (1989: 43–4) from examining multiple-word transfers, and may have also prompted their observation that 'the only items in which clear evidence of modeling can be discerned are individual words'.

is that they are comparable to a single-word calque. This is because, even though they consist of more than one word, in practice they display the internal cohesion expected of single words. Thus, the internal arrangement of words in a bound collocation or idiom calqued by a replica language might in principle violate the syntactic rules of this language, yet I do not consider it a syntactic transfer or innovation unless there is clear evidence that the new pattern is being extended beyond the specific context of the calque. It is quite likely in principle, however, that innovative syntactic patterns introduced in bound collocations or idioms may in time become context-free and productive, in a manner similar to what has been proposed for the borrowing of bound morphemes (cf. Weinreich 1974: 31).

Consider [1–3], attested in Groups 2 and 3, which illustrate what may be bound collocations or idioms:

[1] Estoy quebrada 'I'm broke'   (L19,f22,2,ELA54)
    Span.: No tengo un peso/Estoy en bancarrota
    lit.: (I) don't have one *peso*/(I) am in bankrupt

[2] OK. Eso está bien conmigo   (R17,f21,2,ELA3)
    OK. That's fine with me
    Span.: OK. (Eso) está bien
           OK. Me parece bien
    lit.: OK. (It) to-me seems fine

[3] So él sabrá si se *cambia su mente*.   (D39,f28,3,ELA42)
    lit.: so he'll know if (he) 'se' *changes his mind*[3]
    Span.: Así que él sabrá si *cambia de opinión*.
    lit.: so that he'll know if (he) *changes of opinion*

In Spanish, the verb *quebrar* may mean 'to go bankrupt', and it may be used as in [4]. The corresponding adjectival expression is *en bancarrota* or *en quiebra* (*María está en quiebra/en bancarrota* 'Mary is bankrupt'). The adjective *quebrada* 'broken' refers to fracture, not to financial status as it does in [1], which replicates the English collocation. It has been brought to my attention, however, that in Mexican Spanish the state of being broke may be attributed to a human entity with the verb *andar* 'to go around' (*Ando quebrado* 'I'm broke'). Thus, it is possible that the combination in [1] may involve the substitution of *estar* 'to be' for *andar* (another instance of the extension of *estar* discussed in Chapter 4) rather than the calque of a bound collocation.

[4] *Esa empresa/María quebró/ha quebrado.*
    That company/Mary broke (went bankrupt)/has broken

As indicated by the general Spanish interpretations, the 'unusual' elements in [2] are *conmigo* 'with me' and the expression of the subject *eso* 'that', which though

---

[3] The use of *se* in [3] reflects an independent phenomenon of extension of reflexive-type verbs (see Ch. 4).

possible, is highly unlikely to be said. Example [2] is a word-for-word translation of the corresponding English construction.

The word *mente* 'mind' in [3] may be said to have extended its meaning from 'memory, recollection, intelligence' to incorporate one of the senses of *mind* in English, namely 'opinion, view, intention'. No examples are attested of the type of [5], for instance, another possible context for the use of *mente* 'mind' with its extended meaning.

[5] *Soy de mente diferente*
    I'm of a different mind

In general Spanish, the sense of 'I'm of a different mind' would be expressed with *tener ideas/opiniones diferentes* 'to have different ideas/opinions' or *pensar de manera diferente* 'to think differently'. The semantic extension of *mente* 'mind', then, occurs only in the bound collocation *cambiar su mente* 'to change one's mind'.

6.2.5. Lexico-syntactic Calques

These are multiple-word calques that alter semantic and/or grammatical features of the replica language. Furthermore, these calques seem clearly separable into six classes on the basis of the semantic and/or grammatical effect of the transfer on Spanish.

6.2.5.1. Type 1

A multiple-word unit which reproduces one in the source language brings about a change in the meaning of a word in the replica language. The modified word with its extended meaning or meanings does not remain restricted to be used in only one set combination:

[6] Es un modo de *tener un buen tiempo.*   (D39,f28,3,ELA42)
    lit.: (it)'s one way to *have a good time*
    Span.: Es un modo de *pasar un buen momento/pasarlo bien*
    lit.: (it)'s one way to *pass a good moment/pass it well*

[7] . . . pero cuando llegó el *tiempo* que ellos ya querían sus carritos   (H48, m39,3,ELA23)
    lit.: but when arrived the *time* that they already wanted their cars
    Span.: pero cuando llegó el *momento*/la *hora* que ellos ya querían sus carritos
    lit.: but when arrived the *moment*/the *hour* . . .

[8] porque otro *tiempo* - - ando en el carro - - y empecé a notar que no estaba bien   (L19,f22,2,ELA54)
    lit.: because another *time* - - (I) go in the car - - and (I) started to notice that (it) was not fine

Span.: porque otra *vez*/en otra *ocasión* . . .
lit.: because another *instance*/on another *occasion* . . .

The word *tiempo* is quite vulnerable in a Spanish–English contact situation because many but not all the uses of English 'time' overlap with it. This situation probably favours the extension of *tiempo*, basically a durative mass concept in Spanish, to incorporate the notion of one specific point: 'one of several instances, an occasion, an hour, a moment' ([6–8]). In Spanish the phrase *buen/mal tiempo*, in the singular, can only mean 'good/bad weather'. The word *tiempo* may occur in the plural form, as in *buenos/malos tiempos*, with the meaning of 'good/bad periods of time', i.e. it retains the meaning of duration.

The often quoted case of *para atrás* is also an illustration of a lexico-syntactic calque of type 1. The phrase *para atrás* collocates with a number of verbs of movement in Spanish: *mirar para atrás* 'look back', *pasar (X) para atrás* 'pass (X) to the back', *caminar para atrás* 'to walk backwards'. In these collocations, *atrás* conveys its general, standard, traditional locational meaning of 'to the back, behind, back, backwards'.

In Los Angeles Spanish, as in all other varieties of US Spanish, *para atrás* has extended its meaning to include not strictly 'repetition' as Otheguy (1993) suggests, but rather 'in reply' or 'in return', which *back* has in such English verb phrases as 'to call back', 'to come back', 'to send back'. The extension of *para atrás* to include the concept of repetition or return allows it to occur with verbs that did not allow this combinational possibility. Examples attested in my data include *dar para atrás* 'to give back', *llamar para atrás* 'to call back', *pagar para atrás* 'to pay back', *decir para atrás* 'to answer back', *regresar a alguien para atrás* 'to make someone go home', *ir para atrás* 'to go back', *traer a alguien para atrás* 'to bring someone back'. If the extension of the meaning of *para atrás* were attested in Spanish varieties clearly not in contact with English (to my knowledge, it has not been attested), one could more forcefully argue that the mechanism for the change was purely a metaphorical extension. If not, transfer of meaning from English would seem to be a more appropriate explanation.

6.2.5.2. Type 2

A multiple-word unit which reproduces one in the source language brings about a change in combinational restrictions related to, among other things, animacy of the constituents, tense or aspect of the verb, and other semantic constraints on the constituents of the corresponding construction in the replica language. The calque affects the meaning of a word included in this construction. Consider [9, 10], produced by speakers in Group 2:

[9] Y tu carro que compraste, ¿cómo te gusta?   (H22,m21,2,ELA54)
   lit.: and your car that (you) bought, *how to-you pleases?*
   Span.: Y tu carro que compraste, ¿*te gusta?*

lit.: and your car that (you) bought, *to-you pleases?*
and the car you bought, *how do you like it?*

[10] ¿*Cómo te gustó* [la película]?   (A20,f19,2,ELA29)
     lit.: *how to-you pleased* [the movie]?
     Span.: ¿*Te gustó* [la película]?
     lit.: *to-you pleased* [the movie]?
     how did you like it [the movie]?

In Spanish the interrogative word of manner *cómo* does not have the meaning of 'to what extent, amount, or degree' that *how* may have in English. Therefore, as indicated in the general Spanish versions, questions about the extent to which something is or was liked, as in [9, 10], should not include the interrogative word *cómo*, since *cómo*-questions must be answered with a description of the manner in which the situation obtains. This interlinguistic difference in the meaning of *cómo* and *how* accounts for the acceptability of [11*b, c*] as possible answers to [11*a*] in English, for the unacceptability of the corresponding exchange, [12*a, b*], in Spanish, and for the acceptability of [12*c*], which describes in what manner or condition soup is liked, as an answer to [12*a*].

[11] (*a*) How do you like the soup?
    (*b*) I like it, it's good
    (*c*) I like it very hot

[12] (*a*) ¿Cómo te gusta la sopa?
    (*b*) *Me gusta, está buena
        I like it, it's good
    (*c*) Me gusta bien caliente
        I like it very hot

It is clear, then, that the syntactic structure *cómo X gustar Y* exists in Spanish, but since *cómo* does not include the meaning 'to what extent', its distribution is more restricted than English in this respect. Furthermore, neither English nor Spanish may ask about the manner in which a specific *Y* is or was liked. When *cómo* or 'how' is used with the sense of 'in what manner', certain restrictions are imposed on the semantics of the subject (*Y*), which must be non-specific, and on the aspect of the verb, which must be imperfective (see the unacceptability of [13*c*] in both languages). The less restricted meaning of *cómo* in LA Spanish results in less restricted syntax, but the appropriate answer refers to the extent of the liking ([13*b*]), not to the manner ([13*c*]). The answer given to the question in [9], expanded here as [13*a, b*], illustrates; [13*c*], unacceptable in English, is not attested in LA Spanish either.

[13] (*a*) Y tu carro que compraste, ¿*cómo te gusta?*   (H22,m21,2,ELA54)
        and the car you bought, *how do you like it?*

(*b*) Mi carro me encanta   (L19,f22,2,ELA54)
I love my car

(*c*) *Me gusta amplio
*I like it spacious

The semantically less restricted meaning of *cómo* 'how' in LA Spanish is also extended to a declarative context, to the complement of *saber* 'to know'. Here again, the *cómo* in the complement of *saber* 'to know' refers to the manner of a specific situation, as in [14*a*], which could be appropriately followed up by instructions on 'how to', as in [14*b*]. Note, however, that the wider meaning of *how* in English allows it to occur with *to know* when only a general knowledge or skill required to do something is being referred to, as in [15]. While in general Spanish [15] must be translated without *cómo* 'how', this complementizer is acceptable in LA Spanish, as shown by [16].

[14] (*a*) María no sabe *cómo* irse a la universidad
       Mary doesn't know *how* to go to the university

     (*b*) Dile que tome el bus 73
       Tell her to take bus 73

[15] He doesn't know *how* to read yet
     No sabe ∅ leer todavía

[16] Sí sabía *como* hablar español   (D39,f28,3,ELA42)
     lit.: yes knew-3sg *how* speak-Inf Spanish
     Span.: Sí sabía ∅ hablar español
     He did know *how* to speak Spanish

Another example of a lexico–syntactic calque of type 2 is offered by sentences related to measurements of weight, age, etc.:

[17] Mi padre *es* seis pies [de altura]
     lit.: My dad *is* six feet [tall]
     Span.: Mi padre *mide* seis pies
     lit.: My dad *measures* six feet

In Spanish *ser* may select a predicate nominal with the feature [+ specific unit of measurement] only if the subject encodes the measured category (*El largo es cinco pies* 'The length is five feet', *Los años de estudio son cinco* 'The years of study are five', *La edad para empezar es seis años* 'The age to begin is six years old'). Calquing the use of *to be* to attribute a specific unit of measurement to any type of entity brings about the loss of a selectional restriction on the subject NP. Thus in LA Spanish one finds such examples as [17], with the copula *ser* 'to be' relating a specific unit of weight, age, or height to a human subject referent. Examples [18–19] illustrate further:

[18] [la casa] ahora *es* cien mil o ciento veinte mil dólares   (H22,m21,2,ELA11)
     Span.: . . . *cuesta* 'costs'

Now it [the house] *is* one hundred or one hundred and twenty thousand dollars

[19] [la planta] ya *es* como dos, tres años   (V21,f18,2,ELA67)
Span.: . . . *tiene* 'has'
By now it [the plant] *is* about two, three years old

6.2.5.3. *Type 3*

A prepositional phrase in the source language is reproduced with lexical units of the replica language, but the preposition is not the one used in the replica language (e.g. in popular or standard Latin American Spanish). Rather, it corresponds to the preposition used in the parallel source-language phrase (e.g. in English).

Cases of missing prepositions and of uses of prepositions that do not comply with the norm in popular or standard Latin American Spanish are fairly frequent in the data from Groups 2 and 3, an expected condition given the semantic complexity of prepositions in Spanish (as well as in English). The fact that almost every sentence contains a preposition, and thus a possible site for 'an error' or deviation from the norm, appears to be a strong factor in creating the impression, exaggerated in my view, that the syntax of those in Groups 2 and 3 is quite different from those in Group 1. In any case, in most cases these modifications cannot be attributed to direct influence from English, as shown by [20–2].

[20] y ∅ la mañana habló ∅ el trabajo   (A46,f31,3,ELA20)
lit.: and ∅ the morning spoke-3sg ∅ the work
Span.: y *en* la mañana llamó *del* trabajo
and *in* the morning he called *from* work

[21] ¿Qué son tus planes *del* futuro?   (R24,m20,2,ELA50)
lit.: what are your plans *of*-the future?
Span.: ¿Cuáles son tus planes *para* el futuro?
What are your plans *for* the future?

[22] ya empezó su tercer año de medicina *con* UCLA   (R24,m20,2,ELA50)
lit.: just started his third year of medicine *with* UCLA
Span.: ya empezó su tercer año de medicina *en* UCLA
he's just started his third year of medicine *at* UCLA[4]

There are, on the other hand, a number of instances in which the [preposition + NP] in English may be considered a *collocation* (cf. Cruse 1986: 40), in the sense that either only one preposition is allowed to occur in that particular construction or one of several possible prepositions is the one that most frequently co-occurs with the noun or NP in question.[5] If the corresponding construction in LA Spanish

---

[4] A native speaker of English informs me that it would be possible to say '*with* UCLA' in a different discourse context, i.e. if the person had been studying at another university and had changed to UCLA. This is not the case in [22].

[5] I conducted an informal survey of 9 native non-Hispanic speakers of English to examine preposi-tional phrase collocations. These native speakers were told that prepositions included such 'little words

reproduces the English preposition either instead of the expected one in Spanish or when no preposition is required in Spanish, I consider it an instance of a lexico-syntactic calque:

[23] para llegar allá *en tiempo*   (B33,f19,3,ELA29)
      lit.: to arrive there *on time*
      Span.: para llegar allá *a tiempo*

[24] ella estaba *en sus rodillas*   (A20,f19,2,ELA29)
      lit.: she was *on her knees*
      Span.: ella estaba *de rodillas*
      lit.: she was *of* knees

[25] Yo voy a una parte *en los jueves*   (V21,f18,2,ELA16)
      lit.: I go to a place *on the Thursdays*
      Span.: Yo tengo un compromiso ∅ *los jueves*
      I have a commitment *on Thursdays*

[26] no había niños *a cuidar*   (M47,f33,3,ELA52)
      lit.: no there were children *to take care*
      Span.: no había niños *para/que cuidar*
      there were no children *to take care of*

[27] y le echaron como veinte pescados *a* una vez   (R24m20,2,ELA50)
      lit.: . . . *at* one time
      Span.: . . . *de* una vez
      lit.: *of* one time
      and they threw him like about twenty fish *at* once

6.2.5.4. *Type 4*

The subcategorization of a verb in the source language is transferred to the corresponding one in the replica language. Changes in subcategorization occur when the replica language (*a*) reproduces the syntactic-semantic relationship of the arguments of the verb in the source language ([29–34]); (*b*) leaves the required preposition out when none is required in the source language ([35]); (*c*) reproduces the preposition that collocates with the source-language verb with a formally and/

as to, at, under, over, in, on, from, for, above, with, against, without, etc.'. I then asked them to tell me the first preposition that came to mind after hearing the examples I would give them, and illustrated the 'test' with a couple of examples. The phrases given as stimulus and the prepositions supplied most frequently by the speakers consulted were the following (number of times is given in parentheses): in (9) the room, on (8) the road, between (4) you and me, *on* (6) *time*, with (4)/to (4) care, with (4) the baby, in (6) school, *on* (5) *his knees*, in (8) January, on (5) his neck, on (4) the corner, for (5) you, *to* (4)/ *on* (4) *the left*, with (8) sugar, *on* (8) *vacation*, in (4) the stars, *on* (8) *Sunday*. I was particularly interested in the 5 examples italicized. This informal survey supports my claim that these words are strongly associated with the preposition *on* in English, while in Spanish they collocate more frequently with prepositions that do not usually translate as *on* (e.g. *a* 'at', *de* 'of'). Group 2 and 3 speakers, however, frequently use *en* 'on/in' rather than *a* or *de*.

or semantically similar one in the replica language, whether or not a preposition is required in this language ([36, 37]); or (*d*) reproduces the valency of a given verb in the source language ([38]).

The most quoted example of this type of lexico-syntactic calque in books and articles dealing with English influence on Spanish concerns the verb *gustar* 'to like'. In Spanish, *gustar* 'to like' is subcategorized for a subject with the semantic role of 'theme' or 'patient' and an indirect object (introduced by *a* and with an obligatory coreferential verbal clitic *le/les*) which has the semantic role of 'experiencer'. The opposite syntactic-semantic relationship holds in modern English,[6] as the examples below show.

[28] A nadie$_i$ le$_i$ gusta ella$_q$ where i = IO = experiencer
                                                         q = subject = theme

lit.: to no one$_i$ him$_i$ likes she$_q$
No one$_i$ likes her$_q$ where i = subject = experiencer
                                                         q = DO = theme

Speakers in Groups 2 and 3 calque the syntactic-semantic structure of *to like*, although not exactly. Indeed, while the experiencer is coded in the nominative as a subject, in many of the examples attested in the data the theme is not in the accusative as in English. Instead, it is coded as an indirect object, i.e. it is introduced by *a* (variably in the case of infinitival clauses), and it may appear with a coreferential dative Cl, as illustrated in [29–32]. The only instances of exact calquing, i.e. the theme coded as a direct object, with no coreferential Cl and no *a*, are produced by the two speakers at the bottom of the continuum ([33, 34]).

[29] Se llama la Sra X, pero naden [*sic*] le gusta - a ella[7]   (V21,f18,2,ELA16)
     lit.: *se* calls the Mrs X, but no one him/her - likes to her
     Span.: Se llama la Sra X, pero a nadie le gusta - ella
     Her name is Mrs X, but no one likes her

[30] Los cocodrilos les gustaron *a* matar   (R24,m20,2,ELA50)
     lit.: the crocodiles them-liked-3pl to kill
     Span.: A los cocodrilos les gustaba-3sg matar
     Crocodiles liked to kill

[31] No nos gustábamos trabajar   (D36,m45,3,ELA43)
     lit.: not us-liked-1pl work
     Span.: no nos gustaba-3sg trabajar
     we didn't like to work

[32] Ahorita le gusta a - a todo   (M47,f33,3,ELA52)
     lit.: now her - likes to - to everything

---

[6] *To like* and other verbs (e.g. *to think*) patterned like modern Spanish in medieval English.

[7] The speaker pauses briefly after *gusta*. Otherwise, it would have been impossible to tell whether an indirect object marker *a* had been produced in this example.

Span.: Ahorita le gusta todo
Now she likes everything

[33] y gusta golf mucho[8]   (R42,m15,3,ELA30)
   lit.: and likes golf much/a lot
   Span.: y le gusta mucho el golf
   and he likes golf a lot

[34] Yo gusto eso   (N40,f21,3,ELA48)
   lit.: I like-1sg that
   Span.: A mí me gusta-3sg eso
   I like that

Further examples of changes in subcategorization are offered by [35, 36]. [35] omits the required preposition, thus changing the subcategorization of *entrar* 'to go into, to become a member of', intransitive in Spanish, from verb followed by prepositional phrase, [___ + PP], to the transitive structure verb followed by NP, [___ + NP]. I have no evidence that this extension allows this verb to occur with a Cl, as in lo *entras por la izquierda* 'you enter *it* from the left', but the transitive structure opens up this possibility.

[35] y entras ∅ el washroom   (S38,f19,3,ELA31)
   lit.: and enter-2sg the washroom
   Span.: y entras *a/en* el washroom
   and you enter the washroom

[36] reproduces the preposition that collocates with the English verb *to have respect* for *someone*, roughly with the structure [V NP(DO) PP]. This construction translates into Spanish *tener*le *respeto* a *alguien* [V NP(DO) PP(IO)], with an indirect object and its corresponding dative clitic. The use of *para* instead of *a* coincides with a change in syntax in Spanish, inasmuch as prepositional phrases with *para* 'for' do not require a coreferential clitic (∅ *tengo unos libros* para *ellos* 'I have some books for them' as against les *tengo unos libros* a *ellos* 'I have some books for them'). Calquing the preposition *para* in an example like [36] opens up the possibility for this syntactic change in LA Spanish. Note that the preposition change illustrated by [36], produced by a speaker in Group 2, appears to have only a lexical consequence at this stage since the Cl is not blocked. The seed has been planted, however, for a consequent lexico-syntactic modification which could involve either blocking the Cl or allowing Cls coreferential with the NP in a *para* 'for' prepositional phrase.

[36] Nosotros *les* teníamos respeto *para* ellos y todo eso   (R17,f21,2,ELA3)
   lit.: we *them* had respect *for* them and all that
   Span.: Nosotros *les* teníamos respeto (*a* ellos) y todo eso
   We had respect *for* them and all that

---

[8] Because this person speaks slowly, I feel confident that there was no *a* after *gusta*.

Examples involving the substitution of *por* 'for' for *a* 'to' that bring about a lexico-syntactic modification and consequent blocking of the Cl have been reported (Franco, n.d.) as occurring with such verbs as *buscar a* 'to look for' (someone), and *esperar a* 'to wait for' (someone). In US Spanish these verbs have changed from a structure [V + NP] to [V + PP], with the consequent blocking of Cl formation:

[37] ∅ estoy esperando *por* ella
  lit.: am waiting for her
  Span.: *la*ᵢ estoy esperando (*a* ellaᵢ)
  I'm waiting *for* her

Finally, in [38] *visitar* 'to visit', a two-argument verb in Spanish, reproduces the valency of the verb that translates it in English, which may be used intransitively in this language.

[38] El me dijo - cuando mi familia fue allá al Texas *a visitar*   (D36,m45,3,
  ELA43)
  lit.: he told me - when my family went there to the Texas *to visit*
  Span.: El me dijo - cuando mi familia fue allá a Texas *a visitar a los parientes/ de visita*.
  He told me - when my family went there to Texas *to visit (relatives)* / *on a visit*

6.2.5.5. *Type 5*

A pragmatically neutral word order in the source language is reproduced with lexical units of the replica language. (A construction is considered to be pragmatically neutral when its function involves the conveying of information with an informational intonation contour (Silva-Corvalán 1983*c*), without any special connotations of surprise, contrast, sarcasm, etc.) The word order in question is either not allowed in any non-literary style or occurs under very marked pragmatic conditions in the oral mode in the replica language (e.g. contrast, contrary to expectation, sarcasm). In the context where the calque occurs, there is no indication that these pragmatic conditions obtain. Word-order calques are illustrated in [39–43] (see also section 5.4 above).

[39] Ella hablaba como yo más o menos, *machucado español*, mitad las palabras inglés
  y mitad, palabras español   (R50,m46,3,ELA36)
  Span.: . . . *español machucado* . . .
  She spoke like me more or less, *chopped up Spanish*, half in English and half
  in Spanish

[40] es el *número uno gastador* de petróleo   (D39,f28,3,ELA42)
  Span.: . . . *gastador número uno* . . .
  it's the *number one user of oil*

[41] si *cuatro otros alumnos*   (S38,f19,3,ELA30)
Span.: si *otros cuatro alumnos*
if *four other students*

[42] la *más importante persona*   (D36,m45,3,ELA43)
Span.: la *persona más importante*
the *most important person*

[43] esa es una *diferente generación*   (D36,m45,3,ELA43)
Span.: . . . *generación diferente*
that's a *different generation*

It is interesting to note that type 5 calques occur mostly in Group 3. In the samples examined from eleven speakers in Group 2 only two cases were found: [44], produced by V21, a speaker with lower proficiency than most in this group, and [45], provided by L19, who is by contrast quite proficient in Spanish (see Table 2.2) Observe that [45] differs from all the others in that it incorporates a switch to English, 'king-size', a unit of measurement that does not have an exact correspondence in the Hispanic world (a 'cultural borrowing'). This fact would perhaps justify placing [45] in a category other than word-order calque, for instance, a switch to English with a Spanish borrowing (*cama* 'bed') included in the switch. Since I have only one example, I have chosen to consider it a type 5 lexico-syntactic calque, with an adjective–noun (or noun–noun) order.

[44] tengo *dos más meses*   (V21,f18,2,ELA17)
Span.: tengo *dos meses más*
I have *two more months*

[45] pos tengo también 'king', compré una *'king-size' cama*   (L19,f22,2,ELA82)
Span.: pos tengo también 'king', compré una *cama de tamaño 'king'*
Well I have also a 'king', I bought a *king-size bed*

6.2.5.6. Type 6

This type of calque is a form of relexification: by reproducing the source model almost word for word, the calque creates a syntactic structure that is non-existent in the replica language. The lexical units are from the replica language, with possible switches contained in the combination. Examples [46, 47] are illustrative. The genitive marker *'s* is in parentheses in [46] because I cannot discern if it is present or not, given that the following word starts with an *s* and the speaker is talking fairly rapidly. Be that as it may, the construction 'possessor–possessed' does not exist in Spanish.

[46] [Estaba trabajando] . . . abajo de un hermano('s) 'social security'   (D39, f28,3,ELA42)
lit.: . . . under of a brother('s) 'social security'
Span.: . . . con la seguridad social de un hermano

      lit.: . . . with the security social of a brother
      [He was working] . . . under a brother's social security (number)

[47] Yo nací diez millas afuera de la ciudad de Santa Fe   (A37,m57,3,ELA22)
      lit.: I was born ten miles away from the city of Santa Fe
      Span.: Yo nací *a* diez millas de la ciudad de Santa Fe
      lit.: I was born *at* ten miles from the city of Santa Fe

Finally, I have considered as an instance of relexification the calquing of the sequence *that is why*. Even though it may be argued that this is a bound collocation in English, I decided to include its calquing into Spanish as type 6, because it creates a syntactic structure that does not exist in this language:

[48] *Eso es por qué* yo quiero un hijo   (R42,m15,3,ELA30)
      lit.: *that is why* I want a child
      Span.: *Por eso* (*es que*) yo quiero un hijo
      lit.: *for that* (*is that*) I want a child

[49] y *eso es por qué* nosotros fuimos p'allá   (S38,f19,3,ELA31)
      lit.: and *that is why* we went there
      Span.: y *por eso* (*es que*) nosotros fuimos p'allá
      lit.: and *for that* (*is that*) we went there

In the following section, I estimate how widespread multiple-word modelling is across the bilingual continuum.

6.3. Modelling Across the Bilingual Continuum

This section is based on an examination of one- to one-and-a-half-hour samples of speech from each of 4 speakers in Group 1, 11 speakers in Group 2, and 13 in Group 3, i.e. on a total of approximately 33 hours of taped conversations. Interestingly, the analysis shows that the two types of multiple-word modelling that I am concerned with, calques of bound collocations and lexico-syntactic calques (sections 6.2.4 and 6.2.5), distribute differently across the continuum. Group 1 is set apart from the other two groups in that multiple-word modelling is practically non-existent in their speech. Multiple-word modelling is far from being extensive in Group 2, and only a slight increase is noted in Group 3. (I use 'modelling' as a cover term to refer both to calques of bound collocations and to lexico-syntactic calques; note that this last type may include the transfer of form and meaning (type 6 in section 6.2.5).)

In their study of the Spanish of two generations of Cuban Americans in New York, Otheguy *et al.* (1989: table 1) show that, while single-word modelling (in their terminology, 'modelling' means calquing of meaning only) amounts to only 0.1 per cent in a corpus of 7,162 words in the first generation (six Cuban-born adults), it increases considerably to 1.6 per cent of 5,724 words in the second generation (six US-born late adolescents). Of the three types of contact feature they study, loanwords, modelling, and switching, they observe that modelling is what most distinguishes the speech of the second generation from that of the first. Loanwords average 0.8 per cent and the difference between the two groups is of only 0.2 percentage points. Switching is the most prevalent type of phenomenon, but it does not increase as much as modelling from one generation to the next.

I have noted and analysed only cases of multiple-word modelling in my data. The assessment of how extensive modelling might be is based on a simple count of the instances of calques attested in comparable amounts of recorded conversation across speakers. This is obviously not a rigorous assessment of the preponderance of this phenomenon. However, it is an approximation which is more reliable than a completely impressionistic evaluation: it offers some form of quantified information based on the assumption that, given similar topics of conversation across speakers, one may expect the discourses produced to be comparable in terms of the linguistic devices employed. Comparability of discourse topics applies in the case of most speakers except those at the bottom stages of the proficiency continuum (e.g. N40, R42, A46). These speakers are quite aware of the limitations of their linguistic resources in Spanish; they confine their conversation in this language to a number of very reduced concrete topics which they can handle without deviating too much from Spanish norms, and they switch to English if necessary to continue conversing.

This strategy most probably explains the relatively low number of calques used by these speakers. One might even submit that speakers with a very low degree of proficiency in a language do not have the ability to be linguistically creative in this language. More proficient speakers, on the other hand, display the same type of linguistic creativity that characterizes innovations in fully fledged monolingual varieties, e.g. adoption of loanwords, semantic extensions. Observe, in this respect, the skilful extension of the meaning of *descansar* 'to rest' in [50].

[50] They were laying off. So, I didn't get laid off. Ramón, Ramón got laid off. And I quit because he got laid off. Because I was working, and he was working at nights . . .
Dije, 'No, SI LO VAN A DESCANSAR A ÉL *(lit.: if him are-3pl gonna rest him), ¿pa' qué me quedo yo, especial yo?' Yo, de aquí, como, 'onde puedo agarrar trabajo. El, es más difícil, porque* he's not *reglado para 'garrar trabajo.*   (D39,f28,3, ELA42)
I said, 'No, IF THEY'RE GOING TO LAY HIM OFF, why should I stay, especially me?' I'm from here, so I can get a job anywhere. As for him, it's more difficult, because he's not 'fixed' (legalized) to get a job.

As a transitive verb, *descansar* 'to rest/lean/lay' takes an inanimate direct object in Spanish (*descansa tu cabeza en mi hombro* 'rest/lean/lay your head on my shoulder'). Most likely based on the connection between *descansar* and *lay* with the meaning of 'rest/lean', D39 establishes the further link with *lay off*. This has lexico-syntactic consequences because both the meaning of *lay off* and its subcategorization are transferred to *descansar*, which now incorporates the meaning of 'to fire (an employee)' and allows an animate direct object, i.e. it represents a lexico-syntactic calque of type 4.

Only two unquestionable calques are attested in the data examined from the four speakers in Group 1 (E1, R11, C13, J14). One involves the use of *volver para atrás* 'to return', the other is the substitution of *a* 'at' for *en* 'in/on/at' (*Me recogió* A *la biblioteca* 'he picked me up *at* the library'). Both examples occur in E1's speech. The results for Groups 2 and 3 are presented in Table 6.1. The mean is based on an average of the cases attested for every ten minutes of conversation.

Table 6.1 indicates that modelling increases in Group 3 (those in the special Group 3 are italicized). One person in Group 2 does not produce any cases of modelling, and only one evidences an average of more than 1.4 cases every ten minutes. This speaker is V21, whose Spanish has been shown to be further from the norms of Group 1 in other respects as well when compared to other speakers in her group (see Table 2.2). By contrast, all speakers in Group 3 incorporate modelling in their speech, ranging from an average of 0.6 to 2.1 cases per ten minutes of conversation.

I have not focused on loanwords, but I see no reason to believe that loanwords would amount to a much higher percentage in LA Spanish than in Cuban Spanish. Thus, if the major lexical differences between general Spanish and LA Spanish are due to the calquing of meaning only, then one might expect that intelligibility between these varieties would not be badly impaired, especially if the interlocutor has some knowledge of English. This is indeed the case, as my analysis of narrative and hypothetical discourse indicates (see Chapter 3). Regular inferential processes allow both Group 1 speakers and out-group members to draw the necessary semantic connections between the meaning that the items in question have in the more conservative varieties and the usually extended meanings that these items acquire as they calque those in the corresponding items in the source language. It seems to me that the same inferential processes allow speakers of, for instance, Castilian and Chilean Spanish to understand one another even though their lexicons do not exactly correspond. Words are not used in isolation; they are embedded in contexts which usually offer the necessary clues to their interpretation.

6.4. Acts of Conflicting Loyalties: Positive Attitudes and Uncommitted Behaviours[9]

6.4.1. The Study of Attitudes

The attitudes that monolinguals and bilinguals have towards such aspects of societal bilingualism as the issue of the maintenance of two languages, the public and

---

[9] This section owes much to the help of Consuelo Sigüenza, a graduate student and my research assistant in the language attitudes project. Consuelo participated in all stages of the research, and applied the questionnaires in person to almost every one of the respondents. Analysis, generalizations, and conclusions are, however, my sole responsibility.

TABLE 6.1. Types of Modelling Attested in Groups 2 and 3

| | | Modelling types | | | | | | | | |
| | | Bound | Lexico-syntactic calques: type | | | | | | | |
	Time (min)	N[a]	1 N	2 N	3 N	4 N	5 N	6 N	Total	N/10 min.
Group 2										
B27	60								0	0.0
A29	60							1	1	0.2
L28	60		1		1				2	0.3
L19	90	1	3				1	1	6	0.6
M26	90		1			6			7	0.7
A20	90			2	3	2		1	8	0.8
R17	60	3		3		1			7	1.2
R24	60	1	1	1	3	2			8	1.3
E18	60		3	3	2				8	1.3
H22	90	1	1	4		4		3	13	1.4
V21	90	1	2	9	3	5	1	5	26	2.9
Total	910	7	12	19	13	22	2	11	86	0.9
Group 3										
H48	90		*1*		*1*	2		*1*	5	0.6
R50	90		5				*1*		6	0.6
A34	60		1			4			5	0.8
A37	45		2		1			1	4	0.9
N40	40					3		1	4	1.0
A46	45		1			3		1	5	1.1
B33	60		2		4	1			7	1.2
M41	60		1	1	2	1	1	1	7	1.2
M47	60		2	2	2	2			8	1.3
S38	90	1	2	1	2	1	2	4	13	1.4
R42	45		2	1	1	3		1	8	1.8
D39	90	1	3	2	3	4	2	4	19	2.1
D36	90		3		2	4	4	6	19	2.1
Total	865	2	25	7	18	28	10	20	110	1.3

[a] N = no. of cases per 10 mins.

private status assigned to each language, or the linguistic adequacy or correctness of the minority language can throw some light upon the motivations that may promote either the maintenance or the fading away of the minority language. Thus, the study of attitudes has constituted the focus of many research efforts that attempt to predict the future of (usually) a minority language in a bilingual context, as well as to elucidate the symbolic status that the languages involved may have for particular social groups.

The mental position (feelings, emotions) that individuals have, or are willing to disclose, towards a specific fact or state of affairs is not easily measurable. Romaine (1989*b*: 257) notes this problem in her discussion of attitudes towards bilingualism: 'The translation of the notion of "attitude" from the subjective domain into something objectively measurable, and therefore more easily comparable, is a common problem in any research that involves social categorization and perceptual judgements.'

In terms of direct methods, the attitude questionnaire has been one of the devices most used to elicit measurable information about specific aspects of bilingualism, e.g. code-switching, the appropriate domains for use of the languages, self-reports concerning language usage patterns, and level of language proficiency. Questionnaires have a number of undeniable advantages over direct observation or the personal interview: a higher number of people may be surveyed in a shorter period of time, the answers to closed questions make measurement and comparison across individuals easier. Unfortunately, questionnaires are also riddled with pitfalls.

Dorian (1981: 157–60), for instance, notes that some of the problems include not knowing who in fact filled out the questionnaire, and not being able to clarify or expand on the instructions. (Supposedly she refers to questionnaires filled out when the investigator is not present or when they are given to a large group of people at the same time.) Furthermore, the issue of the predictive validity of the instrument used to elicit language attitudes has attracted attention and criticism. According to some researchers (Agheyisi and Fishman 1970; Edwards 1985; Ryan *et al.* 1982), most types of questionnaire are inadequate to obtain data relating to anticipatory behaviour, and therefore lack predictive validity because they focus exclusively on the cognitive and/or affective components of attitude.

Attitudes, however, involve not only a mentalist perspective, which implies that they would have to be inferred from the subject's introspection and/or the researchers' interpretation of overt behaviour, but also actual, overt, observable behaviour (Agheyisi and Fishman 1970). This multiple-component view (cognitive, affective, and conative or action components) dictates the inclusion in the questionnaire of items which elicit information about the various dimensions of language attitudes.

Accordingly, in my study I employed a number of questionnaires modelled mostly on questionnaires used by Dorian (1981), Fishman *et al.* (1971: ch. 5), and Mejías and Anderson's (1988), (MA) and applied them in 1988–9 (i.e. long after

TABLE 6.2. Sample of Respondents to the Questionnaires

	Group 1		Group 2		Group 3		Total sample	
	F	M	F	M	F	M	F	M
Age								
21–30	2	2	5	3	3	1	10	6
31–70	4	4	5	3	3	4	12	11
Total	6	6	10	6	6	5	22	17 = 39

I had completed the recording of conversations). By using a battery of different questionnaires already tested and applied in bilingual contexts I expected to obtain data on the various components of attitudes which could be used for comparative purposes. Appendix 4 contains the English version of the five questionnaires administered (there was also a Spanish version of all the questionnaires except No. III, applied only to Groups 2 and 3).

The questionnaires included mainly closed-question items. This eliminates the problem of respondents failing to focus on the expected dimension, since all they have to do is choose from a set of provided categories, and it also facilitates the quantification and comparison of responses. The questionnaires were administered in an interview setting, with the respondents either writing their answers in the presence of the researcher[10] or asking her to do so. The researcher was there to help facilitate the completion of the questionnaire, and interacted with the respondents in a friendly, interview-like fashion, questioning, explaining, clarifying, and expanding on certain items. Such a method was especially helpful with the older respondents, who either could not read in Spanish or were prevented by poor eyesight from completing the questionnaire without help. Thirty-three questionnaires were applied in person and 9 had to be mailed;[11] of these 9, 4 persons responded. Not all the respondents completed every questionnaire; this is noted when relevant in the ensuing discussion. In addition to these 37 individuals, all included in the sample of 50 bilinguals studied in this book, two additional ones volunteered to participate: B51, f43 (included in the results for Group 2), married to R50; and R52, m45 (included in the results for Group 3), married to E45. Table 6.2 summarizes the information.

Personal contact in a combination of the face-to-face (rather than telephone) interview and questionnaire format offers the interviewer the possibility to focus the attention of the respondent on the desired cue, and to assess and influence the mood of the respondents (thus reducing the chance of boring or irritating them).

---

[10] This researcher was in all cases Consuelo Sigüenza, who is a member of the Mexican-American community investigated.

[11] Questionnaires were mailed to those speakers whose schedule did not allow us to meet with them. Seven of the speakers included in the sample of 50 had moved and could not be contacted; one had died.

Although the researcher's presence risks biasing the respondents, the fact that they are all exposed to the same application method offsets this possible bias, since in principle it should affect all speakers in the same manner. Thus, differences and similarities in the results obtained across speakers can be interpreted as responding to factors other than the researcher's presence. Despite these efforts, the responses to the questionnaires must still be treated with caution, and should be regarded as 'useful only in their general gestalt' (Dorian 1981: 160).

6.4.2. *Questionnaire I*

This questionnaire, admininistered to speakers in Groups 1, 2, and 3, was partly based on and adapted from Dorian (1981), Fishman *et al.* (1971), Gal (1979), and Zentella (1981). Questionnaire I is reproduced in Appendix 4, followed by an arrangement of its 80 items, according to the type of dimension being investigated, into 9 groups (I–IX, A or B, depending on the language about which information is sought).

The 79 closed questions were responded to by 34 persons surveyed, but only 10 of these answered 4 open questions included at the end of the questionnaire (80–3), fairly briefly. The comments with respect to item 80 agree that the inter-locutor is the most crucial factor in determining what language to speak. Most of the respondents agree that they switch languages if the topic calls for the other language, when they 'get stuck' and cannot promptly remember how to say something in one or the other language, or when 'a word [in the other language] better describes a situation' (M25). As for their feelings towards switching, they are reflected in S38's (f19, 3) response. She states that she switches when she is 'among down-to-earth bilingual people I feel comfortable with [because] some thoughts are better expressed in Spanish'.

Item 82 was also commented on briefly. Groups 2 and 3 concurred that when they used Spanish in front of an English-only speaker they did not sense any hostility. Even if they did, however, this would not stop them from using whatever language they cared to speak. One speaker from Group 1, on the other hand, stated that he had once been told that he 'should learn to speak English', to which he responded, in English, 'I know English'. The topic addressed by item 82 came up spontaneously during some of the conversations recorded earlier. Example [51] is illustrative.

[51] R: R50,m46,3,ELA36; C: researcher
    C: Fíjate. Tú poco a poco has ido viendo que ha llegado más y más gente a la policía que son latinos.
    R: Latinos. Como ahora, estaba en el *catering wagon* y, y, y estaba hablando - Un mecánico mejicano le dijo una a la - al que está cocinando en el *catering wagon*, le dijo una de doble sentido, una palabra de doble sentido nomás. *Nothing serious, nothing serious, you know, just a* - No me acuerdo

qué era ni nada. So le hablé yo p'atrás en español. 'Ya te agarré la movida,' le dije, 'Ya te, ya te estoy escuchando.' Y luego este gringo estaba a un lado y luego '*Eh*,' dice, '*don't speak that foreign language around here.*' Es lo que me dice a mí, *you know.* '*What do you mean "foreign language"? That sucker was around here before the English were!*' [R laughs]. *And he says, 'Man, you're right!', he says, 'You're right! OK?*' [R and C laugh]

C: *He had to accept it, uh?*

R: *Yeah, he had to accept it. Two reasons: I'm right, and two, I'm the boss.* [R and C laugh]

C: There you are. Little by little you've been seeing that more and more people have joined the police who are latinos.

R: Latinos. Like now, I was at the catering wagon and, and, and was speaking – A Mexican mechanic said one to the – to the one who's cooking in the catering wagon, he told him a double-sense one, just one double-sense word. Nothing serious, nothing serious, you know, just a – I don't remember what it was. So I talked to him in Spanish. 'I got what you said,' I said, 'I'm, I'm listening to you.' And then this gringo was to one side and then 'Eh,' he says, 'don't speak that foreign language around here.' That's what he says to me, you know. 'What do you mean "foreign language"? That sucker was around here before the English were!' [R laughs]. And he says, 'Man, you're right!', he says, 'You're right! OK?' [R and C laugh]

C: He had to accept it, uh?

R: Yeah, he had to accept it. Two reasons: I'm right, and two, I'm the boss! [R and C laugh]

This passage from a speaker in Group 3 supports in part the opinion expressed by those in Groups 2 and 3. The question remains, however, whether the English monolingual would have agreed with R's statement if the second reason (R is the boss) had not applied.

Table 6.3 displays the results of selected items in the sections (IA and IB; see Appendix 4) probing the respondents' assessment of their use of Spanish with various interlocutors.

The decline in the use of Spanish across groups is evident. This situation seems to apply not only in work and church domains but also within the family environs. While Group 1 speakers report almost exclusive use of Spanish with parents, grandparents, and siblings, some speakers in Groups 2 and 3 speak only frequently or sometimes to their parents and siblings in this language, and four respondents in Group 3 report never using Spanish to communicate with their siblings.

R17 (f21,2,ELA3) spontaneously assessed this situation during the time of the recorded conversations. She told me that when they were small their parents asked them to speak only Spanish at home. However, this 'rule' was frequently

TABLE 6.3. Use of Spanish with Various Interlocutors

Interlocutor	Group 1 (12 respondents)					Group 2 (13)					Group 3 (9)				
	A	F	UO	N	NA[a]	A	F	UO	N	NA	A	F	UO	N	NA
13.[b] Mexican friends	4	5	3			1	2	6	4		2	1	5	1	
40. Mexican becoming friendly	9	3				4	5	2	2		4	3	2	2	
61. Fellow workers	4	3	2		3		3	2	6	2	1	2	3	2	1
62. Supervisor or boss	2	3	2	2	3			2	10	1		1	1	6	1
70. Parents	8				4	6	1	1		5	2	1	3	1	2
71. Grandparents	6				6	3				10	2	1		1	6
73. Siblings	8	3		1	1	1	1	6		5		2	2	4	
28. Priest or minister	6	2	1	1	2	1		3	8	1	1	1	1	7	
79. Hispanic-looking:															
(a) Same or younger	7	1	1	2	1	3		2	7	1	1	2	1	5	
(b) Child	6	1	3	1	1	2	1	3	7		2	1	1	5	
(c) Older	6	3		1	2	6	1	4	2		1	2	3	3	
(d) Salesperson	4	3	1	3	1		1	2	10			1	2	6	
(e) Clerk	2	2	3	4	1		1	2	12				2	6	
(f) Teacher	2	2	3	4	1		1	3	9			1		9	
(g) Restaurant employee	1	2	3	4	1	2	2	3	6			1	3	8	
(h) Police officer	3	1	3	4	1		1		12			3	1	7	1
(i) Car maintenance employee	2		5	4	1	3	1	2	7			3	3	5	1

[a] A = always; F = frequently; UO = usually or sometimes; N = never; NA = does not apply. In addition to ticking the NA box when the situation in fact did not apply in the case of a specific respondent, this box was also ticked when the respondent did not feel comfortable about giving an answer.

[b] Nos. and letters in Tables 6.3–6 correspond to those in the questionnaire (see Appendix 4).

disregarded by the time her younger brother and sister were born. Consequently, the youngest did not learn enough Spanish to interact comfortably in Spanish; the siblings use English among themselves. R herself explains:

[52] . . . y mi hermanita chiquita sí habla español, pero no creo que tiene la voca, el voca, ¿el vocabulario? / *Researcher*: Sí, el vocabulario. / Sí, no tiene mucha vocabulario para, para estar en una conversación. Y, y yo estaba diciendo, 'Pos otra vez necesitamos de esa regla'.

 . . . and my little sister does speak Spanish, but I don't think she has the voc, the voc, the vocabulary? /Researcher: Yes, the vocabulary./ Yes, she doesn't have much vocabulary to, to be in a conversation. And, and I was saying, 'Well, we need that rule again'.

In the work domain, Spanish tends to be used more with fellow workers than with supervisors. Dorian's (1981: 162–3) respondents report the same with respect to Gaelic, a situation which she deems to be a reflection of East Sutherland society, where 'there are simply very few bilinguals in supervisory positions'. This explanation possibly applies in Los Angeles, where those in supervisory positions may be bilinguals, but most frequently English-dominant. It may also be the case, however, that the large numbers of recent Spanish-speaking immigrants working in Los Angeles may stimulate Mexican-Americans to revive their lost linguistic skills, even if the English-dominant bilingual is in the supervisory position. This situation is well reflected in the spontaneous description volunteered by L28 (f37, 2) of her husband's (H48, m38, 3) proficiency in Spanish. L's husband is the son of the owner of the printing company to which [53] refers.

[53] Y digo yo que este señor [her husband] su español era horrible, ¿verdad?, porque lo había perdido cuando se mudaron a ese vecindad. Sí, pero cuando nos casamos entonces ya no era el estudiante, ya se puso a trabajar en la planta. Y en la planta, los hombres que trabajan las imprentas casi todos son hispanoamericanos. Vienen de distintos países, pero todos hablan español. Entonces por su amistad, en la imprenta él pudo aprender español.

And I say that this man his Spanish was horrible, right?, because he had lost it when they moved to that neighborhood. Yeah, but when we got married then he was no longer a student, he started working in the company. And in the company, the men who work at the printing presses are almost all hispanoamericans. They come from different countries, but they all speak Spanish. So then because of their friendship, in the company he learnt Spanish.

In addition to the negative effect that the different neighbourhood (mostly non-Hispanic) had on H's Spanish, his wife surmises that he had also stopped using it because his grandparents had died by then.

In regard to the use of Spanish with strangers, Group 1 speakers hesitate to use this language with individuals who are not necessarily in-group members (e.g. clerk, teacher, police officer). This trend is strengthened in Groups 2 and 3.

No inconsistencies are reported in the corresponding items that concern the use of English in relation to interlocutors. Respondents in Groups 1 and 2 tend to report more reduced use of English in the situations examined (see questionnaire I, section IB) as compared to speakers in Group 3.

Table 6.4 displays the results of questionnaire I, section IIA, followed by Table 6.5, corresponding to section IIB. The two items in Table 6.5, 29 and 32, concerning English, are roughly conversely comparable with 30 and 31 respectively in Table 6.4, concerning Spanish. Note that this comparison does not indicate inconsistencies in the responses. On the other hand, the lack of fitness between the responses given to items 12 and 31, for which I expected nearly exact results, raises the usual questions concerning the reliability of self-report. Overall, however, I am confident that the questionnaires are an accurate reflection of the gradual reduction in use that affects Spanish in this community. This is also revealed by self-report with respect to the use of Spanish according to topic or type of activity in Groups 2 and 3.

Writing and reading in Spanish are reported to be much less frequent than listening activities in this language. For instance, 6 of 12 respondents in Group 1 report reading Spanish publications either always or frequently, 5 write letters in Spanish either always or frequently, but 9 of these 12 speakers listen to Spanish radio programme and music broadcasts either always or frequently. Although there is less reading, writing, and listening in Spanish in the other two groups, 9 of 13 speakers in Group 2 and 4 of 9 in Group 3 report reading Spanish publications 'sometimes'. Letter-writing is also an activity that occurs, though only sometimes, among Group 3 respondents. The maintenance of some degree of literacy in Spanish in this group is encouraging. (No speakers were illiterate in both languages.)

As would be expected given the differing levels of proficiency in Spanish across the continuum, Group 1 speakers evidence strong preferential use of Spanish in response to items 56, 59, 68, and 69 by marking mostly 'always'; speakers in Groups 3 show preferential use of English by selecting mostly 'sometimes' or 'never'; Group 2 falls between these two groups, with responses distributed almost equally between 'frequently', 'sometimes', and 'never'. Preferential use of English increases accordingly across the three groups.

The responses to the items in section VIIIA of questionnaire I show that contact with Mexico remains strong in Groups 1 and 2, and quite solid in Group 3 as well. Table 6.6 displays the answers.

Close contact with Mexico certainly facilitates the maintenance of Spanish, and visits to Mexico motivate Hispanics to learn or improve their knowledge of this language. But regardless of how much reduction Spanish has undergone in terms of domains of use and linguistic resources in Groups 2 and 3, almost every speaker in these groups, as well as in Group 1, responds with an emphatic 'yes' to question 45: 'When I have children, I want them to be able to speak Spanish fluently.' Only

Table 6.4. Use of Spanish in Relation to Topic or Activity[a]

Topic	Group 1					Group 2					Group 3				
	A	F	UO	N	NA	A	F	UO	N	NA	A	F	UO	N	NA
12. Religious service	4	5	1	2		2	1	7	3		1		3	5	
30. Praying	7	3	1	1		1	3	6	3				1	2	6
31. Religious service	3	3	3	1	2	1	1	9	2		1		5	3	
64. Telephone calls	4	4	3		1	1	1	10	1			2	4	3	
65. Local affairs	5	5	1		1	1	1	8	3			2	3	4	
66. National affairs	4	6	1		1	1	1	8	3			1	4	4	
67. Health	5	4	1		2	1		9	1	2		1	4	4	
63. Counting	4	3	3		2	1	3	6	3		1	1	3	3	1

[a] A = always; F = frequently; UO = usually or sometimes; N = never; NA = does not apply.

TABLE 6.5. Use of English in Relation to Topic or Activity[a]

Topic	Group 1					Group 2					Group 3				
	A	F	UO	N	NA	A	F	UO	N	NA	A	F	UO	N	NA
29. Praying	3	1	1	7		7	3	2	1		6	1	2		
32. Religious service	1	1	5	4	1	3	6	3	1		3	2	3	1	

[a] A = always, F = frequently, UO = usually or sometimes, N = never, NA = does not apply.

TABLE 6.6. Contact with Mexico[a]

Activity	Group 1			Group 2			Group 3		
	A	N	NA	A	N	NA	A	N	NA
5. I visited Mexico	9	2	1	10	3		3	5	1
6. Family visited Mexico	8	2	2	11	2		4	4	1
14. Visited from Mexico	9	3		11	2		7	1	1

[a] A = yes; F = frequently; UO = usually or sometimes; N = no; NA = does not apply.

three speakers respond that full fluency is not crucial, 'a little Spanish would be fine' (Group 3: B33, D36, E45). Similarly, all speakers but two in Group 1 (J14, J16) respond 'yes' to question 47: 'When I have children, I want them to be able to speak English fluently.'

6.4.3. Questionnaires II and III

Questionnaires II, administered to Group 1, and III, given to Groups 2 and 3, were based on Dorian's (1981) two versions of her questionnaire II, and on another questionnaire devised by Mejías and Anderson (1988) (MA). Questionnaire II was answered by 12 speakers (6 females, 6 males) and questionnaire III was completed by 16 speakers in Group 2 (10 females, 6 males), and by 11 in Group 3 (6 females, 5 males). Group 1 speakers were asked to select the main reasons they *have* to be happy to know Spanish, while Groups 2 and 3 were asked to choose the main reasons they *would have* if they were ever to try to improve or maintain their Spanish (see questionnaires in Appendix 4).

When presented with the questionnaire, the respondents were instructed to circle the reasons that seemed important to them, draw a line through the least important reasons, put a star next to the most important one or two reasons, and to leave unmarked those that were neutral to them. They were also instructed to write in their main reasons if these were not included in the questionnaire. No respondents added reasons to the ones given (Dorian reports the same for her respondents).

The sixteen-item questionnaire corresponds to the four dimensions of attitude applied by MA in their study of the language attitudes of Rio Grande Valley residents in Texas. The *group-identity* (G) (value 'V' in MA) dimension refers to the use of Spanish as a public symbol of group worth and lasting values and traditions, with ethnic identity at its core, as illustrated by item 6: [If I were ever to try to improve, or maintain my Spanish, my main reasons would be:] 'It would make me feel more a part of the community I live in.' The *sentimental* (S) dimension refers to the private feelings, emotions, and personal satisfaction the bilingual experiences in the use of Spanish, as illustrated by item 4: 'Spanish is a very rich and expressive language.' The *communication* (C) dimension refers to the use of Spanish for public understanding and interpersonal communication, i.e. to the actual transmission and communication of information between people in Spanish, as illustrated by item 5: 'It is necessary for daily communication.' Finally, the *instrumental* (I) dimension refers to the use of Spanish for personal benefits, material profits, and gains, as illustrated by item 14: 'It helps me make money at my job.' The communication and group-identity dimensions represent extrinsic perspectives, through which bilinguals view themselves as identifying the use of Spanish with belonging to a group or community, whereas the instrumental and sentimental dimensions represent intrinsic perspectives, through which bilinguals view themselves as individuals.

These dimensions roughly correspond to some of Dorian's (1981: 165–71) reasons for valuing Gaelic: G = local integrative and tradition, I = operational, S = subjective aesthetic. For purposes of comparison with MA, in the quantitative analysis I have classified items 2 and 16, borrowed from Dorian's questionnaire II, as 'instrumental' rather than 'abstract principle' and 'exclusionary', respectively, as Dorian does.

MA report that, for their entire sample of 293 subjects, using Spanish for communication is strongest among the four attitude dimensions (endorsed by an average of 45.9 per cent of their sample). This is followed by value (22.6 per cent), sentimental (15.2 per cent), and instrumental (13.2 per cent) reasons. On this basis they hypothesize that Spanish will be maintained along with English in Rio Grande Valley, Texas, rather than suffer a shift to English. But they find a contradiction to strong Spanish language maintenance when viewing the variable of generational group. They note that although third- and fourth-generation respondents, whose residence in the USA has been longer, chose more communicative reasons for maintaining Spanish, first- and second-generation respondents chose more sentimental reasons for maintaining Spanish. MA interpret this to indicate a tendency toward language shift away from Spanish among newer residents, i.e. first- and

TABLE 6.7. Most Important Dimension for Valuing Spanish Based on Percentage of Respondents Selecting Reasons in Each

	Group 1 (12)[a] %	Group 2 (16) %	Group 3 (11) %	Total sample (39) %
Group identity	25	12	6	17
Sentimental	27	27	22	26
Communication	21	27	22	23
Instrumental	27	33	50	34

[a] Figures in parentheses indicate no. of respondents.

second-generation respondents. They attribute this to 'a temporary desire to shift from Spanish which will moderate as residency is more established' (p. 406).

In our sample, although much smaller than MA's, we find a different outcome: a higher percentage of our respondents select the instrumental dimension as the most important (34 per cent), with communicative reasons being in third place, selected by only 23 per cent of the sample. As I show below, this difference may be due in part to the inclusion of item 7 (reading in Spanish), a communicative reason, in our questionnaire II but not in MA's, and to the classification of item 2, strongly supported by most respondents, as instrumental. Table 6.7 summarizes the results. For the total sample of respondents, the attitude toward the use of Spanish for instrumental reasons is strongest among the four attitude dimensions. The attitude toward the use of Spanish for sentimental reasons is the next strongest (26 per cent of the sample), followed by communication reasons. Group-identity reasons are the weakest among the four attitude dimensions, with only an average of 17 per cent of the respondents choosing them.

It is evident in Table 6.7 that the communication dimension of attitude increases in importance from Group 1 (21 per cent) to Group 2 (27 per cent). The lower weight given to communicative reasons in Group 1, compared with group-identity and sentimental reasons, may indicate that recent immigrants are still nostalgic about their native land and culture. A different explanation is needed to account for the decline in the value assigned to communicative reasons in Group 3 (22 per cent), however, as compared to Group 2. Indeed, the weakening of the communicative motive as Spanish-language proficiency decreases further also makes sense, given that a person with reduced Spanish productive proficiency will tend not to use this language to read or for oral communication, unless absolutely necessary. For our sample, absolutely necessary cases involve those in which the low-functioning bilingual must communicate with recent Spanish-speaking immigrants or visitors who do not understand English. Otherwise, interaction takes place in the two languages: each interlocutor uses his dominant language knowing that the listener understands both English and Spanish.

In terms of intergenerational and language-proficiency differences, in Group 1, the attitudes toward the use of Spanish for instrumental and sentimental reasons are strongest among the four dimensions (27 per cent). Although a well-balanced group overall, the private, intrinsic attitude dimensions (S and I) are endorsed by Group 1 respondents as the most important for maintaining Spanish, with communicative reasons as the weakest. These results agree in part with those obtained by MA for first-generation immigrants, who also chose more sentimental reasons for maintaining Spanish.

Even though differing in degrees, Group 2 and Group 3's attitude dimension relationships are identical. Instrumental reasons are the most important in the maintenance of Spanish, followed by S and C reasons, while group-identity reasons are the weakest. These overall results seem to point in the direction of possible diversity of bilingual communities across the USA in terms of attitude and motivations toward maintaining Spanish, although many more in-depth and extensive studies using identical questionnaires and methodologies need to be carried out before any firm generalizations may be established. Therefore, the comparisons across communities presented in this chapter are necessarily only tentative.

In the Rio Grande Valley, MA's respondents chose communicative reasons—those that deal with public understanding and interpersonal communication—as the most important for maintaining Spanish in their community, with instrumental reasons being the weakest. In Los Angeles, our sample of respondents chose instrumental and sentimental reasons, those dealing with personal benefits and emotional satisfaction, as the most important reasons for using or maintaining Spanish in their community. And even though the item dealing with reading makes a difference, an examination of the percentage of respondents who starred each item confirms that of the communicative reasons offered (items 5, 11, 12), only 'talking to people from other Spanish speaking countries' is starred equally across the three groups, but it does not receive the strongest support. Table 6.8 presents the percentage of respondents who starred each of the 16 items in questionnaire II. Within each group I have italicized the two items starred by most respondents.

Conspicuous in Table 6.8 is the high value assigned to item 2 in Groups 1 and 2 ('it's broadening to have more than one language'). Dorian proposes this reason as an 'abstract principle', supported only weakly by her respondents. Item 16 ('it is useful to know a second language') is strictly comparable with item 2 only in the version given to Groups 2 and 3. It is somewhat surprising that the responses to these two items are not the same in these two groups: the utilitarian reason for knowing more than one language is favoured by Group 3 (item 16), while the purely intellectual reason (item 2) receives a warmer response from Group 2. The most starred items in the three groups, then, do not pertain specifically to Spanish,

TABLE 6.8. Percentage of Respondents Starring a Reason as
Most Important for Valuing Spanish

Dimension	Group 1 (12)[a] %	Group 2 (16) %	Group 3 (11) %	Total sample (39) %
(G) 1.	·41.7	12.5	0.0	17.95
(I) 2.	75.0	43.7	9.1	43.59
(S) 3.	8.3	0.0	9.1	5.13
(S) 4.	33.3	18.7	0.0	17.95
(C) 5.	33.3	18.7	9.1	20.51
(G) 6.	16.7	0.0	0.0	5.13
(C) 7.	8.3	12.5	0.0	7.69
(I) 8.	16.7	0.0	9.1	7.69
(G) 9.	16.7	12.5	0.0	10.26
(G) 10.	16.7	0.0	9.1	7.69
(C) 11.	8.3	0.0	0.0	2.56
(C) 12.	25.0	25.0	25.0	25.64
(S) 13.	25.0	12.5	0.0	18.32
(I) 14.	0.0	0.0	18.2	5.13
(S) 15.	33.3	25.0	27.3	28.21
(I) 16.	8.3	25.0	45.4	25.64

[a] Figures in parentheses indicate nos. of respondents.

but to the more general or non-specific notion of 'another language'. This elicited
attitude concurs with the spontaneous opinion expressed by one of the speakers in
Group 2:

[54] *Insisten que se - claro, las dos [idiomas]. Somos asi. Es una cosa - bonito hablar
dos idiomas.* It's something that enriches the person. It's something that enriches the society. It's, it's education, it's culture. It gives you two systems of
thinking, you know.   (E18,f27,2,ELA32)
They insist that - of course, the two [languages]. We're like that. It's - nice
to speak two languages.

There is a difference in the number of items that speakers starred which also
points to a fairly disheartening situation. Although all respondents were asked to
star one or two most important reasons for maintaining or improving their knowledge of Spanish, in Group 1, four respondents marked three reasons; in Group
2, two respondents marked three reasons; while no one in Group 3 starred more
than two reasons (nor did they offer other possible reasons in the section of the
questionnaire which encouraged them to do so). This selectional pattern seems
to indicate that Group 1 speakers have more very important reasons to maintain

TABLE 6.9. Percentage of Respondents Crossing Out a Reason as
Least Important for Valuing Spanish

	Group 1 (12) %	Group 2 (16) %	Group 3 (11) %	Total sample (39) %
(G) 1.	0.0	12.5	9.1	7.7
(I) 2.	0.0	0.0	0.0	0.0
(S) 3.	8.3	*43.7*	27.3	28.2
(S) 4.	8.3	12.5	9.1	10.3
(C) 5.	8.3	12.5	18.2	12.8
(G) 6.	33.3	31.2	*36.4*	33.3
(C) 7.	0.0	31.2	27.3	20.0
(I) 8.	*41.7*	*68.7*	*36.4*	*51.1*
(G) 9.	0.0	31.2	18.2	17.9
(G) 10.	16.7	*43.7*	27.3	30.8
(C) 11.	0.0	31.2	27.3	20.0
(C) 12.	0.0	0.0	9.1	2.6
(S) 13.	8.3	6.2	9.1	7.7
(I) 14.	*58.3*	*43.7*	*45.4*	*48.7*
(S) 15.	25.0	0.0	0.0	7.7
(I) 16.	25.0	0.0	0.0	7.7

Spanish, and results in more items being thus marked in the questionnaires from this group, where only item 14 is never starred; fewer items are starred in Group 2 (10), and even fewer in Group 3 (9). This may reflect a weakening of support toward the maintenance of Spanish in Groups 2 and 3.

Furthermore, US-born bilinguals do not consider, overall, that the preservation or protection of tradition and group integration is the most important motive to maintain their ancestors' language. Two G reasons are selected as the most important by only 12.5 per cent of the sample in Group 2, and a low 9.1 per cent of those in Group 3 (i.e. one of 11 respondents) star only one G reason, item 10: 'It's the language of my friends and neighbours.' This item, however, is also crossed out as the least important by three speakers (27.3 per cent) in this same group, as illustrated in Table 6.9. This table shows the percentage of respondents who crossed out each of 16 prompts as the least important reasons why they would like to improve or maintain Spanish (in the case of Groups 2 and 3) and why they are happy to know Spanish (in the case of Group 1). Italicized in Table 6.9 are the reasons marked by a higher percentage of respondents as least important for valuing Spanish.

The three groups agree in their high percentage of rejection of two instrumental motivations which value Spanish as a 'secret language' (item 8), and as a means to

make money at a job (item 14). Although this latter choice obviously depends on
the type of occupation, it seems to be on the whole an accurate assessment, given
the secondary and unofficial status of Spanish in Los Angeles and the primary
status of English, the single official language in California, in education and in the
business world. Likewise, the three groups concur in never crossing out item 2
('It's broadening to have more than one language'), an intellectual motivation
which was also starred by respondents in the three groups.

Generally, then, the results of questionnaires I, II, and III appear to indicate a
correlation between decrease in the number and strength of the motivations or
reasons for maintaining or improving knowledge of Spanish, reduction in the
domains of use of Spanish in the community, and linguistic attrition of this
secondary language.

6.4.4. Questionnaire IV

Questionnaire IV (see Appendix 4), administered to the three groups, was adapted
from Dorian's (1981: 184–5) questionnaire III. For purposes of analysis and quantification, item 4 in section A ('Spanish is a difficult language to learn') was left out:
because this was a 'fact question' (see Questionnaire IV) I was uncertain as to the
attitude that the answer to this item could be interpreted as reflecting. The remaining 29 items were divided into 4 categories: positive attitudes towards Spanish
(11 items); negative attitudes towards Spanish (9 items); positive attitudes towards
English (7 items); and negative attitudes towards English (2 items). The responses
were scored with 1–5 points, decreasing from 'strongly agree' to 'strongly disagree'. Table 6.10 displays the results.

Table 6.10 shows clearly that attitudes towards both English and Spanish remain on the whole quite positive. It is not surprising that Group 1 should favour
Spanish slightly more than the other two groups. Mean strength of agreement with
positive statements about Spanish decreases from 4.1 in Group 1 to 3.7 in Group
2 and to 3.6 in Group 3. Within each subgroup, women and men do not seem to
differ significantly in their support of Spanish. Some minor division of sentiment
appears to occur at the age cut-off point in Groups 2 and 3, where negative
statements about Spanish receive a stronger rejection from the younger respondents (1.7 per cent). This favourable trend may be due to societal changes of
attitude towards bilingualism in general in the last thirty years. Indeed, while older
bilinguals report having been disciplined for using Spanish in school, younger
bilinguals have not had such experience. By contrast, some of them have attended
schools where some form of bilingual education was being promoted.

The favourable responses given to questionnaire IV are somewhat in contrast to
the relatively low value placed by Group 3 on the existence of strong reasons for
maintaining or improving their Spanish (see Table 6.8). These differences do not
indicate inconsistencies, however, since not selecting a reason as most important

TABLE 6.10. Average Agreement with Positive (+) and Negative (−)
Items about Spanish and English

	N^a	+ Span. %	− Span. %	+ Eng. %	− Eng. %
Group 1					
15–30 F	2	4.5	1.9	3.0	3.2
M	2	4.2	2.0	2.7	2.5
31–70 F	4	4.0	2.0	3.2	1.3
M	3	4.1	2.4	3.4	1.8
Total	11	*4.1*[b]	*2.1*	*3.1*	*2.0*
Group 2					
15–30 F	5	3.7	1.7	2.4	1.7
M	3	3.7	1.7	2.5	1.8
31–70 F	4	3.6	2.1	3.1	1.7
M	2	4.0	2.0	3.4	1.5
Total	14	*3.7*	*1.8*	*2.7*	*1.7*
Group 3					
15–30 F	3	3.5	1.7	3.1	1.2
M	1	3.6	1.7	3.7	1.5
31–70 F	3	3.6	2.4	3.5	2.5
M	4	3.7	2.2	3.2	2.0
Total	11	*3.6*	*2.0*	*3.4*	*1.8*

[a] N = no. of respondents in each subgroup.
[b] italics indicate total per cent in each group for each category of attitude.

for maintaining Spanish (questionnaires II and III) does not imply a negative
sentiment towards it.

6.4.5. Questionnaire V

Questionnaire V, administered last to all three groups, was based on Fishman's (in
Fishman *et al.* 1971: ch. 5) 'ten-item commitment scale'. This commitment scale
was used by Fishman to examine the possible 'greater relevance to subsequent
pertinent behavior of commitments than of attitudes or other self-reports' (p. 108).
Sophisticated statistics allowed him to confirm this greater relevance. More important for my purpose, given that I did not incorporate an overt behaviour criterion
in my study (such as the invitation to participate in a Puerto Rican evening
function sent by Fishman to part of his sample), is his observation that language-
attitude and language-usage self-reports do not appear to be guaranteed predictors
of language behaviours unless these self-reports concern 'commitment-type

TABLE 6.11. Degree of Commitment to Act in Order to
Maintain Ancestors' Culture and Language

	N[a]	Total 'yes'[b]	Mean	Questions receiving the 2 highest numbers of 'yes' answers Item (N)	Questions receiving the 2 highest numbers of 'no' answers Item (N)
Group 1					
15–30 F	2	14	.77		
M	2	9	.50		
31–70 F	4	16	.44		
M	3	21	.77		
Total	11		.62[c]	1 (10), 2, 5, 6 (8)	9 (6), 7 (5),
Group 2					
15–30 F	5	33	.48		
M	3	5	.18		
31–70 F	4	26	.72		
M	2	15	.83		
Total	14		.55	6 (10), 2, 8 (9)	7 (13), 4 (7)
Group 3					
15–30 F	3	6	.22		
M	1	1	.11		
31–70 F	3	6	.22		
M	4	16	.44		
Total	11		.24	6 (7), 8 (5)	7, 9 (10), 4 (9)

[a] N = no. of respondents.
[b] 'Yes' = 1 point, 'no' = 0 point.
[c] Italics indicate total mean in each group.

attitude' items. Similarly, Dorian (1981) notes a gap 'between relatively positive *attitudes* toward Gaelic . . . and willingness to see something done to *implement* those attitudes' (p. 174).

Despite possible methodological weaknesses involved in the application of an instrument such as questionnaire V, it seems to me of value to compare the responses obtained from the speakers in my sample, and to venture some explanations for their differing degrees of behavioural commitment to supporting the maintenance and strengthening of Mexican culture and of Spanish as a community language.

Table 6.11 displays the results. The mean value is calculated by scoring 'yes' responses with 1 point, and 'no' responses with zero. Thus, the higher the mean, the stronger the commitment may be interpreted to be. Six speakers (distributed equally in the three groups) responded 'no' to all questions and did not sign the questionnaire. The rest of the sample all signed it, regardless of the number of positive or negative responses.

The results displayed in Table 6.11 indicate clearly that degree of commitment varies within each of the three groups. It is only when global results for each group are compared that the willingness to participate actively in programme-oriented activities organized to promote Spanish language and Mexican culture is seen to decrease steadily and rather dramatically as family length of residence in the USA increases. These results contrast with the positive attitudes towards Spanish that speakers showed in their responses to questionnaire IV. At the same time, they support Dorian's and Fishman's observations that bilingual communities show a dismaying gap between positive attitudes towards a receding or secondary language and willingness to do something or have something done to implement those attitudes.

The commitment scale clearly shows that more respondents in Group 1 agreed in answering 'yes' to a larger number of items. The number of items agreed upon diminishes, however, as we move down the proficiency continuum. This concurs with the results of questionnaires II and III (see Table 6.8), which reveal a descent in the number of most important reasons to maintain Spanish. Notable is the fact that the more intellectual type of activity (question 6: 'Would you agree to attend a lecture or conference on the topic of how persons of Mexican ancestry in Los Angeles can improve their command of Spanish language and Mexican culture?') receives the strongest support in Groups 2 and 3, and also considerable support in Group 1. This response also accords with the support that item 2, the 'abstract principle', received in questionnaires II and III. Consistent with this support is the rejection by most speakers of the more militant proposal 'to join a protest meeting against Los Angeles persons of Mexican ancestry who have stopped speaking and reading the Spanish language'.

Otherwise noteworthy in these responses is the fact that degree of commitment can be almost exactly inverse between siblings or spouses. For instance, J7 (m17, 1) responds 'no' to all 9 questions, while his twin brother, M8 (m17, 1), answers 'yes' to all. Likewise, R17's (f21, 2) sole negative answer is to participating in a protest meeting (item 7), but her sister, V21 (f18, 2), does not commit herself to 4 (5, 7, 8, 9) of the 9 items. One further example comes from L19 (f22, 2), who answers 'yes' only to item 9 (contribution of $15), while her brother, H (m21, 2), answers 'no' to item 9, but 'yes' to items 1, 2, 5, 6, and 8.

6.4.6. Conclusion

On the whole, then, the results of questionnaires I, II, and III indicate a correlation among the following: decrease in the number and strength of the motivations or reasons for maintaining or improving knowledge of Spanish, reduction in the domains of use of Spanish in the community, and linguistic attrition of this secondary language as reflected in the differing varieties characteristic of Groups 1, 2, and 3. Attitudes towards Spanish language and Mexican culture (questionnaire IV, Table 6.10) remain generally very positive. However, the loyalty implicit in these positive attitudes seems to conflict with the uncommitted behaviour revealed by the responses to questionnaire V given by respondents in Group 2 and especially by those in Group 3.

It is necessary to bear in mind, however, Fishman's suggestion (1971: 114) that 'certain populations [language-politicized and language-ideologized populations] can report their language behaviors validly but others [the general population] cannot'. Our sample fits generally the category of 'general population'.

7

Conclusion

7.1. Summary

THREE of the main purposes of this final chapter are: to provide a summary of the linguistic changes which have been examined in this book; in relation to these individual changes, to review how distant the speech of Groups 2 and 3 is from the Spanish dominant norm of Group 1; and to discuss some of the theoretical implications of this book's findings.

Let us first restate briefly that the general hypothesis investigated is that in language-contact situations bilinguals develop strategies aimed at lightening the cognitive load of having to remember and use two different linguistic systems. In the use of the subordinate language, these strategies include: simplification of grammatical categories and lexical oppositions; overgeneralization of forms, frequently following a regularizing pattern; development of periphrastic constructions, either to achieve paradigmatic regularity or to replace less semantically transparent bound morphemes; and direct and indirect transfer of forms from the superordinate language.[1] These strategies facilitate the maintenance of the less used language, they converge towards rendering communication more efficient (cf. Maher 1991: 81), and indeed respond, as proposed by Thomason (1986: 250), to the same factors that make simplifying internal changes natural, namely 'ease of perception, ease of production, and overall ease of learning'.

The linguistic phenomena analysed have illustrated the four strategies referred to. Chapters 2 and 4 have given clear evidence of processes of simplification affecting the verbal system, and the opposition between the copulas *ser* and *estar*, as well as of the concomitant overgeneralization of *estar*, of certain simple tense forms, and of the lexical reflexive verb pattern. Chapter 2 has also demonstrated the trend to develop verbal periphrases (e.g. with *hacer* 'to do/make' + nominal) as a means to facilitate the production of conjugated forms by using simply one conjugational paradigm. The extension of *estar*, as well as the phenomena examined in Chapter 4—the omission of the complementizer *que*, the overall trend to place subjects preverbally, and the differing loss of constraints on subject expression— were offered as possibly illustrating indirect transfer from English. In addition to single-word loans and calques, widely discussed in the existing literature on contact phenomena, direct transfer from English was plainly attested in the cases of multiple-word modelling (with possible syntactic implications) examined in Chapter 6.

---

[1] A fifth strategy, code-switching, has been dealt with only very briefly in Ch. 3.

One further important goal of this book has been the examination of the permeability of Spanish to interference or transfer from English. I have examined innovations in the speech of Groups 2 and 3, identified as such on the basis of a comparison with the norms of the Spanish-dominant bilinguals in Group 1, in an effort to clarify which types of change may be more appropriately explained as intra- or interlinguistically motivated.

In this respect, both spontaneous and non-spontaneous use of tense–mood–aspect morphology reveals a clear trend towards the development of a simplified grammaticalized verb system, independently of English influence (see Table 2.4). In addition, it is intriguing to observe that speakers show a clear inclination to split the verb lexicon in accordance with stative/non-stative lexical aspect, both at the level of bound morphology (Imp for statives, Pret for non-statives) and in the differing development of auxiliary constructions with *hacer* 'to make/do', and with *estar*. These processes find interesting parallels in a good number of diverse studies dealing with language contact (attrition or development) and with language acquisition. Regarding interlinguistic considerations, the generality of the processes identified and the progression of simplification and loss of the different tenses in my data agree in indicating that postulating direct influence from English is not justified.

Chapter 2 has argued that the simplest system of grammaticalized tense appears to be more appropriately accounted for by intralinguistic, cognitive, and interactional considerations (cf. Ferguson 1982: 59). This observation supports the hypothesis that in language-contact situations a number of changes affecting the secondary language have an internal motivation in that (*a*) they are in progress in the 'model' monolingual variety before intensive contact with another language occurs and/or (*b*) they may be spurred by such language-specific features of the secondary language as the semantic opaqueness of certain forms or the relative complexity of a given paradigm. A similar point is made and supported by Mougeon and Beniak (1991: ch. 5) with reference to changes in Ontarian French.

Chapter 4 deals with two independent changes that are also internally motivated in the sense of (*a*) and (*b*) above: the generalization of *estar* 'to be' and Cl placement. Furthermore, transfer from English does not appear to play a role in the various patterns of omission of dative, accusative, and reflexive Cls. The complexity of the Spanish system and reduced use of and exposure to this language emerge as more adequate reasons for these modifications.

Four possible cases of permeation of the syntax of Spanish by English grammatical rules investigated in Chapter 5 lead also to the conclusion that transfer from English is mostly indirect. For instance, knowledge of English probably favours (in the sense that these phenomena are more frequent in the speech of bilinguals in Groups 2 and 3) the non-expression of the complementizer *que* 'that', the slight tendency to place subjects preverbally, and the selective retention of some constraints on subject expression. However, none of these modifications produces ungrammatical structures in Spanish, nor does the omission of so-called 'dative clitics of possession', which corresponds at best to what Mougeon and Beniak (1991: 188–9) call an 'ambiguous change', i.e. one that may be 'predictable both intra- and intersystemically'. Crucially, however, with the exception of the variable omission of the complementizer, the explanation for these modifications is more adequately found in the loss of semantic-pragmatic constraints. The trend towards a more fixed SVX word order, and at the same time towards a lower frequency of subject expression in Groups 2 and 3, two opposing trends if English is taken as the measure for comparison, is further proof that secondary languages do not blindly calque the structures of a superordinate language.

As noted before by numerous linguists, calquing may be more easily identified in the lexicon. A number of single-word and multiple-word items used by bilinguals in Groups 1, 2, and 3, which deviate from the norms of more conservative Group 1 speakers, are shown to be the consequence of direct transfer of forms and/or form meanings from English (Chapter 6).

The comparison of diverse linguistic phenomena across speakers who represent varying lengths of residence in the USA, different degrees of decline of Spanish language use, and dissimilar overall attitudes towards the maintenance of this language reveals the points at which these linguistic phenomena manifest themselves in relation to the extralinguistic factors associated with the bilingual proficiency continuum. Table 7.1 summarizes the linguistic phenomena analysed in the three groups of speakers, as well as extralinguistic information about degree of use of Spanish and degree of commitment to its maintenance as one of the community languages.

The various sections in Table 7.1 have been adapted from tables or text in the preceding chapters as follows: section I is based on Table 2.3. A plus sign between columns in sections I and II is used to indicate that the content of the columns to the left is added to the content of the columns on the right. Sections II, III, and IV are adapted from Tables 4.6, 4.13, and 4.17 respectively. The matrix verbs included in section IV are those that occur frequently enough to allow a comparison across the three groups. Sections V, VI, and VII are based on Tables 5.2, 5.4, and 5.10 respectively. Sections III, V, and VII include the following abbreviations: Refl = reflexive; inan = inanimate; S = subject; PerPro = personal pronoun; NP = noun phrase; OthPro = other pronoun; MorphAmb = morphological ambiguity of the verbal form; Coref = coreferentiality with the preceding subject. Section VIII is from Table 6.1. Section IX comes from section 5.2. Section X contains three subsections. The value for degree of use of Spanish (a) is based on the responses to items 71, 72, 74 of Table 6.3. It is determined by assigning one point if the response is either 'A' (always) or 'F' (frequently), and calculating the percentage of the total number of possible points in each group that the actual points assigned represent. The value for agreement with positive items about Spanish (b) is based on Table 6.10 (scale = 1–5 points). Finally, degree of commitment is based on Table 6.11.

TABLE 7.1. Summary of Some Linguistic and Non-linguistic Phenomena Examined

I. *Loss and simplification of tense morphemes*

	GROUP 1	+	GROUP 2	+	GROUP 3
L:	Fut Perf		Fut		IS
	Cond (tense)		Perf Inf		Cond (modal)
	Cond Perf		PluS		PresPerf
	PPS		Pluperf		PS
	S: IS		S: IS		Imper
			Pret		
			Imp		
			PS		

II. *Extension of estar by adjective type*

GROUP 1	+	GROUPS 2, 3
Age		Moral
Size		Class
Physical		
Colour		

III. *Clitics omitted by clitic type*

	GROUP 1 (No.)	GROUP 2 (No.)	GROUP 3 (No.)
Dative	2	4	15
Obligatory Refl	1	2	11
Accusative		2	13
True Refl		2	6
Indirect Refl			10
Refl with inan S			4
Reciprocal			2
Total (%)	0.1	0.8	3.8

IV. *Preverbal clitics*

Matrix verb	GROUP 1 (%)	GROUP 2 (%)	GROUP 3 (%)
Ir (a)	92	97	92
Estar	91	95	89
Poder	60	95	83
Tener que	57	75	65
Querer	32	55	52

V. Preverbal subjects

	GROUP 1 (%)	GROUP 2 (%)	GROUP 3 (%)
PerPro	85	91	94
NP	56	66	62
OthPro	60	63	83

VI. Subject pronoun expression

GROUP 1 (%)	GROUP 2 (%)	GROUP 3 (%)
33	28	26

VII. Valid constraints on subject expression

	GROUP 1	GROUP 2	GROUP 3
MorphAmb	Yes	Yes	No
Coref	Yes	Yes	Yes

VIII. % modelling in every 10 minutes of speech

GROUP 1 (No.)	(%)	GROUP 2 (No.)	(%)	GROUP 3 (No.)	(%)
2	0.05	86	0.9	110	1.3

IX. % speakers omitting the complementizer

GROUP 1	GROUP 2	GROUP 3
4/13 30.7%	6/11 54.5%	9/11 81.8%

X. (a) Degree of use of Spanish with family members (b) Degree of agreement with positive items about Spanish (c) Degree of commitment to maintain ancestors' language and culture

	GROUP 1	GROUP 2	GROUP 3
(a) Use	.69	.30	.29
(b) Positive items	4.1	3.7	3.6
(c) Commitment	.62	.55	.24

7.2. Discussion and Theoretical Implications

7.2.1. External factors

Conspicuous in Table 7.1 is the correlation between gradual distancing of Groups 2 and 3 from some of the linguistic norms of Group 1 speakers (sections I–IX), a sharp reduction of Spanish language use from Group 1 to 2 and 3, a slight descent in the strength of positive attitudes, and a significant decline in the degree of commitment to act in order to maintain Spanish culture and language. Generally, then, the extralinguistic factors illustrated in section X (Table 7.1) appear to be good predictors of the degree of linguistic attrition of a secondary language in a situation of societal bilingualism, as well as of the stages (according to the differing length of family residence in the USA represented in Groups 1, 2, and 3) at which such strategies as simplification, overgeneralization, and transfer manifest themselves with respect to different linguistic phenomena.

Table 7.1 shows that certain linguistic modifications occur only in the speech of speakers in Group 3. Others are attested in Groups 2 and 3, but never (or only rarely) in the speech of those in Group 1. Interestingly, this is so regardless of whether there has been a certain degree of decline in Spanish language use in this group.

These results support in part our initial hypothesis regarding the correlation between extralinguistic and linguistic factors (see Chapter 1). This hypothesis proposed that changes affecting bilinguals' Spanish were favoured and accelerated by (*a*) absence of normative pressures on the subordinate language, (*b*) restriction in the range of communicative uses of the subordinate language, and (*c*) speakers' positive attitudes towards the superordinate language in contrast to either neutral or negative attitudes toward the subordinate one.

In light of the results, proposals (*b*) and (*c*) may need to be slightly modified. In the case of (*b*), given the absence of changes with respect to the ancestor variety in some speakers in Group 1 who have evidently reduced Spanish usage, the degree of restriction should be determined with more precision. This requirement may also be justified by the very small difference in degree of use of Spanish which emerges from the reports of Groups 2 and 3, although these reports must be taken with caution. Furthermore, it is likely that reduction in use is to a certain extent counterbalanced by the fact that Group 1 speakers have come to the USA after age eleven—i.e. one may assume that they have been exposed to 'normative pressures' in elementary school in Mexico. As for (*c*), the attitudes towards English are positive overall, but no negative attitudes towards Spanish are uncovered in any group. Commitment, by contrast, declines in Group 2 and even more clearly in Group 3. Thus, it appears that changes away from the norms of Group 1 are favoured by—or at least correlate with—either neutral attitudes or weak commitment to maintaining the subordinate language.

These findings support Mougeon and Beniak's (1991: 221) hypothesis that it is possible to account in a predictable and principled way for the association between 'individual instances of change attested in a contact setting' and 'specific thresholds of bilingualism and frequency of use of the minority language'. On the basis of the specific outcome of my research regarding some speakers in Group 1, I would like to suggest that frequency of use in adolescence or adulthood should be considered in relation to the possibility of a stage of pre-adolescent monolingualism in the minority language.

7.2.2. *Universality of the processes*

A number of language processes, including first- and second language-acquisition, foreigner talk, pidginization, creolization, and language loss, have been observed to give rise to language varieties which share reduced or incompletely developed features frequently described in terms of *simplification*[2] (see several contributions in Andersen 1983; Ferguson 1977; 1982; Meisel 1977; 1983*b*; Mougeon and Beniak 1991; Mühlhäusler 1981; Romaine 1988; Trudgill 1983: ch. 6). Furthermore, it has been claimed that these similarities are motivated by psycholinguistic universals which underlie *inter alia* the order of acquisition and possibly also the order of loss of linguistic items (see e.g. Andersen 1989; Menn 1989).

With respect to the issue of universality, it has been observed that the four strategies identified in the preceding chapters—simplification, overgeneralization, transfer, and analysis—are indeed attested across different situations of linguistic stress, and may justifiably be accounted for with reference to cognitive processes which govern language acquisition and use in general.

Assuming that two of Slobin's forty 'operational principles' (cited in Andersen 1989: 387) for first-language acquisition are correct—frequency and the separate mental storage of different units—the outcome of simplification, i.e. a simplified system with fewer categories and oppositions, should obviouly be simpler to store, remember, and use. A simpler system must also make more manageable the rapid retrieval of less frequently used linguistic forms. Likewise, overgeneralization does away with exceptions and restricted subclasses; analytical constructions are semantically more transparent or paradigmatically more regular than synthetic ones; and convergence (when two or more languages are involved) through indirect or direct transfer reduces the task of having to store, remember, and use different linguistic rules. All these strategies converge, then, to lighten the cognitive load of having to use two or more linguistic systems in daily communication and at the same time contribute to rendering communication more efficient under the special circumstances involved (see Chapter 3).

In the context of my work, I have considered linguistic simplification to be a complex process which also implies rule generalization, in the sense that a given form is being expanded to a larger number of contexts at the expense of a receding

---

[2] This observation is not incompatible with the attested existence of contact-induced complicating changes (sometimes alongside simplifying ones), esp. in situations where the affected language is not receding.

form. So defined, simplification of forms, of grammatical categories, and also frequently, though not necessarily, of meanings is widespread in the data examined. It could be easily demonstrated, however, that it is also prevalent in functionally unreduced superordinate languages.[3] While this is indeed the case, there are two important differences between the two situations. One is that receding varieties do not develop linguistic alternatives for reduced or eliminated grammatical categories (although they may for some lexical items). Simplification thus results in simplified linguistic systems or subsystems (e.g. no gender-marking, fewer tense forms, reduced case-marking)[4] (see Taylor 1989: 179, who observes that the speech of not-fully-competent speakers of Gros Ventre 'shows the unreplaced loss of some features, with the result that some things either cannot be expressed, or must be expressed in roundabout ways').

The second difference concerns the speed of simplification in a contracting secondary language. One generation in the life cycle of these languages is equivalent to many more than one in the non-receding corresponding language. The same point about speed of change has been made by Markey (cited by Romaine 1989a: 380) in connection with the evolutionary rate of creoles: 'thirty years in the life cycle of a creole might well be equivalent to three centuries in the life cycle of a non-creole'. In the case of creoles, the rapid changes leading to the development of more complex linguistic systems (a contrast that has led linguists to view attrition as a case of creolization in reverse) may be considered as processes of language creation. Once a creole has reached maturity, so to speak, its rate of change would not necessarily be different from any other language changes.

There seems sufficient evidence to maintain that language contact has the effect of speeding up simplification and diffusion of changes. In regard to minority languages, these tend to be changes already present in the non-contact ancestor variety, i.e. they have intralinguistic roots (such as the rapid extension of *estar* and the internally motivated trend to place Cls preverbally in verbal periphrases). Maandi (1989) argues similarly that contact with Swedish has had the effect of accelerating the internally motivated simplification of the objective case-marking system of Estonian among Estonian immigrants in Sweden.

Among the most debated theoretical issues dealt with by those concerned with language change (in growth, attrition, or 'normal' life of languages) has been the impact that one linguistic system may have on that of another. Concern with the question of transfer (or interference) and substratum or superstratum influence is evident in a number of recent publications (e.g. Thomason and Kaufman 1988;

---

[3] Regarding Spanish in particular, the simplification processes attested in Groups 2 and 3 which affect the verbal system and the omission of Cls (as well as multiple-word modelling with syntactic implications) have no counterparts in monolingual communities using the language; i.e. they probably require some degree of language-use (functional) restriction in a context of daily use of 2 or more languages.

[4] This is the sense in which the term 'simplification' appears to be used most frequently in linguistic writings. Observe that in my framework simplification is viewed as a process which may lead to a simplified system as a result.

TABLE 7.2. Types of Linguistic Changes and Associated Triggering Factors

	Group 1	Group 2	Group 3
Direct transfer			
(*a*) Lexical: with syntactic implications	No	Yes	Yes
without syntactic implications	Yes	Yes	Yes
(*b*) Semantic-pragmatic	Yes	Yes	Yes
Indirect transfer			
Higher frequency of parallel structures	Yes	Yes	Yes
Forgetting or incomplete learning			
Loss of discourse-pragmatic constraints	No	Yes	Yes
Loss of tense–mood–aspect inflections	No	Yes	Yes
Loss of agreement markers (e.g. gender, case)	No	Yes	Yes
Acceleration of intralinguistic processes			
Diffusion of preferred variants of either stable or 'changing' variables in the ancestor varieties	Yes	Yes	Yes

Dorian 1989; Mougeon and Beniak 1991; Seliger and Vago 1991) and in many works of the last hundred years or so (concerning the formation of Latin American Spanish, for instance: Alonso 1939; Catalán 1958; Fontanella de Weinberg 1980; de Granda 1968; 1971; 1991; Henríquez Ureña 1921; Lapesa 1964; Lenz 1893; Lope Blanch 1967; López Morales 1980; Suárez 1966).

In planning her volume, Dorian (1989: 9) explicitly proposed as one of the possible lines of investigation the search for an answer to the following question: 'Is change in dying speech forms the result of interference, convergence, independent autogenetic processes or all of these?' As may be evident by now, my answer would be 'all of these'. More importantly, however, my own research has contributed in this respect by identifying in three groups of speakers some types of change that may be expected to result from direct or indirect transfer, some that probably result from forgetting or incomplete learning caused by reduction in language use, and yet others that are the outcome of acceleration of independent intralinguistic processes (see Table 7.2).

It is clear from Table 7.2 that Groups 2 and 3 are not qualitatively distinct with regard to these broad classes of linguistic change. The dissimilarities are discovered when finer subclasses are distinguished and quantitative analyses performed.

Thomason and Kaufman (1988) and Campbell and Muntzel (1989) (CM) have challenged the view that a grammatical system is impermeable to direct transfer of foreign elements. On the basis of evidence provided by a number of studies, Thomason and Kaufman argue that 'any linguistic feature can be transferred from any language to any other language' (p. 14), but their evidence stems from old contact situations, not ongoing ones. In their consideration of structural changes in obsolescing languages, CM also surmise that 'several grammatical changes in American Finnish can only be attributed to the external influence of English' (p. 190).[5]

A brief examination of the examples provided, however, leads me to a different conclusion. For instance, CM note that Standard Finnish (SF) does not permit agentive phrases, but American Finnish (AF) does, replicating the English '*by* phrase' model. However, the assumed corresponding agentive phrases are not headed by a *by*-type preposition; they contain case inflections or postpositions (translated by CM as 'from (within)', 'from (without)', and 'through') that do not appear strictly to mark agentivity. It is unclear, then, whether the examples provided do in fact represent acts of syntactic reception. The same reservation is raised by another proposed case of syntactic permeation of AF: the occurrence of subjects with infinitival complements of nouns or adjectives. But SF is said to 'not normally permit' this structure, which implies that the structure does exist in SF under certain perhaps more restricted conditions. Could this not be, then, an instance of loss of semantic–pragmatic constraints leading to an extended use of the structure in question?

These reservations and the outcome of my own research lead me to reassert that it may be possible for any linguistic feature to be transferred from any language to any other language as a 'nonce borrowing' in the speech of bilinguals (cf. Weinreich 1974), but only those that are compatible with the structure of the borrowing language (i.e. they correspond to an already existing syntactic variant in this language, see Chapter 5) at any given stage will be adopted, disseminated, and passed on to new generations.

The modifications that occur in a receding language under conditions of intense contact and strong cultural pressure are first and foremost the result of simplification or overgeneralization of grammatical rules that do not introduce elements which cause radical changes in the structure of the language. Since it seems possible that these gradual changes may in time lead to the development of a language fundamentally different from its non-contact ancestor, I would like to reaffirm my proposal that the sociolinguistic history of the speakers is the primary determinant of the language direction and degree of diffusion of the innovations, as well as of the more remote linguistic outcome of language contact; the structure of the languages involved, to a large extent constrained by cognitive and interactional processes, governs the introduction and diffusion of the innovative elements in the linguistic systems. As suggested in Chapter 1, this hypothesis probably accounts for the changes attested in numerous situations of language maintenance and/or shift after several generations of normal language transmission (Thomason and Kaufman 1988).

Weinreich (1974: 4) has stated that 'the cause of the susceptibility of a language

[5] CM (p. 190) follow Jane H. Hill (whom they cite) in calling these changes 'acts of reception'.

to foreign influence [lies] in its structural weaknesses'. By contrast, my research indicates that the permeability of a grammar to foreign influence does not depend on its structural weaknesses but rather on the existence of superficially parallel structures in the languages in contact. It seems to me that my study has offered evidence, on the other hand, to extend Weinreich's (1974: 14) statement about phonological interference to the level of syntax, as follows. Transfer arises when a bilingual identifies a lexical or syntactic structure of the secondary system with one in the primary system and, in reproducing it, subjects it to the semantic-pragmatic rules of the primary language (see Chapters 5 and 6).

While no evidence of direct transfer of productive syntactic forms has been uncovered, the speech of US-born bilinguals gives evidence of incipient transfer of discourse-pragmatic functions from the primary to the secondary language, and of loss of semantic and pragmatic constraints that might be spurred on by the dominant language (indirect transfer). This loss of semantic or pragmatic constraints leads to the overgeneralization of syntactic structures (e.g. certain word order patterns).

I have found evidence of direct transfer (i.e. replacement and incorporation of forms and/or meanings) at the level of the lexicon, which is affected in various manners. Reproductions of multiple-word units, for instance, may have syntactic implications, in that verb subcategorization or combinational possibilities may be modified. Otherwise, the only additions to the syntax of the replica language come through the internal arrangement of words in bound collocations. It is quite likely, however, that innovative syntactic patterns introduced in bound collocations (or in idioms) may in time become context-free and productive, in a manner similar to what has been proposed for the borrowing of bound morphemes (Weinreich 1974: 31).

One question that arises in this connection, therefore, is the justification for the common affirmation that the Spanish of US-born bilinguals is very different from the Spanish of those in Group 1. It seems to me that what creates this impression, exaggerated in my view, is basically simplification of tense–mood–aspect morphology and gender agreement, and confusions in the use of prepositions. The fact that almost every sentence contains one or more of these phenomena, and thus a possible site for deviation from the norms of Group 1, appears to be a strong factor in creating stereotypes of widespread incorrectness and lack of systematicity.

The changes that characterize language loss, the manner in which languages develop ontogenetically, and the evolution of languages in historical time have been proposed as comparable in some respects (see e.g. Slobin 1977). Numerous attempts have been made to investigate child language acquisition and language loss in aphasic subjects in order to ascertain whether one would mirror the other (see Gleason 1982). Likewise, non-pathological language loss (loss resulting from forgetting a less-used language) has been proposed as a special kind of language acquisition (Andersen 1982; 1989; Preston 1982; Seliger 1991) and, further, to be very probably its reverse in terms of the order of retention of a number of language items. In this vein, for instance, and in the context of her study of East Sutherland Gaelic, a 'dying language', Dorian (1982) asks herself whether the loss of language follows a recognizable pattern according to the complexity or frequency of the items in question, and whether this pattern in any way parallels the pattern of acquisition, two very complex questions which she can answer only partially.

One should heed Mougeon and Beniak's (1991: 185) remark that 'simple solutions to complex problems are simply wrong'. However, it is tempting to consider Menn's (1989: 340) four broad levels of acquisition of any language rule or pattern—(0) ignorance; (1) rote or formulaic knowledge; (2) pre-conventional or overgenerative knowledge; (3) full conventionalized knowledge—the mirror image of stages of loss or de-acquisition of the rules of a minority language. Indeed, the extreme degree of functional reduction that characterizes the Spanish of speakers at the lowest levels of the continuum could be seen as a stage of rote or formulaic knowledge. The Spanish they have retained appears to be pinned to a small number of topics and situations which can trigger the use of Spanish in an almost formulaic fashion.

Assuming this parallelism, and assuming that it is due to the workings of similar psychological principles and/or to the freezing, as it were, of the process of acquisition of the minority language at level 1 or 2 of those proposed by Menn, then the linguistic structures retained by those in Group 3 may represent those aspects of a language system that are most regular, frequent, and perceptually salient (cf. Campbell and Muntzel 1989; Menn 1989; Mougeon and Beniak 1991).

I have argued and given evidence that four types of factor—cognitive, social, intralinguistic, and interlinguistic—contribute in complex and interactive ways to the simplification, loss, and transfer of forms or meanings in the various stages of restructuring of a receding language. This result also has implications for general linguistic theory, inasmuch as it gives further evidence of the fact that the structure of language is to a large extent constrained by cognitive and interactional processes. This supports, then, Slobin's (1977) assertions that the study of language during its changing phases 'is an excellent tool for discovering the essence of language itself' (p. 185), and that 'both change and structure are bound by the same psycholinguistic and sociolinguistic constraints imposed by the processing of speech in real time and in social settings' (p. 186).

It is no wonder, therefore, that in language attrition in contact situations we observe the same principles which characterize change in unstressed languages. Our study gives evidence of the workings of at least the following: *generality, frequence, distance,* and *semantic transparency.*

The *principle of generality* predicts that, given two forms with at least one shared structural context and with closely related meanings, the form with a wider structural and pragmatic distribution, or for which there are no other alternatives in the language, will be acquired first, retained, or lost later (see e.g. Maandi 1989; Prince 1992; Seliger 1991).

With respect to the verb system, for instance, this principle correctly predicts the earlier loss of the Cond Perf as opposed to the PluS in Mexican-American Spanish (see Chapter 2). Observe (*a*) that, while the PluS may occur in the protasis and apodosis of past counterfactual conditional clauses, the Cond Perf may occur only in the apodosis,[6] and no other tense may substitute for the PluS in the protasis without a change in meaning ([1]); and (*b*) that, in contexts which refer to possibility in the past, where the PluS does not occur, there are a number of structures which may substitute for the Cond Perf ([2a–c]).

[1] Si *hubiera jugado, hubiera ganado*   (PluS)
   * *habría . . . habría*   (Cond Perf)
   If (he) *had played*, (he) *would've won*

[2] (*a*) Se *habría ido* ya cuando Uds. llegaron   (Cond Perf)
      * *hubiera*   (PluS)
      (He) *must've* already left when you arrived
   (*b*) Se *debía haber ido* ya cuando Uds. llegaron
      (He) *must've* already left when you arrived
   (*c*) *Seguramente* se *había ido* ya cuando Uds. llegaron
      Surely (he) *had left* when you arrived

The principle of generality refers to intralinguistic structural factors. I feel, however, that it is related to circumstances which have to do with the nature of communication. On the one hand, generality has frequency implications. More general forms occur more frequently in discourse and tend, for this reason, to be retained (longer) in receding languages (cf. Dorian 1983: 161), while infrequent forms are either lost or never acquired (cf. Mougeon & Beniak 1991: 220).

On the other hand, consideration of the nature of communication leads me to propose a further related principle, the *principle of distance* (cf. Silva-Corvalán 1985: 565). According to this principle, if a language system has several forms in the same syntactic-semantic sphere, the form which is farthest away from the speaker, in the sense that it refers to objects or events which are the farthest from him in his objective (e.g. actual distance) or subjective (e.g. possibility of actualization) world, will tend to be lost first and acquired later. Interactional, and perhaps also memory factors underlie this principle: since speakers tend to speak about themselves and their immediate objective world rather than about distant and hypothetical situations, the infrequently used forms, if any, will disappear first, while the more frequently used ones will be acquired earlier or retained longer.

Thus, consideration of the principle of distance makes it reasonable to expect that, regarding the possible extension of a copula, *estar* rather than *ser* would be extended because *estar* is the copula associated with concrete and/or immediate experience (v. Ch. 4). My research gives evidence that this is in fact so.

[6] The Cond Perf may occur in the protasis of some varieties of Spanish spoken in northern Spain. It has not, to my knowledge, been reported in this context in any Mexican Spanish variety.

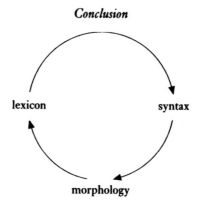

FIG. 7.1. Cycle of changes in unstressed languages.

morphology ————————▶ lexicon ————————▶ (syntax (periphrasis))

FIG. 7.2. Linear changes in language attrition

The development of periphrases and simplification support the cognitively motivated *principle of semantic transparency*, defined by Slobin (1977: 186) as a tendency 'to maintain a one-to-one mapping between underlying semantic structures and surface forms, with the goal of making messages easily retrievable for listeners'. The ideal iconic stage is never reached, however, because linguistic units are not isolated; so changes in one item lead to other changes which frequently result in polysemy. The general trend in language attrition seems to be toward simplification and loss of forms, but the remaining ones may become semantically more complex (although there is also greater reliance on contextual cues).

In conclusion, even though the same principles seem to be at work, there is one major difference between attrition in language contact and complexification and development in child language, creolization, and historical language change. In the latter group of situations, language goes through cycles of simplification, loss, and complexification (see the evolution of future tense forms in the history of Romance in Fleischman 1982). By contrast, in language attrition the changes are linear and lead to extensive reduction. Thus, while Slobin's (1977) four charges to Language—to be clear, processible, quick, and expressive—appear to account in part for the cycle of changes in unstressed languages illustrated in Fig. 7.1, in attrition the cycle is broken and remorphologization does not occur, as shown in Fig. 7.2.

The linear changes in Fig. 7.2 are intended to represent the facts associated with attrition and final language death. I have shown in this book that bilingualism involving Spanish and English is not dying in Los Angeles. Rather, Hispanic communities throughout this city give evidence of the wondrously complex sociolinguistic phenomenon of societal bilingualism: Spanish illustrates a continuum of levels of proficiency along which speakers move, up or down, either in their life-time or across generations. (There is also a clear proficiency continuum in English, characteristic of speakers in Group 1.) This is a dynamic situation which, given enough time depth and favourable social conditions, may lead to a cycle of changes as pictured in Fig. 7.1.

Societal bilingualism offers a wealth of research possibilities. Essential relation-ships between language and society, between language and mind, between lan-guage and language can be found and examined in a situation of this type. Studies of Spanish–English contact have made, and will most certainly continue to make valuable contributions to our knowledge of the nature of the linguistic, cognitive, and social processes underlying both possible changes in language maintenance and changes characteristic of language shift and loss. This book is one more stage in the advancement of our knowledge of the topic, and my impression is that in some areas it has provided some firm foundations upon which we can continue to build.

Appendix 1
Tape Contents and Speaker Coding

Tape Contents

Tape No.	Speaker ID No.	Coding 1	2	3	4	5	6	7	8	9	10
Group 1											
ELA 26, 64	Elisa V. 1	A	B	F	A	C	I	J	N	T	P
ELA 37, 76	Silvia P. 2	A	F	F	A	C	Z	G	N	V	P
ELA 45, 72	Lourdes C. 3	A	F	F	A	C	Z	J	N	T	P
ELA 56	María G. 4	A	B	F	A	C	I	G	N	T	P
ELA 13, 90	Fortino V. 5	A	A	M	A	C	I	G	Z	T	P
ELA 51	Manuel C. 6	A	D	M	A	C	Z	J	N	T	P
ELA 58, 91	José Luis A. 7	A	B	M	A	C	G	G	K	T	P
ELA 59, 91	Moisés A. 8	A	B	M	A	C	G	G	K	T	P
ELA 2, 3, 73	Alicia C. 9	A	C	F	B	C	J	G	N	V	P
ELA 9, 10, 88	Consuelo S. 10	A	D	F	B	C	J	J	N	T	P
ELA 16, 17, 18, 19, 77	Rosa J. 11	A	C	F	B	C	J	H	N	T	P
ELA 27, 28, 44, 92	Eva R. 12	A	C	F	B	C	J	J	N	T	P
ELA 4, 5, 6, 85	Carlos I. 13	A	D	M	B	C	Z	J	N	V	P
ELA 17, 18, 77	Juan J. 14	A	F	M	B	C	Z	G	N	V	P
ELA 28, 44, 95	Phil R. 15	A	B	M	B	C	H	J	N	T	P
ELA 41, 81	Julián C. 16	A	F	M	B	C	Z	G	N	V	P
Group 2											
ELA 3, 4, 67, 68	Rosy J. 17	C	A	F	A	D	I	N	K	R	R
ELA 32, 33, 70	Elsa O. 18	C	A	F	A	D	I	N	Z	R	P
ELA 54, 82	Laura R. 19	A	A	F	A	D	I	N	Z	P	P
ELA 26, 29, 61B, 64	Araceli C. 20	A	A	F	A	D	I	N	K	R	P
ELA 16, 17 67	Virgie J. 21	D	A	F	A	D	I	N	K	R	P
ELA 11, 50, 69	Hector R. 22	A	A	M	A	D	I	N	K	P	P
ELA 49, 71	Hector Z. 23	C	A	M	A	D	I	N	L	R	P
ELA 50	Robert R. 24	C	A	M	A	D	I	N	L	P	R
ELA 55, 87	Mark Anth. R. 25	B	A	M	A	D	I	N	L	P	R
ELA 4, 5, 6, 85	Mercedes I. 26	B	A	F	B	D	J	N	L	R	P

Tape No.	Speaker ID No.	Coding
		1 2 3 4 5 6 7 8 9 10
ELA 21, 22, 94, 22B	Beatrice O. 27	B A F B D J N Z R P
ELA 23, 24, 75	Lucy A. 28	C A F B D J N Z R P
ELA 2, 3, 73	Alberto C. 29	B A M B D G N Z P P
ELA 33, 35, 36, 79	Enrique M. 30	A A M B D H N Z R P
ELA 39, 40	Ed C. 31	A A M B D H N Z P P
ELA 47, 48, 86	Gilberto S. 32	A A M B D G N Z R P
Group 3 ('special')		
ELA 29	Belinda P. 33	C A F A M I N L R P
ELA 46, 83	Ana María G. 34	C A F B M J N Z P P
ELA 7, 8, 94	Rufina O. 35	A B F B M G N Z R P
ELA 43, 90	Diego V. 36	C A M B M P N K P S
ELA 21, 22, 94, 95	Alejo O. 37	B A M B M J N Z R P
Group 3		
ELA 30, 31, 66	Sonia R. 38	C A F A E I N P R R
ELA 42, 61	Dolores Y. 39	C A F A E J N Z R S
ELA 48	Nora S. 40	F A F A E J N Z P P
ELA 34, 74	Marc Andr. A. 41	D A M A E I N Z R P
ELA 30, 63	Rodney R. 42	D A M A E G N L P R
ELA 57, 84	Joe R. 43	D A M A E G N P P R
ELA 62	José Rich. M. 44	F A M A E G N Z P R
ELA 1, 25, 89	Esther Z. 45	D A F B E J N K P S
ELA 19, 20	Alma Ali. C. 46	F A F B E H N Z R P
ELA 52, 53, 80	María O. 47	C A F B E I N Z R P
ELA 23, 24, 75	Henry A. 48	C A M B E J N Z R P
ELA 31, 32, 87	Richard E. 49	B A M B E J N Z P P
ELA 36, 38, 78	Robert Rd. 50	B A M B E H N Z P R

Family Groupings

Parents	Offspring	Other relatives
1. Alicia (Gr1, No. 9)	Alma Ali. (Gr3, No. 46)	
Alberto (Gr2, No. 29)		
2. Rosa (Gr1, No. 11)	Rosy (Gr2, No. 17)	
Juan (Gr1, No. 14)	Virgie (Gr2, No. 21)	
3. Eva (Gr1, No. 12)	Laura (Gr2, No. 19)	Robert (Gr2, No. 24)
Phil (Gr1, No. 15)	Hector (Gr2, No. 22)	Mark (Gr2, No. 25)

Parents	Offspring	Other relatives
4. Carlos (Gr1, No. 13) Mercedes (Gr2, No. 26)		
5. Julián (Gr1, No. 16)	Araceli (Gr2, No. 20)	Hector (Gr2, No. 23 Belinda (Cr3, No. 33) Ana M. (Cr3, No. 34)
6. Lourdes (Gr1, No. 3) Manuel (Gr1, No. 6)		Elisa (Gr1, No. 1)
7.	José L. (Gr1, No. 7) Moisés (Gr1, No. 8)	
8. Beatrice (Gr2, No. 27) Alejo (Gr3, No. 37)		
9. Lucy (Gr2, No. 28) Henry (Gr3, No. 48		
10. Gilberto (Gr2, No. 32)	Nora (Gr3, No. 40)	
11. Robert Rd. (Gr3, No. 50)	Sonia (Gr3, No. 38) Rodney (Gr3, No. 42)	Richard (Gr3, No. 49)

Explanation of Speaker Codings

I. Impressionistic level of language proficiency or fluency

My evaluation is based on such features as: pauses, self-corrections, smoothness and speed of delivery, switching to English, requests for help with vocabulary, and the speaker's own subjective evaluation of the degree of difficulty or ease he has in communicating in Spanish.

1. Spanish: A = native; B = near native; C = good; D = fair; F = very poor.
2. English: A = native; B = near native; C = good; D = fair; F = very poor.

II. Ascribed social features

3. Sex: F = female; M = male.
4. Age: A = 15–29 years; B = 30–65 years.

III. Group by family length of stay in the USA

5. Group 1:
   C = both parents from Mexico; speaker came to the USA after age 11.

Group 2:

D = both parents from Mexico, or one parent from Mexico and the other from New Mexico or Texas; speaker was born in or came to Los Angeles before age 11.

Group 3 ('special'):

M = parents and grandparents from Arizona, New Mexico, or Texas; speaker has lived in Los Angeles for at least 19 years.

Group 3:

E = both parents from California or one parent came to the USA before age 11; speaker has lived in Los Angeles all his life.

Note: Both subgroups (M and E) are referred to as 'Group 3', and treated as one group unless otherwise stated in the text.

IV. Level of formal schooling

6. English:

   G = attending/incomplete high school
   J = high school diploma
   H = technical school beyond high school
   I = attending college
   P = Ph.D. degree
   Z = no formal schooling

7. Spanish as L1:

   G = incomplete elementary
   J = incomplete secondary
   H = technical before completion of secondary
   I = college
   N = not applicable

8. Spanish as L2 in High School and/or College

   Z = zero semesters; K = 2 semesters; L = 3–4 semesters;
   P = 5–6 semesters; N = not applicable.

V. Age at which language acquisition started

9. English:

   P = at birth
   R = 3–6 years
   S = 6–11 years
   T = 12–19 years
   V = after 19 years

10. Spanish:

P = at birth

R = reactivated at adolescence

S = reactivated after 20 years of age

Note: 'Reactivated' means that the speaker states that he made a conscious decision and effort to use Spanish more frequently, and to improve his fluency in this language.

Appendix 2
Verb Test

Ejemplos

1. Creo que no (voy a poder ir) para México el próximo mes.
2. Cuando fui a visitarlos, me (llevaron) a ver una película muy bonita.
3. Al niño le (hablan) puro inglés.

1. Algunas veces . . . . . al parque el domingo en la tarde.
2. Eso lo . . . . . el próximo año.
3. Tus grados no están buenos, hijo, ... estudiar más.
4. Bueno, pues, ella extrañaba porque nunca . . . . . lejos de la casa.
5. Si hubieras ido con nosotros al estadio, ... jugar a Fernando Valenzuela.
6. Es posible que ya . . . . . de hacer los tamales.
7. Yo hacía los dibujos como yo . . . . . .
8. Cuando lo conocí . . . . . unos 20 años, pero no estoy seguro.
9. Nos invitaron a cenar, pero estamos tan atrasados. Seguro que ellos ya . . . . . cuando lleguemos a su casa.
10. La grabación te quedó muy mala . . . . . de hacerla otra vez.
11. A los 20 años mi cuñada ya se . . . . . con mi hermano.
12. Me dijo que yo tenía que contestar la pregunta en la mejor forma que . . . . .
13. No quiero que . . . . . con esos muchachos.
14. Estando en la escuela, tú . . . . . tomado clases de español.
15. No sé qué . . . . . lo que había en la caja.
16. Cuando llegó el policía, le dijeron que alguien . . . . . a robar.
17. Dicen que . . . . . el precio de la carne mañana.
18. Lo llevé a la escuela para que . . . . . con los otros chamaquitos.
19. Decían que él tenía otra mujer, pero no sé si . . . . . verdad o no.
20. Ahora me arrepiento de . . . . . al party.
21. Tú tienes muchas caries, ... ir al dentista.
22. En mi aplicación miraron que yo . . . . . que sabía hablar español.
23. El patio de mi casa . . . . . bastante amplio, pero la yarda de enfrente . . . . . chiquita.
24. Cuando cumplas 5 años de residente, ... ciudadano.
25. ¿Qué edad tiene Pedro?
    . . . . . unos 35, pero no estoy seguro.

26. Lo que mis padres hicieron por mí, lo . . . . . por mis hijos también, pero ya no lo hice.
27. Entonces llegó y le pregunté que si . . . . . y me dijo, 'Sí; me comí unos tacos'.
28. Antes de haber ido tú a ese lugar horrible, me . . . . . preguntado cómo era.
29. Bueno, si tuviera mucho dinero, me . . . . . un Cadillac.
30. No creo que . . . . . para México sin que nadie supiera.
31. Si te sientes mal . . . . . descansar.
32. No sé qué . . . . . lo que hay en esta caja.
33. Es difícil describir mi nariz; ¿cómo la . . . . . tú?

Approximate English translation

Examples

1. I don't think I (am going to be able to go) to Mexico next month.
2. When I went to visit them, they (took) me to see a movie.
3. To the child, they (speak) only in English to him.

1. Sometimes I . . . . . to the park on Sunday afternoons.
2. That I . . . . . next year.
3. Your grades are not good, son, ... study harder.
4. Well, then, she felt homesick because she . . . . . never away from home before.
5. If you'd gone to the stadium with us, you . . . . . Fernando Valenzuela play.
6. It's likely that they . . . . . doing the tamales.
7. I made the drawing as I . . . . .
8. When I met him, he . . . . . about 20 years old, but I'm not sure.
9. They invited us to dinner, but we're so late. Surely they . . . . . already when we get to their place.
10. The recording didn't turn out good. . . . . . do it again.
11. When she was 20, my sister-in-law . . . . . already my brother.
12. He told me that I had to answer the question as best as I . . . . .
13. I don't want you . . . . . with those guys.
14. Being in school, you . . . . . taken Spanish lessons.
15. I don't know what . . . . . that was in the box.
16. When the policeman arrived, they told him that someone . . . . . to rob the house.
17. They say that the price of meat . . . . . tomorrow.
18. I took him to school so he . . . . . with the other children.
19. They say he had another woman, but I don't know whether it . . . . . true or not.
20. Now I'm sorry for . . . . . to the party.
21. You have a lot of cavities, ... go to the dentist.

22. They saw in my application that I . . . . . that I knew how to speak Spanish.
23. My backyard . . . . . quite big, but the front garden . . . . . small.
24. When you've been a resident for five years, you . . . . . a citizen.
25. How old is Peter?
    . . . . . about 35, but I'm not sure.
26. What my parents did for me, I . . . . . for my children as well, but I didn't do it.
27. So then he came home and I asked him if he . . . . . and he told me, 'Yes, I ate some tacos'.
28. Before going to that horrible place, you . . . . . asked me what it was like.
29. Well, if I had a lot of money, I . . . . . me a Cadillac.
30. I don't think that . . . . . to Mexico without having told anyone.
31. If you don't feel well, you . . . . . rest.
32. I don't know what . . . . . that is in this box.
33. It's difficult to describe my nose. How . . . . . it?

Appendix 3
Factors Included in the Coding of Subject Expression

1. *Dependent variable*
   1. Expressed subject
   2. Non-expressed subject
2. *Coreferentiality index with preceding sentence*
   1. Coreference with subject
   2. Coreference with indirect object, switch reference with subject
   3. Coreference with direct object, switch reference with subject
   4. Switch reference with subject, direct object, and indirect object
   5. Sentential subject
   6. After pause
   7. Coreference with oblique complement, switch reference with subject
   8. Non-identifiable subject
3. *Morphological ambiguity of the verbal form*
   1. Ambiguous
   2. Non-ambiguous
4. *Contextual ambiguity**
   1. Ambiguous subject referent despite discourse context
   2. Non-ambiguous subject referent in discourse context
   3. Subject referent identified by the verbal inflection
5. *Contrast*
   1. Subject focus of contrast
   2. Subject non-contrastive
6. *Verb type*
   1. Reflexive form
   2. Non-reflexive form
7. *Verb syntax/semantics*
   1. Estimative (e.g. *pensar* 'to think', *creer* 'to believe', *decir* 'to say')
   2. *Gustar* 'to like' type verbs (e.g. *faltarle* 'to lack', *ocurrírsele* 'to occur to one')
   3. Stative (e.g. *estar* 'to be' locative, *vivir* 'to live', *quedarse* 'to stay', *encontrarse* 'to be located')
   4. Intransitive of activity (e.g. *salir* 'go out', *pasar/ocurrir* 'to happen', *irse* 'to leave', *correr* 'to run')
   5. Copulative verb with nominal or adjectival predicate

6. Presentational (e.g. *aparecer* 'to appear', *llegar* 'to arrive', *asomarse* 'to show up')

7. All others

8. *Decir* 'to say/tell' as a verb of reporting

8. *Second dependent variable: subject word order*
   1. Preverbal: transitive verb with direct or indirect object NP
   2. Preverbal: transitive verb with verbal clitic and no object NP
   3. Postverbal: transitive verb with direct or indirect object NP
   4. Postverbal: transitive verb with verbal clitic and no object NP
   5. Preverbal: intransitive verb
   6. Postverbal: intransitive verb
   7. Non-expressed subject
   8. Copulative verb

9. *Subject type*
   1. *Yo* 'I'
   2. *Tú/usted* 'you-sg. familiar/formal'
   3. *El/ella* 'he/she/it'
   4. *Nosotros/nosotras* 'we-masc./fem.'
   5. *Ustedes* 'you-pl.'
   6. *Ellos/ellas* 'they-masc./fem.'
   7. Noun phrase
   8. Other pronouns
   9. *Tú* 'you' (interlocutor + others)
   10. Ambiguous subject

10. *Turn of speech*
    1. New
    2. Same

11. *Clause type*
    1. Independent
    2. Relative clause
    3. Other subordinate clauses
    4. Infinitival clause

12. *Sentence type*
    1. Declarative
    2. Interrogative
    3. Exclamative
    4. Imperative

13. *Communicative value*
    1. Focal subject
    2. Non-focal subject
    3. Subject and another focal argument

*Although included in the coding chart, the data were not coded for this factor because the very few ambiguous subjects that occurred (four cases in group 3) were captured in 2.8: non-identifiable subject.

Appendix 4
Attitude Questionnaires

Questionnaire I

This questionnaire grouped answers under the following headings: ALWS = always; USULY = usually; OFT = often; SMTMS = sometimes; NVR = never; NA = does not apply. The instruction at the head of the questionnaire read: 'Please tell me which column is correct for you.'

1. I speak both Spanish and English to most Mexican friends my age.
2. Non-Mexicans visit me at my home.
3. I eat typically Mexican foods.
4. I belong to an organization primarily for Mexicans.
5. I have visited Mexico during the past year or two.
6. A member of my household has visited Mexico during the past year or two.
7. I think that being Mexican is different from being another kind of American.
8. I think I might be happier living in Mexico.
9. Most of my good friends are of Mexican ancestry.
10. I speak English to my mother and to other Mexican female adults.
11. I think that being Mexican is different from being another kind of Hispano.
12. When I go to church, I attend a Spanish service.
13. I speak primarily in Spanish to any Mexican friends who know both English and Spanish.
14. Someone from Mexico has visited me or some member of my household during the past year or two.
15. I speak Spanish when I get emotional or upset with a Mexican friend or relative.
16. Education is one of my major interests.
17. Occupational success is one of my major interests.
18. Literature-art-music-drama are an area of prime interest to me.
19. I speak English to them when I want my parents to do me a favour.
20. I speak English to them when I want my grandparents to do me a favour.
21. I speak English to them when I want my children to do me a favour.
22. I think the husband should have the final word on most problems that come up in the family.

23. Finding non-Mexican friends is one of my major interests.
24. I read Spanish publications (newspapers, magazines, church bulletins).
25. Many Americans I have met are prejudiced against Mexicans.
26. Religion is one of my major interests.
27. I read the Bible in Spanish.
28. When I talk to the priest/minister at church I speak to her/him in Spanish.
29. In private I pray in English.
30. In public (or in a group of people) I pray in Spanish.
31. I attend worship services in Spanish.
32. I attend worship services in English.
33. I write poems, songs, or stories in Spanish.
34. I am a *comadre* or *compadre* to someone.
35. I have a *madrina* and/or a *padrino*.
36. I listen to Spanish radio programmes.
37. I feel as much at home among Americans as among Mexicans.
38. I am interested in travelling to places I have never visited before.
39. I write poems, songs, or stories in English.
40. I speak Spanish when I become very friendly or familiar with another Mexican.
41. I like (or would like) to watch Spanish TV programmes.
42. There are some people with whom I try to speak a 'better' kind of Spanish.
43. I think it is important that Mexicans living in Los Angeles preserve their customs and traditions.
44. I go to see Spanish movies or shows.
45. When I have children, I want them to be able to speak Spanish fluently.
46. Some Mexicans/Mexican-Americans give too much emphasis to being Mexican.
47. When I have children, I want them to be able to speak English fluently.
48. There are some people to whom I try to speak a 'better' kind of English.
49. There are some Mexicans/Mexican-Americans who try to act too American.
50. I receive letters from relatives living in Mexico.
51. I rent videos in Spanish.
52. I rent videos in English.
53. I watch the news on TV on a Spanish channel.
54. I listen to Spanish music broadcasts.
55. I listen to radio stations in English.
56. I prefer to speak Spanish.
57. I prefer to speak English.
58. I feel more comfortable speaking English.
59. I feel more comfortable speaking Spanish.
60. I write letters in Spanish.
61. I use Spanish with my fellow workers.
62. I use Spanish with my boss or supervisor.
63. I count in Spanish.

64. I make telephone calls in Spanish.
65. I discuss local affairs in Spanish.
66. I discuss national affairs in Spanish.
67. I discuss health in Spanish.
68. I prefer to speak Spanish with local people younger than myself.
69. I prefer to speak Spanish only if the other person addresses me in Spanish.
70. I use Spanish when I speak with my parents.
71. I use Spanish when I speak with my grandparents.
72. I use Spanish when I speak with my in-laws.
73. I use Spanish when I speak with my brothers and sisters.
74. I use Spanish when I speak with my sisters-in-law.
75. I use Spanish when I speak with my brothers-in-law.
76. I am close with my cousins, uncles, and aunts.
77. I have friends that speak only English.
78. I have friends that speak only Spanish.
79. If I came across a Hispanic-looking individual for the first time, I would speak to her/him in Spanish if the person were:
    (*a*) my age or younger
    (*b*) a child
    (*c*) older than me
    (*d*) a salesperson
    (*e*) a clerk (bank, post office, etc.)
    (*f*) a teacher
    (*g*) a restaurant employee
    (*h*) a police officer
    (*i*) a car maintenance employee
    (*j*) someone on the street wearing a suit
    (*k*) someone on the street wearing jeans and a T-shirt

Open-ended questions

80. Are there times when you should speak only Spanish or only English? Tell me about them.
81. Do you switch from English to Spanish or vice versa? Why do you think you do that? How do you feel about doing that?
82. What do the English speakers who don't know Spanish say when you use Spanish? How do you feel about that?
83. Where do you usually buy your groceries?

Questionnaire I

The items are grouped according to dimensions investigated. Numbers in parentheses correspond to parallel statements about Spanish and English.

IA.   Use of Spanish in relation to interlocutors: 1, 13, 15, 40, 42 (48), 61, 62, 70
        (19), 71 (20), 72, 73, 74, 75, 28, 79.
IB.   Use of English in relation to interlocutors: 10, 19 (70), 20 (71), 21, 48 (42).
IIA.   Use of Spanish in relation to topic or type of oral activity: 12, 30, 31 (32,
        12), 63, 64, 65, 66, 67.
IIB.   Use of English in relation to topic or type of oral activity: 29, 32 (12).
IIIA.   Writing and reading in Spanish: 24, 33 (39), 60, 50.
IIIB.   Writing and reading in English: 39 (33).
IVA.   Preferential use of Spanish: 56 (57), 59 (58), 68, 69.
IVB.   Preferential use of English: 57 (56), 58 (59).
VA.   Listening in Spanish: 36 (55), 41, 44, 51 (52), 53, 54.
VB.   Listening in English: 52 (51), 55 (36).
VIA.   Positive attitudes toward Mexican culture: 3, 4, 7, 8, 9, 11, 22, 34, 35, 43,
        45, 49, 76, 78.
VIB.   Positive attitudes toward mainstream culture: 2, 23, 37, 47, 77.
VIIA.   Negative attitudes toward Mexican culture: 46 (25).
VIIB.   Negative attitudes toward mainstream culture: 25 (46).
VIIIA. Contact with Mexico: 5, 6, 14.
IX.   General attitudes: 16, 17, 18, 26, 38.

Questionnaire II: Spanish Dominants' Form

Instructions

When answering the questions below, circle the ones that seem important to you,
put a star by the most important one or two, and draw a line through any that are
particularly unimportant to you.

Abreviations used in Questionaires II and III

The letters in front of the numbers correspond to the classification of Mejías
and Anderson (1988) (MA): G = group identifying ('V' or 'value' in MA);
I = instrumental; S = sentimental; C = communicative. These roughly correspond
to four of Dorian's (1981: 165–71) reasons: G = local integrative and tradition; I =
operational; S = aesthetic. For purposes of comparison with MA, I have considered items 2 and 16 'instrumental' rather than 'abstract principle' and 'exclusionary',
as in Dorian.

I'm glad I know Spanish because:

G 1.   It's the language of my ancestors.
I 2.   It's broadening to have more than one language.
S 3.   I can enjoy Mexican music better.

S 4. Spanish is a very rich and expressive language.

C 5. It is necessary for daily communication.

G 6. It makes me feel more a part of the community I live in.

C 7. I can read in Spanish, for example, the Bible or newspaper columns.

I 8. It's useful to have a 'secret language' that not everyone else understands.

G 9. This part of the world was always Spanish-speaking and I'm keeping that tradition alive.

G 10. It's the language of my friends and neighbours.

C 11. I can understand the Spanish programmes on TV and radio.

C 12. I can talk to people from other Spanish-speaking countries.

S 13. Spanish is a beautiful language to hear and speak.

I 14. It helps me make money at my job.

S 15. It makes me feel good about myself.

I 16. I use it at my job.

If your main reasons are not given above, please tell me what they are or write them here:

Questionnaire III: English dominants' form

Instructions

When answering the questions below, circle the ones that seem important to you, put a star by the most important one or two, and draw a line through any that are particularly unimportant to you.

If I were ever to try to improve or maintain my Spanish,
my main reasons would be:

G 1. Some or all of my ancestors were Spanish-speaking.

I 2. It's broadening to have more than one language.

S 3. I would be able to enjoy Spanish music better.

S 4. Spanish is a very rich and expressive language.

C 5. Because it is necessary for daily communication.

G 6. It would make me feel more a part of the community I live in.

C 7. I would be able to read in Spanish, for example, the Bible or newspaper columns.

I 8. It's useful to have a 'secret language' that not everyone else understands.

G 9. This part of the world has always been Spanish-speaking in the past, and I would be proud to keep that tradition alive.

G 10. It's the language of my friends and neighbours.

C 11. I would understand the Spanish programmes on TV and radio.

C 12. I would be able to talk with Spanish speakers from other parts of the Spanish-speaking world in Spanish.

S 13. Spanish is a beautiful language to hear and speak.
I 14. It would help me make money at my job.
S 15. Because I do not want to lose my language.
I 16. It is useful to know a second language.

If your main reasons are not given above, please tell me what they are or write them here:

Questionnaire IV

Instructions

For the statements below, please check the box which expresses best how you feel: whether you agree with the statement, are uncertain about it, or disagree with it.

Abbreviations used in Questionaire IV

The letters in front of the numbers correspond to the six groups identified in Dorian's questionnaire III (1981: 172–8). A = fact question; B = attitudes (Spanish); C = goal-directed questions; D = programme-oriented; E = attitudes (English); F = 'special' attitude towards English. A '+' after these letters indicates that the item conveys a positive attitude, a '–' indicates that the item conveys a negative attitude. The questionnaire grouped answers under the following headings: STNGLY AGR = strongly agree; AGR = agree; UNCRTN = uncertain; DISAGR = disagree; STNGLY DISAGR = strongly disagree.

Section A

B+ 1. I like to hear Spanish spoken.
B+ 2. We should work hard to save the Spanish language.
B– 3. As all Mexican people speak English, it is a waste of time to keep up with Spanish.
A 4. Spanish is a difficult language to learn.
B– 5. There are far more useful things to spend time on than Spanish.
B+ 6. Spanish is a language worth learning.
B– 7. Spanish has little value in the modern world.
C+ 8. I should like to be able to read books in Spanish.
B+ 9. Anyone who learns Spanish will have plenty of chances to use it.
B– 10. There is no need to keep up Spanish for the sake of tradition.

Section B

B+ 1. I want to keep up Spanish in order to help the Mexican people.
B– 2. Speaking Spanish won't help you get a job.

B+ 3. You can't be a real Mexican/Mexican-American without Spanish.
D– 4. Learning Spanish or not should be left to a person's own choice.
B+ 5. We owe it to our ancestors to keep Spanish alive.
C+ 6. I should like to be able to understand the Spanish songs on the radio and television.
D– 7. School time should be used for more practical subjects than Spanish.
B+ 8. Spanish has a beauty all its own.
B– 9. It's looking backward instead of forward to try to keep Spanish alive.
D+ 10. More radio and television time should be given in Spanish.

Section C

E+ 1. English should be taught in all countries.
E– 2. Mexicans in the USA should speak Spanish and not a foreign language.
E+ 3. English will take you further than Spanish.
E+ 4. It's wrong to teach in Spanish in the elementary schools when Spanish-speaking children should be learning English.
F+ 5. You are considered to belong to a higher class if you speak English.
E+ 6. Those who don't want to learn English shouldn't come to live in Los Angeles.
E+ 7. English is a beautiful language.
E+ 8. English is better for studying scientific subjects than Spanish.
C– 9. Spanish will become less important in Los Angeles in the future.
E– 10. English will become less important in Los Angeles in the future.

Questionnaire V

Instruction: Please answer my questions with either YES or NO.

1. Would you agree to participate in a small-group discussion, with other persons of Mexican origin in Los Angeles, on the topic of improving your command of Spanish language and Mexican culture?
2. Would you agree to have as your room-mate in college a person of Mexican origin who preferred to speak in Spanish?
3. Would you agree to spend a weekend at the home of another person of Mexican ancestry in Los Angeles who wanted to discuss with you how to improve your command of Spanish language and Mexican culture?
4. Would you agree to invite another person of Mexican ancestry to spend a weekend at your home in order to discuss with her (him) how to improve your command of Spanish language and Mexican culture?
5. Would you agree to join a club for people of Mexican origin in Los Angeles who are interested in improving their command of Spanish language and Mexican culture?

6. Would you agree to attend a lecture or conference on the topic of how persons of Mexican ancestry in Los Angeles can improve their command of Spanish language and Mexican culture?

7. Would you agree to join a protest meeting against Los Angeles persons of Mexican ancestry who have stopped speaking and reading the Spanish language?

8. Would you agree to attend a meeting of a local chapter of a Mexican-American organization for the strengthening of the use of Spanish in Los Angeles?

9. Would you, if asked, agree to contribute $15.00 to help finance the activities of a Mexican-American organization for the strengthening of the use of Spanish in Los Angeles?

10. If you have answered *yes* to any of the above please give your name, address, and telephone number.

References

ADAMS, M. (1987), 'From Old French to the Theory of Pro-drop'. *Natural Language and Linguistic Theory*, 5: 1–32.

AGHEYISI, R., and FISHMAN, J. A. (1970), 'Language Attitude Studies: A Brief Survey of Methodological Approaches'. *Anthropological Linguistics*, 12: 137–57.

AISSEN, J., and PERLMUTTER, D. (1976), 'Clause reduction in Spanish', in H. Thompson *et al.* (eds.), *Proceedings of the Second Annual Meeting of the Berkeley Linguistics Society*, 1–30 (Berkeley, Calif.: Berkeley Linguistics Society).

ALONSO, A. (1939), 'Examen de la teoría indigenista de Rodolfo Lenz', *Revista de Filología Hispánica*, 1: 331–50.

AMASTAE, J., and ELÍAS-OLIVARES, L. (eds.) (1982), *Spanish in the United States: Sociolinguistic aspects* (New York: Cambridge Univ. Press).

ANDERSEN, R. W. (n.d.), 'Interpreting Data: Second Language Acquisition of Verbal Aspect' (MS, Univ. of California at Los Angeles).

—— (1982), 'Determining the Linguistic Attributes of Language Attrition', in R. D. Lambert and B. F. Freed (eds.), *The Loss of Language Skills*, 83–118 (Rowley, Mass.: Newbury House).

—— (ed.) (1983), *Pidginization and Creolization as Language Acquisition* (Rowley, Mass.: Newbury House).

—— (1989), 'The "up" and "down" Staircase in Secondary Language Development', in Dorian (1989: 385–94).

—— (1991), 'Developmental Sequences: The Emergence of Aspect Marking in Second Language Acquisition', in T. Huebner and C. A. Ferguson (eds.), *Crosscurrents in Second Language Acquisition and Linguistic Theories*, 305–24 (Amsterdam: Benjamins).

ANTTILA, R. (1972), *An Introduction to Historical and Comparative Linguistics* (New York: Macmillan).

BARRENECHEA, A., and ALONSO, A. (1977), 'Los pronombres personales sujetos en el español hablado de Buenos Aires', in J. L. Blanch (ed.), *Estudios sobre el español hablado en las principales ciudades de América*, 333–49 (Mexico, DF: Universidad Nacional Autónoma de México).

BAVIN, E. L. (1989), 'Some Lexical and Morphological Changes in Warlpiri', in Dorian (1989: 267–86).

BEHREND, E. (1986), 'The Use of *Ser* and *Estar* by Bilingual Mexican Americans in the Chicago Area: A Languages-in-Contact Study' (MA thesis, Hamburg Univ.).

BENTIVOGLIO, P. (1987), *Los sujetos pronominales de primera persona en el habla de Caracas* (Caracas: Universidad Central de Venezuela).

BENVENISTE, E. (1968), 'Mutations of Linguistic Categories', in Lehmann and Malkiel (1968: 83–94).

BERGEN, J. (ed.) (1990), *Spanish in the United States: Sociolinguistic Issues* (Washington, DC: Georgetown Univ. Press).

BICKERTON, D. (1975), *Dynamics of a Creole System* (Cambridge: Cambridge Univ. Press).

—— (1981), *Roots of Language* (Ann Arbor, Mich.: Karoma).

BILLS, G. (ed.) (1974), *Southwest Areal Linguistics* (San Diego, Calif.: Institute for Cultural Pluralism).

—— (1989), 'The US Census of 1980 and Spanish in the Southwest', in Wherritt and García (1989: 11–28).

BLOOMFIELD, L. (1933), *Language* (New York: Holt, Rinehart & Winston).

BOWEN, J. D., and ORNSTEIN, J. (eds.) (1976), *Studies in Southwest Spanish* (Rowley, Mass.: Newbury House).

BROWN, R. (1973), *A First Language* (Cambridge, Mass.: Harvard Univ. Press).

BYBEE, J. (1985), *Morphology: A Study of the Relation between Meaning and Form* (Amsterdam: Benjamins).

CAMERON, R. (1990), 'Variable Constraints on the Alternation of Subject Pronouns and Empty Subjects in Puerto Rican Spanish' (thesis proposal, Univ. of Pennsylvania).

CAMPBELL, L., and MUNTZEL, M. C. (1989), 'The Structural Consequences of Language Death', in Dorian (1989: 181–96).

CANTERO SANDOVAL, G. (1976), 'Peculiaridades en el empleo del pronombre personal *yo* en el habla culta de la ciudad de México', *Anuario de Letras*, 14: 233–7.

CATALÁN, D. (1958), 'Génesis del español atlántico: Ondas varias a través del Océano', *Revista de Historia Canaria* (La Laguna), 24: 1–10.

CIFUENTES, H. (1980–1), 'Presencia y ausencia del pronombre personal sujeto en el habla culta de Santiago de Chile', in *Homenaje a Ambrosio Rabanales: Boletín de Filología de la Universidad de Chile*, 31: 743–52.

COLEMAN, L., and KAY, P. (1981), 'Prototype Semantics: The English Word *Lie*', *Language*, 57: 26–44.

COMRIE, B. (1976), *Aspect* (Cambridge: Cambridge Univ. Press).

—— (1985), *Tense* (Cambridge: Cambridge Univ. Press).

COPÇEAG, D., and ESCUDERO, G. (1966), '"Ser" y "estar" en español y en rumano', *Revue roumaine de linguistique*, 11: 339–49.

CRUSE, D. A. (1986), *Lexical Semantics* (Cambridge: Cambridge Univ. Press).

DORIAN, N. (1973), 'Grammatical Change in a Dying Dialect', *Language*, 49: 414–38.

—— (1978), 'The Fate of Morphological Complexity in Language Death', *Language*, 54: 590–609.

—— (1980), 'Maintenance and Loss of Same-Meaning Structures in Language Death', *Word*, 31: 39–45.

—— (1981), *Language Death* (Philadelphia: Univ. of Pennsylvania Press).

—— (1982), 'Linguistic Models and Language Death Evidence', in L. Obler and L. Menn (eds.), *Exceptional Language and Linguistics*, 31–48 (New York: Academic).

—— (1983), 'Natural Second Language Acquisition from the Perspective of the Study of Language Death', in Andersen (1983: 158–67).

—— (ed.) (1989), *Investigating Obsolescence: Studies in Language Contraction and Death* (Cambridge: Cambridge Univ. Press).

DuBOIS, J. W. (1985), 'Competing Motivations', in J. Haiman (ed.) *Iconicity in Syntax*, 343–65 (Amsterdam: Benjamins).

EDWARDS, J. (1985), *Language, Society and Identity* (Oxford: Blackwell).

ELÍAS-OLIVARES, L. (1979), 'Language Use in a Chicano Community: A Sociolinguistic Approach', in J. B. Pride (ed.), *Sociolinguistic Aspects of Language Learning and Teaching*, 120–34 (Oxford: Oxford Univ. Press).

ELÍAS-OLIVARES, L. (ed.) (1983), *Spanish in the United States: Beyond the Southwest* (Washington, DC: National Center for Bilingual Education).

ENRÍQUEZ, E. V. (1984), *El pronombre personal sujeto en la lengua española hablada en Madrid* (Madrid: Consejo Superior de Investigaciones Científicas).

FALK, J. (1979), SER *y* ESTAR *con atributos adjetivales* (Uppsala: Almqvist & Wiksell).

FERGUSON, C. A. (1977), 'Absence of Copula and the Notion of Simplicity: A Study of Normal Speech, Baby Talk, Foreigner Talk and Pidgin', in D. Hymes (ed.), *Pidginization and Creolization of Language*, 141–50 (Cambridge: Cambridge Univ. Press).

—— (1982), 'Simplified Registers and Linguistic Theory', in L. Obler and L. Menn (eds.), *Exceptional Language and Linguistics*, 49–66 (New York: Academic).

FERNÁNDEZ, S. (1964), 'Un proceso lingüístico en marcha', in OFINES (1964: ii. 277–85).

FISHMAN, J. A. (1971), 'Bilingual Attitudes and Behaviors', in Fishman *et al.* (1971: 105–16).

—— COOPER, R. L., and MA, R. (1971), *Bilingualism in the Barrio* (Bloomington, Ind.: Indiana Univ. Press).

—— and KELLER, G. D. (eds.) (1982), *Bilingual Education for Hispanic Students in the United States* (New York: Teachers College Press).

FLEISCHMAN, S. (1982), *The Future in Thought and Language: Diachronic Evidence from Romance* (Cambridge: Cambridge Univ. Press).

FONTANELLA DE WEINBERG, M. B. (1980), 'Español del Caribe: ¿rasgos peninsulares, contacto lingüístico o innovación?', *Lingüística Española Actual*, 2: 189–201.

FRAKE, C. O. (1977), 'Lexical Origins and Semantic Structure in Philippine Creole Spanish', in D. Hymes (ed.), *Pidginization and Creolization of Languages*, 223–42 (Cambridge: Cambridge Univ. Press).

FRANCO, J. (n.d.), 'Loan Translation in Prepositions Subcategorized by Verbs in LA Spanish' (MS, Univ. of Southern California).

—— (1991), 'Spanish Object Clitics as Verbal Agreement Morphemes', in J. D. Bobaljik and T. Bures (eds.), *MIT Working Papers in Linguistics*, 14: 99–114.

GAL, S. (1979), *Language Shift: Social Determinants of Linguistic Change in Bilingual Austria* (New York: Academic).

—— (1984), 'Phonological style in bilingualism: The Interaction of Structure and Use', in D. Schiffrin (ed.), *Meaning, Form and Use in Context*, 290–302 (Washington, DC: Georgetown Univ. Press).

GARCÍA, E. (1975), *The Role of Theory in Linguistic Analysis: The Spanish Pronoun System* (Amsterdam: North-Holland).

—— (1983) 'Context Dependence of Language and of Linguistic Analysis', in F. Klein-Andreu (ed.), *Discourse Perspectives on Syntax*, 181–207 (New York: Academic).

—— VAN PUTTE, F., and TOBIN, Y. (1987), 'Cross-linguistic Equivalence, Translatability, and Contrastive Analysis', *Folia Linguistica*, 21: 373–405.

GILI Y GAYA, S. (1970), *Curso superior de sintaxis española* (Barcelona: Bibliograf).

GIVÓN, T. (1976) 'Topic, Pronoun and Grammatical Agreement', in C. N. Li (ed.), *Subject and Topic*, 149–88 (New York: Academic).

—— (1979), 'Prolegomena to Any Sane Creology', in I. F. Hancock (ed.), *Readings in Creole Studies*, 3–35 (Ghent: Story-Scientia).

GLEASON, J. B. (1982), 'Converging Evidence for Linguistic Theory from the Study of Aphasia and Child Language', in L. Obler and L. Menn (eds.), *Exceptional Language and Linguistics*, 347–56 (New York: Academic).

GRANDA, G. DE (1968), *Transculturación e interferencia lingüística en el Puerto Rico contemporáneo (1898–1969)* (Bogotá: Instituto Caro y Cuervo).

——(1971), 'Algunos datos sobre la pervivencia del criollo en Cuba'. *Boletín de la Real Academia Española*, 51: 481–91.

——(1991), *El español en tres mundos: Retenciones y contactos lingüísticos en América y Africa* (Valladolid: Secretariado de Publicaciones, Universidad de Valladolid).

GUMPERZ, J., and WILSON, R. (1977), 'Convergence and Creolization', in D. Hymes (ed.), *Pidginization and Creolization of Languages*, 151–67 (Cambridge: Cambridge Univ. Press).

GUTIÉRREZ, M. (1989), 'Michoacan Spanish/Los Angeles Spanish: Trends in a Process of Linguistic Change' (Ph.D. diss., Univ. of Southern California).

——(1990), 'Sobre el mantenimiento de las cláusulas subordinadas en el español de Los Angeles', in J. J. Bergen (ed.), *Spanish in the United States: Sociolinguistic Issues*, 31–8 (Washington, DC: Georgetown Univ. Press).

HAIMAN, J., and THOMPSON, S. (1984), ' "Subordination" in Universal Grammar', in C. Brugman and M. Macaulay (eds.), *Proceedings of the Tenth Annual Meeting of the Berkeley Linguistics Society*, 510–23 (Berkeley, Calif.: Berkeley Linguistics Society).

HENRÍQUEZ UREÑA, P. (1921), 'Observaciones sobre el español de América', *Revista de Filología Española*, 8: 357–90.

HERNÁNDEZ-CHÁVEZ, E. *et al.* (eds.) (1975), *El lenguaje de los chicanos* (Arlington, Va.: Center for Applied Linguistics).

HILL, J. H. (1989), 'The Social Functions of Relativization in Obsolescent and Non-obsolescent Languages', in Dorian (1989: 149–64).

HOCHBERG, J. G. (1986), 'Functional Compensation for /s/ Deletion in Puerto Rican Spanish', *Language*, 62: 609–21.

HUDSON-EDWARDS, A., and HUDSON-EDWARDS, A. (1986), 'Syntactic, Semantic, and Pragmatic Influences on Judgments of Grammaticality', in K. Ferrara *et al.* (eds.), *Linguistic Change and Contact*, 137–42 (Austin: Univ. of Texas Press).

JACKSON, H. (1988), *Words and Their Meaning* (London: Longman).

JAKOBSON, R. (1938), 'Sur la théorie des affinités phonologiques entre des langues', *Actes du Quatrième Congrès International de Linguistes*, 48–59 (Copenhagen: Munksgaard).

JONGE, B. DE (1987), '*Estar* comes of age', in F. Beukema and P. Coopmans (eds.), *Linguistics in the Netherlands*, 101–10 (Dordrecht: Foris).

KEENAN, E., and COMRIE, B. (1977), 'Noun Phrase Accessibility and Universal Grammar', *Linguistic Inquiry*, 8: 63–99.

KING, R. (1989), 'On the Social Meaning of Linguistic Variability in Language Death Situations: Variation in Newfoundland French', in Dorian (1989: 139–48).

KLEIN, F. (1980), 'A Quantitative Study of Syntactic and Pragmatic Indications of Change in the Spanish of Bilinguals in the US', in W. Labov (ed.), *Locating Language in Time and Space*, 69–82 (New York: Academic).

KLEIN-ANDREU, F. (1986a), 'La cuestión del anglicismo: apriorismos y métodos', *Thesaurus: Boletín del Instituto Caro y Cuervo*, 40: 1–16.

——(1986b), 'Speaker-Based and Reference-Based Factors in Language: Non-past Conditional Sentences in Spanish', in O. Jaeggli and C. Silva-Corvalán (eds.), *Studies in Romance Linguistics*, 99–119 (Amsterdam: Foris).

KLEIN, W. (1986), *Second Language Acquisition* (Cambridge: Cambridge Univ. Press).

—— and VON STUTTERHEIM, C. (n.d.), 'Text Structure and Referential Movement' (MS, Max-Planck-Institut für Psycholinguistik, Nijmegen).

KOIKE, D. A. (1987), 'Code Switching in the Bilingual Chicano Narrative', *Hispania*, 70: 148–54.

LABOV, W. (1972*a*), *Sociolinguistic Patterns* (Philadelphia: Univ. of Pennsylvania Press).

—— (1972*b*), *Language in the Inner City* (Philadelphia: Univ. of Pennsylvania Press).

—— (ed.) (1980), *Locating Language in Time and Space* (New York: Academic).

—— (1981*a*), 'What Can Be Learned about Change in Progress from Synchronic Description?' in D. Sankoff and H. Cedergren (eds.), *Variation Omnibus*, 177–99 (Edmonton: Linguistic Research).

—— (1981*b*), 'Resolving the Neogrammarian Controversy', *Language*, 57: 267–308.

—— (1982), 'Building on Empirical Foundations', in W. P. Lehmann and Y. Malkiel (eds.), *Current Issues in Linguistic Theory*, xxiv: 17–92 (Amsterdam: Benjamins).

—— and WALETSKY, J. (1967), 'Narrative Analysis: Oral Versions of Personal Experience', in J. Helm (ed.), *Essays on the Verbal and Visual Arts*, 12–44 (Seattle: Univ. of Washington Press).

LAMBRECHT, K. (1987), 'On the Status of SVO Sentences in French Discourse', in R. S. Tomlin (ed.), *Coherence and Grounding in Discourse*, 217–61 (Amsterdam: Benjamins).

LANDA, A. (1989), 'Posición de los clíticos en construcciones con perífrasis verbales en el habla culta de Caracas' (MS, Univ. of Southern California).

—— (1995), 'Conditions on Null Objects in Basque Spanish and Their Relation to *Leísmo* and Clitic Doubling' (Ph.D. diss., Univ. of Southern California).

LAPESA, R. (1964), 'El andaluz y el español de América', in OFINES (1964: ii. 173–82).

LAVANDERA, B. (1978), 'Where Does the Sociolinguistic Variable Stop?', *Language in Society*, 7: 171–83.

LEHMANN, W., and MALKIEL, Y. (eds.) (1968), *Directions for Historical Linguistics* (Austin: Univ. of Texas Press).

LENNEBERG, E. H. (1967), *Biological Foundations of Language* (New York: Wiley).

LENZ, R. (1893), 'Beiträge zur Kenntnis des Amerikanospanisch', *Zeitschrift für Romanische Philologie*, 17: 188–214.

LEVELT, W. (1979), 'Linearization in Discourse' (MS, Max-Planck-Institut für Psycholinguistik, Nijmegen).

—— (1982), 'Linearization in Describing Spatial Networks', in S. Peters and E. Saarinen (eds.), *Processes, Beliefs, and Questions*, 199–220 (Lancaster: Reidel).

LEVINSON, S. C. (1983), *Pragmatics* (Cambridge: Cambridge Univ. Press).

LEWIS, E. G. (1978), 'Types of Bilingual Communities', in J. E. Alatis (ed.), *International Dimensions of Bilingual Education*, 19–34 (Washington, DC: Georgetown Univ. Press).

LOPE BLANCH, J. (1967), 'La influencia del sustrato en la fonética del español de México', *Revista de Filología Española*, 50: 145–60.

LÓPEZ MORALES, H. (1980), 'Sobre la pretendida existencia y pervivencia del criollo en Cuba', *Anuario de Letras*, 18: 85–116.

LUJÁN, M. (1981), 'The Spanish Copulas as Aspectual Indicators', *Lingua*, 54: 165–209.

MAANDI, K. (1989), 'Estonian among Immigrants in Sweden', in Dorian (1989: 227–41).

MAHER, J. (1991), 'A Crosslinguistic Study of Language Contact and Language Attrition', in Seliger and Vago (1991: 67–84).

MALKIEL, Y. (1983), 'Multiple versus Simple Causation in Linguistic Change', in *From Particular to General Linguistics*, 251–68 (Amsterdam: Benjamins).

MARTINET, A. (1962), *A Functional View of Language* (Oxford: Oxford Univ. Press).

MEILLET, A. (1926), *Linguistique historique et linguistique générale* (2 vols., Paris: Champion).

MEISEL, J. M. (ed.) (1977), *Langues en contact: pidgins, creoles. Languages in contact* (Tübingen: TBL Verlag Narr).

—— (1983*a*), 'Strategies of Second Language Acquisition: More than One Kind of Simplification', in Andersen (1983: 120–57).

—— (1983*b*), 'Transfer as a Second Language Strategy', *Language and Communication*, 3: 11–46.

MEJÍAS, H. A., and ANDERSON, P. L. (1988), 'Attitude toward Use of Spanish on the South Texas Border', *Hispania*, 71: 401–7.

MENN, L. (1989), 'Some People Who Don't Talk Right: Universal and Particular in Child Language, Aphasia, and Language Obsolescence', in Dorian (1989: 335–45).

MILROY, J., and MILROY, L. (1985), 'Linguistic Change, Social Network and Speaker Innovation', *Journal of Linguistics*, 21: 339–84.

MITHUN, M. (1989), 'The Incipient Obsolescence of Polysynthesis: Cayuga in Ontario and Oklahoma', in Dorian (1989: 243–57).

MORALES, A. (1986), *Gramáticas en contacto: Análisis sintácticos sobre el español de Puerto Rico* (Madrid: Playor).

MORENO DE ALBA, J. (1978), *Valores de las formas verbales en el español de México* (Mexico: Universidad Nacional Autónoma de México).

MOUGEON, R., and BENIAK, E. (1991), *Linguistic Consequences of Language Contact and Restriction: The Case of French in Ontario, Canada* (Oxford: Clarendon Press).

——, ——, and VALOIS, D. (1985), 'A Sociolinguistic Study of Language Contact, Shift, and Change', *Linguistics*, 23: 455–87.

MÜHLHÄUSLER, P. (1981), *Pidginization and Simplification of Language, Pacific Linguistics*, ser. B, No. 26.

MUYSKEN, P. (1981), 'Creole Tense/Mood/Aspect Systems: The Unmarked Case?', in P. Muysken (ed.), *Generative Studies on Creole Languages*, 181–99 (Dordrecht: Foris).

MYHILL, J. (1988), 'The Grammaticalization of Auxiliaries: Spanish Clitic Climbing', in S. Axmaker, A. Jaisser, and H. Singmaster (eds.), *Proceedings of the Fourteenth Annual Meeting of the Berkeley Linguistics Society*, 352–63 (Berkeley, Calif.: Berkeley Linguistics Society).

—— (1989), 'Variation in Spanish Clitic Climbing', in T. J. Walsh (ed.), *Synchronic and Diachronic Approaches to Linguistic Variation and Change*, 227–50 (Washington, DC: Georgetown Univ. Press).

NAVAS RUIZ, R. (1963), *Ser y estar: Estudio sobre el sistema atributivo del español* (Salamanca: Acta Salmanticensia).

NIE, N. H. *et al.* (1975), *Statistical Package for the Social Sciences*, 2nd edn. (New York: McGraw-Hill).

OCAMPO, F. (1989), 'The Pragmatics of Word Order in Spoken Rioplatense Spanish' (Ph.D. diss., Univ. of Southern California).

—— (1990), 'The Pragmatics of Word Order in Constructions with a Verb and a Subject', *Hispanic Linguistics*, 4: 87–128.

OFINES (1964), *Presente y futuro de la lengua española* (2 vols., Madrid: Ediciones Cultura Hispánica).

OTHEGUY, R. (1993), 'A Reconsideration of the Notion of Loan Translation in the Analysis of US Spanish', in A. Roca and J. Lipski, *Spanish in the United States*, 21–45 (Berlin: Mouton).

—— GARCÍA, O., and FERNÁNDEZ, M. (1989), 'Transferring, Switching, and Modeling in West New York Spanish: An Intergenerational Study', in Wherritt and García (1989: 41–52).

PEÑALOSA, F. (1980), *Chicano Sociolinguistics* (Rowley, Mass.: Newbury House).

PFAFF, C., and PORTZ, R. (1979), 'Foreign Children's Acquisition of German: Universals vs. Interference', paper presented at the LSA Annual Meeting, Los Angeles.

POPLACK, S. (1978), *Quantitative Analysis of Constraints on Code-Switching* (New York: Center for Puerto Rican Studies).

—— (1979), '*Sometimes I'll start a sentence in Spanish* y termino en español' (New York: Center for Puerto Rican Studies); repr. in Amastae and Elías-Olivares (1982: 230–63).

—— (1987), 'Contrasting Patterns of Code-Switching in Two Communities', in E. Wande et al. (eds.), *Aspects of Multilingualism: Proceedings from the Fourth Nordic Symposium on Bilingualism, 1984*, 51–77 (Uppsala: Borgstroms).

—— SANKOFF, D., and MILLER, C. (1988), 'The Social Correlates and Linguistic Processes of Lexical Borrowing and Assimilation', *Linguistics*, 26: 47–104.

POUNTAIN, C. (1982), '*Essere/Stare* as a Romance Phenomenon', in N. Vincent and M. Harris (eds.), *Studies in the Romance Verb*, 139–60 (London: Croom Helm).

PRESTON, D. R. (1982), 'How to Lose a Language', *Interlanguage Studies Bulletin*, 6: 64–87.

PRINCE, E. (1992), 'On Syntax in Discourse, in Language Contact Situations', in C. Kramsch and S. McConnell-Ginet (eds.), *Text and Context: Cross-Disciplinary Perspectives on Language Study*, 98–112 (Boston: Heath).

RANSON, D. L. (1991), 'Person Marking in the Wake of /s/ Deletion in Andalusian Spanish', *Language Variation and Change*, 3: 133–52.

REAL ACADEMIA DE LA LENGUA (1973), *Esbozo de una nueva gramática de la lengua española* (Madrid: Espasa Calpe).

RIZZI, L. (1978), 'A Restructuring Rule in Italian Syntax', in S. J. Keyser (ed.), *Recent Transformational Studies in European Languages*, 113–58 (Cambridge, Mass.: MIT Press).

RODRIGO, V. (1991), 'Subject Expression and /s/ Elision in East Andalusia Spanish' (MS, Univ. of Southern California).

ROEPER, T., and WILLIAMS, E. (eds.) (1987), *Parameter Setting* (Dordrecht: Reidel).

ROJO, G. (1974), 'La temporalidad verbal en español', *Verba*, 1 (Universidad de Santiago de Compostela).

ROMAINE, S. (1981), *On the Problem of Syntactic Variation: A Reply to Beatriz Lavandera and William Labov* (Austin, Tex.: Southwest Educational Development Laboratory).

—— (1982), *Socio-historical Linguistics: Its Status and Methodology* (Cambridge: Cambridge Univ. Press).

—— (1988), *Pidgin and Creole Languages* (London and New York: Longman).

—— (1989a), 'Pidgins, Creoles, Immigrant, and Dying Languages', in Dorian (1989: 369–83).

—— (1989b), *Bilingualism* (Oxford: Blackwell).

—— (1992), 'The Evolution of Linguistic Complexity in Pidgin and Creole Languages', in J. A. Hawkins and M. Gell-Mann (eds.), *The Evolution of Human Languages*, 213–38 (Reading, Mass.: Addison Wesley).

ROMO, R. (1983), *East Los Angeles: History of a Barrio* (Austin: Univ. of Texas Press).

ROUSSEAU, P., and SANKOFF, D. (1978), 'Advances in Variable Rule Methodology', in D. Sankoff (ed.), *Linguistic Variation: Models and Methods*, 57–69 (New York: Academic).

RUHL, C. (1989), *On Monosemy: A Study in Linguistic Semantics* (Albany: State Univ. of New York Press).

RYAN, E. B., GILES, H., and SEBASTIAN, R. J. (1982), 'An Integrative Perspective for the Study of Attitudes toward Language Variation', in E. B. Ryan and H. Giles (eds.), *Attitudes towards Language Variation*, 1–19 (London: Edward Arnold).

SÁNCHEZ, R. (1983), *Chicano Discourse* (Rowley, Mass.: Newbury House).

SCHACHTER, J., and RUTHERFORD, W. (1979), *Discourse Function and Language Transfer*, 1–12 (Toronto: Ontario Institute for Studies in Education).

SCHIFFRIN, D. (1981), 'Tense Variation in Narrative', *Language*, 57: 45–62.

SELIGER, H. W. (1991), 'Language Attrition, Reduced Redundancy, and Creativity', in Seliger and Vago (1991: 227–40).

—— and VAGO, R. M. (eds.) (1991), *First Language Attrition* (Cambridge: Cambridge Univ. Press).

SILVA-CORVALÁN, C. (1977), 'A Discourse Study of Some Aspects of Word Order in the Spanish Spoken by Mexican-Americans in West Los Angeles' (MA thesis, Univ. of California at Los Angeles).

—— (1981), 'The Diffusion of Object–Verb Agreement in Spanish', *Papers in Romance*, 3: 163–76.

—— (1982), 'Subject Expression and Placement in Mexican-American Spanish', in Amastae and Elías-Olivares (1982: 93–120).

—— (1983a), 'Tense and Aspect in Oral Spanish Narrative: Context and Meaning', *Language*, 59: 60–80.

—— (1983b), 'Code-Shifting Patterns in Chicano Spanish', in L. Elías-Olivares (ed.), *Spanish in the US Setting: Beyond the Southwest*, 69–87 (Rosslyn, Va.: National Center for Bilingual Education).

—— (1983c), 'On the Interaction of Word Order and Intonation: Some OV Constructions in Spanish', in F. Klein-Andreu (ed.), *Discourse Perspectives on Syntax*, 117–40 (New York: Academic).

—— (1985), 'Modality and Semantic Change', in J. Fisiak (ed.), *Historical Semantics: Historical Word Formation*, 547–72 (Berlin: Mouton).

—— (1986), 'Bilingualism and Language Change: The Extension of *Estar* in Los Angeles Spanish', *Language*, 62: 587–608.

—— (1989), *Sociolingüística: Teoría y análisis* (Madrid: Alhambra).

—— (1990a), 'Cross-Generational Bilingualism: Theoretical Implications of Language Attrition', in T. Huebner and C. A. Ferguson (eds.), *Cross-Currents in Second Language Acquisition and Linguistic Theories*, 325–45 (Amsterdam: Benjamins).

—— (1990b), 'The Pragmastylistics of Hypothetical Discourse', in L. Hickey (ed.), *The Pragmatics of Style*, 87–105 (London: Routledge).

—— (1990c), 'Current Issues in Studies of Language Contact', *Hispania*, 73: 162–76.

—— (1991a), 'Spanish Language Attrition in a Contact Situation with English', in Seliger and Vago (1991: 151–71).

—— (1991b), 'Basic Meanings and Context-Bound Functions of Tense in Spanish', in J. Gvozdanovic *et al.* (eds.), *The Function of Tense in Texts*, 255–70 (Amsterdam: North-Holland).

—— and GUTIÉRREZ, M. (1995), 'On Transfer and Simplification: Verbal Clitics in Mexican-American Spanish', in P. Hashemipour *et al.* (eds.), *Studies in Language Learning and Spanish Linguistics in Honor of Tracy D. Terrell*, 302–12 (San Francisco: McGraw-Hill).

SLOBIN, D. I. (1977), 'Language Change in Childhood and in History', in J. Macnamara (ed.), *Language Learning and Thought*, 185–214 (New York: Academic).

—— (ed.) (1986), *The Cross-Linguistic Study of Language Acquisition* (Hillsdale, NJ: Erlbaum).

SOLÉ, Y., and SOLÉ, C. (1977), *Modern Spanish Syntax* (Lexington, Mass.: Heath).

SUÁREZ, J. A. (1966), 'Indigenismos e hispanismos vistos desde la Argentina', *Romance Philology*, 20: 68–90.

SUBIRATS-RÜGGEBERG, C. (1987), *Sentential Complementation in Spanish* (Amsterdam: Benjamins).

TAULI, V. (1956), 'The Origin of Affixes', *Finnisch-Ugrische Forschungen*, 32: 170–225.

TAYLOR, A. R. (1989), 'Problems in Obsolescence Research: The Gros Ventres of Montana', in Dorian (1989: 167–79).

THOMASON, S. G. (1986), 'On Establishing External Causes of Language Change', in S. Choi *et al.* (eds.), *Proceedings of the Second Eastern States Conference on Linguistics*, 243–51 (Columbus: Dept. of Linguistics, Ohio State Univ.).

—— and KAUFMAN, T. (1988), *Language Contact, Creolization, and Genetic Linguistics* (Berkeley: Univ. of California Press).

TORRES, L. (1989), 'Mood Selection among New York Puerto Ricans', in Wherritt and García (1989: 67–77).

TRUDGILL, P. (1976–7), 'Creolization in Reverse: Reduction and Simplification in the Albanian Dialects of Greece', *Transactions of the Philological Society* (1976–7): 32–50.

—— (1983), *On Dialect* (Oxford: Blackwell).

TSITSIPIS, L. (1981), 'Arvanítika Language Change in Speech Communities in Greece', in H. I. Aronson and B. J. Darden (eds.), *Folia Slavica: Studies in Balkan Linguistics to Honor E. P. Hamp on his Sixtieth Birthday*, 378–83 (Columbus, OH: Slavica).

—— (1988), 'Language Shift and Narrative Performance: On the Structure and Function of Arvanítika Narratives', *Language in Society*, 17: 61–86.

VAN DIJK, T. A. (1980), *Texto y contexto* (first published in English); Spanish translation by J. Domingo Moyano (Madrid: Cátedra).

VAÑÓ-CERDÁ, A. (1982), *Ser y estar + adjetivos: Un estudio sincrónico y diacrónico* (Tübingen: Narr).

VINCENT, N., and HARRIS, M. (1982), *Studies in the Romance Verb* (London: Croom Helm).

WALD, B. (1983), 'Referents and Topic Within and Across Discourse Units: Observations from Current Vernacular English', in F. Klein-Andreu (ed.), *Discourse Perspectives on Syntax*, 91–116 (New York: Academic).

WANG, W. S.-Y. (1969), 'Competing Changes as a Cause of Residue', *Language*, 45: 9–25.

WEINREICH, U. (1974), *Languages in Contact*, 8th printing (The Hague: Mouton).

—— LABOV, W., and HERZOG, M. (1968), 'Empirical Foundations for a Theory of Language Change', in Lehmann and Malkiel (1968: 95–195).

WHERRITT, I., and GARCÍA, O. (eds.) (1989), *US Spanish: The Language of Latinos* (*International Journal of the Sociology of Language*, special issue No. 79).

WOLFSON, N. (1982), *The Conversational Historical Present in American English Narrative* (Dordrecht: Foris).

ZENTELLA, A. C. (1981), ' "Hablamos los dos, we speak both": Growing Up Bilingual in El Barrio' (Ph.D. dissertation, Univ. of Pennsylvania).

Sources of written data examined

ESGUEVA, M., and CANTARERO, M. (eds.) (1981), *El habla de la ciudad de Madrid: Materiales para su estudio* (Madrid: Consejo Superior de Investigaciones Científicas, Instituto Miguel de Cervantes).

INSTITUTO DE FILOLOGÍA ANDRÉS BELLO (1979), *El habla culta de Caracas: Materiales para su estudio* (Caracas: Universidad Central de Venezuela).

RABANALES, A., and CONTRERAS, L. (eds.) (1979), *El habla culta de Santiago de Chile: Materiales para su estudio* (*Boletín de Filología* 2: Universidad de Chile).

UNAM (1971), *El habla de la ciudad de México: Materiales para su estudio* (Mexico, DF: Universidad Nacional Autónoma de México).

—— (1976), *El habla popular de la ciudad de México: Materiales para su estudio* (Mexico, DF: Universidad Nacional Autónoma de México).

Index

Printed in the United Kingdom
by Lightning Source UK Ltd.
107201UKS00001B/98